Gatew

2nd Edition

Anna Cole
Ursula Mallows

macmillan education

B1+

Welcome
Introduction by David Spencer

Before I tell you about *Gateway 2nd Edition*, let me tell you a bit about myself.

After studying Modern Languages, I trained to be a secondary school teacher. And I'm still teaching in a secondary school now, over 25 years later. Being in the classroom every day is a great help when writing a course like *Gateway*. On the one hand, the daily contact with teenagers gives me ideas and inspiration. On the other hand, it keeps me realistic about what actually works in the classroom.

If you don't know *Gateway* already, the course is designed to lead teenage students to success in exams, particularly school-leaving exams. It's also designed to prepare students for further study and the world of work.

In *Gateway 2nd Edition* we've kept many of the features that have made *Gateway* so popular. Each unit has a clear, logical structure. The whole approach to grammar and vocabulary and to the development of the four skills is carefully staged to be both teacher- and student-friendly. Each level offers a wide range of strategies that will help students pass their exams.

But *Gateway 2nd Edition* has several exciting new features. Firstly there are the **Flipped classroom videos**, which bring grammar points from the Student's Book to life. Then there is a whole new focus on **Life skills**, with a special section in each unit preparing teenagers for many, varied facets of life, complete with its own tailor-made video featuring British teenagers.

Meanwhile *Gateway 2nd Edition* offers brand-new, up-to-date texts to motivate you and your students. Reading texts include **Critical thinking** questions to get students reflecting on what they've just read. And for all these features, new and old, we've refreshed the design and made it even clearer and easier to use.

With *Gateway 2nd Edition* we want to support you in the classroom and in your professional development. Via the **Gateway Facebook page**, you can keep in direct contact with me and the *Gateway* team, and with other teachers from around the world. We have news, teaching tips and occasional competitions, plus access to teaching videos and webinars. You can also find out about any upcoming *Gateway* talks in your part of the world. So far I've spoken in over 20 countries and hope to continue being able to share activities and ideas with you all.

I hope you and your students enjoy teaching and learning with *Gateway 2nd Edition*!

Dave

 www.facebook.com/macmillangateway

Key concepts of *Gateway 2nd Edition*

1 Preparation for school-leaving exams

Gateway 2nd Edition prepares secondary school students for both international and school-leaving exams. Throughout the units there are plenty of exam-style activities and preparation tasks as well as **Exam success** tips. These tips lead the students to more in-depth help in the Exam Success section at the end of book. After every two units there are **Gateway to exams** pages which revise the exam techniques they have learnt and give them more practice in doing typical exam tasks. Gateway 2nd edition is closely mapped to the CEFR and the course comes with both a **Test generator** and **printable tests**.

2 Content-based material and critical thinking

Gateway 2nd Edition provides material which helps to develop other areas of knowledge, as well as English-language skills. The most important criteria for choosing texts is that they should be genuinely interesting and appealing to students of the age group. Texts are then used to provide a realistic and meaningful context for the grammar and vocabulary to be studied within the unit. Students are also encouraged to think critically about what they have read, to question the content and personalise the topic of the text.

3 Life Skills

We now have two pages at the heart of each unit which prepare students for life outside the classroom. We help students in areas as wide-ranging as personal and physical well-being, citizenship, social skills, money and finance, and the world of work. Each Life skills section has a motivating video with British teenagers demonstrating the topic and ends with students performing a **Life task**, an activity that has direct relevance to the students' lives outside the classroom.

4 The active role of the learners

Students are encouraged to participate actively in their own learning throughout the course. Here are just some of the ways this is done:

Exam success boxes in the Student's Book and **Study skills** boxes in the Workbook encourage students to reflect on the best way to learn before they are guided to the suggestions at the back of the book.

Students hypothesise about grammar rules before they are directed to the relevant information in the **Grammar reference** section at the end of each unit.

Students are invited to express personal reactions and/or think critically after reading or listening.

On the **Gateway to exams** pages which appear after each two units there is a **'Can Do' Progress Check** where students evaluate their own progress and decide what steps to take next to maximise their learning.

5 Grammar in context

The target grammar in each unit is given meaningful context through the reading and listening texts. The approach is one of guided discovery. Students are then directed to the **Grammar reference** section at the end of the unit to check their hypotheses.

An alternative approach to grammar presentation is now offered by the **Flipped Classroom videos**.

After the grammar presentation stage, the students work through carefully graded exercises which help them to internalise the grammar, starting with exercises where students simply identify correct usage and ending with exercises where students use the grammar in active, oral communication.

The Grammar reference section appears directly at the end of the unit, providing a useful checkpoint for students when reviewing the unit. **Grammar revision** exercises facing the Grammar reference section make this part of the Student's Book interactive and ideal for self-study, for example for revision and self-testing before exams.

6 The Flipped classroom

In the traditional classroom, the teacher explains new content in the class and students do practice at home. The Flipped classroom refers to students learning new content outside the classroom, via video presentations, and then doing practice in the class. This makes it easier for the teacher to give more personalised help and attention during the practice stage. It also means students can go at their own speed during the presentation stage. In **Gateway 2nd Edition** we have created a series of **Flipped classroom videos** to help you to find more time in lessons and to add variety to your teaching. The videos are short grammar presentations linked to one of each unit's **Grammar guides**. Students can watch the presentation at home, as many times as they want. There are interactive

tasks in the *Gateway 2nd Edition* Online Workbook or printable worksheets on the Resource centre to help the students to check that they've understood, and for you to check that they have actually watched the video.

The videos are a flexible teaching tool and can also be used for revision, or when students miss a class, or with the whole class in lesson-time, for variety. The Flipped classroom videos have the added bonus that they encourage students to take responsibility for their own progress and become independent learners.

7 Developing vocabulary

The course revises, extends and practises the most important lexical sets connected to typical topics that appear in school-leaving and international exams, so that students can talk and write about these topics with ease and will have less difficulty reading or listening to texts dealing with these topics. The course also develops the students' active vocabulary unit-by-unit by looking at 'systems' of vocabulary, such as word formation, collocation, phrasal verbs, and dependent prepositions. This approach is a key factor in helping students with Use of English tasks.

8 Developing skills

The emphasis of **Gateway 2nd Edition** is very much on developing the skills, not just testing them. In terms of speaking and writing, the approach taken is step-by-step preparation for the final, exam-style task at the end of the activity. Initial exercises are more receptive, working on a model text or dialogue. Students then analyse the words and expressions used and have guided, controlled practice of these before creating their own texts or performing their own dialogues. Words and expressions that are useful to complete these tasks successfully are highlighted in the **Speaking bank** and **Writing bank**. Pronunciation, an integral part of developing oral skills, is integrated into each unit at the most appropriate stage.

With reading and listening, there is attention to the strategies that help students to understand texts more easily. To develop reading and listening in a comprehensive way, there is a wide variety of text genres and task types.

The *Gateway 2nd Edition* Student's Book offers ten units with Grammar and Vocabulary reference and revision sections in the Language checkpoint at the end of each unit. Exam-style activities appear throughout, with consolidation and practice every two units in the Gateway to exams pages.

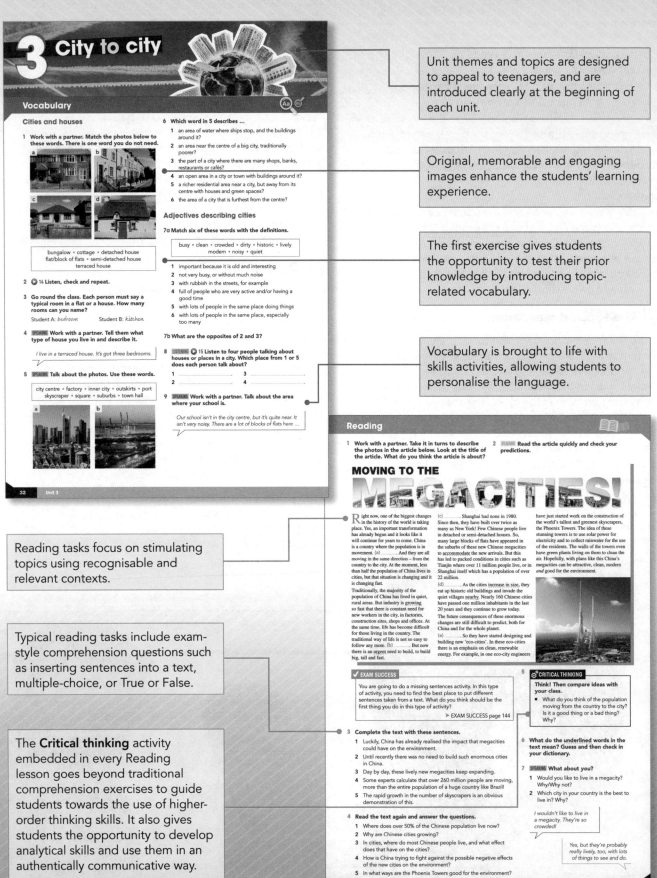

Unit themes and topics are designed to appeal to teenagers, and are introduced clearly at the beginning of each unit.

Original, memorable and engaging images enhance the students' learning experience.

The first exercise gives students the opportunity to test their prior knowledge by introducing topic-related vocabulary.

Vocabulary is brought to life with skills activities, allowing students to personalise the language.

Reading tasks focus on stimulating topics using recognisable and relevant contexts.

Typical reading tasks include exam-style comprehension questions such as inserting sentences into a text, multiple-choice, or True or False.

The **Critical thinking** activity embedded in every Reading lesson goes beyond traditional comprehension exercises to guide students towards the use of higher-order thinking skills. It also gives students the opportunity to develop analytical skills and use them in an authentically communicative way.

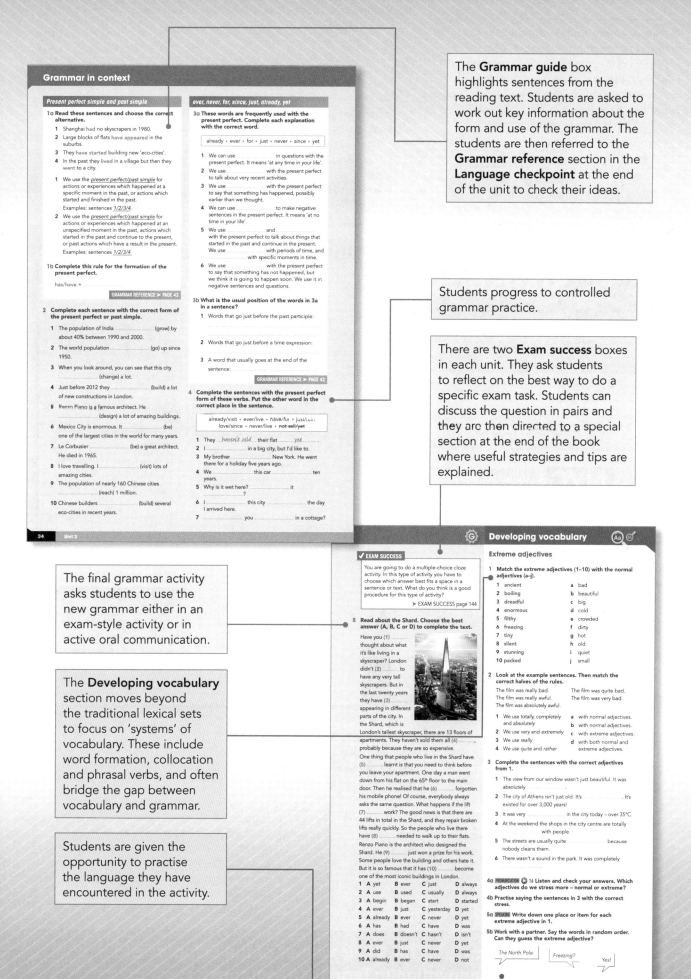

The Grammar guide box highlights sentences from the reading text. Students are asked to work out key information about the form and use of the grammar. The students are then referred to the **Grammar reference** section in the **Language checkpoint** at the end of the unit to check their ideas.

Students progress to controlled grammar practice.

There are two **Exam success** boxes in each unit. They ask students to reflect on the best way to do a specific exam task. Students can discuss the question in pairs and they are then directed to a special section at the end of the book where useful strategies and tips are explained.

The final grammar activity asks students to use the new grammar either in an exam-style activity or in active oral communication.

The **Developing vocabulary** section moves beyond the traditional lexical sets to focus on 'systems' of vocabulary. These include word formation, collocation and phrasal verbs, and often bridge the gap between vocabulary and grammar.

Students are given the opportunity to practise the language they have encountered in the activity.

Grammar in context

Present perfect simple and past simple

1a Read these sentences and choose the correct alternative.

1 Shanghai had no skyscrapers in 1980.
2 Large blocks of flats have appeared in the suburbs.
3 They have started building new 'eco-cities'.
4 In the past they lived in a village but then they went to a city.

1 We use the *present perfect/past simple* for actions or experiences which happened at a specific moment in the past, or actions which started and finished in the past.
Examples: sentences 1/2/3/4.

2 We use the *present perfect/past simple* for actions or experiences which happened at an unspecified moment in the past, actions which started in the past and continue to the present, or past actions which have a result in the present.
Examples: sentences 1/2/3/4.

1b Complete this rule for the formation of the present perfect.

has/have + _____

GRAMMAR REFERENCE ➤ PAGE 42

2 Complete each sentence with the correct form of the present perfect or past simple.

1 The population of India _____ (grow) by about 40% between 1990 and 2000.
2 The world population _____ (go) up since 1950.
3 When you look around, you can see that this city _____ (change) a lot.
4 Just before 2012 they _____ (build) a lot of new constructions in London.
5 Renzo Piano is a famous architect. He _____ (design) a lot of amazing buildings.
6 Mexico City is enormous. It _____ (be) one of the largest cities in the world for many years.
7 Le Corbusier _____ (be) a great architect. He died in 1965.
8 I love travelling. I _____ (visit) lots of amazing cities.
9 The population of nearly 160 Chinese cities _____ (reach) 1 million.
10 Chinese builders _____ (build) several eco-cities in recent years.

ever, never, for, since, just, already, yet

3a These words are frequently used with the present perfect. Complete each explanation with the correct word.

already • ever • for • just • never • since • yet

1 We can use _____ in questions with the present perfect. It means 'at any time in your life'.
2 We use _____ with the present perfect to talk about very recent activities.
3 We use _____ with the present perfect to say that something has happened, possibly earlier than we thought.
4 We can use _____ to make negative sentences in the present perfect. It means 'at no time in your life'.
5 We use _____ and _____ with the present perfect to talk about things that started in the past and continue in the present. We use _____ with periods of time, and _____ with specific moments in time.
6 We use _____ with the present perfect to say that something has not happened, but we think it is going to happen soon. We use it in negative sentences and questions.

3b What is the usual position of the words in 3a in a sentence?

1 Words that go just before the past participle:
_____

2 Words that go just before a time expression:
_____

3 A word that usually goes at the end of the sentence:
_____

GRAMMAR REFERENCE ➤ PAGE 42

4 Complete the sentences with the present perfect form of these verbs. Put the other word in the correct place in the sentence.

already/visit • ever/live • have/for • just/ruin
love/since • never/live • not sell/yet

1 They *haven't sold* their flat *yet*.
2 I _____ in a big city, but I'd like to.
3 My brother _____ New York. He went there for a holiday five years ago.
4 We _____ this car _____ ten years.
5 Why is it wet here? _____ it _____?
6 I _____ this city _____ the day I arrived here.
7 _____ you _____ in a cottage?

34   Unit 3

G **Developing vocabulary** Aa ᴮᴾ

Extreme adjectives

1 Match the extreme adjectives (1–10) with the normal adjectives (a–j).

1	ancient	a	bad
2	boiling	b	beautiful
3	dreadful	c	big
4	enormous	d	cold
5	filthy	e	crowded
6	freezing	f	dirty
7	tiny	g	hot
8	silent	h	old
9	stunning	i	quiet
10	packed	j	small

2 Look at the example sentences. Then match the correct halves of the rules.

The film was really bad.   The film was quite bad.
The film was really awful.   The film was very bad.
The film was absolutely awful.

1 We use *totally, completely* and *absolutely*
2 We use *very* and *extremely*
3 We use *really*
4 We use *quite* and *rather*

a with normal adjectives.
b with normal adjectives.
c with extreme adjectives.
d with both normal and extreme adjectives.

3 Complete the sentences with the correct adjectives from 1.

1 The view from our window wasn't just beautiful. It was absolutely _____.
2 The city of Athens isn't just old. It's _____. It's existed for over 3,000 years!
3 It was very _____ in the city today – over 35°C.
4 At the weekend the shops in the city centre are totally _____ with people.
5 The streets are usually quite _____ because nobody cleans them.
6 There wasn't a sound in the park. It was completely _____.

4a PRONUNCIATION ▶ 16 Listen and check your answers. Which adjectives do we stress more – normal or extreme?

4b Practise saying the sentences in 3 with the correct stress.

5a SPEAKING Write down one place or item for each extreme adjective in 1.

5b Work with a partner. Say the words in random order. Can they guess the extreme adjective?

The North Pole.   Freezing?   Yes!

Unit 3   35

✓ EXAM SUCCESS

You are going to do a multiple-choice cloze activity. In this type of activity you have to choose which answer best fits a space in a sentence or text. What do you think is a good procedure for this type of activity?
▶ EXAM SUCCESS page 144

5 Read about the Shard. Choose the best answer (A, B, C or D) to complete the text.

Have you (1) _____ thought about what it's like living in a skyscraper? London didn't (2) _____ to have any very tall skyscrapers. But in the last twenty years they have (3) _____ appearing in different parts of the city. In the Shard, which is London's tallest skyscraper, there are 13 floors of apartments. They haven't sold them all (4) _____, probably because they are so expensive.

One thing that people who live in the Shard have (5) _____ learnt is that you need to think before you leave your apartment. One day a man went down from his flat on the 65th floor to the main door. Then he realised that he (6) _____ forgotten his mobile phone! Of course, everybody always asks the same question. What happens if the lift (7) _____ work? The good news is that there are 44 lifts in total in the Shard, and they repair broken lifts really quickly. So the people who live there have (8) _____ needed to walk up to their flats.

Renzo Piano is the architect who designed the Shard. He (9) _____ just won a prize for his work. Some people love the building and others hate it. But it is so famous that it has (10) _____ become one of the most iconic buildings in London.

	A	B	C	D
1	A yet	B ever	C just	D always
2	A use	B used	C usually	D always
3	A begin	B began	C start	D started
4	A ever	B just	C yesterday	D yet
5	A already	B ever	C never	D yet
6	A has	B had	C have	D was
7	A does	B doesn't	C hasn't	D isn't
8	A ever	B just	C never	D yet
9	A did	B has	C have	D was
10	A already	B ever	C never	D not

Gateway to life skills lessons equip students with the necessary transferable skills for life beyond the classroom. Each unit has a Life skills lesson that allows students both controlled and freer language practice, using what they have learnt in a cumulative way.

The Life skills lesson is introduced to students with clear objectives.

Students are shown the key concepts of the Life skills lesson in a clear and concise form and have the chance to explore issues of universal interest and importance.

Engaging video activities show real teenagers talking about the Life skills topic in the form of street interviews, presentations and vlogs.

Students have many opportunities to give and share their opinions.

The Life skills lesson culminates in a productive **Life task** such as giving a presentation, creating a poster or making a plan. It gives students the opportunity to use language in an authentic and collaborative context while practising a useful and transferable Life skill.

Students listen to a wide variety of realistic types of recording which may include dialogues, radio programmes, adverts and interviews.

The second Grammar in context lesson functions in the same way as the previous one allowing students to discover grammar rules for themselves.

There is a wide variety of listening tasks, all of which appear in listening exams, such as True/False, completing notes and matching.

Listening

1 SPEAKING Work with a partner. Take turns to describe the photo.

2 LISTENING ▶ 18 Listen to part of a podcast where a student called Deniz describes her experience of the Erasmus project. Answer these questions.

1 Where's Deniz from?
2 Where has she been living?
3 What languages has she been speaking?

3 ▶ 18 Listen again and complete the notes with one or two words.

Notepad

Deniz has been living in this new city since
(a) _____ and she is leaving at
the end of (b) _____. She says the
university there is really (c) _____
and she likes the city because it's quite small,
but very (d) _____. She's seen
two or three good (e) _____
there. She thinks the best part of her
stay has been meeting people from
(f) _____. Every night they make
a (g) _____ from their country.
It has been difficult for Deniz to understand
explanations of (h) _____ in a
different language. Yesterday she finished her
(i) _____.

4 SPEAKING What about you?

1 Would you like to live and study in another country for a year? Why/Why not?
2 Where would you most like to go and study?

I'd like to live abroad. And you?

Yes, I'd like to go to a country where they speak English.

Grammar in context

Present perfect continuous

1a Read these sentences. Which are in the present perfect continuous and which are in the present perfect simple?

1 I've been living here for four months.
2 I've seen two or three brilliant concerts.
3 I've made friends with people from all over Europe.
4 Recently we've been doing lots of exams.

1b Which of the sentences gives more importance to …

a the completion and result of an action?
b the process and duration of an action?
c how many times an action has happened?
d the fact that an action is temporary, incomplete or has finished very recently?

1c Complete this rule for the formation of the present perfect continuous.

has/have + _____ + _____

GRAMMAR REFERENCE ➤ PAGE 42

2 Look at the photos. What have these people been doing?

1 _____
2 _____
3 _____
4 _____
5 _____

The Flipped classroom grammar presentation video provides a versatile and flexible learning tool, and an alternative grammar presentation which gives students greater control over their learning. Ideal for visual learners, research shows that the Flipped classroom can create a more effective language-learning environment.

Photos are used to engage students and bring the grammar to life.

Students are given lots of opportunities to use new grammar in active, oral communication. These activities usually involve personalisation. Students work in pairs or small groups and find out new things about their classmates.

Flipped classroom: watch the grammar presentation video.

3 Are these sentences grammatically correct or not? Why/Why not? If they aren't correct, change them.

1 Ouch! I've been cutting my finger.
2 We've been studying English for eight years.
3 Have you been crying?
4 She's been reading this book three times.
5 My brother has painted his bedroom, but he hasn't finished.
6 We've been waiting for the bus for half an hour and it still hasn't come.
7 Oh no! I've been breaking the window.
8 This week I've been staying with my grandparents but I'm going home tomorrow.

4 Choose the correct alternative.

1 Stop singing that song. You've *sung/been singing* it all afternoon.
2 That's it. I've *done/been doing* all my homework.
3 It's terrible! Max has *had/been having* an accident.
4 She's *looked/been looking* for her keys all day, but she still hasn't found them.
5 Why are you dirty? What have you *done/been doing*?
6 That actor has *made/been making* twenty films.
7 My eyes hurt. I've *worked/been working* on the computer all day.
8 You've *played/been playing* computer games since ten o'clock this morning. It's time to switch off!

5 Complete the dialogue with the present perfect simple or continuous forms of the verbs given.

6 SPEAKING Work with a partner. Take it in turns to ask and answer the questions. Use the present perfect continuous or simple in your answers. Decide which answers are the most imaginative.

1 Why are you hiding behind the sofa?
2 Why are your clothes so dirty?
3 Why are you crying?
4 Why are you so happy?
5 Why are you bored?
6 Why are you so tired?
7 Why aren't you watching your favourite TV programme?

Why are you hiding behind the sofa?

I've been watching a documentary about spiders and I'm really scared of them.

Interviewer:	Silvia, you're Italian, but at the moment you're living here in Bath. How long (a) _____ you _____ (live) here?
Silvia:	For six months. I (b) _____ (study) at the university, but I (c) _____ (not finish) my course yet.
Interviewer:	What (d) _____ you _____ (study)?
Silvia:	Medicine. I (e) _____ (work) in a hospital here, too. That finishes next month.
Interviewer:	Where exactly (f) _____ you _____ (live)?
Silvia:	Well, I (g) _____ (make) two really good friends on the course. We (h) _____ (live) in a house in the suburbs. I love Bath!

Developing speaking

Describing photos – 1

4 Look at photo b and complete the sentences with the words from the Speaking bank.

1 _____ see a quiet road.
2 On the _____, there are some people sitting at a table.
3 In the _____, I can see trees and fields.
4 In the _____ corner, I can see a small blackboard.
5 In the _____ of the photo, there is a blue car.

5 [SPEAKING] Tell your partner which place in photos a and b you prefer. Give reasons for your opinions.

PRACTICE MAKES PERFECT

6 [SPEAKING] Work with a partner. Take it in turns to do the task below. Use some of the expressions in the Speaking bank.

Describe the two photos. Then say which place you would prefer to live in and give reasons for your opinion.

1 [SPEAKING] Look at the photos. Work with a partner. Write at least four words that you could use to describe each one.

2 [LISTENING] ▶ 19 Listen to someone talking about one of the photos and answer the questions.

1 Which photo do they describe?
2 Which words on your list do you hear?
3 What does the speaker think of the place in the photo?

3 ▶ 19 Listen again. Which of the words or expressions in the Speaking bank does the speaker use?

💬 **SPEAKING BANK**

Useful expressions for describing photos
- In the photo I can see …
- The photo shows …
- In the foreground …
- In the background …
- At the top of the photo …
- At the bottom of the photo …
- In the middle of the photo …
- On the right …
- On the left …
- In the top/bottom right/left corner …

> The **Developing speaking** lesson develops students' oral skills with a highly-structured and supportive approach to speaking.

> Students are given extensive practice of the language they have learnt in the **Practice makes perfect** activity.

> The **Speaking bank** highlights and analyses key language for students to refer to during the productive phase of the speaking task.

Developing writing

An informal email describing a place

1 Work with a partner. Do you think these statements about the English city of Birmingham are True (T) or False (F)?

1 Birmingham is the second biggest city in Britain. T/F
2 Birmingham has more canals than Venice. T/F
3 Birmingham has a museum and theme park dedicated to chocolate. T/F
4 Heavy metal music began in Birmingham. T/F
5 Birmingham isn't on the coast, but it has a beach. T/F

2 [READING] Read this email written by Mia from Birmingham and check your answers in 1.

Hi Elena,

Thanks for your last email. It was great to hear from you!

You asked me to tell you something about my home town. Birmingham is actually the second biggest city in Britain. And it has more canals than Venice! In the past, the canals used to be quite dirty because they were next to busy factories. But they've changed a lot.

There's one really famous factory here that everybody likes. It's a chocolate factory. There's even a chocolate museum and theme park. They've just opened a 4D 'chocolate adventure' there!

We also have an enormous shopping centre called the Bullring. It's near the city centre and it's always packed. Oh, and there's a great stadium for concerts, too! People usually say that heavy metal music started in Birmingham.

Some years we've had a beach in the city centre in the summer. Birmingham isn't on the coast, but they fill an area in a main square with sand and you can pretend that you're on a real beach.

Anyway, write back soon. Don't forget to tell me about your home town. Has it changed much in the last few years?

Love,
Mia

3 Would you like to visit Birmingham after reading Mia's email? Why/Why not?

4 Look again at the email in 2. Complete the words and expressions in the Writing bank.

✏️ **WRITING BANK**

Useful words and expressions in informal letters and emails
- Begin with *Dear* or (a) _____ and the person's (b) _____
- Your first sentences can be *Thanks for* (c) _____ and/or *It was great* (d) _____
- Use contractions (e.g. *they're* or (e) _____).
- Use short forms of words (e.g. *Thanks* instead of (f) _____).
- Use interjections like *Well* or (g) _____
- Use exclamation marks (e.g. *It has more canals than Venice* (h))
- Use *Any* (i) _____ to change the subject.
- Use *Write* (j) _____, *All the best* and/or (k) _____ to end.

5 Work with a partner. Make notes about your home town. What type of place is it? What is special about it? Has it changed in the last few years? How?

PRACTICE MAKES PERFECT

6 Look at the task below and write the email. Include all the information and organise your ideas from 5 into paragraphs. Use words and expressions from the Writing bank.

An English-speaking friend has asked you to write them an email about your home town. Write the email. Say what type of place your home town is and what is special about it. Describe any recent changes.

WRITING BANK ➤ PAGE 150

> The **Writing bank** highlights and analyses the key language of the writing task and gives help in planning and organising the information they need to include. Students refer to it during the productive stage.

> Students are given help in planning and organising the information they need to use in their writing activities. Model texts give students realistic examples of different genres of written texts.

> The **Practice makes perfect** activity gives students further practice and refers them to the Writing bank at the end of the book for more extensive support and guidance.

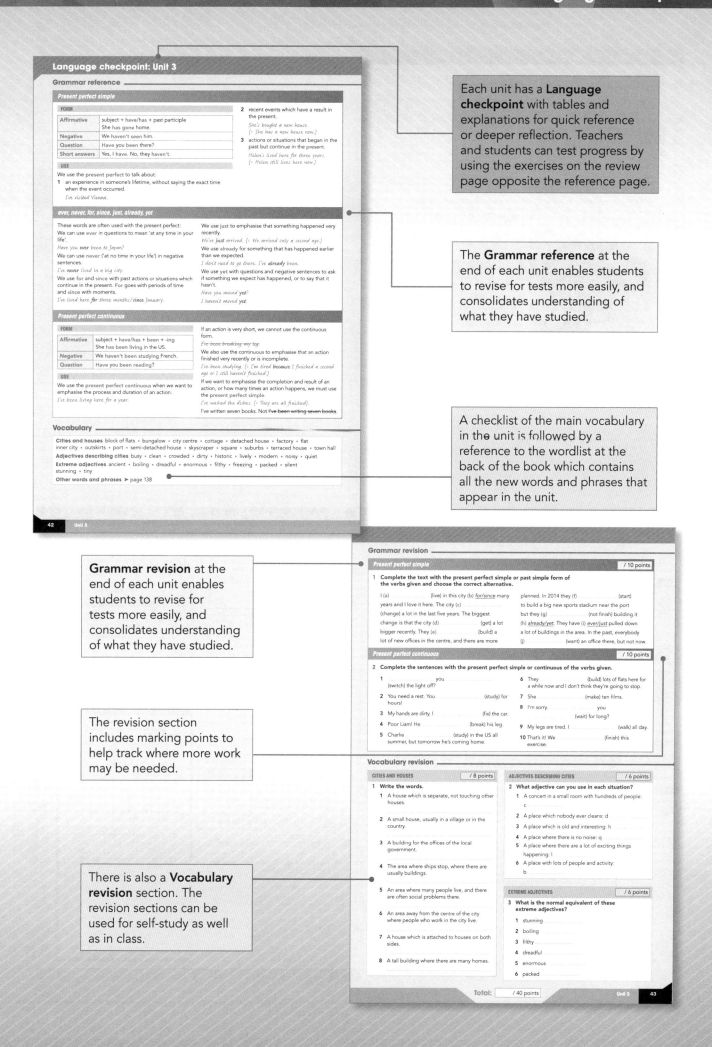

Language checkpoint: Unit 3

Grammar reference

Present perfect simple

FORM	
Affirmative	subject + have/has + past participle She has gone home.
Negative	We haven't seen him.
Question	Have you been there?
Short answers	Yes, I have. No, they haven't.

USE

We use the present perfect to talk about:

1 an experience in someone's lifetime, without saying the exact time when the event occurred.
I've visited Vienna.

2 recent events which have a result in the present.
She's bought a new house.
(= She has a new house now.)

3 actions or situations that began in the past but continue in the present.
Helen's lived here for three years.
(= Helen still lives here now.)

ever, never, for, since, just, already, yet

These words are often used with the present perfect:
We can use ever in questions to mean 'at any time in your life'.
*Have you **ever** been to Japan?*
We can use never ('at no time in your life') in negative sentences.
*I've **never** lived in a big city.*
We use for and since with past actions or situations which continue in the present. For goes with periods of time and since with moments.
*I've lived here **for** three months/**since** January.*

We use just to emphasise that something happened very recently.
*We've **just** arrived.* (= We arrived only a second ago.)
We use already for something that has happened earlier than we expected.
*I don't need to go there. I've **already** been.*
We use yet with questions and negative sentences to ask if something we expect has happened, or to say that it hasn't.
*Have you moved **yet**?*
*I haven't moved **yet**.*

Present perfect continuous

FORM	
Affirmative	subject + have/has + been + -ing She has been living in the US.
Negative	We haven't been studying French.
Question	Have you been reading?

USE

We use the present perfect continuous when we want to emphasise the process and duration of an action.
I've been living here for a year.

If an action is very short, we cannot use the continuous form.
I've been breaking my leg.
We also use the continuous to emphasise that an action finished very recently or is incomplete.
I've been studying. (= I'm tired **because** I finished a second ago or I still haven't finished.)
If we want to emphasise the completion and result of an action, or how many times an action happens, we must use the present perfect simple.
I've washed the dishes. (= They are all finished.)
I've written seven books. Not I've been writing seven books.

Vocabulary

Cities and houses block of flats · bungalow · city centre · cottage · detached house · factory · flat
inner city · outskirts · port · semi-detached house · skyscraper · square · suburbs · terraced house · town hall
Adjectives describing cities busy · clean · crowded · dirty · historic · lively · modern · noisy · quiet
Extreme adjectives ancient · boiling · dreadful · enormous · filthy · freezing · packed · silent
stunning · tiny
Other words and phrases ➤ page 138

Each unit has a **Language checkpoint** with tables and explanations for quick reference or deeper reflection. Teachers and students can test progress by using the exercises on the review page opposite the reference page.

The **Grammar reference** at the end of each unit enables students to revise for tests more easily, and consolidates understanding of what they have studied.

A checklist of the main vocabulary in the unit is followed by a reference to the wordlist at the back of the book which contains all the new words and phrases that appear in the unit.

Grammar revision

Present perfect simple   / 10 points

1 Complete the text with the present perfect simple or past simple form of the verbs given and choose the correct alternative.

I (a) _____ (live) in this city (b) _for/since_ many years and I love it here. The city (c) _____ (change) a lot in the last five years. The biggest change is that the city (d) _____ (get) a lot bigger recently. They (e) _____ (build) a lot of new offices in the centre, and there are more

planned. In 2014 they (f) _____ (start) to build a big new sports stadium near the port but they (g) _____ (not finish) building it (h) _already/yet_. They have (i) _ever/just_ pulled down a lot of buildings in the area. In the past, everybody (j) _____ (want) an office there, but not now.

Present perfect continuous   / 10 points

2 Complete the sentences with the present perfect simple or continuous of the verbs given.

1 _____ you _____ (switch) the light off?
2 You need a rest. You _____ (study) for hours!
3 My hands are dirty. I _____ (fix) the car.
4 Poor Liam! He _____ (break) his leg.
5 Charlie _____ (study) in the US all summer, but tomorrow he's coming home.
6 They _____ (build) lots of flats here for a while now and I don't think they're going to stop.
7 She _____ (make) ten films.
8 I'm sorry. _____ you _____ (wait) for long?
9 My legs are tired. I _____ (walk) all day.
10 That's it! We _____ (finish) this exercise.

Vocabulary revision

CITIES AND HOUSES   / 8 points

1 Write the words.

1 A house which is separate, not touching other houses.

2 A small house, usually in a village or in the country.

3 A building for the offices of the local government.

4 The area where ships stop, where there are usually buildings.

5 An area where many people live, and there are often social problems there.

6 An area away from the centre of the city where people who work in the city live.

7 A house which is attached to houses on both sides.

8 A tall building where there are many homes.

ADJECTIVES DESCRIBING CITIES   / 6 points

2 What adjective can you use in each situation?

1 A concert in a small room with hundreds of people: c
2 A place which nobody ever cleans: d
3 A place which is old and interesting: h
4 A place where there is no noise: q
5 A place where there are a lot of exciting things happening: l
6 A place with lots of people and activity: b

EXTREME ADJECTIVES   / 6 points

3 What is the normal equivalent of these extreme adjectives?

1 stunning _____
2 boiling _____
3 filthy _____
4 dreadful _____
5 enormous _____
6 packed _____

Total: _____ / 40 points   Unit 3   43

Grammar revision at the end of each unit enables students to revise for tests more easily, and consolidates understanding of what they have studied.

The revision section includes marking points to help track where more work may be needed.

There is also a **Vocabulary revision** section. The revision sections can be used for self-study as well as in class.

Gateway to exams: Units 3–4

Reading

1 You are going to read about the coldest city on Earth. Work with a partner. Make predictions about life there.

2 READING Read the text and check your predictions.

YAKUTSK:
life in the coldest city on Earth

At -45°C wearing glasses is not a good idea. 1 _____ I know this because I've just arrived in Yakutsk, a place where friendly local people suggest not wearing glasses when you go outside.

2 _____ It's famous because it is probably the coldest city on Earth. In January, the most freezing month, the *highest* temperature is -40°C. Today it is -43°C and the city is covered in freezing fog which only allows you to see ten metres in front of you. I decided to come to Yakutsk myself to find out how people can survive in the coldest city on Earth.

In January, the highest temperature in Yakutsk is -40°C.

I soon discover that local people describe -40°C as 'cold, but not very cold'. 3 _____ Before I go outdoors in Yakutsk for the first time I put on two pairs of socks, long underwear, two big jumpers, a heavy winter coat with hood, two pairs of gloves, and a hat. And when I walk out, I feel ... fine. In fact, I feel good.

4 _____ Then I just can't feel it, and that is dangerous. Then the cold penetrates my two pairs of gloves and starts to attack my fingers. Next it's my ears. And then my legs. Finally my whole body hurts and I decide to go back indoors. I look at my watch. I've been outside for just 13 minutes.

5 _____ Now it takes six hours by plane. There are no trains to Yakutsk. The other alternatives are a 1,000 mile boat ride up the Lena River (only during summer, when the river isn't frozen) or a 1,200 mile drive on the 'road of bones' (only during winter), which runs over frozen rivers.

6 _____ Workers continue working on building sites up to -50°C. When it gets colder than this the metal becomes too fragile to work with. Children go to school unless it's below -55°C. 'Anyway, it's a nice cold here, because we don't have wind,' says university professor Vasily Illarionov. 'When it's -40°C I like to walk to work. I like our weather, but I don't think I could live somewhere windy.'

7 _____ There are two or three weeks when the temperatures rise to 30 or 35°C. None of the buildings have air-conditioning and the air is full of mosquitoes and other insects. And there's just time to make repairs and prepare for the next winter. 'Of course it's difficult to live here' says Vladimir Fyodorov, editor of the regional newspaper. 'But the people here were born here. It's our home. What can you do about it?'

3 Read the text again. Complete it with sentences a–g.

a The inhuman temperatures are just part of daily life for the residents of the city.

b In the past it took more than three months to get to Yakutsk from Moscow.

c In fact one person told me that last November was exceptionally warm – -25°C!

d Yakutsk is a remote city in eastern Siberia with a population of 200,000.

e But after a few minutes, the cold weather starts to make my face feel uncomfortable.

f The metal sticks to your face and it's extremely painful when you try to take your glasses off.

g Unfortunately, the summers in Yakutsk sound worse than the winters.

Speaking

4 Work with a partner. Make a list of six different places or things to visit in or near where you live.

5 SPEAKING Imagine that a friend from the US called Tom is going to come and visit you for a day. You and your partner must decide which are the two best places in your list in 4 to take your friend and why. Ask for your partner's opinions and respond to them.

What do you think about going to the river with Tom?

Good idea. But to go to the river we need good weather.

> **TIP FOR READING EXAMS**

In reading activities where you complete a text with missing sentences, remember ...
First read the text quickly to get a general idea. Then read the missing sentences and find the sections of the text where you think the sentences go. Read those sections again slowly and carefully.

➤ EXAM SUCCESS page 144

> **TIP FOR SPEAKING EXAMS**

In negotiating activities, remember ...
Work with your partner and take turns to speak. Help your partner to speak if you think you are speaking too much or if your partner is not speaking enough.

➤ EXAM SUCCESS page 144

Use of English

> **TIP FOR USE OF ENGLISH**

In multiple-choice cloze activities, remember ...
Read the complete text first without thinking about the gaps. Then read again and think of words that could go in each gap. Look at the alternatives. Are any words the same as yours?

➤ EXAM SUCCESS pages 144

6 Read this text about genetically-modified foods. What are they? What good and bad aspects of these foods appear in the text?

Genetically-modified (GM) foods are foods which come from plants and animals that scientists (1) _____ changed through genetic engineering. For example, you can make a strawberry plant more resistant to the cold by adding a gene from an alpine plant that is able to live even when the weather is (2) _____ freezing. These organisms are stronger than natural organisms so they can grow in difficult conditions. The biotech companies that make GM organisms say that they will help to end world hunger. But organisations like Greenpeace say (3) _____ that the real reason for their development is so that multinational biotech companies can control food production in the world and make money.

The truth is that nobody knows what the effects of GM foods may be. Scientists have (4) _____ investigating the possible consequences (5) _____ more than ten years, but they still can't predict all the possible impacts on plants, animals and human health. They say that by the time we understand the effects, it will probably be too late and the biotech companies will (6) _____ contaminated the environment so badly that it will be impossible to fix the problem. Because GM organisms grow faster and stronger (7) _____ natural organisms, once they mix with other natural varieties they will probably change these natural species forever. But some scientists have already predicted that we will all (8) _____ eating GM foods in the future because they will be so good for our health.

7 Read the text again. Choose the best answer (A, B, C or D) to complete the text.

	A	B	C	D
1	are	has	have	will
2	really	extremely	quite	very
3	true	convinced	thinking	seeing
4	wanted	had	been	already
5	for	since	already	yet
6	finish	become	be	already
7	that	then	than	with
8	be	are	have	can

Writing

> **TIP FOR WRITING EXAMS**

In transactional activities, remember ...
It is essential to write in the correct style – informal, semi-formal or formal. Only use contractions and informal expressions in informal texts.

➤ EXAM SUCCESS page 145

Hi!
I'm having a party at 8 pm on 18th June to celebrate the end of term and I'd love you to come. You don't need to bring drinks, but I'm asking everyone to bring food. And can you come early to help me get everything ready?
Hope you can make it!
Matt

8 Write a reply to Matt's invitation.

■ Tell Matt what food you are going to bring.
■ Explain why you can't come early to help.
■ Ask if you can bring a friend to the party.
■ Offer to help tidy up after the party.

'CAN DO' PROGRESS CHECK UNITS 3–4   CEF

1 How well can you do these things in English now? Give yourself a mark from 1 to 4.

1 = I can do it very well.
2 = I can do it quite well.
3 = I have some problems.
4 = I can't do it.

a I can talk about past activities using the present perfect simple and continuous.

b I can describe cities and use extreme adjectives.

c I can understand written and spoken texts about city life.

d I can describe different parts of a photo.

e I can write emails describing places.

f I can talk about the future using different verbs and tenses.

g I can talk about meals and describe food.

h I can form new words by adding prefixes.

i I can negotiate with somebody by asking for, giving and responding to opinions.

j I can write simple replies to invitations.

2 Now decide what you need to do to improve.

1 Look again at my book/notes.
2 Do more practice exercises.
   ➤ WORKBOOK Units 3 and 4
3 Ask for help.
4 Other: _____

(Annotation callouts:)

Every two units the **Gateway to exams** pages allow students to test their progress and at the same time develop their skills through targeted training tasks for exams.

Useful exam tips cover all of the skills – **Writing, Speaking, Listening, Reading** and give guidance for **Use of English** tasks, providing invaluable reminders and hints for students to approach their exams fully prepared.

Students are referred to the **Exam success** pages at the back of the book for more detailed exploration of the skills they have been learning and the best way to approach a specific exam task.

The **'Can do' progress check** empowers students by encouraging them to measure their own progress against a checklist of tasks they are able to do successfully after every two units. It also acts as a useful summary of the language topics and skills covered so far.

For students PLUS Gradebook for teachers

The Gateway Digital Student's Book offers a content-rich interactive learning experience for your students, facilitating dynamic and engaging lessons.

Contains:

Interactive Student's Book Activities	Complete class audio	Integrated video	Note-taking function	Automated marking	Gradebook

Students can work through interactive versions of the exercises, developing their language skills through collaborative or individual learning.

Enhanced Student's Book pages are easy to navigate, and contain embedded audio and video, as well as interactive activities.

The Notes functionality enables students to put language into meaningful written practice, take presentation notes, or even add links for further research.

Completed exercises will be automatically marked, and grades synced to your teacher Gradebook when online.

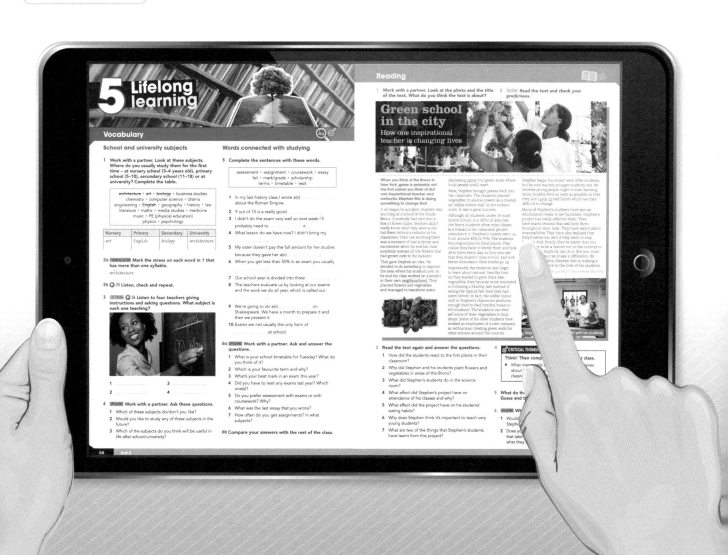

For teachers

Bring *Gateway 2nd Edition* to life in the classroom with your complete presentation and teaching tool.

Contains:

Interactive Student's Book activities

Complete class audio

Integrated video

Additional vocabulary presentation tool

Answer key feature

Note pad feature

Pages contain interactive versions of many of the Student's Book exercises with automated marking offering instant feedback.

Class audio and video can be played at the click of a button.

The built-in tools allow you to annotate and customise your presentation in advance.

The interactive vocabulary presentation tool provides additional support for presenting the Student's Book core vocabulary.

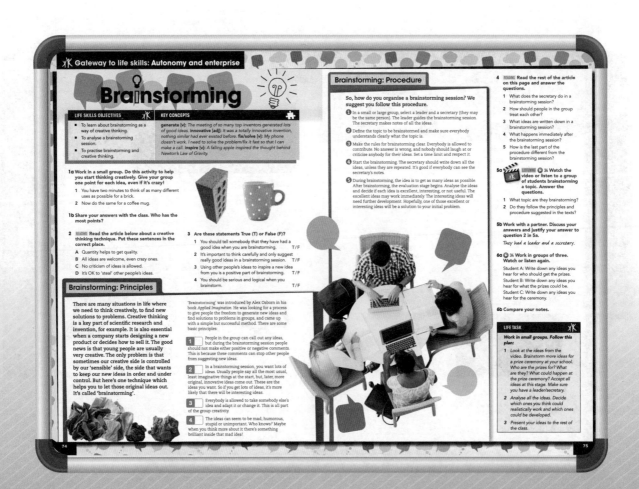

Course components
Videos

Gateway 2nd Edition offers a Flipped classroom grammar presentation video and a Life skills video in each unit. These integrate effectively into Student's Book lesson stages to enrich classes.

Flipped classroom videos

David Spencer, the author of *Gateway 2nd Edition*, delivers engaging grammar presentations that accompany one Grammar in context section for each unit. The presentations take a visual approach, introducing concepts and making new structures accessible through examples, timelines and diagrams.

Flipped classroom approach

By presenting the grammar outside the class, Flipped classroom allows more time for in-class practice. To find out more about the Flipped classroom, go to macmillangateway2.com

Flexible tool

The videos are a versatile and efficient resource for teachers which can also be used flexibly as a useful tool for mixed-ability groups or for revision.

Life skills videos

The Life skills videos form part of the Life skills lessons. They show British teens demonstrating or discussing the Life skills topic in a way that has direct relevance to all students' lives. There are comprehension tasks on the Student's Book page and further exploitation exercises and activities for the video in the Resource Centre. The video formats are fun and appeal to teens, featuring:

- vlogs
- school projects
- street interviews

After watching the video, students complete the Life task - a project or presentation in which they can apply what they have learnt during the Life skills lesson.

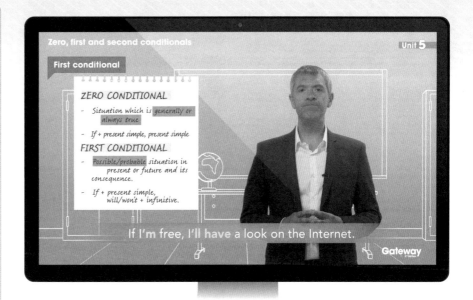

The Workbook offers consolidation of the core language in the Student's Book, with extra listening, Study skills and a special cumulative Revision page in each unit.

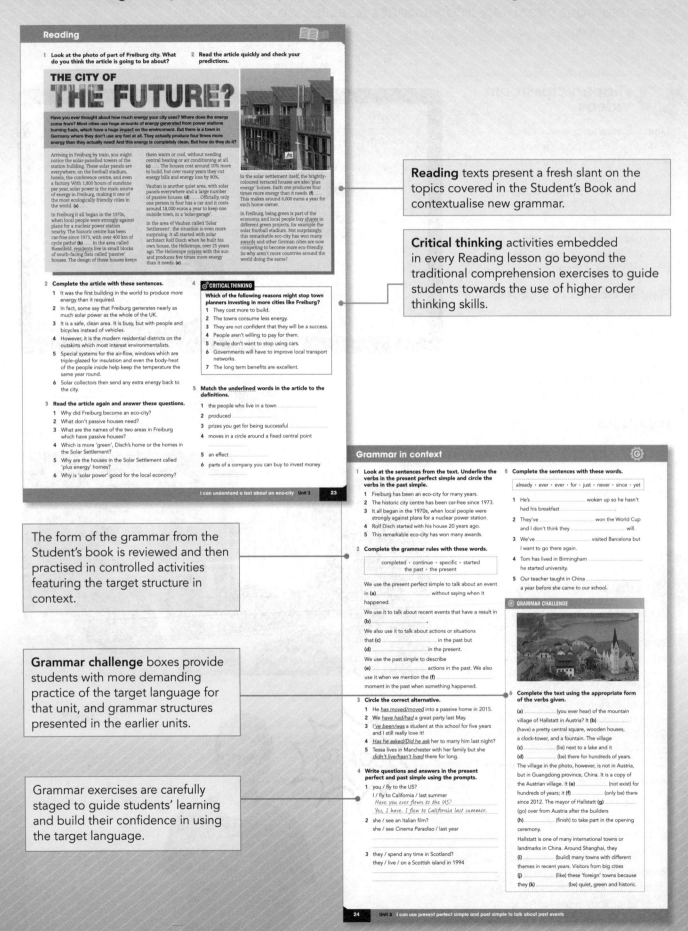

Reading texts present a fresh slant on the topics covered in the Student's Book and contextualise new grammar.

Critical thinking activities embedded in every Reading lesson go beyond the traditional comprehension exercises to guide students towards the use of higher order thinking skills.

The form of the grammar from the Student's book is reviewed and then practised in controlled activities featuring the target structure in context.

Grammar challenge boxes provide students with more demanding practice of the target language for that unit, and grammar structures presented in the earlier units.

Grammar exercises are carefully staged to guide students' learning and build their confidence in using the target language.

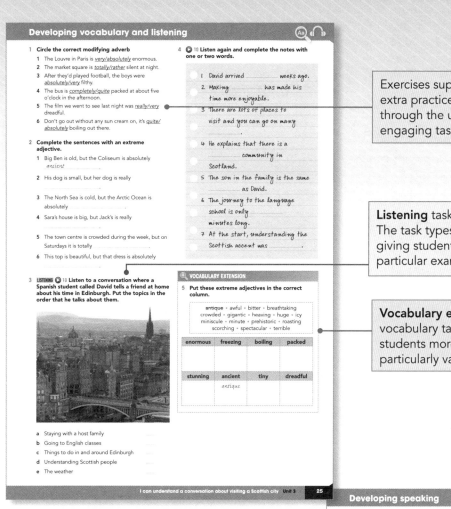

Developing vocabulary and listening

1 Circle the correct modifying adverb

1 The Louvre in Paris is _very/absolutely_ enormous.
2 The market square is _totally/rather_ silent at night.
3 After they'd played football, the boys were _absolutely/very_ filthy.
4 The bus was _completely/quite_ packed at about five o'clock in the afternoon.
5 The film we went to see last night was _really/very_ dreadful.
6 Don't go out without any sun cream on, it's _quite/absolutely_ boiling out there.

2 Complete the sentences with an extreme adjective.

1 Big Ben is old, but the Coliseum is absolutely ancient.
2 His dog is small, but her dog is really
3 The North Sea is cold, but the Arctic Ocean is absolutely
4 Sara's house is big, but Jack's is really
5 The town centre is crowded during the week, but on Saturdays it is totally
6 This top is beautiful, but that dress is absolutely

3 LISTENING 10 Listen to a conversation where a Spanish student called David tells a friend at home about his time in Edinburgh. Put the topics in the order that he talks about them.

a Staying with a host family
b Going to English classes
c Things to do in and around Edinburgh
d Understanding Scottish people
e The weather

4 10 Listen again and complete the notes with one or two words.

1 David arrived _____ weeks ago.
2 Making _____ has made his time more enjoyable.
3 There are lots of places to visit and you can go on many _____.
4 He explains that there is a _____ community in Scotland.
5 The son in the family is the same _____ as David.
6 The journey to the language school is only _____ minutes long.
7 At the start, understanding the Scottish accent was _____.

⊕ VOCABULARY EXTENSION

5 Put these extreme adjectives in the correct column.

antique • awful • bitter • breathtaking
crowded • gigantic • heaving • huge • icy
miniscule • minute • prehistoric • roasting
scorching • spectacular • terrible

enormous	freezing	boiling	packed
stunning	ancient	tiny	dreadful
	antique		

> Exercises support the Student's Book and give extra practice in developing vocabulary, often through the use of images, puzzles and other engaging tasks.

> **Listening** tasks recycle the vocabulary of the unit. The task types match those in the Student's Book, giving students further opportunity to develop particular exam skills.

> **Vocabulary extension** boxes expand on the vocabulary taught in the Student's Book, offering students more challenge. These activities are particularly valuable in mixed-ability classes.

---

1 Look at the photo and write five adjectives to describe it.

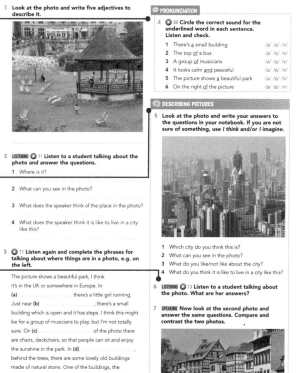

2 LISTENING 11 Listen to a student talking about the photo and answer the questions.

1 Where is it?

2 What can you see in the photo?

3 What does the speaker think of the place in the photo?

4 What does the speaker think it is like to live in a city like this?

3 11 Listen again and complete the phrases for talking about where things are in a photo, e.g. _on the left_.

The picture shows a beautiful park, I think it's in the UK or somewhere in Europe. In (a) _____ there's a little girl running. Just near (b) _____, there's a small building which is open and it has steps. I think this might be for a group of musicians to play, but I'm not totally sure. On (c) _____ of the photo there are chairs, deckchairs, so that people can sit and enjoy the sunshine in the park. In (d) _____ behind the trees, there are some lovely old buildings made of natural stone. One of the buildings, the one (e) _____, looks like a hotel. In (f) _____ the park and the buildings there is a road, I think, as I can see what looks like the top of a bus and a lorry. I'd like to be in that park. It looks calm and peaceful, and a nice way to get away from a lively city.

PRONUNCIATION

4 00 Circle the correct sound for the underlined word in each sentence. Listen and check.

1 There's a small building   /ə/ /ʊ/ /ʌ/
2 The top of a bus   /ə/ /ʊ/ /ʌ/
3 A group of musicians   /ə/ /ʊ/ /ʌ/
4 It looks calm and peaceful   /ə/ /ʊ/ /ʌ/
5 The picture shows a beautiful park   /ə/ /ʊ/ /ʌ/
6 On the right of the picture   /ə/ /ʊ/ /ʌ/

DESCRIBING PICTURES

5 Look at the photo and write your answers to the questions in your notebook. If you are not sure of something, use _I think_ and/or _I imagine_.

1 Which city do you think this is?
2 What can you see in the photo?
3 What do you like/not like about the city?
4 What do you think it is like to live in a city like this?

6 LISTENING 13 Listen to a student talking about the photo. What are her answers?

7 SPEAKING Now look at the second photo and answer the same questions. Compare and contrast the two photos.

> **Pronunciation** boxes help students really focus on an aspect of pronunciation relevant to that speaking topic, heightening their awareness of the common sounds, intonation and stress of English and providing them with an audio model.

> **Describing pictures** sections form part of each Developing speaking page and provide students with carefully staged practice of exam-style image description.

> The audio model gives students examples of useful language and provides guidance on how best to tackle an exam-style task. There is then another image on the same theme, which they can describe using the model to help them.

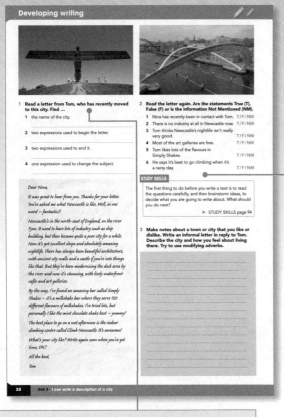

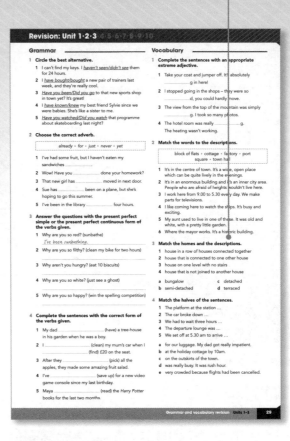

Cumulative revision pages provide essential recycling of language from not only the preceding unit but also earlier units in the book.

Further analysis and highlighting of key language from the same type of writing task as in the Student's Book.

Study skills boxes help students to improve their studying habits.

Gateway to exams pages appear every two units, offering Reading, Listening, Use of English and Writing tasks. The topics and tasks reflect what has been covered in the preceding two units, providing students with the opportunity to further develop their exam skills, while recycling key grammar and vocabulary.

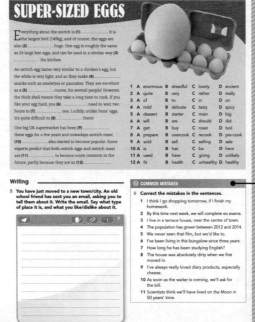

Common mistakes boxes provide error correction practice, with the focus on the language of the preceding two units. They highlight mistakes often made by students at this level, giving them the opportunity to recognise and reflect on any such errors they may be making in their own work.

Course components
Online Workbook

All the Workbook content and more in a fully-interactive format for flexible self-study.

Contains:

Interactive Workbook activities

Complete Workbook audio

Integrated video

Automated marking for instant feedback

Gradebook

Multiple classes and levels can be managed in a single location, and the content-locking feature gives you control over how you set tasks for your students.

Detailed feedback on activity scores and progress all help to create a highly-personalised self-study environment.

Multiple attempts keep students motivated, allowing them to consolidate what they have learned in class in an engaging way. Students can also access the Flipped classroom videos and activities on the Online Workbook, making this an excellent tool for developing independent learning.

The messaging and notification features allow you to correspond with your students, send homework reminders, and notify your classes when results are available.

Results are automatically collated in the Gradebook and displayed in an easy-to-read, easy-to-compare way. Learner progress can be monitored at a glance, highlighting areas where students may require additional support or assistance.

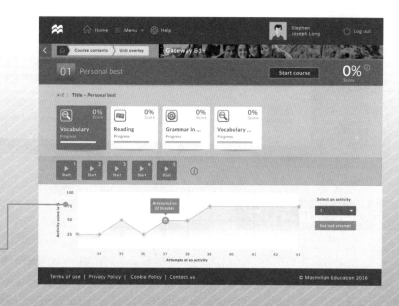

Course components
Teacher's and Student's Resource Centres

The Resource Centres contain a wealth of downloadable worksheets, multimedia assets and additional resources to support your *Gateway 2nd Edition* core course content.

KING ARTHUR AND THE KNIGHTS OF THE ROUND TABLE

Stephen Colbourn

MACMILLAN READERS

Student's Resource Centre

For students, the Student's Resource Centre provides complementary materials to consolidate learning and encourage independent study including:

- Teen-focused culture worksheets to inspire a broader cultural perspective

- A graded Macmillan Reader, with extra activities and extended reading support

- Study skills materials to encourage students to take control of their learning

- Life skills video worksheets and Flipped classroom video worksheets provide additional support for students to use with the videos.

Teacher's Resource Centre

The Teacher's Resource Centre is your go-to place for resources to deliver dynamic lessons, assign for homework assignments and to support you in the classroom. The flexible content includes:

- Audio and video files and scripts

- Complete answer keys

- Teacher tips and videos

- Extra grammar worksheets and communication activities

- Everyday English worksheets

- Optional CLIL and literature lessons

- Teacher notes and guides to accompany all material

Sounds App

This award-winning app helps students practise and play with pronunciation wherever they are. Carefully selected wordlists from the *Gateway 2nd Edition* course are now available to download within the app.

Course components
Testing and assessment materials

For teachers

Extensive resources for assessing your students' progress and preparing them for international and school-leaving examinations.

Test generator

The Test Generator allows you to create customised tests from an extensive database of exercises.

- Aligned closely to CEFR learning outcomes
- Includes a range of reading, writing, speaking and listening tasks typical of international and school-leaving exams
- Comes with the option to save tests in progress and to preview before printing
- Allows for maximum flexibility in choosing the test content
- Teacher-version of tests complete with answer keys

Printable tests

A comprehensive range of printable tests are available on the Teacher's Resource Centre in both PDF and editable Word format. Tests matched to the course level can be selected and then customised to meet the specific needs of your school and classes.

- One diagnostic test per level
- Ten Unit tests, three Review tests and one End-of-year test for tracking progress
- Aligned closely to CEFR learning outcomes and international and school-leaving exams
- Complete answer keys, audio and audio scripts for all tests
- Two levels of difficulty for each test

Teacher support
Dave's top teaching tips

Here are some great teaching tips to help you throughout the year. These tips give you strategies for classroom management, planning and student training that you can use again and again to improve your students' results and get the best out of your teaching.

⚔ TEACHING LARGE CLASSES

One of the potential difficulties in teaching large classes is getting students to participate actively in the learning process. Consider:

- teaching from different points in the classroom to give the students the feeling of being in the middle of the 'action' rather than an observer. Moving around the class makes the room feel smaller and encourages student involvement.
- giving regular feedback by using some of the next class or handouts to clarify points students haven't understood.
- setting up routines (weekly homework assignments of 30 minutes).
- relating what students have learnt to the exam (a common goal).
- giving regular short tests and dictations.
- writing an outline on the board about what will be taught in class.
- giving fast finishers something to do (see Teaching notes for suggestions) or directing them to the Workbook.

🔍 TEACHING EXPRESSIONS

Expressions are multi-word phrases that are very frequently used and function as a unit. They are generally pronounced as if they are one word, or unit, or 'chunk'. Fixed expressions such as expressions of opinions perform specific discourse functions, which are not easily determined by looking them up in a dictionary as individual words. Such sequences play an important role in the production of fluent speech. By learning these fixed expressions students can easily transfer them to a wide variety of different topics or situations.

It is often the case that students learn these expressions, use them in the class and then go back to using just one expression they were already familiar with. Point out to students they can gain more points in an oral exam if they use a variety of expressions.

💬 CUTTING DOWN ON TEACHER TALKING TIME

Teacher Talking Time (TTT) is the amount of time the teacher talks in the classroom. The teacher should be aware of the quality of their TTT and how it is used. A large amount of TTT can slow the pace and student under-involvement leading to a loss of concentration, boredom and reduced learning. Strategies for reducing the amount of TTT include:

- Waiting for an answer when you ask a question. Students need 'processing' time.
- Correcting student responses, but not repeating them. If necessary, gesture to the first student to repeat.
- Asking open-ended questions (e.g. *Wh-* questions) which require longer answers, e.g. *What did you do yesterday?* instead of *Did you go to school yesterday?*
- Varying feedback: students can check activities in pairs. Feedback involving the teacher can be used for more problematic questions rather than every exercise.
- Eliciting explanations from students instead of explaining.
- Presenting students with clear examples and guided questions so that they do not need to be 'told'. Guided discovery leads to better understanding and learning.

A useful guideline is to limit TTT to 30% of class time and no more than ten minutes at a time.

🔍 GAMES IN THE CLASSROOM

Vocabulary games such as Snowman (where the teacher writes a number of gaps on the board and students take turns guessing letters of the word before the snowman is drawn) are useful for practising and reviewing language. They engage the students, who should remember more as a result. When using games, your instructions need to be clear and precise. As with all instructions, you need to do a comprehension check. For example, after explaining what to do, ask the students to explain the game back to you. Another option is to give a demonstration of the game by playing it yourself with a few of the students while the others watch.

When planning games you need to consider what your aims and objectives are. Games are particularly useful for reviewing work from the previous lesson, checking what students know before teaching a new language item, practising a new language item you have just presented, warming up at the beginning of the lesson or filling in at the end of a lesson.

✔ BEING SUCCESSFUL IN EXAMS

In order to be successful in exams, students need to be familiar with the exam format.

- *What type of tasks are there?*
- *How long do students have for each section?*
- *How are the different sections scored?*

Encourage students to analyse different exam tasks and reflect on the sub-skills they need (i.e. skimming and scanning, listening for detailed understanding of numbers and letters, reading quickly for general understanding) and the techniques they need to learn (picking out the important words, ignoring words that aren't important for the question, etc.). If students focus on the language, exam techniques and skills they need for the different tasks in their English exam, it will impact on their exam marks. In addition, it gives students the information they need to be able to organise their time during the exam.

Each section is worth a certain number of points. Remind students not to spend too much time on one particular section. It is better to answer all the questions than to do an excellent job on some and not have enough time to do the others. Advise your students that if they run out of time they should write notes.

By doing model or practice tests, students will become familiar with the exam format (how much time they have for each section, how much each section is worth, how many words they have to write, where they should write their text, etc.) and this will help them allocate their time effectively during the exam. Students will have to decide if they have enough time to write a rough draft, and should try to leave some time at the end to check their work. Help students to prepare a mental checklist for checking their work.

💬 ORGANISING PAIRWORK ACTIVITIES

Pairwork means more speaking time for students. If 30 students speak in turn in a 60-minute class, students speak for an average of two minutes per class. Using pairwork activities, they can speak for 30 minutes. When students are working in pairs, it's a good time to talk to or listen to one student at a time without everyone observing.

If you ask your class to get into pairs, almost inevitably the students will pair up with their friends or the person closest. This is fine sometimes, however, it's good practice to vary the make-up of pair work partners so students have variation in their practice and in working with different personalities.

Certain speaking skills are necessary when working with another person so you should explicitly teach phrases which help students interrupt politely (*Yes, I agree, but…/ May I… So you think …, question tags, etc.*).

You could play some quiet music in the background when students are doing a speaking activity to help students feel more relaxed about speaking in English.

🏃 PERSONALISATION

Personalisation is when students communicate ideas about themselves as opposed to acting out role-plays or imaginary dialogues, etc. when they will be taking on others' opinions and information. Personalisation is important in learning a second language as it makes language more meaningful and therefore memorable to learners. Where possible, extend and adapt activities to give students the opportunity to apply the lesson's language or theme to themselves.

✔ ACCURACY VERSUS FLUENCY

Accuracy is the ability to produce correct sentences using correct grammar and vocabulary. Fluency is the ability to read, speak or write easily, smoothly and expressively. The accuracy/fluency question depends on the purpose of the activity students are doing in the class. Controlled and semi-controlled speaking practice such as drills and information exchanges are working on accuracy. Freer speaking production should focus on fluency.

In general, teachers should avoid correcting too much in a speaking class. This interrupts the student's train of thought and can frustrate the student. The emphasis is on getting students to talk and then keeping them talking, intervening mainly to encourage quiet students to add their point of view. Monitor the students and note down errors to take a few minutes at the end of class for a quick feedback session.

🔍 MAXIMISING YOUR MEMORY

It is likely that students will remember words that they have analysed and evaluated in some way. If they have learnt the word in context and they have fully understood the word rather than just learning it based upon a definition, it is more likely to be remembered long-term.

Discuss with students how they learn words best – do they need to hear them, see them written down or write them down themselves? Some students memorise vocabulary by associating new words with ideas or anecdotes. Good learners create mnemonic devices such as short phrases, tunes or poems. In order to internalise vocabulary, students should also review vocabulary regularly. To really improve vocabulary, students need to study vocabulary in context and that means reading in English. When your students come across a new word, encourage them to look at its place in the sentence, and look at the words that appear with it.

- Are there any patterns?
- Is the context usually formal or casual?
- Is the context written or spoken?
- Is the word typically used for one topic only?

If it's a word your students don't know, teach them to look at context clues to try and deduce meaning. Finally, they can find the meaning in a good dictionary and make a note in their vocabulary notebook.

✏️ WRITING TASKS

Although the writing process may vary depending on the task, the basic steps it includes are the same.

Before beginning to write, students need to consider the purpose of the text and who they are writing to, which will affect the tone (*formal or informal*).

The first phase is when students brainstorm ideas (they can make lists, mind maps, or think of the 'six wise men' – *Why? What? Where? When? How? Who?*). It is important to spend time on this stage as it makes the next steps easier. They then select and order their ideas.

If students are writing a longer text, they may now need to carry out some research into their chosen topic.

Next, students write a first draft as quickly as they can, including all the main points from the brainstorming phase.

The next stage is the revision process when students should take a global look at their text and decide if the text flows in a clear, well-organised way.

The final stage is the editing process. Students should look closely at spelling, grammar, punctuation and word choice. Here is a useful checklist that you can photocopy for students:

CHECKING YOUR WRITING

Check for mistakes with:

- Punctuation
- Capital letters
- Style
- Spelling
- Tenses
- Agreement between the subject and verb, e.g. *He works* … not *He work.*
- Word order
- Content

It can also be useful to use a model text for writing practice. A model is a text that provides a good example of how texts of a particular kind can be written. You should draw their attention to features such as layout, structure and fixed phrases that they can make use of in their own written text. Model texts can also develop useful exam techniques such as planning and self-correction. Always read the model text provided in the Teaching notes with your students and go through the writing tasks in detail so that students are fully aware of why they are writing and who they are writing to.

Teacher support
Teacher development tips index

There are a number of methodological and practical tips which are strategically placed within the teacher's notes in the *Gateway 2ⁿᵈ Edition* Teacher's Book to be of most use to the teacher not just during planning, setting up and evaluating activities, but also helping 'on the spot' in certain language or pronunciation areas.

CLASSROOM TIPS AND PLANNING

Kinaesthetic learners	p88	Reformulating	p117	Carrying out listening tasks (part 2)	p127

LANGUAGE

Negative prefixes and Adjectives	p29	Modal verbs	p80	Reported questions	p115
Effective study of grammar	p31	Giving instructions	p88	Reported commands	p115
Synonyms and partial synonyms	p32	*by* + agent	p90	Modal verbs of speculation and deduction – present	p124
State and action verbs	p35	Using prepositions	p91		
Dictionary skills	p41	Defining relative clauses	p101	Modal verbs of speculation and deduction – past	p124
used to	p47	Phrasal verbs	p102		
Present perfect continuous	p60	Non-defining relative clauses	p105	Third conditional	p128
Use of tenses	p68	Suffixes – jobs	p110	Indeterminate pronouns	p135
Present simple with time expressions	p69	Reported speech	p111	Collocations	p136
		-ing and *-ed* adjectives	p112	*I wish/if only*	p138

STUDENT TRAINING

Recording vocabulary	p29	Asking for and giving information	p49	Letters of application	p85
Inference in reading	p30	Predicting content in text	p55	Paying attention to the task	p85
Carrying out listening tasks (part 1)	p34	Missing sentences reading activities	p55	Matching activities	p89
Portfolio assessment – learning diaries	p35	Informal writing	p62	Predicting text content	p89
		Using adjectives	p67	Multiple-choice listening	p93
Question tags	p36	Finding the meaning of a word in a dictionary	p67	A for-and-against essay	p95
Assessing writing	p38			How to improve your results in grammar exercises	p102
Giving a presentation	p46	Negotiating in an oral activity	p73		
Polite requests	p48	Informal invitations	p74	Being positive in listening tests	p104
How to learn everyday expressions	p49	Reading for general and specific information	p79	Reflecting on the year	p139

PRONUNCIATION

Sentence stress	p31	Emphasis on *do/does*	p50	Syllable stress	p99
Intonation	p32	Emphatic stress	p57	*-ed* adjectives	p113
Question tags	p36	Contracted form *'ll*	p68	Modal verbs of speculation: strong and weak form	p125
Pronunciation of past perfect	p43	Unstressed vowels	p69		
Word stress in phrasal verbs and their noun counterparts	p44	Contractions	p80	Homophones	p133

The Common European Framework of Reference (CEFR) is a widely used standard created by the Council of Europe. *Gateway 2nd Edition* is carefully mapped to the CEFR helping teachers identify students' actual progress and helping them to set their learning priorities.

Gateway 2nd Edition offers a wide range of teaching materials in various components which give teachers the opportunity to develop all aspects of their students' language ability. The CEFR can be used to track their progress.

On pages 25–27 are the B1 and B2 descriptors (description of competences) covered in the B1+ level of *Gateway 2nd Edition*. B2 descriptors are also available in the Gateway B2 Teacher's Book.

A basic level of confidence with the B1 descriptors is expected as students start using *Gateway 2nd Edition* B1+ and, by the end of the course, students should be fully competent with the B1 descriptors and with some of the B2 descriptors.

In the Teacher's Resources you will also find a list of unit-by-unit descriptors with suggested targets which can be used for self-assessment. Students can use these at any point to get a detailed picture of their own individual progress.

WHAT IS A EUROPEAN LANGUAGE PORTFOLIO (ELP)?

The European Language Portfolio (ELP) was developed by the Language Policy Unit of the Council of Europe

- to support the development of learner autonomy, plurilingualism and intercultural awareness and competence;
- to allow users to record their language learning achievements and their experience of learning and using languages.

If you are using portfolios as a way of evaluating your students' coursework over the year, you will find a wide variety of opportunities within each *Gateway 2nd Edition* unit to provide material for the dossier.

A portfolio is a means to document a person's achievements. Artists, architects or designers collect samples of their work in portfolios and students are encouraged to do the same. Most of the time, these samples will be texts created by the students, but they could also include photos of classroom scenes, wall displays, audio recordings and videos. All these documents provide evidence of a student's performance, e.g. during a discussion, an oral presentation or a role-play.

Within each unit, there are several opportunities for students to practise speaking and record their conversations for the dossier in their portfolio. Students could record their conversations, date them and include them in their portfolio. They then assess their performance in each speaking activity and give themselves a mark according to the following self-assessment criteria:

CONTENT (1–5)

Did I say what I wanted to say? Was I interesting? Did I speak in English for a long time? Did I hesitate a lot?

VOCABULARY AND GRAMMAR (1–5)

Did I use different words? Did I use words I've learned recently? Were my sentences well constructed? Did I make a lot of errors?

COOPERATION (1–5)

Did I listen to my partner? Did we help each other if we had problems? Did we both speak for approximately the same length of time?

IN ENGLISH! (1–5)

When I didn't know how to say something, did I use English to solve my problem? Did we use English to talk about whose turn it was to speak?

The portfolio consists of three parts: the **Language Passport** with information about a student's proficiency in one or more languages, i.e. qualifications; the **Language Biography** where students reflect on their learning process and progress and say what they can do in their foreign language(s); and the **Dossier**, which is a collection of materials and data put together by students to document and illustrate their learning experiences.

Although it may be a demanding task to set up in the beginning, the overall aim is for students to be involved in planning, collecting and evaluating their own work, thereby taking responsibility for their own learning. This in turn may lead to increased participation and autonomy on the part of the learner.

Listening			1	2	3	4	5	6	7	8	9	10
		page number										
B1	I can follow clearly articulated speech directed at me in everyday conversation, though I sometimes have to ask for repetition of particular words and phrases.		6	12	32	44	58			104		130
B1	I can generally follow the main points of extended discussion around me, provided speech is clearly articulated in standard dialect.		6	31		50 52	64	75	90		116	
B1	I can understand the main points of radio news bulletins and simpler recorded material on topics of personal interest delivered relatively slowly and clearly.			18 23	32	44 49	63		89			
B1	I can catch the main points in TV programmes on familiar topics when the delivery is relatively slow and clear.		11	23		49			89	101	115	127

	1	2	3	4	5	6	7	8	9	10

Listening

page number

		1	2	3	4	5	6	7	8	9	10
B2	I can understand simple technical information, such as operating instructions for everyday equipment.						70				
B2	I can understand what is said to me in standard spoken language even in a noisy environment.	11				64					127
B2	I can follow a lecture or talk, provided the subject matter is familiar and clearly structured.		24	37		66		90			
B2	I can understand most radio documentaries delivered in standard language and can identify the speaker's mood, tone etc. by using contextual clues.		23	38	49		76	90		115	127
B2	I can understand documentaries, live interviews, talk shows and the majority of films in standard dialect.	11				63	83				127 128
B2	I can follow the main ideas of complex speech on concrete and abstract topics in standard dialect, including technical discussions on familiar topics.				49 50	66	76				
B2	I can use a variety of strategies to achieve comprehension, including listening for main points and checking understanding.	11						89	102 104	116	

Reading

page number

		1	2	3	4	5	6	7	8	9	10
B1	I can understand the main points in short newspaper articles about current and familiar topics.	10	22	36	48		82	91		117	
B1	I can read columns or interviews in newspapers and magazines in which someone discusses a current topic or event and understand the overall meaning of the text.	7 10		33							
B1	I can guess the meaning of single unknown words from the context, thus deducing the meaning of expressions if the topic is familiar.	7	19	33	45	59	71	85	97	111	123
B1	I can skim short texts (for example news summaries) and find relevant facts and information (for example, who has done what and where).	10 15	22	36		62 63		88 89	97	114 119	
B1	I can understand the most important information in short, simple information brochures.		22	36	48	62	74 75		101 105	114	126
B1	I can understand simple messages and standard letters (for example, from businesses, clubs or authorities).					69		93			
B1	In private letters I can understand those parts dealing with events, feelings and wishes well enough to correspond regularly with a pen friend.		27	41	53						
B1	I can understand the plot of a clearly structured story, recognising the most important episodes and events and understanding their significance.		19						111	119	
B2	I can rapidly grasp the content and the significance of news, articles and reports on topics connected with my interests, and decide if a closer reading is worthwhile.	7		33	45 56	59	71	85			
B2	I can read and understand articles and reports on current problems in which the writers express specific attitudes and points of view.	10			45	67	71 79			111	123
B2	I can understand in detail texts within my field of interest or the area of my academic speciality.	7	19	33	45	59	71	85	97	111	123
B2	I can understand specialised articles on unfamiliar topics if I can occasionally check with a dictionary.	10		36		62	74	88	97 101	111 114	
B2	I can read reviews dealing with the content and criticism of cultural topics (films, theatre, books, concerts) and summarise the main points.	10					79	85 93	97 105		
B2	I can read letters on topics within my areas of interest and grasp the most important points.	15	27	41	53						131
B2	I can understand in a narrative or play the motives for the characters' actions and their consequences for the development of the plot.		19						111	119	

		1	2	3	4	5	6	7	8	9	10
Speaking: Spoken Interaction		page number									
B1	I can start, maintain and close simple conversations on topics that are familiar or of personal interest.	6 14	21	32 33	44 52	58 61 65	76	90	96 102	116	122 123 128
B1	I can maintain a conversation or discussion but may sometimes have difficulty when trying to be very specific.	7	19	33	45	61	73	90	104	110 117	
B1	I can deal with most situations likely to arise when making travel arrangements through an agent or when actually travelling.		19 26								
B1	I can give or seek personal views and opinions in an informal discussion with friends.	7 13	19	38 40	45 47 52	58 61	71 73	85 87	96 101	117	122 123
B1	I can agree and disagree politely.				51 52			84 92			
B2	I can initiate, maintain and end discourse naturally with effective turn-taking.	14	26				78				130
B2	I can exchange considerable quantities of detailed factual information on matters within my fields of interest.	14	18	40	50	66		90	104	116	
B2	I can convey degrees of emotion and highlight the personal significance of events and experiences.								104		
B2	I can engage in extended conversation in a clearly participatory fashion on most general topics.	11	23 26		52	59			101	111 116	122
B2	I can account for and sustain my opinions in discussion by giving relevant explanations and arguments.				52		73	92			123
B2	I can keep a discussion going, confirm comprehension and invite others to contribute.				52	61	78	92	103		122
B2	I can carry out a prepared interview, checking and confirming information and following up on interesting replies.	13	31		52 56	58 65 67	73 77	87	96	117	124

		1	2	3	4	5	6	7	8	9	10
Speaking: Spoken Production		page number									
B1	I can narrate a story.								104		
B1	I can give detailed accounts of experiences, describing feelings and reactions.		21			58			104		
B1	I can describe dreams, hopes and ambitions.		23								128
B1	I can explain and give reasons for my plans, intentions and actions.		26	39	51		70				
B1	I can relate the plot of a book or film and describe my reactions.								105	116	
B1	I can paraphrase short written passages orally, using the original text wording and ordering.				45				97		
B2	I can give clear, detailed descriptions on a wide range of subjects related to my fields of interest.		23	32 40		66	78	92	96	115	
B2	I can understand and summarise orally short extracts from news items, interviews or documentaries containing opinions, argument and discussion.								102	116	
B2	I can construct a chain of reasoned argument, linking my ideas logically.	10		33	52		70	92			127
B2	I can explain a viewpoint on a topical issue, giving the advantages and disadvantages of various options.		23		50	66		92			127
B2	I can speculate about causes, consequences and hypothetical situations.			38	47	64 65				118	128 134

		1	2	3	4	5	6	7	8	9	10
Speaking: Strategies		page number									
B1	I can repeat back part of what someone has said to confirm that we understand each other.	14	26								
B1	I can ask someone to clarify what they have just said.		26								130
B1	When I can't think of the word I want, I can use a simple word meaning something similar.	9 14				66		84		110 118	122 127
B2	I can use standard phrases like "That's a difficult question to answer" to gain time and keep the turn while formulating what to say.					67	78	92			

		1	2	3	4	5	6	7	8	9	10

Speaking: Strategies

Level	Descriptor	1	2	3	4	5	6	7	8	9	10
	page number										
B2	I can make a note of "favourite mistakes" and consciously monitor speech for them.		31		57		83		109		135
B2	I can generally correct slips and errors if I become aware of them or if they have led to misunderstandings.						73		96 103		129 130

Vocabulary: Language Quality

Level	Descriptor	1	2	3	4	5	6	7	8	9	10
	page number										
B1	I can keep a conversation going comprehensibly, but have to pause to plan and correct what I am saying – especially when I talk freely for longer periods.		18								
B1	I can convey simple information of immediate relevance, getting across which point I feel is most important.	6		35			70			120 121	132
B1	I have a sufficient vocabulary to express myself with some circumlocutions on most topics pertinent to my everyday life such as family, hobbies and interests, travel and current events.	6 16 17	21 28 29	32 35 42	44 47 54 55	58	73 80	84 94 95	96	113	125
B1	I can express myself reasonably accurately in familiar, predictable situations.	6 9	28 29		54 55	61	73	84	106 107	110	122 135
B2	I can produce stretches of language with a fairly even tempo; although I can be hesitant as I search for expressions, there are few noticeably long pauses.		25		47 57	61		90	99		
B2	I can pass on detailed information reliably.	9	25	42 43	44	58		87		121	
B2	I have sufficient vocabulary to express myself on most general topics.	6 9 17	28 29	32 42	44 47	58 68 69	70 80 81	94 95	99 106 107	113 120	135 132 133
B2	I can communicate with reasonable accuracy and correct mistakes that have led to misunderstandings.		28 29	42	54 55	61	77	87	106 107	110	125

Writing

Level	Descriptor	1	2	3	4	5	6	7	8	9	10
	page number										
B1	I can write simple connected texts on a range of topics within my field of interest and can express personal views and opinions.	15					79 83			119	
B1	I can write simple texts about experiences or events, for example about a trip.		31		53				109	119	
B1	I can write personal letters to friends or acquaintances asking for or giving them news and narrating events.	15	27 31	41	53 57						
B1	In a letter I can express feelings such as happiness, interest, regret and sympathy.	15		41							131
B1	I can reply in written form to advertisements and ask for more complete or more specific information about products (for example, a car or an academic course).					67					
B1	I can convey simple factual information to friends, or ask for information, via letters or e-mails.	15	27		53						
B2	I can write clear and detailed texts (essays, reports or presentations) on various topics related to my interests.						79 83	89			
B2	I can summarise information from different sources and media.		23	37					101		
B2	I can discuss a topic in an essay or "letter to the editor", giving reasons for or against a specific point of view.						83				
B2	I can develop an argument systematically in an essay, letter or report, emphasising decisive points and including supporting details.					67	79 83	93	105		131
B2	I can write about events and real or fictional experiences in a detailed and easily readable way.		27							119	131
B2	I can write a detailed review of a film or a book.								105		

KEY LEARNING OUTCOMES

CEF

Students will be able to:

- talk about routines and what's happening now using the present simple and present continuous
- describe people's appearance and personality
- understand written and spoken texts about identity
- ask for and give personal information
- write a short, informal email about themselves and their friends

UNIT OVERVIEW

Vocabulary
Appearance
Personality

Reading
Special people!
CRITICAL THINKING Agreeing and disagreeing with a statement about geniuses

Grammar in context
Present simple and present continuous
Adverbs of frequency

Developing vocabulary
Synonyms and partial synonyms
PRONUNCIATION Word stress

Life skills
Personal well-being:
Building your confidence

Listening
Personality test

Grammar in context
State and action verbs

Developing speaking
Asking for and giving personal information

Developing writing
An informal email describing people

Exam success
Reading: True/False activities
Listening: Matching the speaker and information

DIGITAL OVERVIEW

Presentation Kit

- **Flipped classroom video Unit 1:** State and action verbs
- **Life skills video Unit 1:** Building your confidence
- ⒱ **Vocabulary tool:** Appearance
- **Interactive versions of Student's Book activities**
- **Integrated audio and answer key for all activities**
- **Workbook pages with answer key**

Teacher's Resource Centre

- **Flipped classroom video Unit 1:** State and action verbs
- **Life skills video Unit 1:** Building your confidence
- **Grammar communication activity Unit 1:** The first sentence
- **Worksheets for this unit, including:**
  – Grammar Practice worksheet Unit 1
  – Flipped classroom video worksheet Unit 1: State and action verbs
  – Literature worksheet Units 1 and 2
  – Culture worksheet Unit 1
  – Life skills video worksheet Unit 1
  – Everyday English worksheet Unit 1

Student's App

Gateway 2nd Edition wordlist for the award-winning Sounds App (available for download)

✓ TESTING AND ASSESSMENT

Resources for exam preparation and measuring student progress

- Test Generator Unit 1
- Printable test Unit 1
- Gateway to exams Units 1 and 2 (end of Unit 2)

Vocabulary p6

Talking about people's appearance and personality

WARMER

In pairs, students discuss the meaning of the unit title *Personal best*. Have students discuss their thoughts in pairs then elicit ideas from around the class.

Suggested answer

The theme of this unit is focused on the individual, looking at appearance and personality. The phrase *personal best* is often used in sport, for an athlete's individual record, but in this unit it refers to making the best of yourself in other ways.

Ⓥ Appearance

1 In pairs, students put the words in the correct columns. Draw their attention to the examples in the table. You may like to provide students with dictionaries to help them with this task.

Answers

Build	Height	Hair	General
overweight	medium-height	bald	cute
strong	tall	blonde	good-looking
well-built		curly	pretty
		dark	
		fair	
		long	
		medium-length	
		spiky	
		straight	
		wavy	

2 **LISTENING** ▶ 01 Play the track for students to listen, check and repeat. See p144 for the audioscript for this exercise.

TEACHER DEVELOPMENT: STUDENT TRAINING

Recording vocabulary

Mind maps are a useful way to record vocabulary. They appeal to visual learners and help to show how words connect and relate to each other. They can also provide a very effective revision tool when students come to exam time.

Ask students to write the key word for this unit (*identity*) in the centre of a blank page in their notebooks. They could then record words related to this theme, organised in categories with subheadings. They can add new words as they learn them through the unit.

3 **SPEAKING** Ask students to work in pairs and take it in turns to describe people in the photos, encouraging them to use the vocabulary from exercise 1. Nominate individual students to say their descriptions to the rest of the class.

Suggested answers

Photo a (Laura Trott): She's thin. She's got long blonde hair. She's very pretty.

Photo b (Eddie Redmayne): He's tall and quite good-looking. He's got short, fair hair. *– two*

Photo c (Usain Bolt): He's well-built and strong. He's got dark hair and brown eyes. *the greatest sprinter of all time!*

100, 200. 4 × 100

TEACHER DEVELOPMENT: LANGUAGE

Negative prefixes

The prefixes *un-*, *in-* and *im-* can form antonyms (opposites) of adjectives in English. The most common prefix is *un-* = 'the opposite of', but there are no hard and fast rules for which prefix students should use (except words that start with the letters *b*, *m* and *p* always take the prefix *im-* rather than *in-*). Advise students to consult a dictionary if they have doubts.

Adjectives

Many adjectives describe qualities that can exist in different degrees, such as size, beauty, age, etc. These adjectives are often called gradable adjectives, because they can be used in comparative or superlative forms, or with grading adverbs such as *very, a little, a bit*, to show that a person or thing has more or less of a particular quality. We can use words like *very* to make gradable adjectives stronger or words like *a little* or *a bit* to make gradable adjectives weaker.

When using more than one adjective to describe a noun, place the adjectives in the following order before the noun: 1 opinion (*interesting*); 2 dimension (*big*); 3 age (*old*); 4 origin (*Spanish*); 5 material (*cotton*). We don't usually use more than three adjectives before a noun.

Personality

4 Students match the personality adjectives with their opposites.

Answers

1 d **2** e **3** a **4** c **5** f **6** b **7** g

5 Draw students' attention to the personality adjectives in the box and drill pronunciation. Ask students to match the adjectives with the definitions 1–8. Check answers as a class. To extend the activity, ask students whether they think each adjective is negative or positive and ask them if they can think of any examples of each adjective.

Answers

1 reliable **2** selfish **3** nice **4** clever **5** shy
6 arrogant **7** bossy **8** confident

6 **LISTENING** ▶ 02 Play the track for students to listen to four teenagers talking about themselves. Ask them to note the adjective of personality that best describes each person. Elicit answers from students around the class and ask them to remember key phrases in the listening that helped them decide on their answers.
See p144 for the audioscript for this exercise.

Answers

1 Rose – lazy   **2** William – arrogant   **3** Jessica – tidy
4 Brandon – impatient

7a SPEAKING Ask students to choose five adjectives from exercises 4 and 5 to describe themselves. Students then tell their partner their adjectives and say why they chose them. Draw students' attention to the example sentence and the use of *quite* and *a bit* to make the adjectives weaker. With a less confident class, ask students to make notes before they do this as a speaking activity.

7b Nominate students to tell the class about their partner. Remind students that they should be positive about their partner and focus on strengths rather than weaknesses.

HOMEWORK

Students write a short text about themselves using the adjectives of appearance and personality they have studied in this lesson.

Assign students page 4 in their Workbook or the relevant section of the Online Workbook.

Reading p7

Reading for specific information

>>> FAST TRACK

You could ask students to read the text at home in preparation for completing exercise 3 together in class.

WARMER

Play *Hot Seat* to start the class. Divide the class into two teams. A volunteer from Team A sits with their back to the board. Choose words from the previous lesson and write them on the board one by one. Team A defines the word for the volunteer to guess in one minute. After one minute, it is the other team's turn to define the word, etc. The team that defines the most words in one minute wins the round.

1 In pairs, students look at the photos in the article and describe what they can see and discuss why they think the two people are special. Elicit answers from the class.

Suggested answers

In the first photo there is a man or boy under water. He isn't moving. Perhaps he's been there for a long time. Maybe he's special because he can stay under water or hold his breath for a really long time.

In the second photo there is a woman playing chess. Chess is a very difficult game and people who play it well are very intelligent.

2 READING Students read the article and check their ideas in exercise 1.

✓ **EXAM SUCCESS** Students discuss good procedure for doing a True/False reading exercise, then compare their answers with the information on page 144.

3 Students read the text again and decide if the statements are true or false. Tell them to write down the number(s) of the line(s) where they found the answer.

Answers

1 F (lines 3–5)   **2** F (lines 9–11)   **3** F (lines 11–14)
4 T (lines (18–19)   **5** T (lines 29–33)   **6** F (lines 35–36)
7 F (lines 36–38)   **8** F (lines 47–52)

4 ⚙ **CRITICAL THINKING** Have students read the quote and work individually to think of their answers to the questions. Encourage students to give reasons to support their opinion. Open the discussion up to the class and have a vote to see how many people agree or disagree with the quote. Nominate individual students to give their reasons.

5 Ask students to look at the underlined words in the text and to guess their meaning. Remind them that it can help to use context to guess meaning by looking at the words before and after the underlined one. Allow students to check their ideas in a dictionary.

Answers

hold his breath = deliberately stop breathing
lungs = organs in your chest you breath with
highly = hugely
prove = show
gradually = slowly

>>> FAST FINISHERS

Ask students to write sentences using the new vocabulary in the text. They can then compare their sentences with other students.

TEACHER DEVELOPMENT: STUDENT TRAINING

Inference in reading

Inference is a key strategy for students when learning English. This can cover inferring the meaning of individual words from their context, and also inference in relationships, bias and tone, for example.

Remind students how to look at context to help them infer meaning by writing the first sentence with the underlined phrase **hold his breath** on the board. Ask students first to look at the types of word there (*hold* = verb, *breath* = noun), then to think of other ways they've used the words before (e.g. *hold a pen*) as this may help them guess. Finally, ask them to look at other words in the sentence and make an 'educated guess' at what someone would be able to do underwater.

6 SPEAKING **What about *you*?** In pairs or in small groups, students discuss the questions. If necessary, provide some suggestions, e.g. *I'm really good at chess. I'd like to be good at ice-skating.*

Grammar in context pp8-9

Talking about life using the present simple, present continuous and adverbs of frequency

>>> FAST TRACK

You could ask students to do exercise 5a at home. Then they could do the pairwork in exercise 5b at the beginning of the next lesson.

Present simple and present continuous

1a Students match sentences a–g with rules 1–7.

Answers

1 c **2** f **3** b **4** e **5** g **6** d **7** a

1b Students look through the article on page 7 for examples of a negative sentence and a question form in the present continuous. Elicit the answers and use this opportunity to remind students of rising intonation patterns in *Yes/No* questions.

Answers

… she isn't teaching them in the same way as her father.
Are we expecting another record attempt?

TEACHER DEVELOPMENT: LANGUAGE

Effective study of grammar

Students should learn structures in context to show how they are used in real-life communication. They should note down any new grammatical item in an example sentence and make sure they know how to say it, write it, where it goes in a sentence and its grammatical function (i.e. *What does it tell us?*). Students should reflect on how grammar structures relate to other familiar structures they know, such as verb tenses. Where feasible, students could do a translation exercise (provided this will not promote interference from L1).

2 Students look at the sentences and choose the correct alternative. Elicit answers from students and have them explain which usage from exercise 1a each sentence shows.

Answers

1 is playing **2** play **3** is becoming **4** need
5 is studying **6** changes **7** wear

Adverbs of frequency

3 Ask students to look at the adverbs of frequency and choose the correct alternative to complete rules 1–4.

Answers

1 after **2** before **3** present simple
4 always, present continuous

4 Ask students to complete the text with the present simple or present continuous form of the verbs and the adverbs given.

Answers

a 's always using **b** doesn't usually play
c 's becoming **d** 's making **e** doesn't usually wear
f has got **g** often say **h** play **i** is changing
j don't often play **k** always do **l** is finishing
m usually plays

5a Tell students to write two true sentences about themselves or a friend using the phrases given. Remind them to write one in the present simple and one in the present continuous, writing negative sentences if necessary. Direct students' attention to the example sentences.

5b Ask students to read their sentences to each other and see how many of their sentences are the same.

6 **SPEAKING** In pairs, students take it in turns to ask and answer the questions. Draw their attention to the example speech bubbles and have two students read them out. Do this activity in open pairs first before students continue in closed pairs.

TEACHER DEVELOPMENT: PRONUNCIATION

Sentence stress

Sentence stress is the 'music' of English. Sentence stress will affect the degree to which a student sounds 'natural' and will make what they say easier to understand.

In any given English utterance there will be particular words that carry more 'volume' (stress) than others. This is not random. The stressed words carry the meaning or the 'content' of the sentence, and for this reason they are called 'content words'. Unstressed words tend to be smaller words that have more of a grammatical significance. They help the sentence function syntactically and for this reason they are called 'function words'.

If we take the function words out of the sentence, it will still have a certain amount of meaning and can be understood. However, if we take out the content words we will remove the meaning.

Content words include: main verbs, nouns, adjectives, adverbs, negative auxiliary verbs, demonstratives, question words

Function words include: pronouns, prepositions, articles, conjunctions, auxiliary verbs, verb *to be*

7 Ask students to write at least three more questions like the ones in exercise 6 and the examples for this exercise, and continue interviewing their partner. At the end of the activity, ask students to read out their questions and interview other students in open class.

TEACHER DEVELOPMENT: PRONUNCIATION

Intonation

Remind students that the intonation goes down at the end of a *Wh-* question (a question that begins with any of the words *who, where, when, what, why* or *how*).

Yes/No questions	Wh- questions
Is his name Juan?	What is his name?
Is she from China?	Where is she from?
Is he the teacher?	Who is the teacher?
Is class at nine?	When does class start?

Refer students to the Grammar reference on page 16 if necessary.

HOMEWORK

Assign students page 6 in their Workbook or the relevant sections of the Online Workbook.

Developing vocabulary p9

Using synonyms and partial synonyms

⋙ FAST TRACK

Students could do exercise 2 as homework, using a dictionary if necessary. Ask them to compare their words in class before doing exercise 3a.

Synonyms and partial synonyms

1 Students look at the words and decide if they have similar meanings or if there is any difference between them. If there is a difference, ask students to say what it is. You may like to provide less confident students with dictionaries for this task.

Answers

All these words describe someone's appearance in a positive way:

attractive – used for describing men and women who are pleasant to look at

beautiful – extremely attractive (usually used of women)

cute – attractive, usually small and easy to like

good-looking – used for describing adults of both sexes and older children who are nice to look at

handsome – usually used for a man or boy (= good-looking)

pretty – usually used for young women and girls who have nice faces

TEACHER DEVELOPMENT: LANGUAGE

Synonyms and partial synonyms

A synonym is a word which means the same as another word. Teaching synonyms is a good way to increase students' vocabulary and encourage them to use more interesting and expressive language. A thesaurus is a useful resource that provides lists of similar or related words.

Partial synonyms are words that are very similar, but with some difference between them. *Slim* is a partial synonym of *thin* because we use it to say that someone is *thin* but in an attractive way. *Elderly* is a more polite way of saying someone is *old*. *Glad* is also a partial synonym of *cheerful/happy* because it means 'to be happy about something'. We tend to use *glad* for events but *happy* for attitude.

Teach students the language they need to describe synonyms: *… is another word for …, … means the same thing as …, … is a synonym for …*

2 Students match the words in the box with the synonyms or partial synonyms.

Answers

cheerful – glad – happy, friendly – outgoing – sociable, difficult – hard, slim – thin, elderly – old

3a PRONUNCIATION In pairs, have students say the words in exercises 1 and 2 aloud. With a less confident class, you might want to say the words first for them to repeat. Ask students to find seven words with three syllables.

Answers

attractive, beautiful, good-looking, difficult, elderly, outgoing, sociable

3b ▶ **03** Play the track for students to listen and check their answers. Then ask students to listen again paying attention to the stress of the word and to write each one in the correct column. See p144 for the audioscript for this exercise.

Answers

Ooo (e.g. *talkative*)	oOo (e.g. *impatient*)
beautiful	attractive
difficult	good-looking
elderly	outgoing
sociable	

3c Students practise saying the words with the correct stress. Play the track again if necessary and have students repeat after each word.

4 Students choose the best alternative in each sentence. If there is no difference, tell them to choose both.

Answers

1 old, elderly **2** (both) **3** cheerful **4** thin
5 (both) **6** (both)

5 Students prepare a description of a famous person using words from exercises 1 and 2 and words from page 6.

6 SPEAKING In pairs, students take it in turns to describe the person they chose in exercise 5 for their partner to guess who it is. Draw students' attention to the example description.

HOMEWORK

Assign students page 7 in their Workbook or the relevant sections of the Online Workbook.

Gateway to life skills pp10–11 🏃

Building your confidence
To look at confidence and self-esteem and identify areas and ways to improve it

≫ FAST TRACK

You could set exercise 1c as homework to be discussed in pairs at the next lesson.

ⓘ BACKGROUND INFORMATION

Self-esteem is how a person thinks of themselves, who they are and what they do. People with a good or high self-esteem will generally think positively about themselves and as a result may achieve more of their goals, find it easier to make friends, be more likely to try new things and to learn from their mistakes. People with low self-esteem, on the other hand, may be reluctant to believe that they deserve or are capable of success, feel anxious in social situations, be reluctant to try new things and deal badly with failure. Teenagers will often experience dips in their self-esteem, so it's a crucial time to look at ways to build and maintain confidence.

WARMER

Draw students' attention to the photo of the girl at the bottom of page 10. Ask if they think she is feeling positively or negatively about herself. In pairs, ask students to brainstorm words connected to the word 'positive' (e.g. *happy, proud, confident*). Allow them to use dictionaries if necessary. Then have them find the antonyms to their positive words. Elicit ideas and write the useful vocabulary on the board. Tell students they will be looking at ways to think positively in this lesson. Allow students time to read through the Life skills objectives and the Key concepts before starting the lesson.

1a In pairs, students look at the picture and decide whether the glass is half empty or half full and what this could represent.

Answers

In English, the expression 'glass half full' is often used to describe someone optimistic with a positive outlook on life, e.g. *His glass is always half full: when his flight was delayed he was happy because he had more time to visit the shops in the airport!*

1b In pairs, students compare their answers from exercise 1a. Students answer the question giving examples to justify their answer. Nominate students to share their opinions.

1c Students take it in turns to give their answers and provide examples that support them. With a less confident class students could write notes before participating in this activity.

2 READING Students read the text about self-esteem and then decide whether it says items 1–5 are good or bad. Allow students to compare their answers in pairs, before nominating individuals to give their answers. Encourage students to identify the part of the text that helped with their answer.

Answers
1 ✓ **2** ✓ **3** ✓ **4** ✗ **5** ✓

3a Give students time to read through the text again and choose three pieces of advice that they think are the best. Remind them to give their reasons.

3b SPEAKING In pairs, students compare and justify their answers for exercise 3a. Nominate pairs to feedback on their discussions.

3c In open class or in small groups, ask students to talk about the ideas in the text that they already do. You could have a class vote on the most effective method.

4 Give students time to look at the photos and situations in exercise 4. In pairs, students then use the ideas in the text and give advice to the people. Refer students back to page 10 to give them ideas and if necessary, review any language needed for giving advice and making suggestions. Nominate pairs to feedback their ideas to the class.

5a LISTENING ▶ 04 Tell students they are going to watch or listen to a video of four teenagers talking about what they are good at. Give 30 seconds to tell their partner what they feel good at. Elicit a few ideas, then ask students what words they might use in front of 'good at' if they were a confident person (e.g. *really, very*) or if they had lower self-esteem (e.g. *not, quite, not very*). Play the video or track and ask students to write down what each speaker is good at. Elicit answers from the class and ask students if they thought each speaker had high or low self-esteem. See p144 for the audioscript/videoscript for this exercise.

Answers
Callum: computer games   **Naomi:** listening to people
Rachel: art and making things   **Toby:** tennis

5b ▶ 04 Tell students they are going to watch or listen to the video again and decide whether the sentences are true or false. Give students time to read through the sentences and underline key words or phrases that they think could help them with the task.

Answers

1 F **2** T **3** T **4** T **5** F **6** F **7** T **8** F

6 SPEAKING In pairs, students discuss who they think is the most and least confident. Encourage them to give reasons.

Listening p12

Listening effectively to identify specific information

TEACHER DEVELOPMENT: STUDENT TRAINING

Carrying out listening tasks (part 1)

Students need to be taught listening as well as practising listening. An ideal listening class should include some instruction about how to listen effectively.

Students need to carefully read the instructions and questions to know what they are listening for, predict content (from key words in the questions or visual clues, etc.), learn to use their intuition, take good notes during the listening and decide on the right answer based on the information they have. At the end of a listening task, try to develop a class discussion based on students' opinions (the *What about* you? section provides questions for discussion based on the listening text).

Ask students to evaluate how well they did, whether they thought it was a difficult task and why. For the European Language Portfolio dossier, students could record the listening activities they have done in class on a self-evaluation sheet. They can write the subject, date and evaluate their progress. (See page 127 for more information on listening.)

WARMER

Draw a simple line drawing on the board, e.g. an eye, and ask students to guess what you could have been thinking about or feeling when you drew it. Elicit suggestions from the class.

1 Ask students to copy the picture from exercise 1 onto a piece of paper. Tell them they have three minutes to draw something on it. Tell them not to think too much about it, but just to draw what comes into their head.

2 LISTENING ▶ 05 Play the track for students to listen to five people talking about what they drew as part of a psychology experiment and what their drawings mean. See p144 for the audioscript for this exercise.

Answers

1 the sun **2** a face **3** a football **4** an eye **5** a flower

✔ **EXAM SUCCESS** Ask students to read through the text in the Exam success box and think about ways they can approach a matching task. Tell students to turn to page 144 and check their ideas.

3 ▶ 05 Play the track again for students to identify the speaker. Give students two or three minutes to look through the table and predict any words or phrases each speaker might use. Play the track again and ask students to tick the correct number from 1–5.

Answers

a Speaker 2 **b** Speaker 1 **c** Speaker 3 **d** Speaker 4 **e** Speaker 3 **f** Speaker 5 **g** Speaker 4 **h** Speaker 5

4 **What about *you*?** Ask students to look back at their drawing in exercise 1 and then answer the two questions. Nominate students to share their ideas.

HOMEWORK

Assign students page 7 in their Workbook or the relevant sections of the Online Workbook.

Grammar in context pp12–13

Using state and action verbs

 Test before you teach: Flipped classroom

Set the Flipped classroom video for homework <u>before the lesson</u>. You can check the students' Flipped classroom video answers in the Online Workbook. This will allow you to assess the needs of the students before the class. Students can then move on to the relevant grammar practice exercises.

Talk to students about the change in classroom model. Go over the guidelines for watching the videos and discuss the procedure in class.

⟫ FAST TRACK

You could ask students to complete exercise 3 at home.

Write the following four categories on the board and ask students to think of as many verbs as they can for each category in a three-minute time limit.

verbs of feeling (emotion)/verbs of thinking/verbs of the senses/verbs of possession

Tell them to open their books at page 16 and check to see they have thought of the state and action verbs in the Grammar reference.

1a Students look at the sentences and decide if they describe states and situations or if they describe actions.

Answer

They all describe states and situations.

1b Ask the students to look at the sentences again and decide if they are in the present simple or present continuous and say why. (They are all in the present simple because action verbs can be used in continuous tenses, but verbs that describe states and situations can't.)

1c Tell students to put the verbs in blue in exercise 1a in the correct list.

Refer students to the Grammar reference on page 16.

Answers

1 love, like   **2** don't believe, know, think
3 looks, smell   **4** have

2 Students decide if each verb describes a state or action and choose the correct alternative.

Answers

1 am looking, Do you know   **2** looks   **3** has got
4 is having   **5** Do you know   **6** don't understand
7 believe   **8** don't like, want

TEACHER DEVELOPMENT: LANGUAGE

State and action verbs

State verbs generally fall into four groups: verbs of feeling (emotion), verbs of thinking, verbs of the senses, verbs of possession. When a verb describes a state and not an action, we do not use the continuous tense. For example, *play* is an action so we can say *playing* whereas *be* is a fixed state which does not change.

Students can be confused by advertising slogans. There is a popular example at the moment which is used by an American restaurant company in their advertising. They simply say for the experience of eating in their restaurant, *I'm loving it.* Grammatically it is not correct to say *I'm loving it.* *Love* is a state verb and so we should say *I love it.*

Some words can be state verbs and action verbs. The meaning of these verbs is then different. Take a look at these:

I have a car. – **state verb** showing possession
I am having a bath. – **action verb** which, in this case, means *taking*
I think you are cool. – **state verb** meaning 'in my opinion'
I am thinking about buying a motorbike. – **action verb** meaning 'considering'

3 Students complete the sentences with the correct form of the verbs.

Answers

1 sounds   **2** smells   **3** seem   **4** looks   **5** tastes
6 feels

4a Students write sentences about the items in the photos. Remind them to use one of the verbs and at least one of the adjectives in the boxes.

4b SPEAKING Students read out their sentences to their partner without saying the name of the items. Their partner must guess which things are being described. Focus students' attention on the model dialogue.

5 Ask students to complete the dialogue with the verbs in the present simple or continuous. Have two students read out the dialogue to check answers.

Answers

a sound   **b** 'm having   **c** 'm staying   **d** remember
e has   **f** belongs   **g** lets   **h** wants   **i** are (you) doing
j 'm getting   **k** cooks   **l** 's making   **m** smells
n 're making   **o** need   **p** 's calling

6 SPEAKING Students complete the sentences about themselves and then predict their partner's answers. Students compare their predictions in pairs.

Students write their answers from the speaking activity in exercise 6, but this time with three false sentences. At the beginning of the next class, students could read out their sentences for their partner to guess which sentences are false.

TEACHER DEVELOPMENT: STUDENT TRAINING

Portfolio assessment – learning diaries

Students can be encouraged to keep a diary where they reflect on how well they feel they are doing. A learning diary can constitute part of a student's European Language Portfolio. Encouraging learners to become active, reflective learners is one of the many strengths of portfolio assessment. It gives learners the opportunity to reflect on their own progress and help them to take responsibility for their own learning. Such autonomous learners become successful learners, and this success can lead to more motivation. Portfolio assessment can support this cycle by contributing positively to each of the three factors: enhanced motivation, active learning and autonomous learning.

An example of a learning diary page:

Your name: ....
Activity: *Page 13 Speaking activity* Date: ....
What was the task? ....
What do you think you did well? ....
What do you think you could improve? ....
What do you think your partner could improve?

....

Other comments ....
1 Needs working on!
2 This could be improved
3 So-so (not good, not bad)
4 OK
5 Great!

Refer students to the Grammar reference on page 16 if necessary.

Refer students to the Grammar reference on page 16 if necessary.

HOMEWORK

Assign students page 8 in their Workbook or the relevant sections of the Online Workbook.

Developing speaking p14

Asking for and giving personal information

⟫⟫ FAST TRACK

You could ask students to complete the sentences in exercise 5 at home. They can then compare their sentences in pairs in the next lesson.

WARMER

Students think of the name of a hobby for each letter of the alphabet except X. Give students five minutes.
Suggested answers

acting, basketball, computers, drumming, embroidery, football, guitar, horse-riding, ice-skating, juggling, kite-flying, listening to music, making models, needlework, origami, photography, quilting, role-playing games, stamps, trainspotting, UFOs, video and computer games, woodwork, yoga, zorbing

1 LISTENING ▶ 06 Play the track for students to listen and say what each person's hobbies are. See pp144–145 for the audioscript for this exercise.

Answers

Megan's hobby: basketball
Ellie's hobbies: swimming, rock music, playing the guitar

2 ▶ 06 Ask students to complete the dialogue. Play the track again if necessary.

Answers

a first **b** basketball **c** swimming **d** rock
e guitar **f** good

3 SPEAKING In pairs, students practise the completed dialogue in exercise 2.

⟫⟫ FAST FINISHERS

Ask students to swap roles and do the activity again, trying to repeat as much as they can from memory.

4 Students look at the sentences in the Speaking bank and read the information about question tags. Students then choose the correct alternative in the statements.

Answers

1 subject pronouns **2** auxiliary verbs and 'to be'
3 negative, affirmative

5 Students complete the sentences with question tags.

Answers

1 haven't you **2** can you **3** doesn't she
4 isn't she **5** is he **6** does he **7** can't they

TEACHER DEVELOPMENT: PRONUNCIATION

Question tags

We can change the meaning of a tag question with our intonation, the musical pitch of our voice. With rising intonation, it sounds like a real question. But if our intonation falls, it sounds more like a statement that doesn't require a real answer.

You don't know where the police station is, do you? ↗

↗ rising = real question
You've got a sister, haven't you? ↘

↘ falling = not a real question

TEACHER DEVELOPMENT: STUDENT TRAINING

Question tags

A question tag is a mini-question at the end of a statement. Question tags are very common in English. We use them at the end of statements when we want to keep a conversation going, or confirm information. They mean something like: 'Am I right?' or 'Do you agree?'

- We form question tags with the auxiliary verb + subject.
- If the main verb in the sentence is positive, the tag is negative. (*You're Spanish, aren't you?*)
- If the main verb in the sentence is negative, the tag is positive. (*You aren't Spanish, are you?*)
- If there is no auxiliary verb in the sentence, we use *do*. (*You live in Spain, don't you?*)

Using question tags well promotes a deep understanding of the use of various auxiliary verbs.

Special cases are:

1 In the present tense, if the subject is *I*, the auxiliary changes to *are* or *aren't*. *I'm sitting next to you, aren't I?*
2 With *let's*, the question tag is *shall we*. *Let's go to the beach, shall we?*
3 With an imperative, the tag question is *will you*. *Close the window, will you?*
4 We use a positive tag question after a sentence containing a negative word such as *never, hardly, nobody. Nobody lives in this house, do they? You've never liked me, have you?*
5 If the main verb in the sentence is *have*, it is more common to use *do* in the question tag. *You have a sports car, don't you?*

6 SPEAKING In pairs, Student A turns to page 147 and Student B turns to page 148. Students take it in turns to read out the first part of a sentence to see if their partner gives the correct question tag.

✚ EXTRA ACTIVITY

Play bingo with question tag endings. Write different tag endings on the board. Ask students to draw a 3 × 3 grid and write different tag endings in the squares. Read out a sentence (e.g. *She went to the supermarket*). If students have a possible ending, they cross it out. The winner is the first student to complete the card.

PRACTICE MAKES PERFECT

7a SPEAKING Individually, students write down five things they think they know about their partner's free-time habits.

7b In pairs, students have a conversation about their hobbies. Encourage them to use their ideas from exercise 7a and question tags to keep the conversation going. Draw students' attention to the model dialogue.

✂ Model dialogue

A: Tell me something about your hobbies.
You like <u>playing tennis</u>, don't you?

B: Yes, I do. I'm in the <u>school tennis</u> club and I play twice a week.

A: Do you play any other sports?

B: I quite like <u>playing football</u>, but I'm not very good.

A: Well, I'm not very good at any sport! I like <u>music</u> though. You don't <u>play an instrument</u>, do you?

B: Yes, I do, <u>I play the guitar and the clarinet</u>.

A: Oh yes, you <u>play in the school orchestra</u>, don't you?

B: Yes, that's right. You <u>play</u> the <u>flute</u>, don't you?

A: Yes. And I really like <u>listening to music</u>.

B: Me too. What kind of music do you like?

A: Oh, I like all sorts, but my favourite <u>band</u> at the moment is <u>5 Seconds of Summer</u>.

B: Great! Come to my house some time and we can <u>listen to music</u>.

A: OK, thanks!

7c Ask students to work with a new partner and produce another dialogue. Use the model dialogue above, by handing out a copy to each pair and having one pair read aloud to the rest of the class. Encourage more confident classes to produce their dialogues without making notes first.

✚ EXTRA ACTIVITY

Students could write sentences with question tags on the end like the ones in exercise 5. At the start of the next lesson, they could take it in turns to test their partner to see if they can give the correct question tag.

HOMEWORK

Assign students page 9 in their Workbook or the relevant sections of the Online Workbook.

Developing writing p15

Writing an informal email describing people

⟫⟫ FAST TRACK

You could ask students to do exercises 2 and 3 at home and check their answers at the start of the lesson. Alternatively, you could set the writing task in exercise 5a as homework.

WARMER

Write these three statements on the board and ask students to discuss if they are true or false.

1 We start an informal email with the word *Dear*.
2 We end an informal email with words like *Take care*, or *Love*, or *Thinking of you*.
3 When we finish an email we write our first and last name.

Answers

1 F (We write *Hi* and the name of the person we are writing to.)
2 T
3 F (We write our first name or nickname.)

1 READING Students read Mia's email to her e-pal and name the different people in the photo. Elicit answers in open class.

Answers

a Rose **b** Mia **c** Olivia **d** Brad

2 Tell students to read the email again and write notes about each person's personality.

Answers

Brad: totally mad, makes people laugh
Rose: extremely clever and helpful
Olivia: always cheerful

ℹ CULTURAL INFORMATION

Students may want to find an English-speaking friend to write to from one of the many pen friend websites. Students often prefer to use email (this kind of pen friend is also called an *e-pal*). There are lots of online organisations that students can join to find a suitable e-pal. As always, students should be reminded about the dangers of online friendships and should use reputable sites.

3 Ask students to complete the sentences in the Writing bank by looking again at Mia's email. Point out that we generally use *rather* instead of *quite* with negative feelings or words.

Answers

1 tired 2 an actress 3 he needs a holiday
4 normal 5 extreme 6 softer

4 Ask students to complete the sentences to describe some of the people in the photo.

Suggested answers

1 clever, long hair
2 happy, mad
3 nice person, friendly
4 shy, he's quite serious

PRACTICE MAKES PERFECT

5a Students find a photo of themselves with friends or family. Tell them to write an email describing the appearance and personality of the people in the photo. Remind them to use the email in exercise 1 as a model and include words and expressions from the Writing bank. Refer students to the Writing bank on page 150.

5b Students show their photo and description to their partner to see if they can identify the people in the photo correctly. For students who are less confident, photocopy the model email below for extra support during the writing task. They can use the model and update the underlined parts.

Model email

Hi Sam!

You asked me to send you a photo of me and my family. So here it is! Can you guess who everyone is? I'm the one in the black T-shirt. You can probably tell that my sister, Alison, is sitting next to me. Everybody says we look a bit like each other. In the photo she's got medium-length brown hair but now it is really short. She is an absolutely fantastic sister, but she is rather bossy sometimes. I'm sitting next to her daughter, Abby. She's very talkative. That's my nephew, Greg, at the top of the table. He's really funny. My mum is at the end of the table. She's really patient and helps us a lot. Then there's my dad next to her; he's always cheerful. The photo was taken when we were on holiday in Puerto Pollença, Mallorca. It's a totally amazing place! I want to go back there one day.

Right, I need to go. I'm going out in about ten minutes! When you send your next email, don't forget to send me a picture of you and your family.

Take care,

Susie

TEACHER DEVELOPMENT: STUDENT TRAINING

Assessing writing

Ask students to assess their performance in each writing activity in the *Developing writing* section and give themselves a mark according to the following self-assessment criteria. Their written work and assessments could form part of the CEF dossier.

- Are your sentences complete?
- Is there subject-verb agreement?
- Is there consistency in verb tense?
- Are pronouns used correctly?
- Are all your words used correctly?
- Are punctuation, capitalisation, spelling and paragraphs used correctly?

Provide students with a key to the marking symbols you use to correct texts to help them grade their or their partner's work:

WF   wrong form
        The movie was the most good WF she had seen.

WW   wrong word
        She smiled happily and sweet WW.

T   wrong tense
        He woke and had jumped T out of bed.

∧   Something is missing.
        She arrived ∧ school on Monday.

Sp   wrong spelling
        The chair was not confortable Sp.

WO   wrong word order
        When I got to the restaurant, she already WO had ordered a meal.

P   wrong punctuation
        Be careful, P The train is coming.

V   wrong verb form
        She drunk V the wine elegantly.

//   new paragraph needed
        They had dinner and went to bed.// Next day when they woke, the sun was shining.

∪   Join the ideas in one sentence.
        She sat down. ∪ She drank the coffee.

?   What does this mean?
        ? They waking up teeth brushed daily. ?

~   change order
        She had brown ~ dark hair.

HOMEWORK

Assign students page 10 in their Workbook or the relevant sections of the Online Workbook.

Language checkpoint: Unit 1

>>> **FAST TRACK**

Students read the Grammar reference and Vocabulary sections on page 16 before completing the revision exercises on the following page.

Grammar revision p17

Present simple and present continuous

1 Students complete the sentences with the correct form of the present simple or present continuous.

Answers

a are (you) wearing **b** don't usually wear
c 'm going **d** 'm starting **e** work **f** 're saving

Adverbs of frequency

2 Students decide if the sentences are correct or not and correct any mistakes.

Answers

1 I **don't** usually **go** to school by bus.
2 (correct)
3 My friends and I **sometimes play** football after school.
4 Adam **is often** late.
5 (correct)
6 He **never** eats meat.

State and action verbs

3 Students choose the correct alternative.

Answers

1 need **2** Do you know **3** Are you having
4 owns **5** don't seem **6** prefer **7** are you looking
8 belongs

Vocabulary revision p17

APPEARANCE

1 Students complete the words to make adjectives. Then they decide the correct category for each word.

Answers

1 attractive (general)
2 well-built (build)
3 medium-height (height)
4 straight (hair)
5 cute (general)
6 overweight (build)
7 bald (hair)

PERSONALITY

2 Students write the opposite of the words.

Answers

1 noisy **2** untidy **3** serious **4** clever/intelligent/bright
5 unfriendly **6** lazy **7** impatient

SYNONYMS AND PARTIAL SYNONYMS

3 Students write a synonym for each underlined word.

Answers

1 clever/intelligent **2** good-looking/handsome
3 hard **4** cheerful **5** sociable **6** elderly

HOMEWORK

Assign students page 11 in their Workbook or the relevant sections of the Online Workbook.

2 Travelogue

KEY LEARNING OUTCOMES

CEF

Students will be able to:

- talk about past events, situations and habits using the past simple, past continuous, past perfect, *used to* and *would*
- talk about trips and travel

- understand written and spoken texts about journeys
- ask to buy a train ticket at a station
- write a blog post about a dream holiday

UNIT OVERVIEW

Vocabulary
Transport and travel
Accommodation

Reading
Notes from a Small Island
CRITICAL THINKING Thinking about an author's intentions

Grammar in context
Past simple, past continuous and past perfect

Developing vocabulary
Phrasal verbs connected with travel
PRONUNCIATION Stress on phrasal verbs

Life skills
The world around you:
Being a responsible tourist

Listening
Travelling around the world

Grammar in context
used to and *would*

Developing speaking
Asking for information

Developing writing
A blog post

Exam success
Speaking: Exchanging information
Writing: Checking your work

DIGITAL OVERVIEW

Presentation Kit
- ▶ **Flipped classroom video Unit 2:** *used to*
- ▶ **Life skills video Unit 2:** Responsible tourism in New Zealand
- ▶ [V] **Vocabulary tool:** Transport and travel; Accommodation
- ▶ **Interactive versions of Student's Book activities**
- ▶ **Integrated audio and answer key for all activities**
- ▶ **Workbook pages with answer key**

Teacher's Resource Centre
- ▶ **Flipped classroom video Unit 2:** *used to*
- ▶ **Life skills video Unit 2:** Responsible tourism in New Zealand
- ▶ **Grammar communication activity Unit 2: What a story!**
- ▶ **Worksheets for this unit, including:**
  - – Grammar Practice worksheet Unit 2
  - – Flipped classroom video worksheet Unit 2: *used to*
  - – Literature worksheet Units 1 and 2
  - – Culture worksheet Unit 2
  - – Life skills video worksheet Unit 2
  - – Everyday English worksheet Unit 2

Student's App
Gateway 2nd Edition wordlist for the award-winning Sounds App (available for download)

✓ TESTING AND ASSESSMENT

Resources for exam preparation and measuring student progress

- ▶ Test Generator Units 1–2
- ▶ Printable test Unit 2
- ▶ Gateway to exams Units 1 and 2 (end of Unit 2)

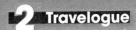

Vocabulary p18

Talking about transport and travel and types of accommodation

>>> FAST TRACK

You could ask students to do exercise 1 at home so that less confident students can take the necessary time to look up the vocabulary in the Macmillan Online Dictionary.

WARMER

Put students in pairs and draw their attention to the four photos in exercise 1. Tell them to think of one positive and one negative thing about each mode of transport. Elicit ideas from students. Tell students that the topic of the unit is *Travelogue* and ask them to brainstorm any themes or ideas they think they will study in this unit.

v Transport and travel

1 In pairs, students write the types of transport they can see in the photos in the correct columns, as in the example.

Answers

Land transport: motorbike
Air transport: rocket, hot-air balloon
Water transport: ferry

2 In pairs, students add the new words to the columns and check they understand the words. Provide dictionaries if necessary. Students then think of other words to write in each column. They then compare their lists with another pair and add any new words to the list. At the end of the activity, elicit all the words students can think of for each list and write them on the board (additional suggestions are in italics in the key).

Answers

Land transport: bike, coach, lorry, tram, underground/ subway, van, *truck, bus, car, taxi, train*
Air transport: rocket, hot-air balloon, *helicopter, plane*
Water transport: ferry, yacht, *ship, boat, canoe*

✚ EXTRA ACTIVITY

Students work in pairs and find out what types of transport their partner usually uses, and one kind of transport he or she never uses. If necessary, give them the form of one or two simple questions, e.g. *What types of transport do you usually/often use? Do you ever travel by train/ride a bike?*, etc.

3 Students complete the text with the words. They could use dictionaries for this task, if necessary. Remind students that *luggage* is an uncountable noun. The most common quantity expression is *a piece of luggage* or a *bag* or a *suitcase*.

4 ▶ 07 Play the track for students to listen and check their answers. See p145 for the audioscript for this exercise.

Answers

a catch   **b** ticket office   **c** single   **d** return
e fare   **f** luggage   **g** platform   **h** miss   **i** delay
j cancel   **k** arrivals   **l** departures

TEACHER DEVELOPMENT: LANGUAGE

Dictionary skills

A wide vocabulary is essential for communicative competence and is important for both production and comprehension. Use this opportunity to review dictionary skills as a key way to develop learner autonomy. You could ask your students these questions in an open-class discussion:

What information does your dictionary provide about new words?

How do you keep a record of the information you look up in a dictionary? (e.g. write two or three example sentences in your notebook, etc.)

Are you familiar with all the symbols, abbreviations and note markers?

Do you use the phonological information?

Remind students that dictionaries provide important information about pronunciation. First, the entire word is phonetically spelt and a stress mark (') shows which syllable is spoken louder than the rest of the word. Long words have a primary stress and a secondary stress because two of the syllables receive more stress than the other syllables.

v Accommodation

5 Ask students what type of accommodation they can see in the photos. Tell them to match the words to the photos.

Answers

a hostel   **b** campsite, caravan, tent
c bed and breakfast (commonly known as a 'B & B')
d hotel   **e** motel

6 **SPEAKING** In pairs, students take it in turns to explain the difference between the words.

Answers

1 A motel is a type of hotel. It's next to a big road. People usually stay there when they drive a long distance and just want to rest and sleep.

2 A hostel is a cheap place where travellers can stay for a short period of time. A hotel is more expensive and has more facilities.

3 A bed and breakfast is a small hotel or private house that provides a room for the night and a meal the next morning.

4 A tent is a structure made of cloth that you sleep in when camping. A caravan is used for living in on holiday and it is pulled behind a car.

5 A campsite is a place where people on holiday can stay in tents or other temporary structures.

7 LISTENING ▶ 08 Play the track for students to listen and choose from the alternatives to say where the people are. Ask for answers in open class and elicit the key words that helped students make their choices. See p145 for the audioscript for this exercise.

Answers

1 This is on the platform at the train station.
2 He is in a bed and breakfast.
3 She is at a ticket office.
4 They are in a caravan.

See p145 for the audioscript for this exercise.

✚ EXTRA ACTIVITY

Ask some follow-up questions: *Why was the train late? How many nights is the man going to stay in the bed and breakfast? Can you describe the bed and breakfast? Why does the ticket officer want to know if the lady is coming back on the same day? What's the weather like on the campsite?*

8 SPEAKING Put students in small groups of four or five and ask them to plan a perfect weekend away. Remind them to include the three things listed as well as as much other detail as they can. You could bring in travel brochures to help them with the task. Have groups present their plans to the rest of the class. Encourage each member of the group to speak. Have a class vote on the best weekend plan.

HOMEWORK

Assign students page 12 in their Workbook or the relevant sections of the Online Workbook.

Reading p19

Reading for specific information and inferring meaning

⋙ FAST TRACK

You could ask students to do exercise 2 at home in preparation for completing exercise 3 together in class.

WARMER

Play *Snowman* with transport-related words. Divide the class into two teams. Team A chooses a word from the previous lesson and a student from that team writes the correct number of spaces for the word on the board. Team B guesses the letters that are in the word, and Team A writes in every letter they guess correctly. For every incorrect guess they draw part of the snowman. If the drawing of the snowman is completed before the word is guessed, the guessing team loses.

1 Draw students' attention to the map of the south-west of England, and have them make suggestions for the best types of public transport for the trip from Exeter to Plymouth, giving their reasons if possible.

2 READING Ask students to read the extract by Bill Bryson and answer the two questions.

Answers

1 trains, buses
2 Exeter to Barnstaple, then back to Exeter

ⓘ CULTURAL INFORMATION

Bill Bryson is an American author (born 1951) who has written numerous books on travel, the English language and science. His style is both humorous and informative and his observant take on English culture, *Notes from a Small Island* (1995) made him famous in the UK.

Choosing texts from writers such as Bill Bryson, who write in an appealing and interesting way, will encourage students to read in the English language and increase their exposure to the language.

3 Ask students to read the extract again and choose the best answers.

Answers

1 a 2 c 3 a 4 b 5 b

4 ⚙ CRITICAL THINKING This critical thinking task will encourage students to think about the purpose and intentions of the writer in producing the piece. Ask students to read through the question and think of their own opinion. Remind them there is not necessarily one right answer. Have a class discussion, encouraging students to share their views.

✚ EXTRA ACTIVITY

Hold a team competition. Divide the class into two teams and read out definitions of words from the text. As soon as someone knows which word you are explaining, they call out the word and that team gets a point. Alternatively, ask students to write five tips for tourists using public transport in their town or city.

5 Students find the words in the text. Ask them to try to infer their meaning from the context and then check their ideas in the dictionary.

Answers

collected = taken, gone to get
announcements = information you hear loudly about trains or other important events
for the benefit of = to help
ritual = something a person always does in the same way
conductor = the person in charge at the train station or on a bus
timetable = the official times and destinations of trains or buses

✚ EXTRA ACTIVITY

Ask students to write five sentences using the new words from exercise 5. Have students read their sentences to each other in pairs.

6 SPEAKING What about *you*? In pairs or small groups, students discuss their preferred means of transport and

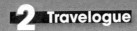

any unusual customs using public transport in their own country.

HOMEWORK

Assign students page 13 in their Workbook or the relevant sections of the Online Workbook.

Grammar in context p20

Using the past simple, past continuous and past perfect

>>> FAST TRACK

Students could do exercise 2a at home before the lesson. Check the answers at the beginning of the lesson.

Test before you teach

Write these three gapped sentences on the board:

1 *Last January, I* .... *to France for two weeks.*
2 *I chose to go to Paris because this is where my mother* .... *grown up.*
3 *I* .... *expecting it to be really busy and elegant.*

Elicit the missing words. Write the first letter if students are stuck. Then ask students to say whether each sentence uses past simple, past continuous or past perfect. If students seem to be very familiar with the form of these tenses, move quickly through the grammar practice activities, eliciting answers from students as an open-class activity.

Answers

1 went/travelled/flew   **2** had   **3** was

1a Students look at the sentences and decide which tenses the verbs are in.

Answers

a past perfect, past simple
b past simple, past simple
c past continuous, past simple

1b Students complete the rules. They then match each sentence a–c from exercise 1a with one of the rules.

Answers

1 past perfect, a   **2** past simple, b   **3** past continuous, c

1c Students rewrite the sentences first in the negative form and then in the question form.

Answers

1 He didn't sit down. Did he sit down?
2 He wasn't eating his sandwich. Was he eating his sandwich?
3 He hadn't eaten his sandwich. Had he eaten his sandwich?

2a Ask students to put the verbs in the correct form of the past simple or past continuous to complete the sentences.

Answers

1 was shining   **2** caught   **3** was riding
4 were waiting   **5** bought   **6** was looking
7 was snowing   **8** heard

2b Students look at the words *while* and *as* in sentences 3, 6 and 8 and decide if they go with the past simple or the past continuous.

Answer

past continuous

3 Students choose the best alternative.

Answers

1 was watching   **2** was leaving   **3** came
4 were driving   **5** were shopping   **6** met
7 were talking   **8** were doing

TEACHER DEVELOPMENT: PRONUNCIATION

Pronunciation of past perfect

If **had** is not completely contracted, it is usually reduced to its weak form in affirmative sentences and questions, sometimes with elision and intrusion.

We had already been:
/wiː həd/ or /wiːjəd/ (the /h/ sound is elided and the /j/ sound intrudes)

You had visited many times:
/juː həd/ or /uːwəd/ (the /h/ sound is elided and the /w/ sound intrudes)

Had they called? /həd/

4 Students write sentences in the past perfect to explain the situations. Draw students' attention to the example sentence. Students compare in pairs before you elicit answers from different students around the class.

Answers

2 Because somebody had stolen it.
3 Because they had had the old one for 15 years.
4 Because I'd never flown before.
5 Because it had snowed the night before.
6 Because she hadn't studied much.
7 Because he had lost his passport.
8 Because he had spent it.
9 Because she hadn't left on time.

Refer students to the Grammar reference on page 28 if necessary

HOMEWORK

Assign students page 14 in their Workbook or the relevant sections of the Online Workbook.

Developing vocabulary p21

Talking about journeys and travel plans

⟫⟫ FAST TRACK

Students could do exercise 2a as homework, using a dictionary if necessary. Ask them to compare their answers in class.

Phrasal verbs connected with travel

1 Students look at the sentences and match the phrasal verbs in bold in the sentences with the definitions a–h below. You may like to provide students with dictionaries for this task.

Answers

1 b **2** h **3** g **4** f **5** d **6** e **7** a **8** c

⟫⟫ FAST FINISHERS

Ask students to write new sentences using each of the phrasal verbs.

✛ EXTRA ACTIVITY

Students make a mind map of all the vocabulary they have seen so far in the unit related to the theme of travel. Provide them with posters and allow them to work in pairs or small groups.

2a PRONUNCIATION Students look at the sentences and decide which of the words in bold are verbs and which are nouns.

Answers

1 verb **2** noun **3** verb **4** noun **5** verb **6** noun

2b ▶ 09 Play the track for students to listen to the sentences and decide which part of the phrasal verb and noun we usually stress. Check the answers in open class. Students then listen to the sentences again and repeat them. See p145 for the audioscript for this exercise.

Answers

The stress in phrasal verbs is usually on the preposition. If they have a noun counterpart, however, the stress is usually on the first part.

✛ EXTRA ACTIVITY

Students look in their dictionaries and find more examples of phrasal verbs and their noun counterparts (*check out/checkout, print out/printout, take over/ takeover*, etc.).

TEACHER DEVELOPMENT: PRONUNCIATION

Word stress in phrasal verbs and their noun counterparts

All words of more than one syllable have what is called word stress. This means that at least one of the syllables is longer and louder than the other syllables. Often, word stress must be learnt when students learn new words. However, there are some rules for word stress, such as stress in phrasal verbs and their noun counterparts.

Phrasal verbs are generally made up of a verb and a preposition. Correct word stress on the preposition is especially important if the phrasal verb has a compound noun counterpart, where the stress will be on the first part.

Note also the word stress on other pairs of two-syllable nouns and verbs, which follows the same pattern. The general rule is that the verb is usually stressed on the second syllable while the noun is usually stressed on the first, e.g. **verb:** *in<u>crease</u>;* **noun:** *<u>in</u>crease.*

3 Ask students to complete the text with the words in the box. Check answers in open class.

Answers

a away **b** off **c** into **d** down
e out of **f** on **g** in **h** off

4a Ask students to prepare notes about a journey that was special to them. Refer students to the question prompts and ask them to include as many of the phrasal verbs from exercise 1 as possible.

4b SPEAKING Put students in small groups and have them tell each other about their journey in exercise 4a. Circulate as students do the task and note any corrections for a feedback session at the end of the lesson.

HOMEWORK

Assign students page 15 in their Workbook or the relevant sections of the Online Workbook.

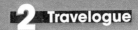

Gateway to life skills pp22–23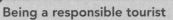

Being a responsible tourist
To appreciate your local and global environment and look at ways to minimise damage

ⓘ BACKGROUND INFORMATION

With the increase in global tourism it is likely that young people will have more opportunities to travel both nationally and internationally as part of university courses, gap years, holidays or volunteering programmes. Though there are many positive aspects to this, such as being exposed to new languages and culture, there are also many negative aspects, the potential damage to the environment being one of them. By encouraging students to consider the impact of travel choices on the local and global environments, they can make decisions to minimise negative effects while still enjoying the experience.

WARMER

Put the following headings on the board: *type of transport to destination, type of accommodation, nature* and *type of transport at destination*. Ask students to think of the last time they travelled abroad or within their own country. Have them write down the types of transport they used both to get there and once they were there, and the type of accommodation they stayed in. Under the heading 'nature', ask them to make note of any interaction they had with the natural world (e.g. going to the beach). At the end of the lesson, ask students to refer back to what they wrote here, and ask them if they could do the trip again, what they would change to be a more responsible tourist.

Before starting the lesson, give students time to read through the Life skills objectives and the Key concepts at the top of the page. Help with pronunciation of *conserve, damage* and *endangered* if necessary.

1   In pairs, ask students to look at the photos and decide which ones show responsible tourism. Encourage them to use the vocabulary from the Key concepts box. Nominate pairs to give their answers, giving their reasons.

Suggested answers
Photo 2 because they are not damaging the environment – they're on bicycles.
Photo 4 because the girl is using a guidebook, which means she's showing interest in the local culture and perhaps she's learning some of the language.

2   Ask students to read the titles from the text and have them match the photos in exercise 1 to four of them. Nominate students to give their answers.

Answers
1 F **2** C **3** E **4** A

3   **READING** Ask students to read the text and match the sections with the titles in exercise 2. With less confident students you might want to pre-teach the words: *consume, refill*.

Answers
Before you travel: **1** D **2** A **3** G
When you are there: **1** B **2** H **3** K **4** E **5** C **6** F **7** J **8** I

≫ FAST FINISHERS

Ask students to number the pieces of advice in the order they think is the most important.

4   Ask students to read the text again and decide whether it says the things are good, bad or dependent on another factor.

Answers
1 it depends – You need to check laws about buying historic artefacts first.
2 bad
3 it depends – You can use it so long as you turn it off when you're not in the room.
4 it depends – Ask permission before you take someone's photograph.
5 good
6 it depends – If your destination is less than 500 km, use a train. If you need to fly, choose airlines that have energy-efficient planes.
7 bad

5   **SPEAKING** In pairs, ask students to discuss which are the three most important or most interesting pieces of advice. Have a feedback session and have students vote on what they think is the most important piece of advice.

6   Ask students to discuss the questions in pairs. After a few minutes, ask students to say what they know about New Zealand and write their ideas on the board.

ⓘ BACKGROUND INFORMATION

New Zealand is a predominantly English-speaking country made up of two main islands in the south-western Pacific Ocean, the North Island, and the South Island, and many smaller islands. The population is about 4.5 million and the capital city is Wellington. Students may know that *The Lord of the Rings* and *The Hobbit* films were filmed in New Zealand, and the country is also famous for its rugby team, the All Blacks.

7   Tell students they are going to watch or listen to a video of a teenager talking about a recent trip to New Zealand. Before they watch or listen to the video, ask them to read through the text and guess any of the missing words. For less confident students, go through the text as a class and elicit suggestions as you go. Elicit possible answers from students.

8 **LISTENING** ▶ 10 Play the video or track for students to fill in the missing words in exercise 7. Play again, pausing after each section if necessary to give students time to write. Allow students to compare their answers in pairs before nominating students to give their answers in open class. See p145 for the audioscript/videoscript for this exercise.

Answers

a food **b** plants **c** soil **d** contaminate **e** rubbish
f Toi Iho **g** environmentally friendly **h** kiwi fruit

✦✦ EXTRA ACTIVITY

Dictogloss

Play the first part of the video or track again for students to do a dictogloss activity. Initially, students work individually to write down as many words as they can hear. Then in pairs or small groups, students combine the versions they have to try to get an accurate version. Play the video or track one more time, and give students two minutes to finalise their version. Have pairs or groups swap with other pairs or groups and display the correct version on the board. Students correct spelling, punctuation and grammar, before swapping back.

LIFE TASK

Tell students they are going to work in small groups and put together a presentation about responsible tourism in an area of their choice.

■ *Step 1*

Ask groups to decide on an area they are going to focus on for their presentation. It could be their own area or somewhere they know well, or somewhere they will be able to find out information about. Draw their attention to the topics and ask them to make notes about each idea, using the ideas in the Student's Book and the Internet to help them.

■ *Step 2*

When students have enough information on all the topics in Step 1, ask them to plan a presentation on responsible tourism in their chosen area. Support students by giving them some help with what to include in their presentation's structure, e.g. an introduction to the area, the type of tourists that visit, tips for tourists coming, summary, etc.

■ *Step 3*

Have each group give their presentation to the class. Encourage other students to ask questions at the end of each presentation. Make notes of any errors to correct at the end of the lesson.

TEACHER DEVELOPMENT: STUDENT TRAINING

Giving a presentation

It can be time-consuming to have each student in a class give an oral presentation so it is important that the experience is a positive and useful one for the whole class. Speaking in front of others is a skill that will be of lifelong benefit to students, but oral presentations can often cause anxiety. When discussing the topic with students, ask them to think about what they can do to reduce anxiety, e.g. knowing what is expected and being well prepared.

Experience builds confidence, which is the key to an effective oral presentation, so it is a good idea for students to practise in pairs before they present their topic to the class. Students may feel more comfortable if they know the assessment criteria beforehand so if possible hand out the grading criteria to them before they do their presentation and ensure they understand what is being looked for.

Listening p24

Listening for specific information and detail

WARMER

Draw students' attention to the two images at the top of the page and ask them to suggest how they think the two may be connected.

Suggested answer

Around the World in 80 Days is a book by Jules Verne. It is based on a real journey. The photo shows men working on the railway. The railway made long-distance travel easier.

ⓘ CULTURAL INFORMATION

The Magellan-Elcano expedition from 1519–1522 is considered to be the first circumnavigation of the world. The expedition set sail from Seville, initially under the command of Ferdinand Magellan. When he died, Juan Elcano took over, sailing via Borneo, the Spice Islands, the Indian Ocean, round the Cape of Good Hope and north along the west coast of Africa, back to Spain three years after they left, in 1522. Though the expedition began with five ships and 270 crew, only one ship, the *Victoria*, completed it with 18 crew.

1 In pairs, students guess the answers to the questions.

2 **LISTENING** ▶ 11 Play the track for students to listen to an expert talking about travelling around the world. Nominate students to give their answers. See pp144–145 for the audioscript for this exercise.

Answers

1 b **2** a **3** c **4** a

3 **LISTENING** ▶ 11 Ask students to read through the text then play the track again for students to correct the six mistakes. In more confident classes, students could try to correct the mistakes from memory, then listen to the track to check their answers.

Answers

20 – 17
1522 – 1519
1870 – 1872
engineer – businessman
fast – took a long time
just over two days – less than 32 hours

HOMEWORK

Assign students page 15 in their Workbook or the relevant sections of the Online Workbook.

Grammar in context pp24–25

Using used to and would

>>> FAST TRACK

You could ask students to complete exercise 2 at home.

Test before you teach: Flipped classroom
Set the Flipped classroom video and tasks for homework <u>before the lesson</u>. This will allow you to assess the needs of the students before the class. Students can then move on to the relevant grammar practice activities.

WARMER

Write these sentences on the board:

It used to take weeks, months or even years to travel around the world.

It didn't used to be easy to travel around the world.

The first person to travel around the world was the Portuguese sailor Ferdinand Magellan.

Really the first person to travel around the world used to be the Spanish captain Juan Sebastián Elcano.

Did it used to take much longer?

Put students in small groups and hold a grammar auction. Tell students that some of the sentences are grammatically correct and some are incorrect and that as a team they need to 'bid' to buy the correct ones. Give each team a budget of 1,000 euros and have a maximum bid of 250 euros on each. Start the auction at 50 euros and keep increasing until each sentence is 'sold' to the highest bidding team. At the end of the auction, correct the incorrect sentences as a class. The team that bought the correct sentences can add the amount they paid for each onto their 1,000 euro total, and deduct the amount they paid if they bought an incorrect one.

This warmer is a useful way to see what students may already know about the target grammar.

Answers

1 (correct)
2 It didn't use to be easy to travel around the world.
3 (correct)
4 Really the first person to travel around the world was the Spanish captain Juan Sebastián Elcano.
5 Did it use to take much longer?

used to

1a Students look at the sentences then match the correct halves of the rules.

Answers

1 b **2** c **3** a

1b Students write the negative and question form of the sentence.

Answers

They didn't use to travel by horse across the US. Did they use to travel by horse across the US?

TEACHER DEVELOPMENT: LANGUAGE

used to

Point out to students that *used to* only exists in the past to talk about something that happened regularly or went on for a time in the past but no longer happens. Both the past simple and *used to* can describe past habits, events and states. However, we prefer *used to* when we want to emphasise repetition of actions/situations that are now finished.

You could give students some more examples:

I used to live in the country. (= 'Once/A long time ago I lived in the country. Now I don't.')

Sam used to spend his summer holidays in Italy. (= 'now he doesn't')

Students may confuse *used to* with the verb *use* in the past (e.g. *I used my dictionary to look up the words.*) so point out this difference in meaning and pronunciation. Note the pronunciation /juːst/ and /juːs/ of *used to* whereas the past of the verb *to use* is pronounced: /juːzd/.

2 Students complete the sentences with the correct form.

Answers

1 used to **2** Did people use to **3** didn't use to
4 used to **5** didn't use to **6** Did people use to
7 used to **8** Did people use to **9** didn't use to
10 used to

3 Students decide if the sentences describe a past habit, a single action in the past or a present habit. Students complete the sentences with the correct form of *used to*, the past simple or the present simple.

Answers

1 went **2** used to go **3** cycles **4** didn't use to like
5 used to play **6** didn't use to go

4 Students look at the picture of a Wild West scene in 1870. Ask them to find eight historical mistakes in the picture and write as many sentences as possible, affirmative and/or negative. Direct students' attention to the example sentences.

Suggested answers

They didn't use to play football.

They didn't use to ride motorbikes, they used to ride horses.

They didn't use to listen to MP3 players.

They didn't use to use tablets. They used to use pen and paper and books.

They didn't use to wear sunglasses, they used to wear hats.

They didn't use to eat take away pizza.

They didn't use to fly helicopters. They used to have hot-air balloons.

would

5 Ask students to choose the correct alternative.

Answers

a can **b** can't **c** can **d** can't

6 Students replace *used to* with *would* when possible.

Answers

1 would **2** would **3** no change
4 no change **5** would **6** no change

7a **SPEAKING** In pairs, students make notes about how life was different in their country fifty years ago using the topics. Remind them to use *would* and *used to*. Walk round, monitoring students and helping them with any language difficulties they may have.

7b Students report back to the class with their ideas. Students could come up and write their sentences for each topic on the board. Draw students' attention to the example sentences.

✚ EXTRA ACTIVITY

Students expand their ideas and notes from exercises 7a and b to write a short text using *used to/didn't use to/would*.

Refer students to the Grammar reference on page 28 if necessary.

HOMEWORK

Assign students page 16 in their Workbook or the relevant sections of the Online Workbook.

Developing speaking p26

Asking for information

>>> FAST TRACK

You could ask students to complete the conversation in exercise 2 without listening to the track again.

WARMER

Divide the class into small teams. Give them a five-minute time limit to think of words connected to the unit theme of transport for each letter of the alphabet. They can look back in the unit for ideas.

Suggested answers

arrival, bed and breakfast, coach, destination, engine, fare, get off, horse, island, journey, kayak, lorry, miss, navigate, one-way ticket, passport, queue, return, single, train, underground, van, weather, X'trapolis, yacht, zeppelin

1 Students look at the British train ticket and complete the information.

Answers

1 London **2** Oxford **3** 22nd September
4 One adult **5** Single **6** Standard
7 £24.00

2 **LISTENING** ▶ 12 Play the track for students to listen to a conversation between a girl and a ticket agent and complete the information. See p146 for the audioscript for this exercise.

Answers

1 Canterbury **2** Today **3** 3.55 pm
4 Change trains at London St Pancras
5 Return, coming back next Wednesday **6** £41
7 Debit card **8** Platform 9

3 ▶ 12 Play the track again for students to tick the expressions they hear in the Speaking bank.

Answers

Could you tell me the time of the next train to Canterbury?

… can you tell me which platform it is for the train to London?

Pardon?

Sorry, I didn't catch that.

TEACHER DEVELOPMENT: STUDENT TRAINING

Polite requests

Give students practice of polite requests in English, by encouraging their use in the classroom (e.g. *Can I use the bathroom? Could you pass me the dictionary, please?*).

Tell students you will help them if necessary, but only if they use a polite request (e.g. *Could you tell me how to say that in English?*).

4 Ask students to make the requests more polite using the expressions from the Speaking bank. Draw their attention to the example given. Elicit answers from the class and drill the sentence paying attention to intonation.

Answers

1 Could you tell me if it's possible to pay by debit card?
2 Could you tell me what the cheapest fare is?
3 Could you tell me if it's a direct train?
4 Could you tell me what time it is?
5 Could you tell me what time the train arrives?

TEACHER DEVELOPMENT: STUDENT TRAINING

How to learn everyday expressions

Encourage students to listen to the radio, especially talk shows or news programmes. Elicit what activities they can carry out in English on the Internet, e.g. listen to podcasts, videos and audio presentations online, listen to songs and find lyrics, chat and participate in forums, etc. Remind students that they can learn a lot of new expressions by playing games and doing puzzles such as crosswords and word searches. If possible, students can try to watch films in English or with English subtitles.

5 In pairs, students prepare the dialogue using the guide given.

PRACTICE MAKES PERFECT

6 **SPEAKING** Students look at the task. Divide the class into two teams: A and B. All students from Team A find someone from Team B to be their partner. Students A and Students B look at page 147 for the information they need.

They then role-play a conversation in the train ticket office. Remind them to show that they understand or don't understand by using expressions from the Speaking bank. For students who are less confident, photocopy the model dialogue above and demonstrate with a strong student. Then instruct students to read aloud in pairs, alternating between roles A and B. Then ask them to read it again, changing the underlined information so that it is true for the task.

Model dialogue

Ticket officer: Good morning. Can I help you?
Customer: Yes, please. I'd like to go to <u>Newcastle</u>. Could you tell me the times of trains?
Ticket officer: OK. Well, there's one at <u>2.15</u>, and the next one is at <u>5.25</u>.
Customer: Are they both direct trains?
Ticket officer: Yes, all the trains to <u>Newcastle</u> are direct trains.
Customer: OK, I'll take the <u>4.25</u> please. How much is that?
Ticket officer: Would you like a single or a return?
Customer: Return please, coming back on <u>Saturday</u>.
Ticket officer: OK. Let's see. The cheapest fare for a return ticket on that train is <u>£100</u>.
Customer: OK. How can I pay?
Ticket officer: You can pay by cash or card.
Customer: Here's my card.
Ticket officer: Thank you.
Customer: Oh, could you tell me which platform it is?
Ticket officer: Yes, it's platform <u>4</u>.
Customer: OK. Thanks a lot.
Ticket officer: Thank you, and have a good journey.

✓ EXAM SUCCESS Ask students to discuss ideas for doing speaking exam exercises where they need to ask for and give specific information, then compare their ideas with the information on page 144.

TEACHER DEVELOPMENT: STUDENT TRAINING

Asking for and giving information

In speaking exam exercises, remind students to avoid giving short, uncommunicative replies. Elicit the difference between a closed question (you can answer *yes/no* without any further explanation) and an open question (one that begins with a question word). Remind students to say when they understand or if they don't understand. Remind them that the examiner is on their side and is there to help them.

✚ EXTRA ACTIVITY

Students make a mind map of all the words they can think of connected to a train station. It could include information like the following:
Useful phrases:
What time does the train leave?
When is the next/last train?
Which platform does the train leave from?
Do I have to change trains?
Verbs: *get on/get off, get in, travel, arrive, depart*
My ticket: *Place of departure, destination, single/return, first class/standard, price, date, fare*
General: *office, lost property office, information office, toilets, passenger, luggage, luggage trolley, ticket officer*

HOMEWORK

Assign students page 17 in their Workbook or the relevant sections of the Online Workbook.

Developing writing p27

Understanding and writing a blog post

>>> FAST TRACK

You could ask students to do exercises 2 and 3 at home and check their answers at the start of the lesson. Alternatively, you could set the writing task in exercise 6 as homework.

WARMER

Ask students to think of words they associate with Dubai, prompting them to think of the weather, the architecture, the natural world. Elicit ideas and then ask them if it's somewhere they would like to visit.

1 SPEAKING Students work with a partner and answer the questions.

2 READING Ask students to read Ryan's blog post and answer the question. Elicit answers from different students.

3 Ask students to read the blog again and write what Ryan said about the four topics.

Answers

1 It was long. It took seven hours. They watched films and played video games.
2 It was his favourite attraction. They spent hours there on the rides.
3 It's one of the biggest in the world. There was an aquarium. There was a spectacular show in the evening.
4 Dubai's indoor snow park is enormous.

4 Students look at the Writing bank and complete the examples with words from Ryan's blog. Explain that *so* and *such* make the meaning of the adjective stronger, and that *do, does, did* are used here for emotive or contrastive emphasis. We do not usually use them in an affirmative sentence.

Answers

a brilliant place   **b** long   **c** a great time   **d** did like

5 Ask students to make the sentences more emphatic by using the word given.

Answers

1 What a busy city!
2 It was such a great flight.
3 We were so tired when we arrived.
4 I do love New York.
5 We did have a good time.
6 We were so happy to get back.
7 What a great holiday!
8 It's such a fantastic place for shopping.

TEACHER DEVELOPMENT: PRONUNCIATION

Emphasis on *do/does*

When we are using the auxiliaries *do* and *does* for contrastive or emotive emphasis like this, we give them extra stress to make them sound louder, longer or higher in tone. When you see the words used in this way in print, they will normally be in italics or bold type or in capital letters. Drill sentences 4 and 5 above with extra word stress on *do* and *did*, and have students practise in pairs.

6 Students choose an amazing holiday destination and make notes for a blog post. Tell them to use the questions to give them ideas.

PRACTICE MAKES PERFECT

7 Students use their notes from exercise 6 to write their blog post. Remind them to use the expressions from the Writing bank to add emphasis and interest. For students who are less confident, photocopy the model blog post in the next column for extra support during the writing task. Refer students to the Writing bank on page 150.

Model blog post

So, today I'm writing this blog to you from Peru ... finally! The journey was so stressful, we had a big delay at Cusco airport and it took ages to get our luggage, but we did eventually arrive and it's such a beautiful place. Yesterday we visited the Qurikancha (temple of the sun) and the Cathedral. I'd recommend them both. Tomorrow, we're going on a three-hour train journey to Aguas Calientes, about 25 minutes from the incredible Machu Picchu.
I can't wait to get on the Inca Trail! What a busy and exciting few days ahead.

✓ **EXAM SUCCESS** Students think of the different things they need to check before they hand in a piece of writing in the exam, then compare their answers with the information on page 144. Suggest that they could compile a checklist based on these suggestions, and use it every time they hand in a piece of work.

HOMEWORK

Assign students page 18 in their Workbook or the relevant sections of the Online Workbook.

Language checkpoint: Unit 2

>>> FAST TRACK

Students read the Grammar reference and Vocabulary sections on page 28 before completing the revision exercises on the following page.

Grammar revision p29

Past simple and past continuous

1 Students complete the sentences.

Answers

1 stopped **2** was waiting **3** put **4** got
5 were crying **6** were watching **7** dropped

Past simple and past perfect

2 Students join the sentences with a time expression and put one of the verbs in the past perfect.

Answers

1 By the time she arrived at their house, they had already left.
2 When he had finished using the computer, he switched it off.
3 After they had bought their tickets, they went into the cinema.
4 As soon as she had done her homework, she went to bed.
5 When we had eaten our meal, we paid the bill.
6 They went into the house after they had unlocked the door.

used to and would

3 Students choose the correct alternative. Remind students that in one sentence, both alternatives are correct.

Answers

1 use **2** didn't use to **3** usually **4** won
5 used to **6** both **7** would take

Vocabulary revision p29

TRANSPORT AND TRAVEL

1 Students write a simple explanation for each word.

Answers

1 a type of transport that goes on the road and takes a lot of people from one city to another
2 the place where you stand to catch a train
3 the situation when something happens later than planned
4 the money that you pay for a journey
5 a type of sea transport that takes people and cars on journeys that are not very long
6 a ticket for a journey where you go and come back to the same place as you started
7 when you arrive too late for a bus, train or other type of transport
8 when you stop something that was going to happen

ACCOMMODATION

2 Students write the names of the types of accommodation.

Answers

1 motel
2 bed and breakfast
3 campsite
4 tent
5 caravan
6 (youth) hostel

PHRASAL VERBS CONNECTED WITH TRAVEL

3 Students choose the correct alternative.

Answers

1 in **2** off **3** in **4** into **5** down **6** away

HOMEWORK

Assign students page 19 in their Workbook or the relevant sections of the Online Workbook.

Reading p30

> ### ➤ TIP FOR READING EXAMS
>
> Ask students to read the tip and discuss, then look at Exam success on page 144 and compare their ideas.

1 READING Students read the text quickly and then answer the questions.

Answers

Chris Hadfield is an astronaut.
1 Moscow – favourite city
2 Barbados – a scuba diving holiday with family
3 Tintagel – his favourite place in the British Isles, he did a trip there
4 Portugal – his best holiday
5 The Caribbean – the next holiday

2 Ask students to read the text again and decide whether the statements are True (T) or False (F). Remind them to write the line number(s) where they found their answer.

Answers

1 T (lines 1–3) **2** T (line 8) **3** F (lines 19–21)
4 F (lines 26–27) **5** F (line 35) **6** F (lines 47–48)
7 T (lines 55–58) **8** F (lines 62–63)

3 SPEAKING What about *you*? Give students time to read the questions. Then either have them discuss their answers in pairs or small groups or nominate individual students to share their answers in open class.

Speaking p31

> ### ➤ TIP FOR SPEAKING EXAMS
>
> Students read the tip fand then turn to Exam success on page 144 for more ideas.

4 Ask students to read through the questions and make notes for their own answers. Remind them not to write full sentences. You could set a time limit for this to encourage students not to write too much detail.

5 In pairs, students imagine that they are in the 'personal information' part of the speaking exam. Students take it in turns to ask and answer the questions. Allow students to refer to their notes from exercise 4, but remind them not to just read them out.

Listening p31

> ### ➤ TIP FOR LISTENING EXAMS
>
> Students read the tips for carrying out matching activities then turn to Exam success on page 144 for more ideas.

6 In pairs, students discuss what problems people have with travel or accommodation when they go away on holiday.

7 LISTENING 13 Play the track for students to listen to four people talking about travel problems. Ask students to match the statements with the person who said them. Remind them that there is one extra statement which they do not need to use. See p146 for the audioscript for this exercise.

Answers

Speaker 1 d   Speaker 2 a   Speaker 3 e   Speaker 4 c

Writing p31 ✏️ ✏️

> ### ➤ TIP FOR WRITING EXAMS
>
> Brainstorm with students what to look for when they are checking for mistakes before handing in their texts. Ask students to read the tip and look at Exam success on page 144 for more ideas.

8 Students imagine that the people in the photo are some new friends they made on holiday and write an email to their family telling them about their new friends. Remind them to describe their appearance and personality using their imagination and the words and phrases given. For students who are less confident, photocopy the model email below for extra support during the writing task and ask them to adapt the descriptions to match the photo.

✂ -
Model text

Hi everyone,

I'm having such a great time here – Paris is so amazing and the people are brilliant. I've made lots of new friends here at the language school. Here's a picture of three of them. Anna is really nice, she's the one in the middle with long, black hair. She's very friendly and cheerful, that's why we're such good friends. Eddy is the guy on the left, he's very funny, but he can be a bit arrogant and quite bossy sometimes! The boys are just mad, totally crazy, especially Jan – he's the one in the black and white striped T-shirt with short dark hair. He's really hard-working and clever – he's working on a computer program he designed at the moment. Right, I've got lots of homework to do for my lessons tomorrow, so I need to go now.

Hope you're all well. Don't forget to write soon! Missing you lots.

Julie
- -

> ### HOMEWORK
>
> Assign students pages 20–21 in their Workbook or the relevant sections of the Online Workbook.

---

1 Ask students to mark from 1–4 how well they can do these things in English.
2 Ask students to look at their marks and decide what they think they need to do to improve. Elicit other suggestions.

3 City to city

KEY LEARNING OUTCOMES

CEF

Students will be able to:

- talk about past activities which are relevant in the present using the present perfect simple and present perfect continuous
- describe cities and use extreme adjectives
- understand written and spoken texts about city life
- use expressions to describe different parts of a photo
- write informal emails describing places

UNIT OVERVIEW

Vocabulary
Cities and houses
Adjectives describing cities

Reading
Moving to the megacities!
CRITICAL THINKING Discussing the pros and cons of moving to a city

Grammar in context
Present perfect simple and past simple
ever, never, for, since, just, already, yet

Developing vocabulary
Extreme adjectives
PRONUNCIATION Emphatic stress

Life skills
Numeracy:
Explaining statistics

Listening
A podcast

Grammar in context
Present perfect continuous

Developing speaking
Describing photos – 1

Developing writing
An informal email describing a place

Exam success
Reading: Missing sentences activities
Use of English: Multiple-choice cloze

DIGITAL OVERVIEW

Presentation Kit

- ▶ **Flipped classroom video unit 3:** Present perfect continuous
- ▶ **Life skills video unit 3:** Explaining statistics
- ▶ V **Vocabulary tool:** Cities and houses
- ▶ **Interactive versions of Student's Book activities**
- ▶ **Integrated audio and answer key for all activities**
- ▶ **Workbook pages with answer key**

Teacher's Resource Centre TRC

- ▶ **Flipped classroom video Unit 3:** Present perfect continuous
- ▶ **Life skills video Unit 3:** Explaining statistics
- ▶ **Grammar communication activity Unit 3:** If this is the answer, what's the question?
- ▶ **Worksheets for this unit, including:**
  - Grammar Practice worksheet Unit 3
  - Flipped classroom video worksheet Unit 3: Present perfect continuous
  - Literature worksheet Units 3 and 4
  - CLIL worksheet Unit 3
  - Life skills video worksheet Unit 3
  - Everyday English worksheet Unit 3

Student's App
Gateway 2nd Edition wordlist for the award-winning Sounds App (available for download)

✓ TESTING AND ASSESSMENT

Resources for exam preparation and measuring student progress

- ▶ Test Generator Units 1–3
- ▶ Printable tests
  Unit 3 and Review (Units 1–3)
- ▶ Gateway to exams Units 3 and 4 (end of Unit 4)

Vocabulary p32

Talking about and describing cities and houses

>>> **FAST TRACK**

Ask students to do exercise 1 at home so that less confident students can take the necessary time to look up the vocabulary in the Macmillan Online Dictionary.

WARMER

In pairs, students discuss the meaning of the unit title *City to city* and what they think the unit is going to be about (different topics related to the places where we live). Ask students to define the word *city* and discuss the difference between a city, a town and a village. (Cities are generally larger and more densely populated than towns and have industrial, commercial and residential areas. Most cities also perform administrative functions. A town is smaller than a city but larger than a village.) *City to city* refers to travelling from place to place and also comparing different cities.

v Cities and houses

1 In pairs, students match the photos with the words.

Answers

a semi-detached house b terraced house
c detached house/bungalow d cottage

2 ▶ 14 Play the track for students to listen, check and repeat. Draw attention to the stress on *bungalow* and *cottage*. See p146 for the audioscript for this exercise.

ⓘ **CULTURAL INFORMATION**

In Britain, the main types of houses are:
- detached (not joined to another house)
- semi-detached (joined to one other house)
- terraced (part of a row of houses)
- flats (apartments)
- maisonettes (two-level flats in a small building)
- bungalows (one-level houses, usually detached or semi-detached)

It is common for young people in the UK to live in shared, rented accommodation away from the family home while at university and in their early twenties. Renting is also becoming a more viable option for people in later life due to recent increases in the cost of buying a house relative to salary.

➕ **EXTRA ACTIVITY**

Students think of the names of other places people call home (*igloo, villa, chalet, castle, farm, ranch, lighthouse,* etc.).

3 Ask students in turn to name a room in a flat or house and as they do so write a list on the board. Alternatively, divide the class into small groups and ask them to make lists in their groups. Then find out which group has the longest list and get them to write their list on the board.

Suggested answers

kitchen, bedroom, study, lounge (or living room), bathroom, dining room, hall, garage, attic, office

4 **SPEAKING** In pairs, students tell each other what type of house or flat they live in and describe it. Draw students' attention to the example sentences.

5 **SPEAKING** Students talk about the photos using the words given.

Suggested answers

a This is a city centre. You can see some very tall skyscrapers in the background. In the foreground you can see the town hall.
b This is on the outskirts of the city but it doesn't show the suburbs. You can see the port and some factories.

6 Students look at the definitions and match them with a word in exercise 5.

Answers

1 port 2 inner city 3 city centre 4 square 5 suburbs
6 outskirts

Adjectives describing cities

7a Students match the words with the definitions.

Answers

1 historic 2 quiet 3 dirty 4 lively 5 busy
6 crowded

7b Students decide the opposites of 2 and 3 in exercise 7a.

Answers

noisy, clean

8 **LISTENING** ▶ 15 Play the track for students to listen to four people talking about houses or places in a city and decide which type of place each person talks about. Ask for answers in open class and elicit the information that helped students make their choices. With a less confident class, pre-teach *a building* – a structure such as a house that has a roof and walls. See p147 for the audioscript for this exercise.

Answers

1 a block of flats 2 a bungalow 3 the suburbs
4 the inner city/city centre

9 **SPEAKING** In pairs, students talk about the area where their school is. Draw students' attention to the model sentences.

>>> **FAST FINISHERS**

In pairs, ask students to brainstorm the type of furniture in each room (*kitchen: sink, cupboards, table,* etc.).

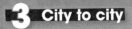

HOMEWORK

Assign students page 22 in their Workbook or the relevant sections of the Online Workbook.

Reading p33

Predicting content and reading for cohesion and logical textual links

≫ FAST TRACK

You could ask students to read the article at home using a dictionary to help them with any new vocabulary.

WARMER

Play *Hot Seat* to start the class. Divide the class into two teams, A and B. A volunteer from Team A sits with their back to the board. Write a word related to the house theme from the previous lesson on the board. Team A defines the word for the volunteer student to guess in one minute. After one minute, it is Team B's turn to define a word. The team that describes the most words in one minute wins the round.

1 In pairs, students look at the photo and take it in turns to describe it. Elicit descriptions from around the class. Tell students to look at the title of the article and guess what the article is about before they read.

2 READING Students read the article and check their predictions. Tell them not to pay attention to the gaps in the text. Set a two-minute time limit to prevent students from getting stuck on vocabulary at this stage.

Answer

The text is about megacities (very large cities) in China.

TEACHER DEVELOPMENT: STUDENT TRAINING

Predicting content in text

Poor readers often read the text word by word, underlining words they are not sure of, without predicting what the text will be about. Poor readers look for unfamiliar words instead of looking for the gist of the whole passage.

Good readers use a variety of strategies. What the student does *before* reading can improve comprehension. Predictions encourage active reading and keep students interested, whether or not the predictions are correct. Students can look at the pictures, photos, headings, maps, diagrams, and other features to make predictions about a text and activate prior knowledge. On first reading, they can look for words or phrases that confirm or contradict their predictions.

ⓘ **CULTURAL INFORMATION**

A megacity is defined as a city with over ten million people. In 2015, there were around 30 megacities in the world, with Shanghai being the fourth largest in terms of population. By 2030, 12 more cities are expected to reach megacity status. Though there are some advantages of living in megacities (such as multiculturalism, high level of cultural activities, public transport systems and many opportunities for investment), these are often outweighed by disadvantages such as pollution, overcrowding, high cost of living, crime and social fragmentation.

✔ **EXAM SUCCESS** Students discuss what they think should be the first thing they do in this type of activity, then look at Exam success on page 144 and compare their ideas.

TEACHER DEVELOPMENT: STUDENT TRAINING

Missing sentences reading activities

These activities test students' complete understanding of the text. Students should identify the key ideas in the sentences and then scan each paragraph for the overall sequence of ideas in the text. A key strategy is to look for matching vocabulary. This can be another clue as to where to put the new sentence. Students can also compare the missing sentence and the paragraphs to see if the second sentence is a direct explanation of the first. Finally, students should put the missing sentences where they think they should go in the text and reread it to see if it makes logical sense.

3 Students put sentences 1–5 into gaps a–e. Elicit answers from students around the class and discuss which strategies students employed to decide on the correct answer.

Answers

1 e **2** b **3** d **4** a **5** c

4 Students read the text again and answer the questions.

Answers

1 They live in the countryside.
2 Because industry is growing and people are moving to the cities to get jobs.
3 They live in large blocks of flats. That means the cities are very crowded.
4 They are building eco-cities.
5 They use solar power, they collect rainwater and the walls have green plants living on them which clean the air.

➕ **EXTRA ACTIVITY**

In pairs, students write three questions each to test each other's reading comprehension. (*How many Chinese cities have more than one million inhabitants?*, etc.)

5 ⚙ **CRITICAL THINKING** Ask students to look at the questions and think about their own answer. Then have a discussion in open class for students to compare their answers.

6 Ask students to look at the underlined words in the text and guess what they mean. Allow them to check in their dictionaries.

Answers

growing = getting bigger

urgent = is important and must happen quickly

accommodate = to give someone a home, make space for someone

increase in size = become larger

nearby = close, not far away

7 SPEAKING **What about *you*?** Ask students to read the questions and the example dialogue and think of their own answers and then discuss in pairs. Elicit answers from different pairs, and see which is the most popular city in your country for students to live in.

HOMEWORK

Assign students page 23 in their Workbook or the relevant sections of the Online Workbook.

Grammar in context pp34-35

Using the present perfect simple and past simple

⋙ FAST TRACK

You could ask students to do exercise 1a at home and compare their answers at the start of the next lesson.

Test before you teach

Write these two sentences on the board and ask students to unscramble them.

moved 2011 She Spain in to

years He three worked here has for

Ask students to say which sentence is in the present perfect simple or past simple and find out how confident they are with these tenses. If students are already familiar with them, move quickly through exercises 1a and 1b eliciting answers from students in open class.

Answers

She moved to Spain in 2011. (past simple)

He has worked here for three years. (present perfect simple)

Present perfect simple and past simple

1a Students look at the sentences and choose the correct alternative.

Answers

1 past simple (sentences 1, 4)

2 present perfect (sentences 2, 3)

1b Students complete the rule for the formation of the present perfect.

Answer

past participle

2 Students complete each sentence with the correct form of the verb in the present perfect or past simple.

Answers

1 grew **2** has gone **3** has changed **4** built
5 has designed **6** has been **7** was **8** have visited
9 has reached **10** have built

ever, never, for, since, just, already, yet

3a Students complete each explanation with the best word from the list. These are words frequently used with the present perfect.

Answers

1 ever **2** just **3** already **4** never
5 for, since, for, since **6** yet

3b Students decide what the usual position of the words from exercise 3a is in a sentence.

Answers

1 already, ever, just, never
2 for, since
3 yet

4 Students choose the correct verb to complete the sentences with the present perfect. Students then put the other word in the correct place in the sentence. If necessary, revise the use of *ever* first. *Ever* (= 'sometime before now') is used in questions, e.g. *Have you ever/ Haven't you ever …?* and in negative statements with the subject *nothing/nobody*, etc., e.g. *Nobody has ever travelled there before. Ever* is also used with *the first time*, e.g. *This is the first time I've ever been to New York.*

Answers

2 've never lived **3** 's already visited **4** 've had, for
5 Has (it) just rained **6** 've loved, since
7 Have (you) ever lived

⋙ FAST FINISHERS

Ask students to look at the list of irregular past participles in the back of their books and find examples of verbs that are:

1 the same in the base form, past simple and in the past participle (e.g. *cost – cost – cost*)

2 the same in the past simple and past participle (e.g. *catch – caught – caught*)

3 the same in the base form and the past participle (e.g. *become – became – become*)

4 the same in the base form and the past simple (e.g. *beat – beat – beaten*)

✓ EXAM SUCCESS **Students work in pairs to discuss the best way to approach the task. They then turn to page 144 of the Student's Book to compare their answers.**

5 Students read the text and choose the best answer. You could time this activity to give students practice for the time constraints they will have under exam conditions.

FAST FINISHERS

Students write some comprehension questions about the text, e.g. *Did London have lots of skyscrapers in the past? Why haven't they sold all the apartments yet? Does everyone think positively of the building?*

Answers

1 B **2** A **3** D **4** D **5** A **6** B **7** B **8** C
9 B **10** A

✚ EXTRA ACTIVITY

For homework or to round off the class, students write sentences about themselves using the present perfect and each of these words at least once (*already, for, just, never, since, yet*). Students make two of their sentences false. In pairs, students read out their sentences to each other for their partner to guess the false sentences.

Refer students to the Grammar reference on page 42 if necessary.

HOMEWORK

Assign students page 24 in their Workbook or the relevant sections of the Online Workbook.

Developing vocabulary p35

Describing things using extreme adjectives

>>> FAST TRACK

Students could do exercise 1 as homework, using a dictionary if necessary. Ask them to compare their words in class before doing exercise 2.

Extreme adjectives

1 Students look at the extreme adjectives and match each one to a normal adjective (a–j).

Answers

1 h **2** g **3** a **4** c **5** f **6** d **7** j **8** i **9** b
10 e

2 Students look at the example sentences and match the correct halves of the rules.

Answers

1 c **2** a/b **3** d **4** a/b

3 Students complete the sentences with the appropriate adjectives from exercise 1.

Answers

1 stunning **2** ancient **3** hot **4** packed **5** dirty
6 silent

4a PRONUNCIATION ▶ 16 Students listen and check their answers. Ask whether we stress normal adjectives or extreme adjectives more. See p147 for the audioscript for this exercise.

Answers

We stress extreme adjectives more.

4b In pairs, students practise saying the sentences in exercise 3 with the correct stress on the extreme adjective. For example, *The view from our window wasn't just beautiful. It was absolutely stunning.*

5a SPEAKING Ask students to write down one place or item for each extreme adjective in exercise 1.

5b In pairs, students say their words from exercise 5a in a random order. Their partners have to guess the extreme adjective. Draw students' attention to the example dialogue.

TEACHER DEVELOPMENT: PRONUNCIATION

Emphatic stress

Sometimes there is a change in the standard stress pattern within a sentence. If you want to emphasise something, you can change the stress from the principal noun to another content word such as an adjective (*big, difficult*, etc.), intensifier (*very, extremely*, etc.) or extreme adjective (*stunning, ancient*, etc.).

This emphasis is called emphatic stress. The speaker calls the listener's attention to what he or she wants to emphasise.

✚ EXTRA ACTIVITY

Students write a short text to describe places in their city or country using their ideas from exercise 5a.

HOMEWORK

Assign students page 25 in their Workbook or the relevant sections of the Online Workbook.

Gateway to life skills pp36–37

Explaining statistics

To look at different ways of presenting statistics; To learn how to talk about and express statistics; To find and present information using statistics

>>> FAST TRACK

You could set exercises 1 and 2 as homework to be checked in pairs at the next lesson.

ⓘ BACKGROUND INFORMATION

Understanding statistics is not just important for studying mathematics, but also for many other disciplines such as marketing, business, social studies, banking and accounting. It can also help to understand how numerical values are used in day-to-day life, in advertising and surveys, for example. The aim of this lesson is to learn vocabulary specific to statistics and to look at ways of presenting statistical findings. Students research a city of their choice and put together a presentation.

1 In pairs, students guess the answers to the questions about New York. Elicit some answers from students, but don't confirm them yet.

2 **READING** Students look at the information presented and check their answers to exercise 1.

Answers

1 -0.3 degrees Celsius   2 24.9 degrees Celsius
3 higher   4 by subway   5 yes

3 Ask students to look again at the information in exercise 2 and match the names of the infographics. For less confident students, you could help by explaining the vocabulary *pie, line* and *bar*, in English, which may help them select the correct option.

Answers

1 D   2 B   3 A   4 C

4 Ask students to read the statements about the information in exercise 2 and then choose the correct alternative. Allow students to use a dictionary if necessary. Elicit answers from students.

Answers

1 rising   2 a quarter   3 over   4 Approximately
5 slightly   6 stays the same   7 increased steadily

5a Draw students' attention to the diagrams. Check that they can remember the names of the types of diagrams. Then ask them to match the parts of the sentences with the diagrams.

Answers

a 4   b 2   c 3   d 6   e 1   f 5

5b Students complete the sentences in exercise 5a using information from exercise 2.

5c Students compare their answers.

Answers

1 The average temperature stays approximately the same between July and August.
2 Just over a third of New Yorkers use the subway.
3 Under a quarter of New Yorkers travel to work by car.
4 One in ten New Yorkers walk to work.
5 About two thirds of people in New York don't travel to work by subway.
6 The number of tourists going to New York / The temperature in New York is rising.

6 Tell students that they are going to watch or listen to a video of two students presenting information about social media use in New York. Students guess the answers to the questions before they listen. Nominate students to give their guesses, but don't confirm anything yet.

7 **LISTENING** ▶ 17 Before students watch or listen to the video, ask them to think about what words or phrases they may hear to answer the questions in exercise 6. Being prepared for particular vocabulary will help them select the correct answers. Play the video or track. Check answers in open class. Ask students if any of their guesses were correct. See p147 for the audioscript/videoscript for this exercise.

Answers

1 Age 25–34, maybe because they use the technology more frequently.
2 55–64, maybe because they are older and they don't know the technology.
3 women

8 ▶ 17 Tell students they are going to watch or listen again and decide if the statements are true or false, then correct the false ones. Play the video or track again. Then check answers. More confident students may want to attempt the task before watching the video for a second time, then using the repeat to check their answers.

Answers

1 F (About two thirds of users are between 13 and 34.)
2 T   3 F (Over a quarter ...)
4 F (... between the ages of 55 and 64)
5 T   6 T   7 F (... falls quite dramatically ...)
8 F (... slightly more women than men.)

9 **SPEAKING** In pairs, ask students to say whether any of the information in the video surprised them. Encourage them to give their reasons.

LIFE TASK

Tell students they are going to put together and present some statistics about a city of their choice.

- **Step 1**

  Ask each group to think of a city they want to research. Encourage them to think of a different one from other groups.

- **Step 2**

  Give students time to research statistics about the city. With less confident students, you could suggest particular topics for them to look at. Ask students to look for charts, graphs and tables to represent their data, and if they can't find any, to put together their own, making sure they choose a suitable one to show the statistic.

- **Step 3**

  Ask students to work individually or together to write about what the chart, graph or table shows. Remind them to use words from exercise 4.

- **Step 4**

  Have students present their information to the class as a poster or as a computer presentation. Encourage other groups to ask questions.

Listening p38

Listening for specific information

WARMER

In pairs, ask students to make a 'vocabulary pyramid' with words they have learnt in the unit so far, with three-syllable words at the bottom and one-syllable words at the top. Give students three minutes and then write their suggestions on the board, reminding students of pronunciation where necessary. For example: three syllables: *enormous, historic;* two syllables: *ancient, boiling;* one syllable: *clean, square.* You could use this opportunity to pre-teach vocabulary from the listening (e.g. *residence, typical*) by writing the words in the correct place in the pyramid.

1 SPEAKING In pairs, students take it in turns to describe the photo. Ask them to say if they think the people are having a good time or not.

Suggested answer

The photo shows a group of young people sitting around a table. Some of them are eating and drinking. In the foreground, there are two bowls of food. Everyone looks really happy. I think this might be lunchtime at college. They all look happy and as if they're enjoying themselves.

2 LISTENING ▶ 18 Tell students to read the information in the task. Play the track for students to listen to a podcast about the Erasmus project and answer the questions. See p147 for the audioscript for this exercise.

Answers

1 Turkey **2** Salamanca, Spain **3** English and Spanish

ⓘ CULTURAL INFORMATION

The Erasmus Project is a European Union (EU) student exchange programme established in 1987 to give students a foreign exchange experience at some of Europe's most prestigious universities and institutions. Students can study at an institution in another participating country for a period of three to 12 months. The time they spend in the foreign institution counts towards the length of their initial course of study in their home country.

3 18 Play the track again for students to listen and complete the notes.

Answers

a October **b** May **c** famous **d** lively **e** concerts **f** different countries **g** typical dish **h** physics **i** exams

4 SPEAKING **What about *you*?** Students take it in turns to ask and answer. Draw students' attention to the example dialogue and pre-teach *abroad* if necessary.

✚ EXTRA ACTIVITY

Students set aside a page at the back of their notebooks and note down as many useful expressions and structures for describing a photo as they can remember.

HOMEWORK

Assign students page 25 in their Workbook or the relevant sections of the Online Workbook.

Grammar in context pp38–39

Using the present perfect continuous

⋙ FAST TRACK

You could ask students to complete exercise 3 at home and compare their answers in class.

 Test before you teach: Flipped classroom
Set the Flipped classroom video and tasks for homework <u>before the lesson</u>. This will allow you to assess the needs of the students before the class. Students can then move on to the relevant grammar practice activities.

WARMER

In small teams, students make as many English words as they can from ERASMUS PROJECT in three minutes. The team with the most words wins.

Present perfect continuous

Point out to students that the present perfect continuous has basically the same meaning as the present perfect simple (*I've lived here for 20 years and she's been living here for 12 years.*). However, we use the present perfect continuous when we want to emphasise the process and duration of an action (with *for* or *since*). For that reason, if the action is very short, we can't use the continuous form.

In speaking and informal writing, we often use contractions (e.g. *I've, she's*). Remind students that when a verb has more than one auxiliary, the first auxiliary changes its form to agree with the subject of the verb. It is also the first auxiliary which is used to form questions and negative statements.

Some verbs are rarely or never used in the continuous form (state verbs) so we use the present perfect simple:
I've wanted to visit Australia for years.
I've known him for seven years.

1a Students look at the sentences from the dialogue and decide which are in the present perfect continuous and which are in the present perfect simple.

Answers
Present perfect continuous: 1, 4
Present perfect simple: 2, 3

1b Students match the two tenses to the explanations a–d.

Answers
1 b **2** c **3** a **4** d

1c Students complete the rule for the formation of the present perfect continuous.

Answer
been + verb + *-ing*

2 Students look at the photos and write about what the people have been doing.

Answers
1 She's been running.
2 They've been shopping.
3 He's been studying all night. / He's been working on the computer.
4 She's been decorating/painting her house.
5 They've been playing tennis.

3 Students look at the sentences and decide if they are correct or not and say why/why not. If the sentences aren't correct, students change them. Students could compare in pairs before you elicit answers from the class.

Answers
1 I've cut my finger. (The action is very short.)
2 Correct (The emphasis is on the duration of the activity.)
3 Correct (The emphasis is on an action finished very recently.)
4 She's read this book three times. (The emphasis is on how many times the action happens.)
5 My brother has been painting his bedroom, but he hasn't finished. (The emphasis is on an action that is incomplete.)
6 Correct (The emphasis is on the duration of the action.)
7 I've broken the window. (The emphasis is on the result of the action.)
8 Correct (The action is incomplete.)

4 Students choose the correct alternative.

Answers
1 been singing **2** done **3** had **4** been looking
5 been doing **6** made **7** been working
8 been playing

5 Students complete the dialogue with the present perfect simple or present perfect continuous.

Answers
a have you been living **b** 've been studying
c haven't finished **d** have you been studying
e 've been working **f** have you been living
g 've made **h** 've been living

+ EXTRA ACTIVITY

In pairs, ask students to read the dialogue and then extend it by two lines each.

6 SPEAKING In pairs, students take it in turns to ask and answer the questions, using the present perfect simple or present perfect continuous. Draw students' attention to the example dialogue. When they have finished, students decide which answers are the most imaginative. Elicit answers from students around the class.

+ EXTRA ACTIVITY

Students write simple questions using the present perfect simple and present perfect continuous with common verbs such as *live, study, play* (e.g. *How long have you been living in this town?*). In pairs, students take it in turns to ask and answer each other's questions.

Refer students to the Grammar reference on page 42 if necessary.

HOMEWORK

Assign students page 26 in their Workbook or the relevant sections of the Online Workbook.

Developing speaking p40

Describing photos

>>> FAST TRACK

Students could do exercise 1 at home, setting their own time limits, and compare their words in pairs in class.

WARMER

Ask students to work in pairs to see what words and phrases they can remember to describe a photo.

1 SPEAKING In pairs, students make a list of at least four words to describe each photo. Set a time limit of two minutes. Elicit words from around the class.

Suggested answers

Photo a: busy, crowded, noisy, dirty, inner city, town centre

Photo b: historic, quiet, clean, terraced houses, village

✚ EXTRA ACTIVITY

Students play *Just a minute*. Ask students to describe a photo for a minute to practise speaking under exam conditions. Their partner can time them with their watch. Remind them to use hesitation devices to 'buy' time to think (*mmm, let me see/well, let me think …*, etc.) and to paraphrase if they are not sure of the exact word (*it's similar to/it's a kind of*, etc.).

2 LISTENING ▶ 19 Ask students to read the questions, then play the track for students to listen to someone talking about one of the photos. Have students note down the answers as they are listening. Elicit answers from the class. See p148 for the audioscript for this exercise.

Answers

1 photo a

2 skyscrapers, busy, packed, dangerous, interesting, lively, noisy, dirty, crowded

3 He wouldn't like to live there because he thinks big cities are too noisy, dirty and crowded.

3 ▶ 19 Play the track again for students to decide which of the words or expressions in the Speaking bank they hear.

Answers

In the photo I can see …

On the right …

In the background …

In the foreground …

In the middle …

On the left …

In the top right corner of the photo …

4 Ask students to look at photo b and complete the sentences with words from the Speaking bank.

Answers

1 In the photo you can   **2** right   **3** background

4 bottom left   **5** middle

5 SPEAKING In pairs, students tell their partner which place they prefer and give reasons for their opinion. Remind them that they can use comparative and superlative structures to compare the places, e.g. *-er than …, more … than …, as … as …, not as … as …*

PRACTICE MAKES PERFECT

6 SPEAKING Students look at the task. In pairs, they take it in turns to describe the two new photos and say which place they would prefer to live in and why. Remind them to use the useful words and expressions in the Speaking bank. For students who are less confident, photocopy the model description below and read it aloud. Then instruct students to take turns to read aloud in pairs. Then ask them to read it again, changing the underlined information so that it is true for themselves.

Model description

The first photo shows a city next to a river or a canal. The river is in the foreground, and a row of old terraced houses is in the background. In the middle of the photo there are a few boats. It looks quite busy. The second photo, on the other hand, shows a very old house. The house is on the left of the photo and on the right of the photo there is a field. The house is detached or semi-detached and it's in the countryside. It looks very peaceful. Personally, I'd prefer to live <u>in the first house because I think there are lots more people and things to do. The second house looks peaceful, but it could be lonely</u>!

✚ EXTRA ACTIVITY

Write some expressions of opinion (or ask the students to do it!) on small pieces of card (*In my opinion, Personally, For me, I think, I don't think, I believe*). Brainstorm topics for debate and write them on the board (*mobile phones, relationships, climate change, advertising on TV*, etc.). In small groups, students deal out the cards from their pack of 'opinion cards'. Each group chooses a topic from the board. Every time a student gives an opinion they can 'spend' a card. The student's argument has to begin with what is written on the card. The first student to get rid of all of his/her cards wins the round.

HOMEWORK

Assign students page 27 in their Workbook or the relevant sections of the Online Workbook.

Developing writing p41

Writing an informal email describing a place

>>> FAST TRACK

You could set the writing task in exercise 5 as homework so that students who live in the same place can personalise their descriptions as much as possible.

ℹ BACKGROUND INFORMATION

Birmingham is a city in the West Midlands of England. Aside from London, it is the most populated city in the UK with around one million residents. The city came to prominence in the late 18th century during the Industrial Revolution when it made advances in science and industry.

The residents of the city are affectionately known as 'Brummies', a term that stems from the city's nickname 'Brum'. The accent is very distinctive and unlike many other parts of the Midlands.

In cultural terms, Birmingham is thriving, with the City of Birmingham Symphony Orchestra, the Birmingham Royal Ballet, the Birmingham Repertory Theatre, the largest municipal library in Europe and the Barber Institute of Fine Arts amongst other internationally renowned institutions.

Famous people associated with Birmingham include the author J. R. R. Tolkien who grew up there.

WARMER

In pairs, ask students to look at the photo of Birmingham and brainstorm as many words as they can think of to describe the city (e.g. *canal, water, busy, skyscraper*). Write their ideas on the board and then ask if students know anything about Birmingham.

1 In pairs, students decide whether the statements about Birmingham are true or false.

2 **READING** Students read an email written by somebody from Birmingham and check their answers to exercise 1.

Answers

1 T **2** T **3** T **4** T **5** T

>>> FAST FINISHERS

Ask students to find two more facts about Birmingham from the email.

Suggested answers

There is a big shopping centre called the Bullring. The canals are cleaner now than in the past.

3 Ask students whether they would like to visit Birmingham, having read Mia's email. Ask them to give their reasons.

4 Ask students to read the email in exercise 2 again and complete the expressions in the Writing bank.

Answers

a Hi
b name
c your last email
d to hear from you
e they've
f Thank you
g Oh
h !
i way
j back soon
k Love

TEACHER DEVELOPMENT: STUDENT TRAINING

Informal writing

Other features of informal writing are the high frequency of Anglo-Saxon words (e.g. phrasal verbs), common words and simple sentences. Focus on the difference in register and why it is useful to be able to write in both styles. Discuss situations where students would need to write a formal letter (e.g. a cover letter with a CV, a letter of complaint, exam essays, etc.) and when they would write an informal letter (to a friend, e-pal, etc.).

5 In pairs, have students make notes about their home town. Ask them to think about the questions given. Draw their attention to the diagram and tell students this is often a good way to prepare for a writing task.

PRACTICE MAKES PERFECT

6 Students read the task and note what information they must include in their informal email. They then include all the information and organise their notes from exercise 5 into paragraphs. Remind them to use the information in exercise 4 and words and expressions from the Writing bank. For students who are less confident, photocopy the model email below for extra support during the writing task. Refer students to the Writing bank on page 150.

Model text

Hey Natalie,

Thanks for your last email. It was great to hear your news. You told me about your home town so now I'm going to tell you a bit about my city. Most people think of the Olympics when they hear the name of my city, Barcelona, but there really is a lot more to discover.

Actually, Barcelona has changed a lot since the Olympic Games, in 1992. Many parts of Barcelona used to be dirty and depressing. Then, lots of new roads and buildings were built. Since then, thousands of people from different parts of the world have come to live in Barcelona and changed it into a more cosmopolitan city. Now there are many trendy bars and restaurants.

Next to the Olympic Village there have been a lot of changes – the Diagonal Mar developments. I don't like this part of the city much. It's too new and it seems to be empty; there are lots of open spaces and not many people. I prefer the city centre. There is some fantastic modernist architecture (particularly that of Antoni Gaudí), narrow streets, medieval buildings and fashionable shops. The night life is amazing.

Anyway, write back soon and tell me when you are going to come and visit!

Love,

Joe

✛ EXTRA ACTIVITY

In pairs, students could check each other's writing and comment on things they think their partner could improve on and expand on. If you have access to the examination criteria for marking writing, give students a copy and ask them to grade each other's work.

HOMEWORK

Assign students page 28 in their Workbook or the relevant sections of the Online Workbook.

Language checkpoint: Unit 3

>>> **FAST TRACK**

Students read the Grammar reference and Vocabulary sections on page 42 before completing the revision exercises on the following page.

Grammar revision p43

Present perfect simple

1 Students complete the text with the correct present perfect simple or past simple form of the verbs given and choose the correct alternative.

Answers

a 've lived   **b** for   **c** has changed   **d** has got
e 've built   **f** started   **g** haven't finished   **h** yet
i just   **j** wanted

Present perfect continuous

2 Students complete the sentences with the present perfect simple or present perfect continuous form of the verbs.

Answers

1 Have (you) switched   **2** 've been studying
3 've been fixing   **4** 's broken
5 has been studying   **6** 've been building
7 's made   **8** Have (you) been waiting
9 've been walking   **10** 've finished

Vocabulary revision p43

CITIES AND HOUSES

1 Students write the words to match the descriptions.

Answers

1 detached   **2** cottage   **3** town hall   **4** port
5 inner city   **6** suburbs   **7** terraced   **8** block of flats

ADJECTIVES DESCRIBING CITIES

2 Students write what adjectives describe the situations.

Answers

1 crowded   **2** dirty   **3** historic   **4** quiet   **5** lively
6 busy

EXTREME ADJECTIVES

3 Students write the normal equivalent of the extreme adjectives.

Answers

1 beautiful   **2** hot   **3** dirty   **4** bad   **5** big
6 busy/crowded

HOMEWORK

Assign students page 29 in their Workbook or the relevant sections of the Online Workbook.

4 Feed your mind

KEY LEARNING OUTCOMES

CEF

Students will be able to:

- talk about the future using different verbs and tenses including the future perfect and future continuous
- talk about food and meals and describe them
- form new words by adding prefixes
- understand written and spoken texts about food
- negotiate with somebody by asking for, giving and responding to different opinions
- write simple replies to informal invitations

UNIT OVERVIEW

Vocabulary
Food and meals
PRONUNCIATION Word stress
Describing food

Reading
The future of food?
CRITICAL THINKING Discussing the pros and cons of a new food product

Grammar in context
will, be going to, present continuous and present simple for future

Developing vocabulary
Prefixes

Life skills
Physical well-being: Preparing food

Listening
Food in the future

Grammar in context
Future continuous and future perfect

Developing speaking
Negotiating

Developing writing
Replying to informal invitations

Exam success
Speaking: Negotiating
Writing: Transactional tasks

DIGITAL OVERVIEW

Presentation Kit
- ▶ **Flipped classroom video unit 4:** Future continuous and future perfect
- ▶ **Life skills video unit 4:** Preparing food
- ▶ **Vocabulary tool:** Food and meals; Describing food
- ▶ **Interactive versions of Student's Book activities**
- ▶ **Integrated audio and answer key for all activities**
- ▶ **Workbook pages with answer key**

Teacher's Resource Centre

TRC
- ▶ **Flipped classroom video Unit 4:** Future continuous and future perfect
- ▶ **Life skills video Unit 4:** Preparing food
- ▶ **Grammar communication activity Unit 4:** The right response
- ▶ **Worksheets for this unit, including:**
  - Grammar Practice worksheet Unit 4
  - Flipped classroom video worksheet Unit 4: Future continuous and future perfect
  - Literature worksheet Units 3 and 4
  - Culture worksheet Unit 4
  - Life skills video worksheet Unit 4
  - Everyday English worksheet Unit 4

Student's App
Gateway 2nd Edition wordlist for the award-winning Sounds App (available for download)

✓ TESTING AND ASSESSMENT

Resources for exam preparation and measuring student progress

- ▶ Test Generator Units 1–4
- ▶ Printable test Unit 4
- ▶ Gateway to exams Units 3 and 4 (end of Unit 4)

Vocabulary p44

Talking about and describing food and meals and how food tastes

>>> FAST TRACK

You could ask students to do exercise 3a at home so that less confident students can take the necessary time to look up the vocabulary in the Macmillan Online Dictionary. Students can then compare their lists in class.

WARMER

In pairs, students discuss the meaning of the unit title *Feed your mind* and what they think the unit is going to be about. Elicit the pronunciation of the word *food* and practise the long sound /fuːd/.

Suggested answers

Feed your mind can be taken literally and metaphorically. Literally, it could be about foods that are good for the brain, but metaphorically it could describe ways to nourish and engage your mind. The unit is about different aspects of the theme of food.

v Food and meals

1 Students look at the photos and say how many food and drink items they can see using the words from the box.

Answers

chicken, cream, olive, pea, pie, rice, sweetcorn, tuna

2 In pairs, students put the words in the correct place in the table. Tell them to use their dictionaries if necessary. Explain that *semi-skimmed milk* is milk from which half the fat has been removed.

Answers

Fruit: peach, plum
Vegetables: carrot, lettuce, olive, pea, sweetcorn
Meat/Fish/Seafood: chicken, lamb, prawn, tuna, turkey
Dairy products: cream, semi-skimmed milk
Sweets/Bakery products: pancake, pie
Other: oil, rice

3a Students read the questions and check they understand the words in red. To check comprehension, ask students to give you an example of each word. Ask students which words they could use to talk about the photos in exercise 1.

Suggested answers

Photo a: dessert
Photo b: main course, dish
Photo c: starter, snack

3b PRONUNCIATION Ask students to mark the stress in each word, then say which one is the odd one out.

Answer

de**ssert** (the stress is on the second syllable)

3c ▶ 20 Play the track for students to listen, check and repeat. See p148 for the audioscript for this exercise.

3d SPEAKING Students work in pairs and ask and answer the questions in exercise 3a.

>>> FAST FINISHERS

Students could write more questions similar to the ones in exercise 3a to ask their partners. Alternatively, you could write these questions on the board for students to ask their partners: *How often do you cook? What did you eat for lunch today? What is your favourite food? What food don't you like?*

v Describing food

4 Students match the words with the definitions.

Answers

1 spicy **2** tasty **3** raw **4** healthy/unhealthy
5 frozen **6** fried **7** boiled **8** baked **9** roast
10 fresh **11** fast **12** stale

5 In pairs, students choose one or two types of food that they think can go with each of the words in exercise 4. Draw students' attention to the example.

Suggested answers

healthy – semi-skimmed milk
roast – chicken

>>> FAST FINISHERS

Students think of other adjectives used to describe food and match them with types of food (*sour – lemons, salty – pizza, creamy – ice cream*, etc.).

6 LISTENING ▶ 21 Play the track for students to listen to six short dialogues and choose a word from exercise 4 to describe the food. Ask different students around the class and elicit the information in the listening that helped students make their choices. With a less confident class, pre-teach these words: *pan*: a round metal container with a handle that is used for cooking; *lime*: a fruit with a hard green skin and sour juice; *pepper*: a green, yellow or red vegetable with white seeds in it; *ruin*: to spoil or destroy something. See p148 for the audioscript for this exercise.

Answers

1 fried **2** raw **3** spicy **4** fast/unhealthy **5** stale
6 roast

+ EXTRA ACTIVITY

Ask some follow-up questions: *When is the chicken ready to eat? How do they prepare the raw fish? Have you tried raw fish? Did you like it? Why is the dish spicy? Do you like hot (spicy) food? Where are they eating junk food? Why is it bad for you? Do you like junk food? How often do you eat junk food?*

7 SPEAKING In pairs, students describe a type of food or drink and see if their partner can guess it. Draw students' attention to the example.

TEACHER DEVELOPMENT: STUDENT TRAINING

Using adjectives

In oral examinations, students often need to be able to describe something, what it looks like, and its function or purpose. When they are describing food, they will need to use adjectives for taste, aroma, flavour, shape, colour, origin, texture. Remind them to be careful with adjective order. You could brainstorm useful associated verbs (*smell, taste, mix*, etc.).

✚ EXTRA ACTIVITY

Students make a mind map of all the vocabulary related to the theme of food. They can add to this over the following lessons.

Suggested categories:

Meals: *breakfast, lunch, dinner, snack, dish, main course, starter, dessert*

Adjectives to describe food: *fresh, fried, frozen, junk, spicy*

Types of food: *fruit, dairy products, vegetables, bakery products*

Cooking utensils: *pan*

HOMEWORK

Assign students page 30 in their Workbook or the relevant sections of the Online Workbook.

Reading p45

Making predictions about content and reading for detail and specific information

⟫⟫ FAST TRACK

You could ask students to do exercises 1 and 2 at home in preparation for completing exercise 3 together in class.

WARMER

Students draw the table from exercise 2 on page 44 of the Student's Book or write the column headings in their notebooks. Organise the class into small teams, and choose a letter of the alphabet (e.g. *C*). The teams write a word beginning with that letter for each category.

Fruit	Vegetables	Meat/ Fish/ Seafood	Dairy products	Sweets/ Bakery products	Total
cherry (20)	carrot (10)	chicken (10)	cream (20)	chocolate (10)	70

The team that finishes all the categories first shouts STOP! All the other students stop writing. The teams compare their words and allocate points according to the following criteria:

words repeated by two teams = 20 points
words repeated by three or more teams = 10 points
words that are not repeated by anyone = 50 points
Choose another letter for the next round. At the end of the game, all the subtotals are added and the team with the highest score is the winner.

1 First, ask students to look at the photos and title of the article. What do they think the article is going to be about?

2 READING Ask students to read the article and check their predictions to exercise 1.

3 Students read the article again and decide if the statements are true or false. Tell students to write the number(s) of the line(s) where they found the answer. Ask fast finishers to correct the false statements.

Answers

1 T (lines 4–5) **2** T (lines 16–20) **3** F (lines 30–31)
4 T (lines 33–35) **5** T (lines 40–43) **6** T (lines 63–65)
7 F (lines 70–72) **8** F (lines 76–77)

4 ⚙ CRITICAL THINKING Ask students to consider their own response to the critical thinking question and then share their answers with the class.

TEACHER DEVELOPMENT: STUDENT TRAINING

Finding the meaning of a word in a dictionary

Regular use of a monolingual dictionary helps expand students' vocabulary and aids student autonomy.

- Words are printed in large bold type at the upper top left-hand and right-hand corner of any page to help you quickly find a word in the dictionary.

- Many words have more than one meaning, and each different meaning is shown by a number. Some words have many different meanings so their entries can be long. In the Macmillan Online Dictionary, entries with five or more meanings have a 'menu' at the top to make it easier to find the specific meaning you are looking for.

- The International Phonetic Alphabet shows you how a word is pronounced. Stress marks tell you which part of a compound to stress when you are saying it.

- Examples in *italics* show you how a word is used in context.

- Abbreviations in italics indicate the part of speech, e.g. *adj.* (adjective). A list of abbreviations is usually included on one of the first pages of a dictionary.

Monolingual dictionaries specifically aimed at learners of English give clear definitions and contextualised examples. Bilingual dictionaries on the other hand tend to give translations without giving contextualised examples, but they do offer the possibility to compare the mother tongue and the target language.

5 Ask students to look back at the underlined words in the article and guess their meaning. Allow them to check in the dictionary.

Answers

wasting = throwing something useful away when you could use it for something else

nutrients = important food groups that make the body work well, found in fruit, vegetables and grain

powder = light, dry substance, you can dissolve it in water

benefits = advantages

developing = improving; becoming more advanced or better

fad = popular for a short period

✦✚ EXTRA ACTIVITY

Ask students to close their books and write the numbers: 90, 80, 20s and 35 on the board. Ask students to work in pairs to say why these numbers are relevant to the reading text.

Answers

Rob ate Soylent for 90% of his meals for one year.

80% of all water goes to farms.

Rob is in his twenties.

There are 35 essential nutrients in Soylent.

6 SPEAKING **What about *you?*** In pairs or small groups, students discuss the questions.

HOMEWORK

Assign students page 31 in their Workbook or the relevant sections of the Online Workbook.

Grammar in context pp46–47

Using will, be going to, and the present continuous and present simple to talk about the future

⟫⟫ FAST TRACK

You could ask students to do exercise 1b and compare their answers in pairs.

Test before you teach

Write the following sentences on the board and ask students whether they refer to the past, present or future. Then ask them to complete each sentence with a tense that they think is correct for the situation. If students are already familiar with these expressions of future time, move quickly through exercises 1a and 1b, eliciting answers from students as an open-class activity.

It's _____ (snow) soon. The clouds are very grey and low in the sky.

Perhaps I _____ China one day. (visit)

What time _____ tomorrow? (leave/you)

The train _____ at 8.00 this evening. (arrive)

Answers

going to snow, 'll visit, are you leaving, arrives

1a Students match the sentences and the rules (1–4).

Answers

1 b **2** a **3** c **4** d

1b Students read the sentences and complete rules 1–4 with *will*, *be going to* or the present simple.

Answers

1 will (sentence d)

2 will (sentence c)

3 the present simple (sentence a)

4 be going to (sentence b)

TEACHER DEVELOPMENT: PRONUNCIATION

Contracted form *'ll*

Remind students that we usually use the contracted form *'ll* in spoken English. Contractions are the reductions in word sounds made by dropping a letter or letters in a word.

'll is pronounced with the dark /l/ sound, i.e. it sounds like the *ull* in *full* rather than the /l/ in *light*. Ask students to note and drill the weak form of *will: 'll* in the following sentences:

I'll be there at 7 pm. It'll probably snow. Who'll get the phone?

What'll you do when he comes home? Where'll you go to eat?

There'll be doughnuts and cakes for breakfast.

James'll do it.

TEACHER DEVELOPMENT: LANGUAGE

Use of tenses

Present simple is used to talk about a future event that is part of a timetable or routine. This is because a timetable is true in the future, but it is also true in the present. These sentences usually contain future words, or the future is understood from the context. Only a few verbs are used in this way, e.g. *be, open, close, begin, start, end, finish, arrive, come, leave, return.*

The train leaves at 8 pm.

Present continuous is used to talk about future arrangements or plans that have been confirmed. Since these constructions can imply present as well as future meaning, a time adverbial is usually employed to help specify the meaning. English teachers often call the present continuous future form the 'diary form' because you can use it for anything written in your diary or agenda. Fixed arrangements can also use *going to*, but the present continuous is more common.

On 14th September I'm seeing my dentist.

be going to:

a When the speaker is making a prediction based on evidence.

b When the speaker already has an intention or plan. The *going to* future is generally found in informal spoken English. *Be going to* constructions often imply an intention and therefore an expectation that the intention will be carried out.

will:

a When the speaker is making a prediction.

b For decisions that we make at the moment of speaking. Another, less common alternative to *will* is *shall* (negative form *shan't*). While *will* can be combined with subjects of all three persons, the usage of *shall* is restricted to first-person pronouns.

✚ EXTRA ACTIVITY

Copy this table onto the board and ask students to complete it individually in their notebooks using the verb *arrive* with *will* and *going to* (the example below is completed).

	Affirmative	Negative	Question
will			
(all forms)	will arrive	won't arrive	Will you arrive?
going to			
I	am going to arrive	'm not going to arrive	Am I going to arrive?
you/we/they	are going to arrive	aren't going to arrive	Are you going to arrive?
he/she/it	is going to arrive	isn't going to arrive	Is he going to arrive?

2 Students complete the sentences with the correct form of the present simple or *will*.

Answers
1 comes, will order   **2** will call, finishes
3 will do, makes   **4** go, will … buy
5 come, will make   **6** gets, will clean
7 have, will eat   **8** won't take, is
9 come, will make   **10** boils, will add

TEACHER DEVELOPMENT: LANGUAGE

Present simple with time expressions

Remind students that we use a comma in the clause with the present simple when it comes first in the sentence:
When + present simple, will + infinitive
When the waiter comes, we'll order some food.

3 Students write predictions for what they think is going to happen in each situation, using the verbs supplied. Remind less confident students which tense they need to use for predictions based on evidence.

Suggested answers
1 She's going to cut herself.
2 He's going to drop the plates.
3 His food is going to burn.
4 She's going to catch a (lot of) fish.

TEACHER DEVELOPMENT: PRONUNCIATION

Unstressed vowels

Ask students to underline the stressed syllables in the sentences in exercise 3. Elicit the pronunciation of the unstressed words. Words that usually have weak stress are called 'function words': words that contribute more to the function of a sentence than to its meaning. Function words in English are articles, conjunctions, prepositions, auxiliary verbs and modal auxiliaries. Some examples are *a, the, but, for, are, is, and, was, do, can*.

Words that are unstressed are generally pronounced with vowels that are 'neutral' rather than clear, often with a *schwa* sound /ə/.

Choral drill the sentences to practise the rhythm and contracted or unstressed form of *be* in the *going to* sentences.

4 Students look at the poster and make as many present continuous sentences as they can. Draw students' attention to the example sentences.

Suggested answers

It's starting at 6 pm.
The first speaker is talking about her new film. They are showing the preview at 7 pm.
The second speaker is explaining his solution to the food crisis at 8 pm.
They're having a snack at 8.30 pm.
At 9 pm, they're holding the prize-giving ceremony.
On Friday 12th at 7 pm, a programme about the talk is being shown on Channel 8.

5 Students look at the pairs of sentences and questions and choose the correct alternative. If they think both are correct, they should mark both, but be prepared to explain any difference in meaning.

Answers
1b Correct
2a Correct
3a Correct
4a is correct because it's a prediction based on evidence.
4b is correct because it's a general prediction.
5a Correct
6a is correct because the present simple is used for timetables.
6b is correct because the present continuous is used for confirmed plans. There's no difference in meaning between 6a and 6b.

6a In pairs, students make notes on the topics with predictions for this year. Walk round the class, monitoring and helping students with any language difficulties.

6b SPEAKING Students compare their predictions in a group and find out if they are similar or different. Draw students' attention to the model dialogue. Elicit predictions from different students around the class.

Refer students to the Grammar reference on page 54 if necessary

Developing vocabulary p47

Understanding and using prefixes

Prefixes

1a Students look at the words and match them with the definitions.

| Answers

1 undercooked **2** recooked **3** precooked
4 overcooked

1b Draw students' attention to the red parts of the words in exercise 1a. Tell students these are called prefixes. Students say what the function of a prefix is.

| Answer

Prefixes change the meaning of the word.

2 Students match the prefixes and their meanings.

| Answers

1 e **2** f **3** d **4** h **5** c **6** g **7** a **8** b

3 Students complete the sentences by adding the correct prefix to the word in red.

| Answers

1 inter **2** re **3** mis **4** dis **5** over **6** under **7** co

4a Students complete the questions with words from exercises 1 and 3.

| Answers

1 misunderstood **2** disadvantages
3 precooked/recooked **4** international

4b SPEAKING In pairs, students take it in turns to ask and answer the questions in exercise 4a.

Gateway to life skills pp48–49

Preparing food

To think about why it's important to know how to cook; To learn about food safety; To learn how to prepare a simple, healthy dish

1 In pairs, students discuss the questions. Nominate different pairs to feedback to the class.

2 READING Ask students to read the article by a top chef and match the titles with the correct section.

| Answers

1 H **2** E **3** D **4** J **5** G **6** A **7** C **8** B **9** I
10 F

3 Ask students to read the statements and write which section of the article gives the information about each advantage. Ask students to underline the part of the text that gave them the information. With a less confident class, you could read the statements together to check they understand the vocabulary.

Answers

a 5 (… eating out is nearly always more expensive than eating at home.)

b 8 (… make your friends happy and show them your skills …)

c 4 (… give you a great sense of freedom.)

d 7 (You can have a great time just by being imaginative and creative in the kitchen.)

e 10 (Maybe you'll become a professional chef, …)

f 3 (… limit the amount of sugar and fat in each meal.)

g 1 (… with just a few basic, natural ingredients you can make delicious meals …)

h 9 (Cooking … can teach you about different countries …)

i 2 (… when you cook dishes yourself, you know exactly what they contain, …)

j 6 (Just increase the quantities and you'll have enough to freeze and eat another day.)

4 In pairs, students decide what they think are the three best reasons for learning to cook. They can use the ideas from the text or add reasons of their own. They also think of the least important reason. Nominate pairs to give their answers, giving their reasons.

✛ EXTRA ACTIVITY

Before playing the video properly, play it with the volume turned down. Ask students what problem they think each person in the video has. This is a good opportunity to help students with any vocabulary they may need.

5 **LISTENING** ▶ 22 Tell students they are going to watch or listen to a video of teenagers cooking. Students write what each chef is making. See p148 for the audioscript/videoscript for this exercise.

Answers

1 Jasmine: special fried fish   **2** Ben: Italian salad

6 ▶ 22 Tell students they are going to watch or listen again and find something that each chef is doing incorrectly in the kitchen. Before they watch or listen, have students read through the Problem column and guess what the problem could be. Play the video or track again for students to write notes.

Suggested answers

olive oil – oil is slippery when it's on the floor, you could slip with a knife or hot food in your hands (Ben)

apron and hair – hygiene, hair must be tied back or covered and wear an apron because it keeps you and food clean (Jasmine)

jewellery – you can't wash your hands and make them 100% clean if you are wearing jewellery (Jasmine)

knife and chopping board – wash knife and chopping board after cutting meat, don't cut salad in same place as meat, get food poisoning (Ben)

7 In pairs, students say what they think of the advice in the video and any other food safety advice they can think of.

✛ EXTRA ACTIVITY

In pairs, students make a poster highlighting important food safety and hygiene rules.

LIFE TASK

Tell students they are going to find or invent a recipe for a tasty and healthy salad.

■ *Step 1*
   In small groups, students either invent or find a recipe for their salad.

■ *Step 2*
   Read through the criteria students need to include in their presentation, then give them time to prepare.

■ *Step 3*
   Groups give their presentations, then the class vote on the healthiest and tastiest.

Listening p50

Listening for gist and overall understanding

WARMER

Elicit all the prefixes students can remember and write them on the board. Students play *Word tennis* in pairs. The first student 'serves' a prefix and the other student must provide a correct word for the prefix to win a point. Then they serve a prefix back to their partner. The student with the most points wins the game. Prefixes: *pre-, over-, mis-, inter-, dis-, co-, re-, under-, im-*

1 SPEAKING In pairs, students look at the photos showing futuristic ideas about food and take it in turns to describe what they see.

2 LISTENING ▶ 23 Play the track for students to listen to four people talking about their predictions for what we will be eating in the year 2050. Tell students to match each speaker to a photo in exercise 1. See pp148–149 for the audioscript for this exercise.

Answers

1 d **2** c **3** a **4** b

3 ▶ 23 Play the track again for students to listen and match the speakers and the opinions.

Answers   1e ?

a 2 **b** 1 **c** 4 **d** 2 **e** 3 **f** 4 **g** 3 **h** 2

4 SPEAKING What about *you*? Students discuss which of the predictions about the future they agree with in an open-class discussion. With a less confident class, students could write notes before participating in this speaking activity.

Grammar in context pp50–51

Using the future continuous and the future perfect to talk about the future

⟩⟩⟩ FAST TRACK

You could ask students to complete exercise 3 at home.

Flipped classroom

Set the Flipped classroom video and tasks for homework <u>before the lesson</u>. This will allow you to assess the needs of the students before the class. Students can then move on to the relevant grammar practice activities.

1a Students look at the sentences and decide which are in the future continuous and and which in the future perfect.

Answers
1 future perfect **2** future continuous
3 future continuous **4** future perfect

1b Students choose the correct alternative.

Answers
1 future continuous **2** future perfect **3** by

1c Students complete the rules.

Answers
1 continuous, -*ing* **2** perfect, past participle

2a Students complete the predictions.

Answers
1 will be having	**5** will be speaking
2 won't be driving	**6** will be doing
3 won't be eating	**7** won't be growing
4 will be working	

2b In pairs, students discuss which predictions in exercise 2a they agree with. You could build this into a class discussion.

3 Students complete the predictions about the year 2050 using the future perfect. Tell students to make affirmative or negative predictions depending on their opinion.

Suggested answers
1 won't have found	**5** will have landed
2 will have stopped	**6** won't have invented
3 will have become	**7** will have got
4 will have disappeared	**8** will have changed

✚ EXTRA ACTIVITY

In pairs, students compare their predictions and discuss any differences of opinion. Elicit opinions from students around the class.

4a Students look at the diary of a busy chef for next Monday.

4b Students complete the sentences with either the future continuous or future perfect using the verbs.

Answers
1 will have got up	**5** will be going
2 will be running	**6** will have filmed
3 will be having	**7** will have eaten
4 will have had	**8** will be talking

4c Ask students to write one more sentence in the future continuous and one in the future perfect about Oliver's day.

5 SPEAKING In pairs, students take it in turns to ask and answer questions about what they will be doing or will have done at different times tomorrow. You could do this activity in open pairs first before students proceed in closed pairs. Draw students' attention to the example dialogue.

6a SPEAKING Students think about their life when they are 30 years old. Individually, students make notes about what they will/won't be doing and what they will/won't have done using the ideas and events from the box.

6b In pairs, students take it in turns to ask and answer their questions from exercise 6a about how they imagine their life when they are 30. Draw students' attention to the example dialogue. With a less confident class, go through the ideas and events in the box and drill the question form for each one. (*Do you think you …'ll be studying/ will have become famous/will have bought a house/will have got married/will be living at home/will be living in a different country/will have made a lot of money/will be studying/will be working.*) You could do this activity as an open-class activity before students do the exercise in closed pairs.

✚ EXTRA ACTIVITY

Play *Past participle bingo.* Write the list of verbs below on the board. Tell students to draw a 3 x 3 grid in their notebooks, choose nine of the verbs and write the past participle form in the squares in the grid. Read out the verbs in a random order. If students have the past participle form on their bingo 'card' they cross it out. The first student to complete his/her grid shouts 'Bingo!'
Verbs: *do, eat, have, live, drive, grow, speak, work, find, use, become, disappear, land, invent, get, change, get up, run, have, talk, meet*

Refer students to the Grammar reference on page 54 if necessary.

Developing speaking p52

Negotiating and responding to and giving opinions

⟩⟩⟩ FAST TRACK

Ask students to prepare for exercise 1 at home and make a list of places they like to eat at to discuss in class.

WARMER

With books closed, ask students to write down in English as many types of places where they can eat. Elicit the phrase 'eating out' for when you eat somewhere that isn't your own house.

Suggested answers

canteen, restaurant, café, snack bar, your own house, outdoor picnic, fast food restaurant

1 SPEAKING Students work with a partner and look at the photos. Students discuss which places they eat at and what they think of them.

2 LISTENING ▶ 24 Play the track for students to listen to two students doing a collaborative task in a speaking exam. Tell students to answer the two questions. See p149 for the audioscript for this exercise.

Answers

Which of these five places do you think is the best place for your end-of-term meal?

the outdoor picnic area

3a ▶ 24 Play the track again for students to make notes about what the students say for each place in exercise 1. Draw their attention to the example and remind them not to write full sentences.

Answers

2 School canteen: we eat there every day, we should choose somewhere we don't usually go

3 Outdoor picnic area: good idea – could go to park or somewhere special, picnics aren't expensive, easy for a larger group

4 Exclusive restaurant: food and service are good, but they're expensive, most people won't want to spend a lot of money on the meal

5 Classmate's house: cheap, comfortable, can have music and move about, but a house is small and it isn't very special

3b SPEAKING In pairs, students compare their notes and say whether they agree or disagree with the final decision.

4 Ask students to match the headings with the expressions from the Speaking bank.

Answers

1 C **2** B **3** A

✓ EXAM SUCCESS Students read the information and discuss if they should speak more than their partner in this type of activity, then turn to page 144 to compare their answers.

TEACHER DEVELOPMENT: STUDENT TRAINING

Negotiating in an oral activity

In this type of activity, students have to show an ability to negotiate and collaborate with their partner. Remind students to ask their partner for his/her opinion rather than simply stating their own. Tell them to focus on asking some *'What do you think …?'* type questions rather than simply making *'I think …'* type statements. Encourage students to listen carefully when their partner is speaking and show interest in his/her comments by responding to what he/she says. This is called active listening. *'That's an interesting point.' 'I see what you mean, but …' 'But don't you think …'*

Students should also help their partner speak if they feel he/she is not speaking enough, rather than dominating the conversation.

PRACTICE MAKES PERFECT

5 SPEAKING In pairs, students look at the instructions and diagram on page 148. Remind students to justify their opinions and come to a joint decision using phrases from the Speaking bank. Draw their attention to the examples. Photocopy the model dialogue below for less confident students and allow them to read it first.

✂ -

Model dialogue

A: Hi, Tom. I've started thinking about planning the end-of-year school event. What do you think about a sports day? That could be fun.

B: I agree, but what about people who don't like sport?

A: Yes, you're right.

B: Personally, I think we should do something that everyone can take part in. What about a meal in a restaurant?

A: That could be expensive. In my opinion, we need to do something that everyone can afford.

B: OK. How about a concert at school? We could make the tickets for entrance really cheap and ask local bands to volunteer.

A: That's a great idea!

- -

Developing writing p53

Writing an email to accept an informal invitation

>>> FAST TRACK

You could ask students to do exercise 1a at home and check their answers in exercise 1b at the start of the lesson.

WARMER

In pairs, students tell their partner about the last time they were invited to an event or a special occasion. You could start the class by describing an event to which you were invited to and how you were invited to provide a model for this activity.

1a **READING** Students read the email invitation and underline the important information that Matt wants from Sam.

Answers

Could you come a bit earlier? Are you doing anything then? (on Sunday) Write back to tell me if you can come or not.

1b Students compare their answers in exercise 1a with a partner.

2 In pairs, ask students to imagine they are Sam and make a list of what information they should include in their reply. Elicit answers from the class and write a complete list up on the board.

Suggested answers

Say 'Hi!'
Say how he is.
Can he bring his MP3 player?
Can he come earlier – what time?
Can he help? Yes or no?
Is he free on Sunday?
Say something nice about the party.

3 Ask students to read the reply and check all the information from exercise 2 has been included.

4 Ask students whether they think the emails are formal or informal. Ask them to give reasons for their opinion.

Suggested answers

Informal – The emails use contracted forms and informal expressions.

5 Students complete the examples in the Writing bank by looking again at the invitation and reply.

Suggested answers

Invitations: Nina can make it, to see you, back
Replies: Thanks, sorry, Would, looking forward

✓ EXAM SUCCESS Students discuss what information and what style is important in an email reply then turn to page 145 to compare their ideas.

TEACHER DEVELOPMENT: STUDENT TRAINING

Informal invitations

In this lesson, students are made aware of differences in register and appropriacy of language, while building up a stock of suitable phrases they can use in more informal texts. Point out that students should always read the instructions carefully to find out whether a formal or informal style is expected.

You could use this opportunity to brainstorm key features of formal and informal texts. Usually students are more comfortable with writing a friendly, informal letter or email, but remind them that they should not become too informal or colloquial in a piece of writing for an exam.

PRACTICE MAKES PERFECT

6a Students look at the task and underline the important information that the writer wants.

6b Ask students to reply to the invitation including all the necessary information. Remind them to use the correct style and expressions from the Writing bank. For students who are less confident, photocopy the model reply below for extra support during the writing task.

Model text

Hello Ella,

I'm fine, thanks. My exams finished yesterday, too.

Thanks for the invitation. I'll definitely be there on Saturday. It'd be nice to say 'bye' to your brother.

I can bring some cakes. What type do you want me to bring?

I will probably arrive at about 6.30 pm because I have a tennis game until 6 pm. I can definitely help to tidy up after the party.

I'm looking forward to it!

All the best,

Joe

✚ EXTRA ACTIVITY

When students have finished writing, ask them to use a writing checklist and grade their partner's invitations, using the checklist as a guideline.

1 Did they answer the task?
2 Did they make good use of structures and expressions?
3 How accurate were they?
4 Did they use appropriate style?

HOMEWORK

Assign students page 36 in their Workbook or the relevant sections of the Online Workbook.

Language checkpoint: Unit 4

>>> FAST TRACK

Students read the Grammar reference and Vocabulary sections on page 54 before completing the revision exercises on the following page.

Grammar revision p55 ─────────

Present simple for future

1 Students complete the dialogue with the present simple or *will*.

Answers

a does (your train) leave **b** arrive **c** will look
d Will (you) remember **e** get **f** 'll call

will, be going to, present continuous for future

2 Students choose the correct alternative.

Answers

1 'm having, 'll call **2** going to rain **3** will get **4** will be
5 will win **6** 'm going

Future continuous and future perfect

3 Students look at the situations and complete the sentences using the future continuous or future perfect.

Answers

1 I will have done my homework
2 she will be studying English
3 I will be sleeping
4 I will have left the dentist
5 we will have given him the money
6 I will be running
7 he will have read the book

Vocabulary revision p55 ─────────

FOOD

1 Students put the letters in order to make names of food. Then they write what type of food each one is.

Answers

1 lettuce (vegetable) **2** turkey (meat)
3 carrot (vegetable) **4** plum (fruit)
5 cream (dairy product) **6** prawn (fish/seafood)
7 pancake (sweet)

DESCRIBING FOOD

2 Students complete the sentences with the words. Remind them there are two words they do not need.

Answers

1 fresh **2** stale **3** fried **4** boiled **5** spicy **6** raw

PREFIXES

3 Students underline the prefix and write the meaning of the prefix.

Answers

1 dis, 'the opposite' **2** re, 'again' **3** co, 'with'
4 under, 'not enough' **5** inter, 'between'
6 mis, 'wrong' **7** over, 'too much'

HOMEWORK

Assign students page 37 in their Workbook or the relevant sections of the Online Workbook.

Reading p56

1 In pairs, students make predictions for the text they are going to read about the coldest city on Earth.

2 READING Students read the text and check their predictions. Remind them not to pay any attention to the gaps at this stage.

3 Students read the text again in more detail and put sentences a–g in the gaps.

Answers
1 f **2** d **3** c **4** e **5** b **6** a **7** g

Speaking p56

4 In pairs, ask students to make a list of six different places or things to visit near where they live.

5 SPEAKING Ask students to read the task and ask for their partner's opinions. Refer students to the example dialogue on the page. For students who are less confident, photocopy the model dialogue below and either read it aloud yourself or allow students to practise it in pairs.

Model dialogue

A: What do you think about taking Tom to the cinema?

B: Good idea, but let's see what type of films he likes. I think bowling would be good, too.

A: I agree. Bowling is always fun. Let's check when everyone can go.

B: OK. I'll email everyone tonight. How about going for a walk near the river, too? It's really beautiful there.

A: Yes, you're right. Why don't we go there in the afternoon?

B: Personally, I think it's nicer in the morning when it's less busy.

A: OK. Then in the afternoon we could take him ice-skating.

B: Great idea. After that we could go to the natural history museum.

A: Hmm. In my opinion, that museum is a bit boring.

B: Well, why don't we wait to see what Tom wants to do on Saturday?

A: OK.

Use of English p57

6 Students read the text about genetically-modified foods and discuss what they are and the good and bad aspects of them. Tell them to ignore the gaps at this stage.

7 Students read the text again and decide which answer best fits each gap.

Answers
1 C **2** A **3** B **4** C **5** A **6** B **7** C **8** A

Writing p57

8 Students write a reply to Matt's invitation following the task instructions. Remind them to write in an informal style, using contractions and informal expressions. For students who are less confident, photocopy the model reply below for extra support during the writing task.

Model text

Hey Matt,

Thanks for the invitation to the party. I'd love to come. Unfortunately, I will be there at 9 pm because I've got the end-of-term football match that afternoon. I'm sorry that I won't be able to help you get the party ready. But don't worry. I promise I'll stay late and help you tidy up after the party. Oh, a quick question! Can I bring my friend, Jason? He'll be staying with us that weekend. I'll bring some pizzas and a big salad to eat, too!

Hope it's OK.

Thanks,

Alicia

HOMEWORK

Assign students pages 38–39 in their Workbook or the relevant sections of the Online Workbook.

1 Ask students to read the 'can do' statements and mark from 1–4 how well they can do these things in English.

2 Ask students to look at their marks and decide what they think they need to do to improve. Elicit other suggestions.

5 Lifelong learning

KEY LEARNING OUTCOMES

CEF

Students will be able to:

- talk about obligation, prohibition, advice and permission using modal verbs
- talk about real, possible and imaginary situations and their consequences using zero, first and second conditionals

- talk about different aspects of life at school and university
- understand written and spoken texts about the web
- give simple oral presentations
- write a formal letter applying for a scholarship

UNIT OVERVIEW

Vocabulary
School and university subjects
PRONUNCIATION Word stress
Words connected with studying

Reading
Green school in the city
CRITICAL THINKING Discussing the text's message about bringing the outside world into the classroom

Grammar in context
Modal verbs of obligation, prohibition, advice and permission

Developing vocabulary
Noun suffixes -er, -or, -ist, -ian, -ee
PRONUNCIATION Stress on noun suffixes

Life skills
ICT: Get the best from the Web

Listening
Extracurricular activities

Grammar in context
Zero, first and second conditionals

Developing speaking
A presentation

Developing writing
A formal letter of application

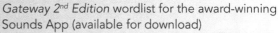
Exam success
Speaking: Giving a presentation
Writing: Thinking about the reader

DIGITAL OVERVIEW

Presentation Kit
- ▶ **Flipped classroom video unit 5:** Zero, first and second conditionals
- ▶ **Life skills video unit 5:** Evaluating web sources
- ▶ ⓥ **Vocabulary tool:** School and university subjects
- ▶ **Interactive versions of Student's Book activities**
- ▶ **Integrated audio and answer key for all activities**
- ▶ **Workbook pages with answer key**

Teacher's Resource Centre
- ▶ **Flipped classroom video Unit 5:** Zero, first and second conditionals
- ▶ **Life skills video Unit 5:** Evaluating web sources
- ▶ **Grammar communication activity Unit 5:** Do's and don'ts crossword
- ▶ **Worksheets for this unit, including:**
  - – Grammar Practice worksheet Unit 5
  - – Flipped classroom video worksheet Unit 5: Zero, first and second conditionals
  - – Culture worksheet Unit 5
  - – Life skills video worksheet Unit 5
  - – Everyday English worksheet Unit 5

Student's App
Gateway 2nd Edition wordlist for the award-winning Sounds App (available for download)

✔ TESTING AND ASSESSMENT

Resources for exam preparation and measuring student progress

- ▶ Test Generator Units 1–5
- ▶ Printable test Unit 5
- ▶ Gateway to exams Units 5 and 6 (end of Unit 6)

Vocabulary p58

Talking about school, university and studying

>>> **FAST TRACK**

You could ask students to do exercise 1 at home so that less confident students can take the necessary time to look up the vocabulary in the Macmillan Online Dictionary.

WARMER

In pairs, students discuss the meaning of the unit title *Lifelong learning*. You could take this opportunity to discuss with students how they will continue their English studies when they have finished school or university. They need to keep working at their English in order to maintain and improve their level.

Answer

Lifelong learning means the ongoing learning process that goes on throughout one's lifetime.

School and university subjects

1 In pairs, complete the table with the subjects. Check answers as a class.

Answers

Nursery: music

Primary: maths, PE (physical education)

Secondary: chemistry, drama, geography, history, literature, physics

University: business studies, computer science, engineering, law, media studies, medicine, psychology

2a **PRONUNCIATION** Ask students to mark the stress on each word in exercise 1 with more than one syllable. For less confident students, you could drill the words as a class first.

Answers

architecture, biology, business studies, chemistry, computer science, drama, engineering, English, geography, history, literature, media studies, medicine, music, physical education, physics, psychology

2b ▶ 25 Play the track for students to listen, check and repeat. See p119 for the audioscript for this exercise.

>>> **FAST FINISHERS**

Students add other subjects in the appropriate column in the table (e.g. their own language as a school subject, another language as a school subject, any other subjects that students could study at school or at university, etc.).

3 **LISTENING** ▶ 26 Play the track for students to listen to four teachers giving instructions and asking questions. Elicit what subject each one is teaching and elicit the information in the listening that helped students make their choices. With a less confident class, pre-teach these words: *transmit* – to pass on information, attitudes or beliefs to other people; *experiment* – a scientific test

to find out what happens to something or someone in particular conditions; *gills* – organs behind the head of a fish that allow it to breathe. See p149 for the audioscript for this exercise.

Answers

1 drama **2** chemistry **3** biology **4** maths

4 **SPEAKING** In pairs, students find out their partner's opinion of different subjects, if they like studying them or would like to study them one day. With a less confident class, do this activity first as open pairs to model the dialogue and then as closed pairs.

Words connected with studying

5 Students complete the sentences with the words.

Answers

1 essay **2** mark/grade **3** resit **4** timetable
5 scholarship **6** fail **7** terms **8** coursework
9 assignment **10** assessment

➕ EXTRA ACTIVITY

In pairs, students discuss whether they think exams are better than coursework for monitoring and assessing understanding of a subject. Encourage students to think of pros and cons for each.

6a **SPEAKING** In pairs, students ask and answer the questions. Tell them to make a note of their partner's answers.

6b Students report back to the class with information about their partner. Elicit some answers from different students around the class to round off the activity.

>>> **FAST FINISHERS**

Students could write more questions similar to the ones in exercise 6a to ask their partners.

HOMEWORK

Assign students page 40 in their Workbook or the relevant sections of the Online Workbook.

Reading p59

Predicting content, reading for general and specific information

>>> **FAST TRACK**

You could ask students to do exercise 3 at home, and then check answers together in class.

WARMER

Ask students to think of the positive and negative ways that their school influences and affects their local community. Elicit some ideas.

1 In pairs, ask students to look at the photo and the title of the text and predict what it's about.

2 READING Ask students to read the text and check their predictions.

Answers

How growing plants in the classroom has changed students' lives.

3 Students read the text and answer the questions. You could set a time limit to give students practice for exams, when time will be limited.

Answers

1 They were surprised and excited.

2 They wanted to do something to improve the area where they lived.

3 They created an edible indoor wall.

4 Attendance improved. It went up from around 40% to 93% because students felt responsible for the plants.

5 As they started to grow their own vegetables, they became more interested in following a healthy diet instead of eating fast food.

6 He believes young people ought to start learning about heathy diets as early as possible so that they don't pick up bad habits which are difficult to change.

7 They have learnt about responsibility. They have also learnt that they need to eat well to stay healthy and that you don't have to be a farmer in the country to grow plants.

TEACHER DEVELOPMENT: STUDENT TRAINING

Reading for general and specific information

Effective reading means being able to change reading strategies to suit the reading task. Skimming is a reading technique that helps you read information quickly to get the gist or general idea of a text. Sometimes skimming is confused with scanning. Both involve speed and learning to read only important words, but when students scan, the objective is different – to look for specific information. On the other hand, while skimming, you usually read quickly all the way through to the end to understand all the main ideas of the text. One key technique in skim reading is to read the first sentence for each paragraph where the main idea of the paragraph is often stated.

By setting a time limit you encourage students to read the text faster. One of the key skills in speed reading is to look at phrases and groups of words instead of individual words. Many students need training in speed reading.

Reading for comprehension is to gain a general to specific understanding of a text, and this is one of the most commonly taught reading skills. After students get an idea of what the text is about, they are usually asked to read it more carefully and produce detailed answers to comprehension questions.

4 CRITICAL THINKING Ask students to consider their own answer to the question and then discuss in open class.

5 Ask students to look back at the underlined words in the text and guess their meaning. Allow students to check their answers in the dictionary.

Answers

bulbs = small round plant seeds that grow into flowers

neighbourhood = the area where you live

spots = places or areas

edible = can be eaten

pick up = learn

>>> FAST FINISHERS

Students can find two or three more words in the text and check definitions for them which they can teach the rest of the class at the end of the task.

6 SPEAKING **What about** *you*? Ask students to consider their own answer to the questions, then ask and answer in pairs.

✚ EXTRA ACTIVITY

Students think of a community project that their school or class could get involved in. Ask students to research the idea, say why it's a necessary project and then come up with a three-step plan for what the school could do to help.

HOMEWORK

Assign students page 41 in their Workbook or the relevant sections of the Online Workbook.

Grammar in context pp60–61

Using modal verbs to talk about obligation and prohibition and to give advice and permission

>>> FAST TRACK

Ask students to do exercise 1a before the lesson, and compare their answers in class.

Test before you teach

Write these sentence stems on the board:
You should …, You shouldn't …, You must …,
You mustn't …, You have to …, You don't have to …,
You can …, You can't …

In pairs, students complete the sentences to write the rules for a game they like playing (football, basketball, etc.). Walk round the class, monitoring students to see if they are familiar with the form and use of these modal verbs. If so, you could choose to move quickly through exercises 1a and 1b, eliciting answers from students in open class.

1a Students read the sentences and complete the rules with the words in blue.

Answers

1 must, have to **2** don't have to **3** mustn't, can't

4 should, ought to, had better **5** can

1b Students say if the sentences are true or false.

Answers

1 T **2** T **3** F **4** T

Modal verbs

Obligation

We use *have/has to* for obligation. Remind students that we can also say *I have got to …* with the same meaning.

Have to/Must mean the same when we are talking about rules and obligations, i.e. external obligation. But *must* generally refers to internal obligation (i.e. the speaker feels something is necessary).

Must is not very common in question forms. Remind students that *must* is followed by the infinitive without *to*. Remind students of the silent 't' in *mustn't*.

No obligation

Students often confuse *don't/doesn't have to* with *mustn't* which is a prohibition. *Don't have to* means 'it is not necessary to do something, but you can do it if you wish'.

Advice

Should/Shouldn't is used when we want to give a strong opinion, telling someone the best thing to do. We can ask for someone's opinion with *Do you think I should …?* or using the modal verb *Should I …?* Remind students of the silent letter 'l' in *should* and *shouldn't*.

Remind students that *should/shouldn't* and *had better* are followed by the infinitive without *to*.

Ought to is a semi-modal verb. This is because unlike modal verbs the main verb is followed by 'to', but like modal verbs the form of the main verb does not change with the person. *Ought to* is slightly more formal and less commonly used than *should*.

Had better is a two-word modal verb which refers to the present or the future (but can't be used to talk about the past). We can contract 'had' (e.g. *you'd better*). *Had better* has the same meaning as *should* and *ought to*, but it also implies more strongly that there will be a problem if you don't follow this advice.

Permission

The modal verb *can* is used to convey the idea of permission (*can* also conveys the ideas of possibility and ability). We can also use *could*, *may* and *might* for permission.

Contractions

Contractions are the reductions in word sounds by the dropping of a letter or letters in the word. *Would* and *had* are both contracted to *'d*, so the listener must rely on the context of the sentence to determine if the speaker means *would* or *had*. Write the following sentences on the board and ask students to decide which word is meant in each sentence. Drill the pronunciation.

I'd say it was more expensive than the other one.
(= would)

You'd better go now. (= had)

I'd already left when she arrived. (= had)

2a Students complete the sentences using the correct form of the word(s) given and any other words.

Answers

1 have to be **2** have to go **3** can't vote
4 don't have to be **5** must be **6** can't change
7 have to be

2b Ask students if they know the legal ages for the things in exercise 2a in their own country. Encourage them to use the target grammar when they answer.

✚ EXTRA ACTIVITY

In pairs or small groups, students research legal ages and rules in another country and present them to the rest of the class using modals of obligation.

3 Students complete the sentences for the situations using *should, shouldn't, ought to, had better* and the expressions from the box. Check answers as a class.

Answers

1 shouldn't study all night
2 had better look for a job there
3 ought to use a dictionary
4 should walk to school
5 had better/should get ready to go
6 shouldn't go out without an umbrella
7 ought to rest and have a coffee

4 Ask students to write rules for their school using the modal verbs and the phrases in the box. Nominate students to read out one of their rules. You could also ask students if they think each rule is fair or unfair.

5 Ask students to read the text and choose the correct alternative.

Answers

a have to **b** should **c** shouldn't **d** have to
e don't have to **f** ought **g** had

6a SPEAKING In pairs, students read the task and prepare advice for a friend. Encourage students to speak first, and then make notes after they have discussed ideas. Remind them to list some things that are essential to do and not to do, and to use all the modal verbs listed. Draw students' attention to the examples in exercise 6b.

6b SPEAKING Pairs compare their advice with another pair.

✚ EXTRA ACTIVITY

In pairs, students tell each other what they think they want to do as a job one day. Students write a list of advice for each other using *must, mustn't, have to, should, shouldn't, had better, ought to*. They then tell their partner and see if he/she agrees with their advice.

Refer students to the Grammar reference on page 68 if necessary.

Refer students to the Grammar reference on page 68 if necessary.

HOMEWORK

Assign students page 42 in their Workbook or the relevant sections of the Online Workbook.

Developing vocabulary p61

Talking about jobs and employment using noun suffixes (-er, -or, -ist, -ian, -ee)

>>> FAST TRACK

Students could do exercise 2 as homework, using a dictionary if necessary. Ask them to compare their words in class before doing the listening exercise in 3a.

Noun suffixes

1 Students look at the words with suffixes which make nouns. They decide if they are nouns for people or things.

Answer

people

2 Students match the words in exercises 1 and 2 with the definitions.

Answers

1 professor   **2** instructor   **3** employer
4 technician   **5** journalist   **6** trainee

3a PRONUNCIATION ▶ 27 Play the track for students to listen to the words, mark the stress and decide which is the only noun suffix we stress. See p150 for the audioscript for this exercise.

Answers

director, employee, farmer, instructor, scientist, technician, electrician, employer, journalist, librarian, photographer, physicist, professor, trainee
-ee (employee, trainee) is the only noun suffix we stress.

3b Students practise saying the words in exercises 1 and 2 with the correct stress.

4 Students match one word from list A to one from list B.

Answers

wildlife photographer, company director, university professor, driving instructor, computer technician

5 SPEAKING In pairs, students take it in turns to say which of the jobs in exercise 4 they would like to do or not giving reasons. Draw their attention to the example sentences.

✛ EXTRA ACTIVITY

Students write definitions similar to those in exercise 2 with the other words from exercise 4 (e.g. *wildlife photographer: someone who takes photos of birds and animals in the natural environment*).

HOMEWORK

Assign students page 43 in their Workbook or the relevant sections of the Online Workbook.

Gateway to life skills pp62–63

Get the best from the Web

To evaluate and use web sources effectively for information and schoolwork

>>> FAST TRACK

You could set the Internet research part of exercise 3 as homework. Students compare their findings in pairs at the next lesson.

ⓘ BACKGROUND INFORMATION

Internet research for essays, homework, projects and exams is a vital skill for all students at each stage of their academic career. The Internet contains a wealth, and seemingly endless, amount of information on almost every subject imaginable. Though this provides students with accessible material, it can be overwhelming. Students, therefore, need to learn how to be selective when using the Internet for research and also how to choose the most reliable sources and disregard those that aren't. An over-reliance on the Internet can also have serious consequences, and students should be encouraged to think about the implications of plagiarism and using other people's work.

WARMER

Play a quick game of *Snowman* to elicit the word *source*. Discuss the meaning of the word with students in relation to studying, then ask them to work in pairs to think of useful sources for writing a school essay (e.g. the Internet, encyclopaedia, journals, newspapers, interviews, etc.).

Tell students the lesson is going to focus on the use of the Internet as a source and allow them time to read though the Life skills objectives and the Key concepts before starting the lesson.

1 In pairs, students discuss the questions. Nominate different pairs to share their answers with the class.

2 READING Students read the first part of the website article and answer the questions.

Answers

1 It means thoughtful, asking questions, and not just believing everything we read or hear immediately.
2 Because anybody can put anything on the Internet, just because it is there it doesn't mean it is true.
3 It can show you the country the website originated from, and whether it is a government agency, a charity or non-profit organisation, an academic institution, or a commercial organisation or a company.

3 In pairs, students look for three websites about the subject 'global warming'. Have them note down the websites they find with a view to discussing them with the rest of the class. In class, you could ask students how they went about finding their websites. Write some of the website addresses on the board and analyse their appropriacy with the class by looking at the different elements of the websites. Ask students to say what they know about each one. Discuss whether they think they will be good sources for an assignment on global warming, giving their reasons.

4 READING Ask students to read the second part of the text and say whether the statements are true or false. Have fast finishers correct the false sentences.

Answers

1 T **2** F (you should check the information using a different source) **3** T **4** T **5** T **6** F (you should always look for the contact details for the website creator)

5 In pairs, students look back at one of the websites they found in exercise 3 and use the questions in the text to evaluate their websites. Have pairs feedback to the class about what they found.

6 SPEAKING Tell students they are going to watch or listen to a video of two students talking about how to use web sources. With a partner, ask students to predict what they are going to say about each of the subjects.

7a LISTENING ▶ 28 Play the video or track. Ask students to put the things in exercise 6 in the order they are mentioned. See p150 for the audioscript/videoscript for this exercise.

Answers

1 b **2** a **3** d **4** c

7b ▶ 28 Give students time to read through the questions first before playing the video or track again.

Suggested answers

1 an encyclopaedia that is written by experts

2 as an example to show that copying it doesn't mean you understand it

3 It is plagiarism and it's stealing unless you write whose words they are.

4 Teachers can detect plagiarism by the ideas, the writing style and they also use special online services to see where the material comes from.

Listening p64

Listening for general understanding and specific information

1a In pairs, students name the different extracurricular activities they can do at school. Refer students to the photos for ideas.

1b Ask students to look at the photos and name the activities.

Answers

a break dance/street dance **b** quidditch **c** cookery **d** capoeira

2 LISTENING ▶ 29 Play the track for students to listen to four dialogues about extra-curricular activities. Students match each dialogue to a photo. See p150 for the audioscript for this exercise.

Answers

1 d capoeira   **2** b quidditch   **3** a dance   **4** c cookery

ⓘ CULTURAL INFORMATION

Many students participate in extracurricular activities at university as a good way to meet new people. These activities tend to be athletic, social or philanthropic rather than academic. Students often organise and direct these activities under faculty sponsorship; although student-led initiatives – such as student magazines or student radio stations – are common. Students can join in with student voluntary work and projects, get involved in running the Students' Union or have fun while raising money for charity through different schemes.

3 ▶ 29 Play the track again for students to listen and complete the sentences with one or two words. Encourage students to look at the gaps first to predict what word or type of word they may hear.

Answers

a dance   **b** Thursdays   **c** timetable (yet)
d football pitch   **e** run   **f** relax   **g** biggest
h Beginners   **i** modern   **j** street   **k** can't   **l** eat out
m together (afterwards)

4 SPEAKING **What about *you*?** Students discuss the questions. With a less confident class, students could write notes before participating in this speaking activity.

✚ EXTRA ACTIVITY

Students choose an extracurricular activity they know something about and prepare a presentation on this activity. They then present their activity in class and students vote on which activities they think sound the most interesting.

HOMEWORK

Assign students page 43 in their Workbook or the relevant sections of the Online Workbook.

Grammar in context pp64–65

Using zero, first and second conditionals

⟫⟫ FAST TRACK

You could ask students to complete exercise 5a at home in preparation for their class discussion in exercise 5b.

Test before you teach: Flipped classroom
Set the Flipped classroom video and tasks for homework <u>before the lesson</u>. This will allow you to assess the needs of the students before the class. Students can then move on to the relevant grammar practice activities.

1a Students look at the sentences and say which are zero conditionals, first conditionals and second conditionals.

Answers

1 second conditional   **2** first conditional
3 second conditional   **4** zero conditional

1b Students write which tense each rule applies to: zero conditional, first conditional, second conditional or all.

Answers

1 S   **2** F   **3** Z   **4** F   **5** Z   **6** S   **7** A   **8** S

2 Students put the verbs given in the correct form to make zero or first conditional sentences.

Answers

1 doesn't come, 'll ring   **2** don't go, calls
3 is, 'll lend   **4** have, 'll go   **5** don't get, fail
6 arrive, will get

3 Students complete the dialogues with the verbs in the second conditional.

Answers

a would (you) do   **b** were   **c** would spend   **d** did
e would get   **f** didn't go   **g** would have

4 Students complete the text with the verbs in the correct form of the zero, first or second conditional.

Answers

a don't like   **b** limits   **c** were   **d** would play
e don't have   **f** are   **g** weren't/wasn't
h would think   **i** were   **j** wouldn't cost   **k** show
l pay   **m** visit   **n** 'll be able to   **o** have   **p** 'll talk

5a Students complete the sentences with their own ideas.

5b In pairs, students compare their sentences from exercise 5a and choose the three best ones. Elicit answers from students around the class and vote which are the most imaginative answers.

6a Students write questions to ask their partner. Tell them they must write a minimum of three questions beginning *What will you do if …?* and three questions beginning *What would you do if …?* Draw students' attention to the example questions.

6b SPEAKING In small groups, students interview different students with their questions. Students choose the best answers and report them back to the class.

✚ EXTRA ACTIVITY

Ask students to tell their partner what they would do if they won a TV talent show. Students could write a short text for homework and read it out to their partner in the next class.

Refer students to the Grammar reference on page 68 if necessary.

HOMEWORK

Assign students page 44 in their Workbook or the relevant sections of the Online Workbook.

Developing speaking p66

Preparing and giving a presentation

>>> FAST TRACK

You could ask students to prepare exercise 1 by doing some research on home schooling before the class. Students can then make notes to compare in pairs.

WARMER

In pairs, students try to make the longest string of sentences using the second conditional. Start with an example *If I won the lottery* and ask a student to complete the sentence, e.g. *I'd travel around the world.* Ask another student to continue, e.g. *If I travelled around the world* and point to another student to complete this sentence, e.g. *I'd visit Australia.*

Write two more half sentences on the board for students to continue in pairs:

If I met my favourite film star, …; If I lost my job, …

When students have finished, elicit some conditional chains from different pairs around the class.

1 **SPEAKING** In pairs, students think of the advantages and disadvantages of homeschooling and make notes of their ideas.

2 **LISTENING** ▶ 30 Play the track for students to listen to somebody giving a presentation on homeschooling and answer whether she thinks it's a good or bad idea. Ask the students if any of their ideas were included in the presentation. See pp150–151 for the audioscript for this exercise.

Answer

a bad idea

3 ▶ 30 Ask students to listen again and tick the expressions they hear in the Speaking bank. Give them time to read through the expressions first.

Answers

I'm going to talk about …
I'd like to begin by saying …
Firstly,
First of all,
Secondly,
Another thing is that …
It's also true that …
What's more,
For example,
For instance,
Take …
To sum up,
The point (that) I'm trying to make is …

4 **SPEAKING** In pairs, students put the stages of giving a presentation in the correct order. Play the track again if necessary.

Answers

1 d **2** e **3** b **4** g **5** f **6** a **7** c

✔ **EXAM SUCCESS** Ask students to read through the Exam success box and think about advice for giving a presentation. Then ask students to turn to page 145 to compare their answers.

PRACTICE MAKES PERFECT

5a Ask students to choose one of the topics and prepare a presentation using the advice in exercise 4. For less confident students, you could brainstorm three or four ideas for each topic to get them started.

5b **SPEAKING** Students give their presentations to the class.

HOMEWORK

Assign students page 45 in their Workbook or the relevant sections of the Online Workbook.

Developing writing p67

Writing a formal letter of application for a scholarship

>>> FAST TRACK

You could ask students to do the writing task in exercise 4a at home and check their letters at the start of the lesson. It's important to provide less confident students with the model answer in advance, so make sure students have the opportunity to compare their answers with the model answer in class.

WARMER

Write the word *Scholarship* on the board and elicit the meaning ('an amount of money that an organisation gives to someone so that they can study at a particular school or university'). Point out to students that we usually use the verb *award* with *scholarship* – *Sophie was awarded a scholarship to attend Edinburgh University.* In pairs, students make as many words as they can from the letters in *scholarship*. Set a time limit of two minutes. The pair with the most words wins.

1 **READING** Students read the information about a scholarship at a college. Ask them to underline the qualities an ideal candidate should have. Elicit from students if they think that they would be good candidates for the scholarship. Ask them to say why or why not.

Answers

a special interest in British history, would like to study in England, must have good grades, be active in extracurricular activities such as sports and debating, have an interest in travel

2 READING Students read the letter of application for the scholarship. Ask students if they think the person is a good candidate for the scholarship and tell them to make a list of reasons saying why or why not.

Answers

He is a good candidate because:
his best subjects are English and history
he wants to study in the UK and find out more about the country
his grades have been very good
he loves sports – especially football: he is captain of his school football team
he organises social activities to raise money for the team

TEACHER DEVELOPMENT: STUDENT TRAINING

Letters of application

Writing a letter of application is a popular task in many exams.

A letter of application is formal and this affects students' choice of grammar and vocabulary. Learning the phrases from the Writing bank by heart will help students score higher marks in an exam. Letters of application are usually short and simple; remind them it is not a CV. Students can write three or four paragraphs with three or four sentences per paragraph.

The most common format includes an introduction, a body and a concluding paragraph. The introduction is the most important part of the letter. It should provide an explanation to support their application. The body of the letter should provide more details (experiences and accomplishments) to support the statement made in the introductory paragraph. In the conclusion, students should give a brief summary and say they are looking forward to a response.

3 Students look again at the letter in exercise 2 and complete the information in the Writing bank.

Answers

a Sir **b** Madam **c** faithfully **d** contractions
e I would be very grateful to receive the chance ...
f look forward

PRACTICE MAKES PERFECT

4a Students read the task carefully and write their letter. For a less confident class, photocopy or read out the model letter below. Refer students to the Writing bank on page 150.

Model letter

Dear Sir or Madam,

I am writing in regard to the scholarship at your institution.

I believe that I would be the perfect candidate for this scholarship. My chosen subject is journalism and English has always been one of my favourite subjects. I would love to study at a university in the UK or the US one day.

My academic marks have been excellent this year in all subjects. I love music and have played the piano since I was five. I now play in a small band. I am also a member of a reading club. I enjoy all types of team sports and play hockey for the school team.

I would be very grateful to receive the chance to study on the Combined English Scholarship programme and am sure that I would take advantage of this fantastic opportunity.

I look forward to receiving your reply.

Yours faithfully,

James Anderson

TEACHER DEVELOPMENT: STUDENT TRAINING

Paying attention to the task

Effective exam writing involves identifying essential clues provided in the task:

- Who is writing: the student is asked to assume a role (applicant for a scholarship)
- Who you are writing to (Combined English Scholarship administrators)
- The purpose of writing the text (e.g. applying for a scholarship, showing yourself to be an ideal candidate)
- The format (letter of application) and number of words required (150–180 words)

This information guides the students' choice of style, content and tone. Encourage students to underline the key words in the task. In exams, points are awarded for appropriate response to the task.

4b Students exchange their letters with a partner. Tell them to prepare five questions to ask each other in an interview to get the scholarship. Draw students' attention to the example statement and question.

4c SPEAKING Students role-play their interviews and decide if they would give their partner the scholarship or not.

✓ EXAM SUCCESS Ask students who they are writing to, what style they should use and why it is important to know this information in an exam. Tell students to go to page 145 to compare their ideas.

✛ EXTRA ACTIVITY

Students write a reply to the interviewee in exercise 4c to say if their application has been successful or not and explain why.

HOMEWORK

Assign students page 46 in their Workbook or the relevant sections of the Online Workbook.

Language checkpoint: Unit 5

>>> FAST TRACK

Students read the Grammar reference and Vocabulary sections on page 68 before completing the revision exercises on the following page.

Grammar revision p69

have to, don't have to, must, mustn't, can, can't

1 Students rewrite the sentences using the modal verbs in the list.

Answers

1 I can't go to the match.
2 Students don't have to wear a uniform.
3 You mustn't make a loud noise.
4 You have to/must write your name here.
5 You can't/mustn't copy in exams.
6 I must/have to leave now.
7 My little brother can ride his bike alone.

should, shouldn't, ought to, had ('d) better

2 Students decide if the sentences are correct or not. If not, they correct them.

Answers

1 They shouldn't to go out at the weekend.
2 You had better walk to school.
3 I think you ought to go to the dentist.
4 (correct)
5 (correct)

Zero, first and second conditionals

3 Students complete the sentences with the verbs in the correct tense.

Answers

1 'd tell 2 will buy 3 would … say 4 give
5 asked 6 were/was 7 don't go 8 had

Vocabulary revision p69

SCHOOL AND UNIVERSITY SUBJECTS

1 Students write the correct word for each question.

Answers

1 physics 2 medicine 3 media studies
4 architecture 5 law 6 engineering 7 drama

WORDS CONNECTED WITH STUDYING

2 Students write simple explanations for each word.

Suggested answers

1 a way to see your progress like an exam
2 money for being a very good student in order to go to a good school
3 when you don't pass
4 when you have to do an exam again
5 a piece of coursework, or homework, such as a project
6 a plan showing the times and days of each lesson at school
7 the percentage or number you get for a test or an assignment, showing how good you are

NOUN SUFFIXES

3 Students add the suffixes to the stems to make words for people.

Answers

1 scientist 2 instructor 3 technician 4 employee
5 employer 6 librarian

HOMEWORK

Assign students page 47 in their Workbook or the relevant sections of the Online Workbook.

6 Pure science

KEY LEARNING OUTCOMES

CEF

Students will be able to:

- talk about processes using different forms of the passive and *have something done*
- name everyday inventions and how to use them
- understand written and spoken texts about inventions and technology
- compare and contrast two photos orally
- write a for-and-against essay

UNIT OVERVIEW

 Vocabulary
Everyday inventions
Operating technology

 Reading
First laugh, then think!
CRITICAL THINKING Discussing the useful and serious sides of inventions

 Grammar in context
The passive
PRONUNCIATION Sentence stress

 Developing vocabulary
Prepositional phrases with adjectives

 Life skills
Autonomy and enterprise: Brainstorming

 Listening
Smart homes

 Grammar in context
have something done
Gerunds and infinitives

 Developing speaking
Comparing and contrasting photos

 Developing writing
A for-and-against essay

 Exam success
Reading: Matching activities
Listening: Multiple-choice activities

DIGITAL OVERVIEW

Presentation Kit

- ▶ **Flipped classroom video unit 6:** *have something done*
- ▶ **Life skills video unit 6:** Brainstorming
- ▶ **V** **Vocabulary tool:** Everyday inventions; Operating technology
- ▶ **Interactive versions of Student's Book activities**
- ▶ **Integrated audio and answer key for all activities**
- ▶ **Workbook pages with answer key**

Teacher's Resource Centre **TRC**

- ▶ **Flipped classroom video Unit 6:** *have something done*
- ▶ **Life skills video Unit 6:** Brainstorming
- ▶ **Grammar communication activity Unit 6:** What's the connection?
- ▶ **Worksheets for this unit, including:**
  - – Grammar Practice worksheet Unit 6
  - – Flipped classroom video worksheet Unit 6: *have something done*
  - – Literature worksheet Units 5 and 6
  - – Culture worksheet Unit 6
  - – Life skills video worksheet Unit 6
  - – Everyday English worksheet Unit 6

Student's App
Gateway 2nd Edition wordlist for the award-winning Sounds App (available for download)

✓ TESTING AND ASSESSMENT

Resources for exam preparation and measuring student progress

- ▶ Test Generator Units 1–6
- ▶ Printable tests Unit 6 and Review (Units 4–6)
- ▶ Gateway to exams Units 5 and 6 (end of Unit 6)

Vocabulary p70

Talking about everyday inventions and how to operate technology

>>> FAST TRACK

Students could do exercise 4 at home using the Macmillan Online Dictionary, and check their answers in exercise 5 in class.

WARMER

In pairs, students discuss the meaning of the unit title *Pure science* and what they think the unit is going to be about. Ask them to brainstorm 'science' vocabulary to describe the kind of things they think they will learn about in a unit about science.

v Everyday inventions

1a SPEAKING In pairs, students talk about the photos using as many of the words in the box as they can. Draw their attention to the example dialogue.

1b Ask students to check that they know the meanings of the words. Allow them to use a dictionary.

2 SPEAKING Ask students to work with a partner and take it in turns to say what they can do with the items in exercise 1a, for their partner to guess. Draw their attention to the example dialogue.

3 SPEAKING Students work with a partner to ask and answer the questions. Read out the examples with a confident student first. Elicit answers from the class.

v Operating technology

4 Ask students to match the words to the pictures.

Answers
a select a programme **b** connect X to Y
c press a button **d** charge/recharge (a battery)
e switch/turn on/off **f** plug in **g** insert
h tap (the screen)

5 ▶ 31 Ask students to listen and check their answers. Play the track again for students to listen and repeat. Remind students of the pronunciation of *charge* and the correct stress on *insert*. See p151 for the audioscript for this exercise.

TEACHER DEVELOPMENT: CLASSROOM TIPS AND PLANNING

Kinaesthetic learners

You can adjust your teaching style to appeal to kinaesthetic learners when introducing the vocabulary in exercises 1 and 4, by teaching students a simple gesture or movement to go with each action. Do the action as you repeat each word and encourage students to do the same. Associating a relevant action with the word will help reinforce the meaning.

6 LISTENING ▶ 32 Students listen to three dialogues about an everyday invention. Ask students to identify which invention they are talking about. See p151 for the audioscript for this exercise.

Answers
1 vacuum cleaner **2** mobile phone **3** dishwasher

TEACHER DEVELOPMENT: LANGUAGE

Giving instructions

Instructions are usually written using the imperative form of the verb. The imperative is formed by using the verb without *to* or any noun or pronoun in front of it, e.g. *Switch on your mobile phone.*

Sequence is important in giving instructions. Elicit some common sequencing expressions (*first, second, then, next, finally,* etc.).

An alternative way of giving instructions would be to use continuous text with *You should …*

7a SPEAKING In pairs, ask students to write basic instructions for how to operate the items. Encourage them to use as many words from exercise 4 as possible.

Suggested answers
1 Firstly, press power to switch it on. Then press open. Wait for the tray to come out. Put the CD in the tray. Press close. Wait for the tray to go in. Press play.

2 First of all, press the button to open the microwave door. Then, put the food in the microwave. Close the door. Select a programme (for example: full power) and the time and press start. Lastly, take the food out of the microwave.

3 Plug in the lead to charge the mobile phone. Turn the mobile on. Select `camera'. Take a photo. Connect the mobile phone to the computer and download the photo.

7b Ask a student from each pair to read out a set of instructions to the class. The rest of the class has to guess which invention they're talking about.

✦✦ EXTRA ACTIVITY

Students could think of an everyday invention that they would like to have. You could help stimulate ideas by asking them questions: *What invention would save you a lot of time at home? What are some of the problems with inventions that already exist? Could everyday objects be more environmentally friendly?* Ask them to draw a diagram of the parts and instructions on how to use it. Students could present their inventions to their partner at the start of the next class.

HOMEWORK

Assign students page 48 in their Workbook or the relevant sections of the Online Workbook.

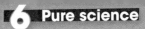
Reading p71

Skimming and scanning a text to find specific information

>>> FAST TRACK

Ask students to do the matching activity in exercise 3 at home and then check their answers in pairs at the beginning of the next lesson.

WARMER

Play *Hot Seat* to start the class. Divide the class into two teams. Ask a volunteer from Team A to sit with his/her back to the board. Choose a word from the everyday inventions in the previous lesson and write it on the board. Team A defines the word for the volunteer to guess in one minute. After one minute, it is Team B's turn to define the word, etc. The team that describes the most words wins the round.

1 In pairs, students predict the answers to the questions. Refer students to the photos to help them understand the topic. Ask students what they think the answers are, but do not confirm them yet.

2 READING Students read the text and check their answers.

Answers

1 You stop talking.
2 If you wash your hair with hot water from copper pipes.
3 Smaller because we begin with small numbers to the left.
4 Cows with names because they feel more relaxed.

✔ **EXAM SUCCESS** Students discuss what strategies they use to help them in matching activities. Elicit answers and tell students to go to page 145 to compare their ideas.

TEACHER DEVELOPMENT: STUDENT TRAINING

Matching activities

In this task, students are asked to match the meaning of a whole paragraph to specific pieces of information from the text. The first step is to read the specific pieces of information carefully and underline key words. Next, students should read the text to identify key words that help them connect the paragraphs to the specific pieces of information from the text. Students may find it useful to underline key words and ideas in each paragraph as they are reading. Remind students that the topic sentence of a paragraph is usually the first sentence or near the beginning of the paragraph.

A useful technique for students, if they are not sure which statement matches which paragraph, is to write down the ones they think might match with a question mark next to them (e.g. A? D?) and move on to the next statement. When they have matched the other statements to the paragraphs, they can go back to these and make a final decision.

3 Students read the text again and match paragraphs A–F

to the correct information.

Answers

1 A **2** D **3** B **4** C **5** F **6** A **7** D **8** E

TEACHER DEVELOPMENT: STUDENT TRAINING

Predicting text content

Discuss why the idea of predicting is important. Prediction helps readers use critical thinking skills and problem-solving. By actively predicting while reading, readers reflect and evaluate the text, thereby extracting deeper meaning. Elicit how in everyday life we constantly make predictions and use our background knowledge to help us make educated guesses. Elicit from students how thinking about the significance of the headline, title, subtitles, pictures and vocabulary in a text starts engagement with key concepts and helps them to have a clear understanding of what they are about to read and why. Before-reading activities also revise vocabulary students already know and introduce new vocabulary they will come across in the text.

In real life, we constantly revise our predictions based on new evidence. Predicting and revising helps students actively engage in reading texts, as they pay attention to see if they were right in their predictions. Having students revise their prediction supports 're-reading', an important component of comprehension.

++ EXTRA ACTIVITY

Students write one or more comprehension questions on the text to test other students.

4 ⚙ **CRITICAL THINKING** Ask students to think of their own response to the question then compare their ideas with the rest of the class.

5 Students look at the underlined words in the text and guess their meaning. They then check their ideas in a dictionary.

Answers

research = a study to find out new facts
aware of = know about
journal = a special magazine with articles from experts
turned = changed, became
copper = type of metal that has an orange colour but goes green with heat or oxygen
analysed = studied to find out what is in it
taps = the way water comes into the home from outside
reacting with = changing when it touches a substance

++ EXTRA ACTIVITY

Students choose other words from the text and look up their definitions. They could test each other by reading out the definitions for their partner to find the word in the text.

6 SPEAKING **What about *you*?** In pairs or small groups, students discuss the question.

Grammar in context pp72–73

Using the passive

⟫⟫ FAST TRACK

Students could do exercise 1b before the class.

Test before you teach

Write these sentences on the board and ask students to fill each gap with a suitable word.

Cars _____ invented in 1885.

Air conditioning _____ invented in 1902.

Lots of everyday inventions are _____ researched.

If students are confident with the basic form you could quickly move through the initial exercises, eliciting answers from students in open class.

Answers
were, was, being

1a Students look at the sentences and decide which sentence is not in the passive.

Answer

Sentence 3 (past simple, active)

1b Students choose the correct alternative to make the rules.

Answers
1 action   **2** isn't   **3** don't always know

1c Students look at the sentences in exercise 1a again and answer the questions.

Answers
1 present simple, past simple, future (*will*), present continuous, present perfect
2 the verb *to be*
3 *by*

2a PRONUNCIATION Students look at the sentences and decide which words are stressed in each sentence. Elicit the words and ask students to explain why they are stressed.

Answers
1 The <u>gadget</u> was <u>invented</u> last <u>year</u>.
2 The <u>new phones</u> are <u>sold here</u>.
3 <u>Ten prizes</u> were <u>given</u>.
4 The <u>disc</u> was <u>inserted</u>.
5 <u>Emails</u> are <u>sent</u> every <u>day</u>.

2b ▶ **33** Students listen to check their answers. Elicit what happens to the verb *to be*. See p151 for the audioscript for this exercise.

Answers

The verb *to be* is not stressed, the words can't be heard clearly.

2c ▶ **33** Play the track again for students to listen and repeat the sentences. Tell them to pay attention to the stress in each sentence.

➕ EXTRA ACTIVITY

Practise the stress-timed nature of English by writing these numbers on the board. Clap out a rhythm and ask students to say the numbers to the beat. Add another word in and then practise saying it <u>to the same rhythm</u>. Add more words in, but keep the same beat. Students will clearly see how the function words are said more quickly to keep the rhythm.
1 2 3 4
1 and 2 and 3 and 4
1 and a 2 and a 3 and a 4
1 and then a 2 and then a 3 and then a 4

3 Students add one word to each sentence to make a correct passive sentence and then decide which tense it is.

Answers
2 have (present perfect)   **3** will (future *will*)
4 were (past simple)   **5** are (present simple)
6 watched (past simple)   **7** was (past simple)

➕ EXTRA ACTIVITY

Students mark the stressed words in the sentences in exercise 3 and practise saying them correctly.

4 Students change the sentences from active to passive.

Answers
1 Dynamite was invented by Alfred Nobel in 1867.
2 The first Nobel prizes were given in 1901.
3 The first electric-powered washing machine was produced by the Hurley Machine Company of Chicago in 1908.
4 This invention has been used since 1908.
5 This invention is being used right now.
6 Perhaps electricity won't be used in the future.
7 The first photo was taken by Joseph Niépce in 1826.
8 A lot of photos are taken on holidays.

TEACHER DEVELOPMENT: LANGUAGE

by + agent

In sentences 2, 4, 5, 6 and 8 in exercise 4 we can leave out the agent, e.g. *by people*. Many English passive sentences do not contain *by* + agent after the verb. Encourage students to omit the agent wherever possible. In many cases, *by* + agent sounds wrong and adds no extra information to the sentence, e.g. *This invention has been used since 1908.* (The agent is completely unnecessary.)

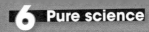

5 Students complete the sentences with the passive or active form and the correct tense of the verbs given.

Answers

1 are built   **2** gave   **3** have been won
4 was made   **5** discovered   **6** is being watched
7 will be spent   **8** has created

6 Students complete the text with the correct passive or active form of the verbs given.

Answers

a are found   **b** are being used   **c** put
d were invented   **e** made   **f** was introduced
g have been sold   **h** designed   **i** was inspired
j will be

7a SPEAKING Students discuss the questions with a partner and see if they know the answers.

Answers

1 Germany   **2** Suzanne Collins   **3** Queen

7b In pairs, students prepare questions for a quiz using the words in the table and their own ideas.

7c SPEAKING Students take it in turns to ask and answer the questions with another pair of students.

> **✚ EXTRA ACTIVITY**
>
> Students could prepare more questions for homework to ask each other at the beginning of the next lesson.

Refer students to the Grammar reference on page 80 if necessary.

> **HOMEWORK**
>
> Assign students page 50 in their Workbook or the relevant sections of the Online Workbook.

Developing vocabulary p73

Talking about yourself using adjectives and prepositional phrases

> **⟫⟫ FAST TRACK**
>
> Students could do exercise 2 as homework, using a dictionary if necessary. Ask them to compare their answers in class before doing the rest of the exercises.

Prepositional phrases with adjectives

1 Students decide what preposition we use after each adjective in this exercise. Tell students to find the adjectives and prepositions in the text on page 71 and check their answers.

Answers

aware *of*, interested *in*, ready *for*

> **TEACHER DEVELOPMENT: LANGUAGE**

Using prepositions

A preposition links nouns, pronouns and phrases to other words in a sentence. The word or phrase that the preposition introduces is called the object of the preposition. A prepositional phrase is made up of the preposition, its object and any associated adjectives or adverbs. Elicit some common prepositions (*about, after, against, along, at, by, down, for, from, in, like, of, off, on, onto, out, over, to, up*, etc.). Remind students that we use a noun or a gerund after prepositions. A gerund is a verbal form that ends in *-ing* and functions as the object of the preposition.

2 Students match the adjectives with the prepositions they usually go with and check they understand the meaning.

Answers

1 b/d   **2** a/e   **3** f   **4** a   **5** a   **6** b   **7** c   **8** c/g
9 e/f

3 Students complete the sentences with the correct prepositions.

Answers

1 at   **2** in   **3** of   **4** of   **5** with   **6** for   **7** of
8 to, from   **9** about   **10** for   **11** with/of

4 SPEAKING Students take it in turns to ask and answer the complete questions from exercise 3. Focus students' attention on the example dialogue. Elicit from students if their answers were the same or different and why.

> **HOMEWORK**
>
> Assign students page 51 in their Workbook or the relevant sections of the Online Workbook.

Gateway to life skills pp74–75

Brainstorming

To learn how to generate new ideas through brainstorming and creative thinking

> **⟫⟫ FAST TRACK**
>
> Ask students to complete the reading task in exercise 2 as homework, and check their answers in class.

> **ⓘ BACKGROUND INFORMATION**

The ability to think creatively is a favourable skill in the classroom, in exam situations, in further education and in many types of employment. 'Brainstorming' refers to a particular technique where either an individual or a group list ideas to a question or problem in a spontaneous way. In this lesson, students look at the principles of brainstorming and the best way to hold a brainstorming session before applying what they've learnt to a group task.

1a In small groups, students do the creative thinking activity.

Suggested answers

A brick: to keep a door open, to hold books in place on a shelf, to stop papers blowing away

A coffee mug: for holding pencils and pens, as a vase, for storing safety pins

1b Write the students' ideas up on the board – the team with the most ideas for each activity is the winner.

2 READING Students read the text about a creative thinking technique and then put the sentences in the correct place.

Answers

1 C **2** A **3** D **4** B

3 Ask students to look at the statements and decide if they are true or false. Fast finishers can correct the false sentences.

Answers

1 F (*during the brainstorming session people should not make either positive or negative comments*)

2 F (*In a brainstorming session you want lots of ideas.*)

3 T

4 F (*The ideas can seem mad, humorous, stupid or unimportant.*)

4 READING Ask students to read the second part of the article and answer the questions.

Answers

1 The secretary makes notes of all the ideas.

2 They should not laugh at anybody or criticise anybody for their ideas.

3 All the ideas are written down.

4 The group evaluates the ideas they have collected.

5 It is different because you decide which ideas are good and bad, reject some and develop others.

5a 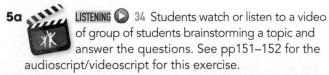 LISTENING ▶ 34 Students watch or listen to a video of group of students brainstorming a topic and answer the questions. See pp151–152 for the audioscript/videoscript for this exercise.

Answers

1 prizes for an award ceremony, what/who should the prizes be for, what the prizes could be, how should the ceremony be

2 yes

5b In pairs, students discuss their answers and justify their answer to question 2 in exercise 5a. Draw their attention to the example sentence. Then ask students what they have decided.

Suggested answers

They listened to everybody. They didn't criticise. They wrote everything down. They developed their ideas at the end.

6a 34 Put students in groups of three and give them time to read the task and decide whether they are A, B or C. Play the video or track again and give students time to write their notes.

6b Students compare their notes in their group. Then elicit answers in open class.

Suggested answers

Student A: a prize for each subject, one overall prize to the best boy or girl in the class, prizes for sports, music and art, prize for other things people do at school not just academic work, prize for student who tries the hardest, prize for the best teacher

Student B: like an Oscar, book or e-reader, money, MP3 player

Student C: like the Oscar ceremony, get a famous actor or TV presenter to present and give prizes, have a red carpet, a photographer, post photos on school website, get the local newspaper to cover the story

LIFE TASK

Tell students they are going to work in groups and brainstorm ideas for a prize ceremony at school.

■ *Step 1*

In small groups, students look at the ideas from the video and then brainstorm more ideas for a ceremony. Ask each group to choose someone to act as a leader or secretary. Remind them to accept all ideas at this stage.

■ *Step 2*

Ask groups to analyse their ideas and decide which ones could work and be developed. Encourage students to give reasoning for their decisions.

■ *Step 3*

Students present their ideas to the class. They can do this orally or with a visual presentation.

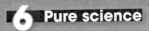

Listening p76

Listening for gist and specific information

WARMER

Draw students' attention to the photo and ask what they think is special about this home. Elicit ideas from students.

1 **SPEAKING** In pairs, students discuss what they think a smart home is and what technology it could have.

2 **LISTENING** ▶ 35 Play the track. Ask students if any of their ideas from exercise 1 were mentioned. See p152 for the audioscript for this exercise.

✓ EXAM SUCCESS Tell students that they are going to do a multiple-choice activity. Ask them to think of the answers to the questions in the Exam success box, and then turn to page 145 to check their ideas.

TEACHER DEVELOPMENT: STUDENT TRAINING

Multiple-choice listening

Students should always read the options before the first listening. In exams, students usually get time to read the questions at the start of each section so they know in advance all the questions they are going to hear. Then time is allowed again at the end of the section to check their answers. When students read the questions at the beginning they can usually predict some of the types of answer that they will hear. A good strategy, at this point, is to try and guess the correct answer before listening and eliminate options that are clearly wrong. If you want to make this into a fun activity, you could ask students to bet on which answers they think are going to be correct before they listen for a second time.

An important tip is to answer all the questions as they hear them, not wait until later. Students cannot remember six answers in a row. Remind them to guess when there is no penalty for guessing. If you are answering a multiple-choice question with three options, you will still have a 33% chance of being correct!

3 ▶ 35 Give students time to read through the options before playing the track again. Nominate students to give their answers.

Answers
1 c **2** b **3** c **4** a **5** c **6** c

4 **SPEAKING** **What about you?** Ask students to ask and answer the questions in pairs.

HOMEWORK

Assign students page 51 in their Workbook or the relevant sections of the Online Workbook.

Grammar in context pp76–77

Describing having or getting something done and using gerunds and infinitives

>>> FAST TRACK

Students could do exercises 2 and 3 as homework. It is important to make sure they have understood correctly, so provide answers and feedback in the next lesson.

Test before you teach: Flipped classroom
Set the Flipped classroom video and tasks for homework <u>before the lesson</u>. This will allow you to assess the needs of the students before the class. Students can then move on to the relevant grammar practice activities.

have something done

1a Students look at the sentences and decide who does the action – the subject at the start of the sentence or somebody/something else.

Answer

In all three sentences, somebody/something else does the action.

1b Students look at the sentences again and answer the questions.

Answers
1 the object of the sentence (i.e. the noun)
2 past participle
3 Yes – in sentence 1 *have* is in the present simple, in 2 *have* is in past simple and in 3 *get* is in the future with *will*
4 *by* introduces the agent

2 Students write sentences using the verbs in the box to say what the people in the pictures had done last week.

Answers
b He had his car fixed.
c She had her eyes tested.
d She had her bedroom painted.
e She had a dress made.
f He had a pizza delivered.

3 Students put the words in order to make questions.

Answers
1 How often do you get your hair cut?
2 Can you fix your computer yourself?
3 Have you ever had a pizza delivered to your house?
4 When was the last time you had your eyes tested?
5 Do you like having your photo taken?
6 Have you ever had clothes made for you?

4 Students rewrite the sentences using *have something done* in the correct tense. Remind students that if we know who did the action, we use the preposition *by*.

Answers

1 We're having the kitchen painted on Saturday.
2 My sister is going to have her car serviced next week.
3 She has her mobile phone bills paid by her parents.
4 My friend had a swimming pool built in her/his garden last summer.
5 We had our computer fixed last week.
6 He had the operating system reinstalled on his computer.
7 I had my files rescued by a computer specialist.

5a SPEAKING Students ask their partner the questions in exercise 3. Remind students to ask follow-up questions to find out more information. Draw students' attention to the question words.

5b Students choose three interesting things they found out about their partner and report them back to the class.

✚ EXTRA ACTIVITY

Students could think of three more questions with *have something done* to ask their partner. You could write these prompts on the board to give students ideas: *pizza / deliver / to your home / hair / cut / a completely different style / take / blood pressure / at the doctor's / bag / stolen*

Gerunds and infinitives

6 Ask students to match the sentences (a–f) with the rules (1–6). They then choose the correct alternative in each rule.

Answers

1 b (gerund) **2** f (infinitive) **3** a (gerund)
4 c (gerund) **5** e (infinitive) **6** d (gerund)

7 Students complete the sentences with the correct form of the verb given.

Answers

1 cycling **2** learning **3** reading **4** playing
5 to learn **6** to get

8 SPEAKING In pairs, students talk about the sentences in exercise 7, saying whether they are true for them or not.

Refer students to the Grammar reference on page 80 if necessary.

HOMEWORK

Assign students page 52 in their Workbook or the relevant sections of the Online Workbook.

Developing speaking p78 💬 💬

Comparing and contrasting photos

≫ FAST TRACK

Students could make notes about the photos in exercise 1 to compare in class.

WARMER

Students look at the photos on page 78 and discuss what they can see in each one. Brainstorm key words to describe each photo and discuss what they think the connection is between the four of them.

1 SPEAKING In pairs, students look at the two photos and decide which style of lesson they would prefer. They should give one or two reasons for why they made their choice. Elicit answers from students.

2 LISTENING ▶ 36 Play the track for students to listen to a student talking about the two photos and the lesson she prefers. Elicit students' answers and opinions. See p152 for the audioscript for this exercise.

Answer

The second lesson because it's more exciting to do things than listen.

3 ▶ 36 Play the track again for students to complete the sentences.

Answers

1 Both **2** whereas **3** difference **4** similarity

4 Students complete the Speaking bank with the phrases from exercise 3.

Answers

Comparing: Both of the photos show, One other similarity between the photos is that
Contrasting: whereas in the second photo, Another important difference between the photos is that

PRACTICE MAKES PERFECT

5a SPEAKING In pairs, students look at the photos and make a list of the similarities and differences between them.

5b In different pairs, students look at the task and take it in turns to compare and contrast the images using expressions from the Speaking bank. For students who are less confident, photocopy the model answer below for extra support during the speaking task.

Model answer

One thing that the photos have in common is that they show a group of young people using technology. Another similarity is that in both photos the teenagers look quite relaxed. In the second photo the people are all on their phones. However, in the first photo they are using a laptop. Another difference is that in the second photo they are each using their phones individually, and in the first photo they are working together as a group on the laptop. The teenagers in the first photo are all smiling, but the ones in the second photo are not.

HOMEWORK

Assign students page 53 in their Workbook or the relevant sections of the Online Workbook.

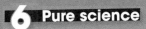
Developing writing p79

Writing a for-and-against essay

You could ask students to do exercise 3 at home and check their answers at the start of the lesson. Alternatively, you could set the writing task in exercise 5b as homework.

WARMER

> **In pairs, students take it in turns to look at the photos on page 79 and describe what is happening in each one.**

1 In pairs, students make a list of arguments for and against the statement.

2 READING Students read the essay to see if it contains any of their ideas from exercise 1.

3 Students read the essay again and write a title or short description of the content in each paragraph.

Suggested answers

Paragraph 1: Introduction – state the topic of the essay
Paragraph 2: Arguments for/Advantages – justifications and reasons
Paragraph 3: Arguments against/Disadvantages – justifications and reasons
Paragraph 4: Conclusion – gives the writer's opinion

TEACHER DEVELOPMENT: STUDENT TRAINING

A for-and-against essay

A for-and-against essay is a formal piece of writing in which a topic is considered from opposing points of view. Students should not use an informal style (e.g. short forms, colloquial language, etc.) or strong language to express their opinion. Point out to students that this type of essay presents both sides in a fair way by discussing them objectively and in equal detail.

A for-and-against essay is structured into paragraphs to make the meaning and progression clear for the reader. Information is grouped in a logical way to distinguish between different information and students use adverbs and conjunctions to establish cohesion within paragraphs.

4 Students look at the linkers and use them to complete the Writing bank.

Answers

a Secondly, **b** Furthermore, **c** What's more,
d However, **e** To sum up,

PRACTICE MAKES PERFECT

5a Students look at the task and plan their essay in pairs. Remind them to organise their ideas into paragraphs. Refer students to the Writing bank on page 151.

5b Individually, students write their essays. Remind them to use linkers and expressions from the Writing bank. For students who are less confident, photocopy the model essay below for extra support during the writing task.

Model essay

When we talk about depending too much on computers, it is important to realise that 'too much' can mean different things for different people.

Firstly, some people's jobs rely on using a computer. Many industries would be a lot slower and less reliable if computers didn't exist. Computers also give people enjoyment; they can be used for games, films and research and many other things. Using a computer can also be a social activity, though people may disagree with this. What would be 'too much' for some people would be normal for other people and it's possible to be happy and healthy and use a computer a lot.

However, some people become very dependent on computers. In the workplace when a computer breaks, sometimes people don't know what to do. Using a computer to find information is also too easy; people can get lazy and not read books instead. In addition, some people spend too much time with virtual friends online and don't know how to make friends in real life.

Io sum up, there are advantages and disadvantages to using a computer a lot. What 'too much' is can be different for each individual, but if a computer is preventing someone from having a normal healthy life, then it is too much.

++ EXTRA ACTIVITY

> **Students review their text (or their partner's text) giving themselves a grade from 1–5 according to these criteria related to organisation of the text:**
> - **My ideas are structured clearly, with sentences organised into appropriate paragraphs.**
> - **I use separate paragraphs to structure my main ideas clearly throughout the text. I make sure the organisation I use supports my purpose (e.g. logical links between paragraphs).**
> - **I think carefully about the way I develop ideas in the text (e.g. closings refer back to openings; I develop ideas in different ways).**
> - **Within paragraphs/sections, I use a range of devices to support cohesion (e.g. pronouns, connectors, etc.).**

HOMEWORK

> **Assign students page 54 in their Workbook or the relevant sections of the Online Workbook.**

Language checkpoint: Unit 6

>>> FAST TRACK

Students read the Grammar reference and Vocabulary sections on page 80 before completing the revision exercises on the following page.

Grammar revision p81

The passive

1 Students complete the sentences with the correct form of the passive using the verbs given.

Answers

1 were stolen   2 is taught   3 is visited
4 will be built   5 was invented   6 will be played
7 has been translated   8 is spoken

have something done

2 Students complete the second sentences using *have something done*.

Answers

1 She had it decorated by professionals.
2 He will have it fixed at a garage.
3 She has it done at the hairdresser's.
4 We had it painted.
5 They had it built by an expert.
6 He had it translated by a friend.
7 They haven't had it tested by an optician.

Gerunds and infinitives

3 Students choose the correct alternative.

Answers

1 listening   2 to read   3 to see   4 watching
5 Fixing

Vocabulary revision p81

EVERYDAY INVENTIONS

1 Students complete the names of the everyday inventions and write if they are usually used for pleasure (P) or housework (H).

Answers

1 dishwasher (H)   2 headphones (P)
3 vacuum cleaner (H)   4 washing machine (H)
5 MP3 player (P)   6 microwave oven (H)
7 remote control (P)

OPERATING TECHNOLOGY

2 Students complete the text with the words.

Answers

a plug … in   b turn … on   c insert
d select   e press   f switch … off

PREPOSITIONAL PHRASES WITH ADJECTIVES

3 Students choose the correct alternative.

Answers

1 with   2 about   3 to   4 of   5 of   6 for   7 at

HOMEWORK

Assign students page 55 in their Workbook or the relevant sections of the Online Workbook.

Reading p82

1 READING In pairs, students read the text and match the pictures to the Ig Nobel prize winners.

Answers

A 3 **B** 1 **C** 2 **D** 4

2 Students read the text again and say which paragraph tells the reader about each thing.

Answers

1 C **2** D **3** A **4** B **5** D **6** C **7** A **8** B

Speaking p82

3 Students have five minutes to prepare a presentation on the topic, before giving their presentation to the rest of the class.

Listening p83

4 LISTENING ▶ 37 Play the track for students to listen to a programme talking about teenage students and choose the best answers. See pp152–153 for the audioscript for this exercise.

Answers

1 b **2** a **3** a **4** a **5** c

5 SPEAKING What about you? Students think of their own answers, then ask and answer the questions in pairs.

Writing p83

6 Students work with a partner and discuss what they think about school uniform, thinking about the advantages and disadvantages.

7 Students read the writing task and write an article for their school magazine, giving the reasons for and against school uniform. For students who are less confident, photocopy the model article below for extra support and allow them to read it before beginning the writing task.

Model article

Many students do not like wearing school uniform. In my opinion, there are advantages and disadvantages to wearing school uniform.

Firstly, it is much easier to get ready for school in the morning when you don't have to think too much about what you are going to wear. Secondly, everyone in the school looks the same. There is less competition between students for who has the most expensive or trendiest clothes, and personally I think that it is good for students to be more equal. In some schools where there is no uniform, students feel that they have to spend a lot of money on clothes for school, and I think that is a bad thing. Finally, some people think that students look smarter when they wear a school uniform instead of jeans.

On the other hand, some students think they should be able to express their personality by choosing their own clothes. Furthermore, they have to buy their own clothes to wear at the weekend and in the holidays, so it would be more sensible to wear the same clothes for school. Finally, in my opinion school uniform does not look very smart. Students don't care about their school uniform clothes, and so they don't try to look nice.

To sum up, there are arguments for and against school uniform, but as far as I'm concerned, I would rather wear my own clothes for school.

HOMEWORK

Assign students pages 56–57 in their Workbook or the relevant sections of the Online Workbook.

'CAN DO' PROGRESS CHECK p83

1 Ask students to read the 'can do' statements and mark from 1–4 how well they can do these things in English.

2 Ask students to look at their marks and decide what they need to do to improve. Elicit other suggestions.

7 Play on!

KEY LEARNING OUTCOMES

Students will be able to:

- give extra information about people, things or places using defining or non-defining relative clauses
- talk about sports and use phrasal verbs connected with sports

- understand written and spoken texts about sports
- take part in a debate expressing agreement and disagreement
- write an article on a topic related to their life

UNIT OVERVIEW

Vocabulary
Sports and sports venues
PRONUNCIATION Stress on long words
Sports equipment and scores

Reading
The game before the game
CRITICAL THINKING Discussing the author's and students' own opinions about superstition in sport

Grammar in context
Defining relative clauses

Developing vocabulary
Phrasal verbs connected with sport

Life skills
Physical well-being:
Looking after your heart

Listening
The origin of basketball

Grammar in context
Non-defining relative clauses

Developing speaking
A debate

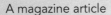

Developing writing
A magazine article

Exam success
Use of English: Cloze activities
Listening: True/False activities

DIGITAL OVERVIEW

Presentation Kit
- ▶ **Flipped classroom video Unit 7:** Defining relative clauses
- ▶ **Life skills video Unit 7:** Looking after your heart
- ▶ V **Vocabulary tool:** Sports and sports venues; Sports equipment and scores
- ▶ **Interactive versions of Student's Book activities**
- ▶ **Integrated audio and answer key for all activities**
- ▶ **Workbook pages with answer key**

Teacher's Resource Centre
- ▶ **Flipped classroom video Unit 7:** Defining relative clauses
- ▶ **Life skills video Unit 7:** Looking after your heart
- ▶ **Grammar communication activity Unit 7:** Sets of three
- ▶ **Worksheets for this unit, including:**
  - Grammar Practice worksheet Unit 7
  - Flipped classroom video worksheet Unit 7: Defining relative clauses
  - Literature worksheet Units 7 and 8
  - Culture worksheet Unit 7
  - Life skills video worksheet Unit 7
  - Everyday English worksheet Unit 7

Student's App
Gateway 2nd Edition wordlist for the award-winning Sounds App (available for download)

✓ TESTING AND ASSESSMENT

Resources for exam preparation and measuring student progress

- ▶ Test Generator Units 1–7
- ▶ Printable test Unit 7
- ▶ Gateway to exams Units 7 and 8 (end of Unit 8)

Vocabulary p84

Talking about different sports and sports venues, sports equipment and scoring in sports

You could ask students to do exercise 1 at home so that less confident students can take the necessary time to look up the vocabulary in the Macmillan Online Dictionary. Encourage students to discuss their answers in class.

WARMER

In pairs, students discuss the meaning of the unit title *Play on!* and what they think the unit is going to be about. Tell students that 'Play on' is an expression used in many sports to mean 'continue with the game'. Write these questions on the board and tell students to ask and answer the questions in pairs:

Are you a member of any sports team? If not, have you ever been? What sports are you good at?

Do you like to watch sports on TV?

Elicit answers from different students around the class.

v Sports and sports venues

1 SPEAKING In pairs, students match as many of the words as possible to each category. Provide dictionaries if necessary.

Answers

1 team sports: baseball, basketball, football, ice hockey, rugby, volleyball

2 individual sports: athletics, climbing, cycling, diving, golf, gymnastics, horse-riding, ice skating, sailing, skiing, snowboarding, swimming, tennis, weightlifting

3 ball sports: baseball, basketball, football, golf, rugby, tennis, volleyball

4 water sports: sailing, swimming

5 winter sports: ice hockey, ice skating, skiing, snowboarding

6 combat sports: judo, karate

7 indoor sports: gymnastics, ice hockey, judo, karate, weightlifting

2a PRONUNCIATION Students put the words in the correct column, according to the stress.

Answers

O	Oo	Ooo	oOo
golf	baseball climbing cycling diving football judo rugby sailing skiing swimming tennis	basketball horse-riding ice hockey ice skating snowboarding volleyball weightlifting	athletics gymnastics karate

2b 38 Students listen and check their answers. They then practise saying the words with the correct stress. See p153 for the audioscript for this exercise.

TEACHER DEVELOPMENT: PRONUNCIATION

Syllable stress

In words of more than one syllable, there is always one syllable which is more heavily stressed than the others. We say that this syllable carries the primary stress (e.g. *ath**let**ics*). In some longer words, other syllables may carry secondary stress. The most important thing for students to recognise is where the primary stress falls – and remember that it can change between words derived from the same base (e.g. *photograph, photographer, photographic*). Incorrect syllable stress can make students difficult to understand. Encourage students to pay attention to how a word is stressed when they first learn how to pronounce it and to mark in the word stress when they record new vocabulary, e.g. by marking the stressed syllable with a coloured highlighter.

✚ EXTRA ACTIVITY

Ask students to add one word connected with sport to each column.

3 Students complete the sentences with the words.

Answers

1 pool **2** gym **3** slope **4** court **5** pitch **6** rink **7** track **8** course

v Sports equipment and scores

4 Students look at the photo and find pieces of equipment from the box.

Answers

ball, net, racket, trainers

5 In pairs, students think of as many sports as they can for each piece of equipment in exercise 4. Draw students' attention to the example sentence.

Suggested answers

You need a ball to play baseball, basketball, football, golf, rugby, tennis, volleyball …

You need a bat to play baseball, table tennis …

You need boots to go skiing, play football …

You need a club to play golf …

You need a goal to play football, ice hockey …

You need goggles to go swimming, play water polo, go diving …

You need a net to play tennis, table tennis, volleyball …

You need a racket to play tennis …

You need skates to go ice skating, rollerblading, skating …

You need skis to go skiing …

You need trainers to do athletics, play tennis, volleyball …

6 Students name one sport where they can do each of the things with a ball.

Suggested answers

bounce – basketball, catch – baseball, head – football, hit – baseball, kick – football, pass – rugby, throw – athletics

7 Students choose the correct alternative. Point out that in one sentence both answers are correct.

Answers

1 beat **2** won **3** both **4** drew **5** scored **6** point

8 LISTENING ▶ 39 Play the track for students to listen and decide which sport in exercise 1 is the subject of each conversation. See p153 for the audioscript for this exercise.

Answers

1 volleyball **2** ice hockey **3** football **4** diving

9 SPEAKING Students work in small groups. One student thinks of a sport; the others must find out what it is by asking a maximum of 20 questions, but the first student can only answer *yes* or *no*.

✚ EXTRA ACTIVITY

Write the first part of these extreme sports on the board and ask students to write the other half of each word. They then classify the sports in the correct column in exercise 2a, acccording to the stress.
scuba (diving), hang- (gliding), rock (climbing), bungee (jumping), sky (diving), mountain (biking)

HOMEWORK

Assign students page 58 in their Workbook or the relevant sections of the Online Workbook.

Reading p85

Skimming for specific information and reading for detail

≫ FAST TRACK

You could ask students to read the text and complete the table at home, then check their answers together in class.

WARMER

Play *20 questions*. Tell students you are thinking of a famous sports star. They can ask up to 20 questions to find out who he or she is. You can only answer *Yes* or *No*. When they have guessed the answer, brainstorm the names of other famous sports stars students know from the sports they looked at in the previous lesson.

---

1 In pairs, students discuss the questions. Elicit answers from different students around the class. Tell students to look at the text title and the photo and predict what they think the text is going to be about.

Suggested answer

A belief that certain things that you do, or that happen to you, will bring good or bad luck.

ⓘ CULTURAL INFORMATION

Superstitions have often evolved from ancient religions or ceremonies. In Britain, it is considered lucky to meet a black cat or to find a clover plant with four leaves, and a horseshoe hung over the door is thought to bring good luck.

Friday is considered to be an unlucky day. The number 13 is also considered unlucky and Friday the 13th is a doubly unlucky day. Another superstition is that if you break a mirror, you will have seven years' bad luck. This superstition is supposed to go back to ancient mythology where mirrors were the instruments of Roman gods.

---

2 READING Students read the text and complete the table.

Answers

Footballer	Country	Most important superstition
1 Laurent Blanc	France	kissed the goalkeeper's head at the start of every match
2 Pelé	Brazil	needed a lucky shirt
3 Kolo Touré	Ivory Coast	had to arrive last on the pitch
4 Pepe Reina	Spain	always fills car with petrol on the way to each match, eats the same kind of sandwich the night before a match, touches the pitch, goal posts and crossbar after warming up
5 Kim Little	Scotland	always puts her left sock and boot on before her right

---

3 Students decide if the statements are true or false and write the number(s) of the line(s) where they find the answer.

Answers

1 F (lines 8–10) **2** T (lines 14–22) **3** F (lines 41–44) **4** F (lines 54–55) **5** F (line 65–67) **6** F (lines 71–73)

4 ⚙ CRITICAL THINKING Ask students to think of their own answer to the questions and then share their thoughts with the class.

5 Ask students to look at the underlined words in the text and guess their meaning. Allow students to use their dictionaries.

Answers

changing room = the place where players put on or take off their sports clothes
irrational = without logic or reason
hosted = received or managed something
gave away = offered to someone for free
teammates = other players in the same team
refused = said no, did not agree
crossbar = the metal pole across the top of the goal post

6 **SPEAKING** **What about *you*?** Ask students to look at the questions and then ask and answer in pairs.

✚ EXTRA ACTIVITY

In pairs or small groups, students research interesting superstitions in other countries and present what they find to the rest of the class.

HOMEWORK

Assign students page 59 in their Workbook or the relevant sections of the Online Workbook.

Grammar in context pp86–87 Ⓖ

Using defining relative clauses

≫ FAST TRACK

You could ask students to do exercise 4 at home and write down their sentences. They could use the Macmillan Online Dictionary to check the words in italics, if necessary. Students can compare their answers in class.

Test before you teach: Flipped classroom
Set the Flipped classroom video and tasks for homework <u>before the lesson</u>. This will allow you to assess the needs of the students before the class. Students can then move on to the relevant grammar practice activities.

1a Students look at the relative pronouns marked in blue in the sentences. Tell students to use them to complete the rules. Check students' answers and make sure they have copied the correct information into their notebooks.

Answers

1 who, that **2** that, which **3** whose **4** where
5 when

1b Ask students why we call these 'defining' relative clauses and what they define. Elicit why we can omit *that* in sentence e but not in f.

Answers

1 The purpose of a defining relative clause is to define clearly who or what we are talking about. Without this information, it would be difficult to know who or what is meant.
2 The relative pronoun can be omitted when it is the *object* of the clause.

TEACHER DEVELOPMENT: LANGUAGE

Defining relative clauses

Defining relative clauses give essential information to define or identify the person or thing we are talking about. Some key points students should know about these clauses are:

- Commas are not used in defining relative clauses.
- *Who*, *whom* and *which* can be replaced by *that*. This is very common in spoken English.
- *Whom* is very formal and is only used in written English.
- The relative pronoun can be omitted when it is the *object* of the clause. This is especially common in spoken English.
- Relative clauses with *who*, *which*, *that* as subject pronouns can be replaced with a participle. This makes the sentence shorter and easier to understand, e.g. I told you about the boy *who lives* next door. I told you about the boy *living* next door.

2 Students choose the correct alternative. If they think that both are correct, they should mark both.

Answers

1 which/– **2** where **3** who **4** whose **5** when
6 who/that **7** which

✓ **EXAM SUCCESS** Ask students to think about what they need to do for a cloze activity. Ask them to turn to page 145 to compare their ideas.

3 Students complete the text with the correct words.

Answers

a that/which **b** whose **c** but **d** to **e** which/that
f the **g** where **h** whose

4 Students match the sentence halves and add a relative pronoun. Allow students to use a dictionary if necessary to check the words in italics.

Answers

1 d The winner in a gymnastics competition is the person **whose** mark is the highest.
2 g A *referee* is the person **whose** job is to control football matches.
3 e 2024 is a year **when** there will be Olympic Games.
4 h A *dojo* is the place **where** you do judo.
5 f *Time out* is a moment in a basketball match **when** the players stop playing.
6 a A *black belt* is a thing you get **when** you are really good at judo or karate.
7 b In football, *goalkeepers* are often the players **whose** shirt has a number 1 on the back.
8 c The *puck* is the thing **–/that/which** you hit in an ice hockey match.

5 Students complete the sentences with a relative pronoun and information. Draw their attention to the example.

Suggested answers

2 A net is something which marks the middle of the court in tennis.
3 Wimbledon is a place where you can watch a famous tennis tournament.
4 Summer is the season when you do athletics at school.
5 PE is a subject which you study at school.
6 The ice rink is a place where you can skate or play ice hockey.
7 Swimming is an activity which you can do in a pool or in the sea.
8 2014 was the year when the Winter Olympics were in Russia.

TEACHER DEVELOPMENT: STUDENT TRAINING

How to improve your results in grammar exercises

If students improve their knowledge of grammar, they are more likely to get better results in language exercises and tests. As teachers, we can help raise students' awareness of achievable goals, help them identify the common grammatical errors they make and offer ways for students to learn how to correct them. We can provide both finely tuned input that requires students to pay attention to the relationships between form, meaning and use for a specific grammar rule, and more general input that allows students to encounter the grammar rule in a variety of contexts.

6a SPEAKING In pairs, students read out the definitions and guess the answers.

Answers

1 instructor **2** campsite **3** check in

6b In pairs, students choose words from the Student's Book so far to write six more definitions like the ones in exercise 6a. Ask students to read out their definitions in open class for other students to guess.

✚ EXTRA ACTIVITY

Students could research and prepare two True/False sentences about sports with relative pronouns for a 'grammar auction' to practise defining relative clauses (e.g. *Football is the …*). Divide the class into four or five teams, each with a team leader. Collect in the True/False sentences and explain that they are now for sale. Read out the sentences (acting like an auctioneer adds an element of fun to this game) for each team to decide if the definition is true and make a bid for it. To buy the definition, one team must offer more money than all the other teams. Tell students that they have a total of 1,000, for example. Every time they win a bid, they must keep a count of the amount they have left. At the end of the auction, tell the students which sentences were true and tell them to count the number of true sentences they have bought. The winner of the game is the team that buys the highest number of true definitions.

Refer students to the Grammar reference on page 94 if necessary.

HOMEWORK

Assign students page 60 in their Workbook or the relevant sections of the Online Workbook.

Developing vocabulary p87

Talking about sports and hobbies using phrasal verbs

▶▶▶ FAST TRACK

Students could do exercise 2 as homework, using a dictionary if necessary. Ask them to compare their sentences in class.

Phrasal verbs connected with sport

1 Students look at the sentences and match the phrasal verbs in red with their definitions.

Answers

1 e **2** a **3** g **4** d **5** b **6** c **7** f

2 Students complete the sentences using the appropriate form of the phrasal verbs from exercise 1.

Answers

1 take up **2** knocked (us) out **3** join in
4 gives in **5** go for **6** warm up **7** work out

3 SPEAKING Students complete the sentences with the appropriate form of the phrasal verbs from exercise 1 and then ask their partner the questions.

Answers

1 work **2** join **3** go, give **4** knocked **5** warm
6 take

TEACHER DEVELOPMENT: LANGUAGE

Phrasal verbs

Phrasal verbs are usually two-word phrases consisting of verb + adverb or verb + preposition. Encourage students to learn them as vocabulary and to note them down in an example sentence to help them remember the meaning. Many phrasal verbs have more than one meaning. Students also need to learn to use phrasal verbs. Some phrasal verbs require a direct object (e.g. *go for* + something, *take up* + something), and some do not (e.g. the other verbs in exercise 1). Some phrasal verbs can be separated by the object, while others can't.

✚ EXTRA ACTIVITY

Ask students to write a text using as many phrasal verbs connected with sport as possible.

HOMEWORK

Assign students page 61 in their Workbook or the relevant sections of the Online Workbook.

Gateway to life skills pp88–89

Looking after your heart

To learn about heart disease, some of the causes and how to protect yourself from it

>>> FAST TRACK

You could set exercises 3 and 4 as homework to be discussed in pairs at the next lesson.

ⓘ BACKGROUND INFORMATION

Looking after your heart

In the UK, heart disease is responsible for over 70,000 deaths each year and by 2020 it is likely to be the leading cause of death worldwide. Heart disease in many cases is preventable with changes to diet, exercise and lifestyle, so teaching young people how to look after their heart is vital in minimising the disease.

WARMER

Write the following gapped sentences about the heart on the board:

Women's hearts typically beat .... *than men's.*

In an average lifetime, a heart will beat .... *times.*

Ask students to work in pairs to guess how to complete the facts. Help with any vocabulary necessary then elicit their guesses. Tell students the answers and ask if any of them were surprising.

| Answers

| faster, 2.5 billion

Allow students time to read through the Life skills objectives and the Key concepts before starting the lesson.

1a Draw students' attention to the leaflet. In pairs, students discuss what they can see and the message of the leaflet.

1b Ask students for ideas for looking after their heart. Encourage them to use *should/shouldn't*.

2 Students match the numbers and information. Ask them to guess the answers, but don't confirm them until exercise 3.

3 READING Ask students to read the first part of the leaflet and answer the questions.

| Answers

| 1 d **2** a **3** e **4** c **5** b

4 Students read the second part of the leaflet and complete parts 3 and 4, then check their answers on page 148.

Answers

Part 3

Things we can change:

1 B stop smoking

2 C eat the right foods and relax; reduce our salt intake

3 D lose weight

4 G do more exercise

5 H eat the right foods with low cholesterol

6 I try to rest and relax

Things we can't change:

1 A family history

2 E Gender

3 F Age

Part 4

1 D **2** C **3** G **4** H **5** B **6** I

5 Students work in pairs to guess what each of the words and expressions is.

Answers

Your heart rate: how many times your heart beats per minute

Beats per minute: BPM – the number of times your heart beats in one minute

A heart-rate monitor: a device with sensors which measures your heart rate electronically

The radial artery: the artery on the inside of the wrist where you can see a heartbeat

The carotid artery: the artery on the side of your neck

✚ EXTRA ACTIVITY

Ask students to work in groups to find out another interesting fact about the heart, and explain it to another group.

6 LISTENING ▶ 40 Tell students they are going to watch or listen to a video of two students presenting an assignment about calculating their recovery heart rate. Ask students to listen for the words and expressions from exercise 5 and check whether their answers were correct. See p153 for the audioscript/videoscript for this exercise.

7 ▶ 40 Allow students time to read through the questions before playing the video or track again.

Answers

1 You take your pulse when you have been resting for 15 minutes.

2 You do moderate to high intensity activity like running or cycling or playing a competitive sport for a short while. You stop and take your pulse immediately then wait 60 seconds and take it again. The second number minus the first gives you your recovery heart rate.

3 Your recovery heart rate tells you how fit you are.

Tell students they are going to create a campaign to raise awareness about taking care of your heart.

- **Step 1**

  Students choose one of the risk factors in part 2 of the text and do some more research about it.

- **Step 2**

  Ask students to think of an interesting and original way to present the information. Go through the ideas listed and ask students to think of their own if they want to. If possible, bring some examples of leaflets and posters in.

- **Step 3**

  Students present the information to the rest of the class.

Listening p90

Making predictions or guesses and then listening for specific information

ⓘ CULTURAL INFORMATION

Basketball is one of the few sports whose exact origin is definitely known. In the winter of 1891–1892, Dr James Naismith invented the game of basketball to provide indoor exercise and competition for the students between the football and baseball seasons. US soldiers brought basketball to Europe in World War I, and it soon became a worldwide sport.

WARMER

In pairs, students brainstorm words they know connected to basketball. Elicit vocabulary from the students. Write these words on the board: *ball, hoop, backboard, forward, guard*. Ask students to make a sentence to define each word with a relative pronoun, e.g. *It's a thing that/which ...; It's someone who ...*, etc.

✓ **EXAM SUCCESS** Students discuss what they should do if they miss an answer to a question in a True/False listening activity. Ask students to turn to page 145 to compare their ideas.

1 In pairs, students look at the statements about the origin of basketball and decide if they are true or false. Tell them that if they don't know, they should guess.

TEACHER DEVELOPMENT: STUDENT TRAINING

Being positive in listening tests

Remind students to write notes as they listen and answer as much as they can when they hear the recording for the first time. Then they can check their answers and listen for any missing answers when they hear the recording a second time. A lapse of concentration during a listening can make students lose the sequence of answers and start to panic. It can be helpful to point out to students that the answers usually appear in the conversation in the same order as the questions. Students should also remember that they do not have to understand everything while listening: some of the parts of the listening may not be tested. If they miss an answer to a question, they mustn't panic. Remind them to keep a positive attitude and keep listening for the next answer. If, at the end of the activity, they are still not sure, they should guess an answer (there is a 50% chance they will be right!).

2 LISTENING ▶ 41 Play the track for students to listen and check their answers to exercise 1. Talk about the answers and any disagreements there might be. With a less confident class, pre-teach the words from exercise 1 before students do the listening activity. You could also practise saying the time expressions in the True/False statements to help students listen out for this in the activity. See p154 for the audioscript for this exercise.

Answers

1 T **2** F **3** T **4** F **5** T **6** T **7** F **8** T

3 ▶ 41 Play the track again for students to answer the questions.

Answers

1 He had 14 days.
2 Because of the cold winters in Massachusetts.
3 They didn't have holes in the bottom so they had to stop the game each time someone scored.
4 A game lasted 35 minutes.
5 It was played at universities.
6 To invent a sport that people would enjoy, and above all to keep people fit and healthy.

4 SPEAKING **What about *you*?** Ask students to think of their own answers to the questions, then ask and answer with a partner.

HOMEWORK

Assign students page 61 in their Workbook or the relevant sections of the Online Workbook.

Grammar in context pp90–91

Using non-defining relative clauses

You could ask students to complete exercise 3 at home, and find out any more information they can about Mo Farah online. Ask them to discuss their answers in class.

Test before you teach
Find out what students already know about non-defining relative clauses. Write these pairs of sentences on the board and ask students to combine each pair to make one sentence.

Valencia is a great place to live. Valencia is on the coast of Spain.

James lives in London now. James left university last year.

If students are confident with non-defining relative clauses, move quickly through exercises 1 and 2 in open class.

1 Students look at the sentences and answer the questions.

Answers
1 sentences a, d, e, f   **2** non-defining clauses
3 No, we can't.   **4** a comma

TEACHER DEVELOPMENT: LANGUAGE

Non-defining relative clauses

In a non-defining clause, the information given is not essential. It tells us more about someone or something, but it does not help us to identify them or it. It might be helpful for students to think that the essential information might be followed by the words *by the way*, i.e. it is additional information and could be presented as two separate statements.

- Non-defining relative clauses are always separated from the rest of the sentence by commas. The commas have a similar function to brackets.
- In non-defining clauses, you cannot use *that* instead of *who, whom* or *which*.
- You cannot leave out the relative pronoun, even when it is the object of the verb in the relative clause: *He gave me the present, which was wrapped in pink paper. He gave me the present, which I opened immediately.*
- The preposition in these clauses can go at the end of the clause, e.g. *This is John, who you have all heard about.*
- Non-defining clauses can be introduced by expressions like *all of, many of* + relative pronoun, e.g. *There are a lot of friends in my class, many of whom I have known for years.*

Students research specific vocabulary in English to describe their favourite sport.

2 Students complete the sentences with non-defining relative clauses including the information given. Draw students' attention to the example sentence. When checking answers, remind students to pause at the commas, and read each part of the sentence with its own short intonation curve. Compare with a defining relative clause, which has no commas and a single intonation curve for the whole sentence.

Answers
2 who is a Formula 1 world champion
3 whose brother Jamie also plays tennis
4 when Liverpool won the Champions League
5 where two different teams play
6 whose grandmother is Queen Elizabeth II

3 Students read the text about Mo Farah and choose the best answer to complete the text.

Answers
1 D **2** B **3** D **4** A **5** B **6** B **7** B **8** C **9** D
10 B

4 Students join the pairs of sentences. Remind them to check if they need to write a defining or non-defining clause. Focus students' attention on the example sentences.

Answers
3 Petra Kvitová, who is from the Czech Republic, is a great tennis player.
4 The athlete who broke the world record won the race.
5 Last Saturday, when my team won the final, was great.
6 Anna, whose mum is a PE teacher, is good at lots of sports.
7 The swimming pool where I go at the weekend is great.

5a Students write short, simple sentences with information about people, places, things, activities and events in the book. Draw students' attention to the example sentences.

5b SPEAKING Students read their sentences to their partner. He/She adds extra information to the sentences using non-defining relative clauses.

Refer students to the Grammar reference on page 94 if necessary.

Assign students page 62 in their Workbook or the relevant sections of the Online Workbook.

Developing speaking p92

Preparing and taking part in a debate

>>> FAST TRACK

Ask students to make the list in exercise 1 at home to compare in pairs in class.

WARMER

Write the names of three or four famous people on the board that students are likely to know. Ask students to work in pairs and write anything positive or negative they know about each of them. Ask students if each of the celebrities are people that young people want to be like or not.

1 SPEAKING In pairs, students read the definition of *role model* and make a list of people who they think are good role models for young people. Tell students that these people don't necessarily have to be celebrities. Compare ideas in open class.

2 SPEAKING Students read the statement and say whether they agree or disagree, giving their reasons why.

3 LISTENING ▶ 42 Play the track for students to listen to a girl and boy discussing the statement in exercise 2. Ask students whose opinion is closer to theirs and why. See p154 for the audioscript for this exercise.

4 ▶ 42 Students look at the expressions in the Speaking bank and write the word that comes after expressions for partially disagreeing. Play the track again if necessary.

Answer

but

5 Students prepare six sentences about sport or sports stars. Tell students they don't have to agree with the statements. Draw their attention to the example sentences.

6 SPEAKING In small groups, students listen to each other's statements and give their honest opinions using expressions from the Speaking bank.

PRACTICE MAKES PERFECT

7a SPEAKING Students read the statement. Choose half of the class to agree and half to disagree. Students prepare a list of points to support their opinion. For students who are less confident, photocopy the model arguments opposite for ideas.

Model arguments

Agree

- Being a footballer is not very demanding and therefore the job is overpaid.
- Football is entertainment. It doesn't contribute to society like teaching, or medicine – but footballers are paid more than the people in these professions.
- Top footballers get lots of freebies and sponsors – they don't need that much money.

Disagree

- Not all footballers are paid enormous sums of money. Only the really top players are and they have to play really well.
- Footballers have to train for hours to be good and be able to win. They deserve the money.
- Footballers can't play for many years, but when they play it puts a lot of stress on their bodies – they can suffer dangerous injuries.

7b Students have a class debate using expressions from the Speaking bank.

7c Students have a vote to see what the class really thinks about the statement.

✚ EXTRA ACTIVITY

Students write a short text using their notes answering the question: 'Are top footballers paid too much?'

HOMEWORK

Assign students page 63 in their Workbook or the relevant sections of the Online Workbook.

Developing writing p93

Writing a magazine article about sport

>>> FAST TRACK

You could set the writing task in exercise 6 as homework.

WARMER

In pairs, students discuss what types of magazines there are and what types of article might be in each of them.

1 In pairs, students read the announcement and discuss their answers to the questions.

2 READING Students read the article and say whether it included their answers from exercise 1. Ask fast finishers to write two or three sentences to say whether they agree or disagree with the author's opinion.

3a Students complete the article with the words in the box.

Answers

a Personally,   **b** convinced   **c** see   **d** view   **e** far

3b Students add the completed expressions from exercise 3a to the Writing bank.

Answers

Personally, I think

I'm convinced that

As I see it

My view is (that)/It is my view (that)

As far as I'm concerned

4   Students match the paragraphs with the descriptions of the content.

Answers

Paragraph 1 b   **Paragraph 2** a   **Paragraph 3** d
Paragraph 4 c

5   With a partner, students read the article again and answer the questions. Nominate pairs to give their answers.

Suggested answers

1 By asking questions.

2 By encouraging the reader to try some sports.

PRACTICE MAKES PERFECT

6   Students look at the announcement and write their article, using the information in exercise 4 and expressions from the Writing bank. Refer students to the Writing bank on page 151.

Model article

My favourite sport

Do you enjoy being outside in the open air, and do you love being part of a team? Would you like to increase your fitness levels? If so, I'd like to tell you something about my favourite sport, and encourage you to try it out.

I play rugby for a local rugby club. Rugby is a sport that is played all over the world, in fact one of the most famous teams, the All Blacks, comes from New Zealand. My team is the best in the area. We train two evenings a week, and usually play a match against teams from all over the country on Sunday. I love the team spirit in my rugby club, and I enjoy all aspects of the sport.

In my opinion, rugby is a sport that you can play at any age, and there are teams for both boys and girls. You don't have to be big or strong to play rugby, but you have to be a fast runner and a competitive player. As far as I'm concerned, rugby is a game which is both exciting to play and thrilling to watch. Many people think rugby is a dangerous sport, because it involves a lot of physical contact, unlike football or basketball, for example. Personally, I have never been hurt playing rugby and you can avoid injury if you are careful and learn the rules of the game.

In conclusion, I would encourage you to watch a rugby match live or on TV and see if you think you would enjoy being part of your local rugby team. If there isn't a team near you, why not start your own rugby team? You can get together with some friends and practise playing rugby in a park or at school. If you can't find a coach, you can download the rules of the game from the Internet. Don't forget the oval ball!

✚ EXTRA ACTIVITY

Students review their article (or their partner's article), giving themselves a grade from 1–5 according to these criteria related to paragraph organisation and the text as a whole:

- Do they get the reader's attention?
- Do they give reasons for their favourite sport?
- Do they give an overall opinion?
- Is there a conclusion?

HOMEWORK

Assign students page 64 in their Workbook or the relevant sections of the Online Workbook.

Language checkpoint: Unit 7

>>> **FAST TRACK**

Students read the Grammar reference and Vocabulary sections on page 94 before completing the revision exercises on the following page.

Grammar revision p95

Defining relative clauses

1 Students complete the sentences. If it is possible to have no word, students put –.

Answers

1 – **2** whose **3** who **4** when **5** – **6** where

Non-defining relative clauses

2 Students decide if the sentences are correct or not. If they are incorrect, students correct them.

Answers

1 The driver, whose car wasn't very fast, never won a race.
2 This sport, which was invented two years ago, is becoming very popular.
3 correct
4 That house, which I lived in when I was small, now belongs to my uncle.
5 correct
6 My neighbours, who are really nice, have got a big garden.

Defining and non-defining relative clauses

3 Students write two sentences for each of these things, people, times or places. One must contain a defining relative clause and the other a non-defining relative clause.

Vocabulary revision p95

SPORTS AND SPORTS VENUES

1 Students write the name of one sport they can play or do at each venue.

Suggested answers

1 golf **2** tennis **3** gymnastics **4** football
5 ice hockey **6** snowboarding **7** athletics

SPORTS EQUIPMENT AND SCORES

2 Students write the words.

Answers

1 bat **2** boots **3** goggles **4** club **5** draw **6** beat
7 nil

PHRASAL VERBS CONNECTED WITH SPORTS

3 Students match the parts to make phrasal verbs and then match them to their meaning.

Answers

1 warm up – c **2** knock out – b **3** join in – a
4 give in – d **5** go for – f **6** take up – e

HOMEWORK

Assign students page 65 in their Workbook or the relevant sections of the Online Workbook.

8 Smart art

KEY LEARNING OUTCOMES

Students will be able to:

- report what people have said, asked or commanded using reported speech
- discuss art, theatre and music
- understand written and spoken texts about art
- describe past events and explain what order they happened in
- write a simple film review

UNIT OVERVIEW

Vocabulary
Art, theatre, music
Artists

Reading
Extreme art!
CRITICAL THINKING Discussing whether knowing about an artist's life affects how their work is received

Grammar in context
Reported speech – statements

Developing vocabulary
Adjectives ending in -*ing* and -*ed*
PRONUNCIATION -*ed* adjectives

Life skills
Art and culture:
Appreciating art

Listening
An artwork

Grammar in context
Reported speech – questions and commands

Developing speaking
Describing a past event

Developing writing
A film review

✓

Exam success
Speaking: Describing past events
Writing: Following the instructions

DIGITAL OVERVIEW

Presentation Kit
- ▶ Flipped classroom video unit 8: Reported speech – questions
- ▶ Life skills video unit 8: Appreciating art
- ▶ [v] Vocabulary tool: Artists
- ▶ Interactive versions of Student's Book activities
- ▶ Integrated audio and answer key for all activities
- ▶ Workbook pages with answer key

Teacher's Resource Centre
- ▶ Flipped classroom video Unit 8: Reported speech – questions
- ▶ Life skills video Unit 8: Appreciating art
- ▶ Grammar communication activity Unit 8: Friends
- ▶ Worksheets for this unit, including:
  - Grammar Practice worksheet Unit 8
  - Flipped classroom video worksheet Unit 8: Reported speech – questions
  - Literature worksheet Units 7 and 8
  - Culture worksheet Unit 8
  - Life skills video worksheet Unit 8
  - Everyday English worksheet Unit 8

Student's App
Gateway 2nd Edition wordlist for the award-winning Sounds App (available for download)

✓ TESTING AND ASSESSMENT

Resources for exam preparation and measuring student progress

- ▶ Test Generator Units 1–8
- ▶ Printable test Unit 8
- ▶ Gateway to exams Units 7 and 8 (end of Unit 8)

Vocabulary p96

Talking about art, the theatre, music and artists

>>> FAST TRACK

Students could prepare exercise 2 at home, using their Macmillan Online Dictionary, and compare their answers in pairs in class.

WARMER

In pairs, students discuss the meaning of the unit title *Smart art* and discuss what they think the unit is going to be about. Tell students that *smart* can mean the opposite of *casual*, but it can also mean 'intelligent'.

Art, theatre, music

1 In pairs, students use the words in the box to talk about the photo.

2 Students read the sentences and check they understand the words in red. If necessary, they should look them up in a dictionary. Encourage them to use the context to deduce the meaning first. Ask fast finishers to write sentences using the new words.

3 Students put the words in exercises 1 and 2 in the correct column. Remind students that some words can go in more than one column.

Answers

Art: drawing, sketch, self-portrait, still life, abstract painting, exhibition, gallery, masterpieces, sculptures, landscapes

Theatre: lighting, performance, play, stage, scene, main character

Music: lighting, performance, stage, tune, lyrics, orchestra, concert

v Artists

4 In pairs, students complete the words in red with *-or*, *-er*, *-ian* or *-ist*.

Answers

1 actor   **2** musician   **3** conductor   **4** director
5 performer   **6** vocalist, guitarist, drummer   **7** composer
8 singer-songwriter   **9** artist, painter, sculptor

TEACHER DEVELOPMENT: LANGUAGE

Suffixes – jobs

Unfortunately, there are no rules for which suffix goes with which job. Some general guidelines can be given, for example many common jobs derived from a verb end in *-er*, whereas those in scientific or medical professions are often denoted with *-ist*, but there are many exceptions. Point out to students that the noun and verb forms relating to common occupations ending in *-er* and *-or* are closely linked: writers write, actors act, sculptors sculpt, conductors conduct, etc.

5 SPEAKING In pairs, students take it in turns to think of a famous

person and their partner answers with the profession. Draw students' attention to the example dialogue.

6 LISTENING ▶ 43 Play the track for students to listen for the order in which they hear the people or things in the box. Students check their answers in pairs before you elicit answers from different students around the class. See p154 for the audioscript for this exercise.

Answers

1 an orchestra   **2** one musician (guitarist)
3 an audience (clapping)   **4** an actor performing
5 a conductor   **6** a band on stage   **7** a sculptor
8 a portrait painter   **9** the cast of a play
10 a composer

✚ EXTRA ACTIVITY

Students write definitions for three of the professions using a relative clause (e.g. *This is a person who pretends to be someone else. This is a person who helps a group of musicians.*, etc.). They then see if their partner can guess.

7 SPEAKING In pairs, students ask and answer the questions. Remind them to ask follow-up questions after each question to get more information. You may like to practise this in open pairs across the class before students continue in closed pairs.

✚ EXTRA ACTIVITY

Students research one of the famous people they talked about in exercise 5 and write a short text about his/her life and work.

HOMEWORK

Assign students page 66 in their Workbook or the relevant sections of the Online Workbook.

Reading p97

Reading for gist and specific information

>>> FAST TRACK

Students could read the articles and do the matching task in exercise 2 at home in preparation for completing exercise 3 in class with a partner.

WARMER

Write the questions below on the board. Students ask and answer the questions in pairs. Elicit answers from different students around the class.
Can you draw pictures well?
Do you like paintings?
Do you prefer art, music or the theatre?

1 In pairs, students look at the photos and take it in turns to describe what they can see. Elicit suggestions from different students around the class.

2 READING Students read the three articles and match two of them with the photos in exercise 1.

Answers
Article 1 – photo 2
Article 3 – photo 1

3 Students think of a suitable photo to illustrate the remaining article.

4 Students read the articles in more detail and choose the best answers.

Answers
1 b **2** b **3** c **4** a **5** a **6** b

5 CRITICAL THINKING **Ask students to read the question and think of their own answers before sharing their ideas with the class.**

6 Students find the underlined words in the text and guess their meaning from the context. Elicit guesses from students around the class and then ask students to check their answers in the dictionary.

Answers
fascinating = extremely interesting, makes you want to know more
blends into – becomes a part of something so that it doesn't show
passers-by = people walking past in the street
airtight = does not allow air in or out
gigs = live concerts usually with a band playing
accurate = with the correct information and detail

7 SPEAKING **What about *you*?** In pairs or small groups, students discuss which articles they enjoyed reading most and why.

HOMEWORK

Assign students page 67 in their Workbook or the relevant sections of the Online Workbook.

Grammar in context pp98–99

Using reported statements

⟫ FAST TRACK

You could ask students to do exercise 1a before class and check their answers in pairs.

Test before you teach
Write the following direct statement on the board and ask students to relay what Pierre said using reported speech *Pierre: 'I like modern art.'* Point out the difference between quoted speech – when we keep the speaker's exact words and use quotation marks, and reported speech where we express the idea by changing the tense, pronouns, etc. If students seem very familiar with reported speech, you could choose to quickly move through the initial exercises in open class.

Answer
Pierre said he liked modern art.

1a Students match the sentences in reported and direct speech.

Answers
1 c **2** g **3** b **4** d **5** a **6** e **7** f

1b Students choose the correct alternative.

Answers
1 Pronouns **2** change **3** don't need **4** need
5 don't always need

TEACHER DEVELOPMENT: LANGUAGE

Reported speech
When we use reported speech, we have to take into account how circumstances have changed since the speaker originally spoke the words. For instance, we may now be reporting what was said from the point of view of a different time or place, or the person reporting the speech may be different from the original speaker. This will affect our choice of pronouns or adverbials of time and place. The tense of the verb changes when they go into reported speech, usually going one tense 'back' and pronouns and possessive adjectives often have to change, depending on who says what.

- Remind students that if the statement is a general statement about things which are still true and will be true, the tense of the verb in the second clause of the statement usually stays the same, e.g. *He said that every holiday he usually visits several art museums.*
- Generally speaking, the past simple and continuous don't always need to be changed if there is a time context which makes everything clear.
- The most common verbs used to report statements are *say* and *tell*. When *tell* is used in reported speech, it is always followed by a noun or a pronoun indicating the person spoken to, e.g. *Jane said (that) we were going to the cinema on Saturday. Jane told us (that) we were going to the cinema on Saturday.*
- Other reported speech verbs commonly used are: *add, admit, claim, declare, explain, indicate, mention, observe, point out, state, reply,* etc.

2 Students complete the table with the tense change, in reported speech.

Answers
2 present continuous – past continuous
3 present perfect – past perfect
4 past simple – past perfect
5 *will – would*
6 *can – could*
7 *may – might*
8 *must/have to – had to*

✛✛ EXTRA ACTIVITY

To give students further practice you could drill a simple sentence and ask a student to report it, e.g. *'I like chocolate.'* She said she liked chocolate. Repeat this going around the class.

3 Students complete the table.

Answers
1 that **2** here **3** today **4** the day before
5 tomorrow **6** that night
7 the following (week/month/year)
8 the previous (week/month/year)
9 a (week/month/year) ago

4 Students choose the correct alternative.

Answers
1 – **2** reporters **3** told **4** said **5** – **6** said
7 me

5 Students put the reported speech in exercise 4 into direct speech (i.e. what the people actually said), as in the example.

Answers
2 'I'm going to play a concert on the moon.'
3 'I've just finished a new picture of New York.'
4 'I hope you won't let the band out of the box.'
5 'The actress is making a new film next month.'
6 'The exhibition is going to be a great success.'
7 'They took/have taken away my paper.'

6 Students look at the statements made by famous people and write them in reported speech. Do the first one together as an example.

Answers
1 Banksy said that people either loved him, or they hated him, or they didn't really care.
2 James Dean said that being an actor was the loneliest thing in the world.
3 Sylvia Plath said she wrote only because there was a voice within her that would not be still.
4 Andy Warhol said that in the future everyone would be world-famous for 15 minutes.
5 Oscar Wilde said that he was so clever that sometimes he didn't understand a single word of what he was saying.
6 Vincent Van Gogh said the only time he felt alive was when he was painting.
7 Damien Hirst said he had wanted to be stopped, but no one would stop him.
8 Sir Ian McKellan said that he was only an actor and that all he had ever done was learn the lines and say them.

7a Students write down things people have said or told them yesterday or today, at home, at school or anywhere they like.

7b SPEAKING In pairs, students tell each other the things that people have said. Their partner guesses who said them. Draw their attention to the model dialogue.

+ EXTRA ACTIVITY

Students prepare three personal statements about art to tell their partner. Ask them to write two true statements and one false one, e.g. *I have painted a portrait of my mother. I have been to the Metropolitan Museum in New York. My favourite artist is Picasso.*

Students tell each other their statements. Students report back to their partner and tell him/her which statement they think is false, e.g. *You said you had painted a portrait of your mother. I think this is true. You said you had been to the Metropolitan Museum in New York. I think this is false. You said your favourite artist was Picasso. I think this is true.*

+ EXTRA ACTIVITY

For homework, ask students to find an interview (video or print) with their favourite celebrity, politician or sportsperson and report back to class what he/she said.

Refer students to the Grammar reference on page 106 if necessary.

HOMEWORK

Assign students page 68 in their Workbook or the relevant sections of the Online Workbook.

Developing vocabulary p99

Describing people and things using -ing and -ed adjectives

>>> FAST TRACK

Students could do exercise 2 as homework, using their Macmillan Online Dictionary if necessary. Ask them to compare their words in class before doing exercise 3a.

Adjectives ending in *-ing* and *-ed*

1 Students look at the words in red in the two sentences. Elicit which adjective describes how someone feels and which adjective describes why they felt this way.

Answers
1 *Amazing* (i.e. adjectives ending in *-ing*) describes why someone feels this way.
2 *Amazed* (i.e. adjectives ending in *-ed*) describes how someone feels.

TEACHER DEVELOPMENT: LANGUAGE

-ing and *-ed* adjectives

Point out to students that adjectives ending in *-ing* describe the effect that something has on your ideas and feelings. Like other adjectives, *-ing* and *-ed* adjectives can be used in front of a noun, modified by adverbials such as *quite*, *really* and *very*, and can be used in the comparative and superlative (e.g. *This is one of the most boring books I've ever read.*).

If students find this concept difficult, give them two more examples and ask them to compare the sentences and explain the difference in meaning.
My best friend is bored. (My best friend feels bored.)
My best friend is boring. (My best friend is a boring person.)
I am confused. (I don't understand something.)
I am confusing. (I will cause you to be confused.)

2 Students look at the adjectives and decide which ones are positive (+) or negative (−). Ask them to state which word could be either.

Answers

Positive (+): amazed, excited, fascinated, inspired, interested, relaxed, surprised (can also be negative)
Negative (−): bored, confused, depressed, disappointed, disgusted, embarrassed, frightened, tired, uninspired, worried

3a PRONUNCIATION Students look at the adjectives in exercise 2 again and decide in which adjectives we pronounce -*ed* as /ɪd/.

Answers

disappointed, disgusted, excited, fascinated, interested

3b ▶ 44 Play the track for students to listen and check their answers. Elicit which letter comes before -*ed* in all those adjectives. See p155 for the audioscript for this exercise.

Answer

the letter 't'

3c Drill the adjectives in exercise 2.

TEACHER DEVELOPMENT: PRONUNCIATION

-*ed* adjectives

Remind students that -*ed* adjectives follow the same pronunciation rules as regular past tense endings:
Voiced sound: if the stem ends with a vowel sound or the consonant *b, g, l, m, n, th, v* or *z*, we pronounce the -*ed* ending /d/, but if the stem ends with *d* or *t*, we pronounce the -*ed* ending /ɪd/.
Voiceless sound: if the stem ends with *f, p, k, s, sh, ch, x* or *h* we pronounce the -*ed* ending /t/.
A simple explanation of voiced consonants is that they use the voice. Ask students to test this by putting their finger on their throat. If they feel a vibration, the consonant is voiced. Voiceless consonants do not use the voice. They are hard sounds and there is no vibration in your throat, just a short explosion of air.
However, tell students that the difference between /d/ and /t/ is insignificant phonetically and that the important thing is to remember when to pronounce /ɪd/.

4 Students choose the correct alternative.

Answers

1 inspired   **2** disgusting   **3** tiring
4 confused   **5** boring   **6** embarrased
7 disappointing   **8** excited

5a Students prepare things to say about the topics. With a less confident class, you could brainstorm some ideas for each topic first.

5b SPEAKING In pairs, students discuss the topics with their partner. Remind them to ask questions to keep the conversation going. Elicit the question words and write them on the board as prompts: *who, what, why, where, when* and *how*.

5c Students tell the class what their partner told them about the topics. Draw students' attention to the example.

Write these words on the board and ask students to make notes with their opinions. In pairs or small groups, students compare their ideas and make full sentences.
art museums, Irish music, Picasso, a TV documentary about the history of art, going on a sculpture course

HOMEWORK

Assign students page 69 in their Workbook or the relevant sections of the Online Workbook.

Gateway to life skills pp100–101

Appreciating art
To look at ways to describe and appreciate art, and to analyse two works of art

⋙ FAST TRACK

You could ask students to do exercise 1 at home and write down their reactions, using their Macmillan Online Dictionary for reference if necessary. Students can compare their answers in class.

ⓘ BACKGROUND INFORMATION

Art appreciation may be considered a 'highbrow' topic for many students, but learning how to look at art and to discuss it and articulate their feelings can be interesting and enriching. This lesson looks at ways students can discuss their initial reactions to art, how to describe the more technical aspects of art and also the cultural context in which a piece of art was produced.

WARMER

In pairs, give students two minutes to think of as many artists and types of art as they can.
Elicit ideas from the class. Allow students time to read through the Life skills objectives and the Key concepts before starting the lesson.

1 In pairs, students look at the three works of art and say their first reactions to each one. With less confident students, help with relevant vocabulary first.

2 SPEAKING Ask students to read the questions in the text and then work with a partner and use the questions to discuss the paintings in exercise 1.

3 Students say which of the three works they prefer and why.

4 **LISTENING** ▶ 45 Tell students they are going to watch or listen to a video of three students talking about the paintings in exercise 1. Ask students to predict what words they might use. Play the video or track for students to match the speakers to the pictures. See p155 for the audioscript/videoscript for this exercise.

Answers

Olivia: painting 3   Jack: painting 2   Luke: painting 1

5 ▶ 45 Students read the reasons and choose the correct speaker. Play the video or track again if necessary.

Answers

1 Jack **2** Luke **3** Olivia **4** Jack **5** Olivia **6** Luke
7 Olivia **8** Jack **9** Luke

6a Ask students to read the statements and say if they agree or disagree. Encourage students to give their reasons.

✚ EXTRA ACTIVITY

Divide the class into two and hold a class debate about the use of art, with one side arguing that art is not important to society and the other defending art's role in society. Remind students that they may have to argue an opinion that is not necessarily their own.

6b SPEAKING Students compare their answers to exercise 6a in small groups. Ask students to add their own reasons.

LIFE TASK

Tell students they are going to turn their classroom into an art gallery.

- **Step 1**
  Students choose two paintings by two different artists and use the questions on page 101 to think about the paintings. Ask them to make notes.
- **Step 2**
  Students research the artists.
- **Step 3**
  Students use their notes to make a poster, including images of the paintings and their personal response to them.
- **Step 4**
  Display the posters around the classroom. Encourage students to walk around and give their opinions.

Listening p102

Listening for general understanding and specific information

WARMER

In pairs, ask students to discuss any controversial modern art that they have heard of. Elicit answers from the class.

1 Students look at the photo and say what they think it shows.

2 LISTENING ▶ 46 Play the track for students to listen to check their predictions in exercise 1. With a less confident class, pre-teach these words before students do the listening activity: *explode*: when something breaks out of its package or shell in a very violent way; *publicity*: the attention someone or something gets for something, usually an event; *rubber*: a natural material which is useful because it's often waterproof and highly elastic. It's often used in erasers and tyres for cars. See pp155–156 for the audioscript for this exercise.

3 ▶ 46 Students listen again and choose the best answers.

Answers

1 c **2** a **3** c **4** a **5** b **6** b

4 SPEAKING **What about *you*?** Students discuss what they think about the Giant Rubber Duck. Elicit suggestions from students around the class.

✚ EXTRA ACTIVITY

Write this statement on the board: *Modern art is rubbish.* You could bring in some pictures of modern art to help stimulate the debate. Divide the class into two groups (for and against) and give them five minutes to prepare their arguments. Open the debate by asking each side to present their arguments. At the end of the debate, ask students to vote if they agree or not with the statement by raising their hands.

Suggested arguments

Against: A lot of modern art is difficult to understand, although it really makes you think. The ideas are usually very intelligent.

For: Modern art often looks like the work of a child because it is so simple. Most of the time it's meaningless.

HOMEWORK

Assign students page 69 in their Workbook or the relevant sections of the Online Workbook.

Grammar in context pp102-103

Using reported speech, questions and commands

⟫⟫ FAST TRACK

You could set exercise 1 for homework, and check answers in class.

 Test before you teach: Flipped classroom
Set the Flipped classroom video and tasks for homework <u>before the lesson</u>. This will allow you to assess the needs of the students before the class. Students can then move on to the relevant grammar practice activities.

Reported speech – questions

1 Students look at the direct and reported questions and decide if the rules are true or false.

Answers

1 T **2** T **3** T **4** F **5** T

TEACHER DEVELOPMENT: LANGUAGE

Reported questions

- Point out to students that reported questions are not real questions and therefore do not need question marks.
- *Yes/No* questions in reported speech begin with the word *if* or *whether*. Information questions (*who, what*, etc.) in reported speech begin with the question word and also use the statement word order. The most common verb to report questions is *ask*.
- The intonation in reported speech questions usually falls at the end.

2 Students choose the correct alternative.

Answers

1 where he was **2** if **3** he had
4 he worked **5** had **6** he would do

3 Students complete the reported questions.

Answers

1 She asked him if he (had) liked the exhibition.
2 She wanted to know who his favourite artist was.
3 She asked him if he often visited art galleries.
4 She asked him if he would recommend the exhibition to other people.
5 She wanted to know why he had decided to see the exhibition.
6 She wanted to know if he was going to buy anything in the shop.
7 She asked him if he had ever bought an original painting.

4a SPEAKING Students write five questions to ask a partner about art, theatre or music.

4b Students take it in turns to ask and answer the questions.

4c Students change partners and tell their new partner the five questions their first partner asked them and their answers. Refer students to the example.

➕ EXTRA ACTIVITY

Students write the conversation they had in exercise 4c in reported speech. In pairs, students take it in turns to practise reading aloud the reported conversation with the correct intonation.

Reported speech – commands

5 Students look at the direct and reported commands and then answer the questions.

Answers

1 The most common verbs are *ask* and *tell*. *Ask* is a request and *tell* is an order.
2 We use *to* + infinitive in the reported command (i.e. the imperative changes to the infinitive).
3 *Not* comes before *to* + infinitive, i.e. *not to do*.

TEACHER DEVELOPMENT: LANGUAGE

Reported commands

- In reported commands, the pronouns and other words change in the same way as in reported statements.
- Verbs we often use in reported commands are *order, recommend, instruct, warn* and *command*, i.e. verbs that indicate commands. Remind students that *tell* is used to report commands and instructions and *ask* is used for more polite requests.
- In English we report commands, orders, requests and suggestions to other people in a five-part format:
  1 somebody (he, she, etc.)
  2 told/ordered/asked
  3 somebody else (her friend, me, etc.)
  4 to/not to
  5 infinitive (+ something)

6 Students report the commands.

Answers

1 The teacher told the class to pay attention.
2 The man at the entrance asked them to give him their tickets.
3 His mum told him not to shout.
4 The guide asked the visitors not to take photos inside the museum.
5 His dad told him not to come home late.
6 The art teacher told Jake to use a bigger brush.
7 The teacher asked the students to write a description of the painting for homework.

7 SPEAKING Divide the class into two teams. The teams take it in turns to try and remember things that teachers asked or told them to do this week. They score one point for each correct sentence. Draw students' attention to the example sentences.

EXTRA ACTIVITY

Students write the teachers' instructions as reported commands. In pairs, students take it in turns to practise reading aloud the reported commands.

Refer students to the Grammar reference on page 106 if necessary.

HOMEWORK

Assign students page 70 in their Workbook or the relevant sections of the Online Workbook.

Developing speaking p104

Describing a past event

>>> FAST TRACK

Students could do exercise 6 at home and compare their answers in class.

WARMER

Write the following groups of three words from the unit on the board. Students find the odd one out in each group and give reasons. Students could then invent another odd one out with vocabulary from the unit.

classic masterpiece portrait

sculpture painting still life

gallery museum gig

composer musician audience

Answers

A *classic* and a *masterpiece* are both important works of art, so *portrait* is the odd one out.

A *still life* is a kind of *painting*, so *sculpture* is the odd one out.

A *gallery* and a *museum* are both places, a *gig* is a musical event, so *gig* is the odd one out.

A *composer* and a *musician* both produce music, the *audience* listens, so *audience* is the odd one out.

1 SPEAKING In pairs, students discuss the questions.

2 SPEAKING In pairs, students look at the pictures and take it in turns to describe what they can see.

Suggested answers

a The picture shows a group of children at an art exhibition. There is a guide next to the paintings.

b A group of young people are in the audience in a theatre or cinema. They are clapping and looking happy.

c An orchestra with a conductor on a stage.

d A girl is taking a photo of two friends in Paris. The Eiffel Tower is behind her.

3 LISTENING ▶ 47 Play the track for students to listen to a teenager talking about a school trip that was special to her. Tell students to choose which pictures are similar to her experience. See p156 for the audioscript for this exercise.

Answers

Pictures b and c

4 ▶ 47 Students look at the diagram and make notes about what the teenager says. Play the track again if necessary.

Suggested answers

Where we went: to see a play in English with English teacher

What happened at first: the play was quite boring, but after about half an hour, two musicians came on stage

Something special that happened: went up on the stage to sing, everyone clapped and kept asking for more songs

How I felt and why: frightened because it was embarrassing; nervous then more relaxed; enjoyed myself

5 ▶ 47 Play the track again for students to tick the expressions in the Speaking bank that they hear.

Answers

At first (x 3), Next, Then, Later, Later on, After about half an hour, After a minute or two, Finally, In the end (x 2)

✓ EXAM SUCCESS Students discuss how they can prepare for a speaking exam in which they have to talk about a past event. Tell students to turn to page 146 to compare their ideas.

6 Individually, students think about a memorable school trip they went on. Students copy the diagram from exercise 4 and make notes in the boxes.

PRACTICE MAKES PERFECT

7a SPEAKING In pairs, students take it in turns to do the task. Tell students to ask questions to find out details and to help their partner continue talking. Let students look at one anothers' diagrams. Remind students to use the words and expressions from the Speaking bank to make the order of events clear. Monitor students, noting important errors and good use of language to go over in a short feedback slot at the end of this activity. For a less confident class, photocopy the model description below.

7b SPEAKING Students change partners and do the task again. They should try to improve on their first performance.

Model description of a past event

I remember a school trip when I was <u>in my first year at secondary school</u>. We went to <u>Paris</u> with <u>my class</u> and <u>our French teacher</u>. At first, <u>the trip was great</u>. The weather was fantastic and we did a lot of sightseeing – we visited <u>all the most important monuments in Paris</u>.

A few days later, we visited the Georges Pompidou Centre and we sat outside to have our lunch. We were <u>watching some street performers</u>. After about <u>half an hour</u>, I noticed that my school bag was missing. Then <u>I noticed that I couldn't see my jacket</u>. A few <u>seconds</u> later, <u>my friend said he couldn't find his jacket or bag</u>. <u>Somebody had stolen our things! We told the teacher and</u> in the end, <u>we went to the police station</u>. <u>We spent the rest of the day there</u>. Finally, we went <u>back to the hotel</u>. <u>The next day</u>, we went home. <u>I enjoyed the first part of the school trip, but I didn't like the last part!</u>

TEACHER DEVELOPMENT: CLASSROOM TIPS AND PLANNING

Reformulating

When students have practised the speaking task, they change partners and talk about the trip again. This is a good opportunity for them to think about what they could improve and to put their ideas into practice by reformulating their description. Monitor students the first time they describe their trip and give feedback on students' performance (correct important errors, praise students for good active listening techniques, use of intonation, organisation of ideas, etc.).

HOMEWORK

Assign students page 71 in their Workbook or the relevant sections of the Online Workbook.

Developing writing p105

Writing a film review

≫≫ FAST TRACK

You could ask students to do exercise 2 at home and check their answers at the start of the lesson. Alternatively, you could set the writing task in exercise 6 as homework. Allow students to read each other's reviews in the next lesson.

WARMER

Write the word *review* on the board and ask students where you usually see them (online, in newspapers, magazines, etc.). Ask students if they think they usually contain facts or opinion or a mixture of both. Have a show of hands to see how many students look at reviews before they go to see a film, or go to a restaurant or buy music, etc.

1 SPEAKING Students work in pairs and talk about the last film they saw.

2 READING Students read the film review and answer the questions.

Answers

The writer liked the plot, but generally he/she loved everything about the film – an inspiring film, with great characters and excellent actors.
The writer recommends the film to people who like emotional stories about characters you care for.

3 Students match the paragraphs with the descriptions of their content.

Answers

1 c **2** b **3** d **4** a

4 Students read the review again and answer the questions.

Answers

1 present simple tense **2** no **3** no **4** yes

5 Students put the headings in the correct place in the Writing bank. Check that students understand the words and expressions in the box.

Answers

1 b **2** c **3** a **4** d

PRACTICE MAKES PERFECT

6 Students look at the task and write their reviews using the Writing bank and the paragraph plan in exercise 3. For a less confident class, photocopy the model review on the next page and let students read through it before attempting the task. Refer students to the Writing bank on page 151.

✚ EXTRA ACTIVITY

In small groups, students read out their review without saying the name of the film. The other students have to guess which film it is and say whether or not they agree with the review.

✓ EXAM SUCCESS Ask students to think of their answer to the question, then turn to page 146 to compare their ideas.

Model review

The most important film of the year!
The Imitation Game is a 2014 film based on true events starring Benedict Cumberbatch and Keira Knightley. It tells the story of Alan Turing, a mathematician who ends up working at Bletchley Park, a top secret government location during the Second World War. He and a team of code-breakers race against time to break the German's Enigma code.
The plot is exciting as the team work so hard despite lots of obstacles and people not believing in them. It is also a little bit sad as Alan Turing had a lot of difficulties in his personal life both in his childhood and after the war. There are some funny parts to the film too and Keira Knightley is inspiring playing the role of Joan Clarke, one of the few female code-breakers at the time.
I really enjoyed this film, as the acting is excellent and it makes you think about real historical events and how they affected the world.
To sum up, this film is definitely worth seeing for people who like drama and history and also for people who like a bit of romance, too!

HOMEWORK

Assign students page 72 in their Workbook or the relevant sections of the Online Workbook.

Language checkpoint: Unit 8

>>> **FAST TRACK**

Students read the Grammar reference and Vocabulary sections on page 106 before completing the revision exercises on the following page.

Grammar revision p107

Reported speech – statements

1 Students rewrite the sentences in reported speech.

Answers

1 She said she was happy to be there that day.
2 She told me she was writing a play.
3 She said she had never written a play before.
4 She said that when she had finished she would choose the actors herself.
5 She told me she was inspired by a trip to California the previous year.
6 She said she might go to the US again the following year.
7 She said she had to go then because her manager was waiting for her.

Reported speech – questions

2 Students rewrite the reported questions in direct speech.

Answers

1 'What are you doing here?'
2 'When did you arrive?'
3 'Do you know what the answer is?'
4 'Have you ever written a poem?'
5 'What will you do with the money?'
6 'How many pages has the book got/does the book have?'
7 'Is that bag yours?'

Reported speech – commands

3 Students write the direct commands.

Answers

1 'Get out of the car!'
2 'Don't panic!'
3 'Do the exercise carefully!'
4 'Please don't sing that song!'
5 'Get ready!'
6 'Please don't interrupt me!'
7 'Give me the bag, please!'

Vocabulary revision p107

ARTISTS

1 Students complete the words to match the definitions.

Answers

1 conductor **2** drummer **3** singer-songwriter
4 composer **5** sculptor **6** vocalist

ART, THEATRE, MUSIC

2 Students complete the definitions.

Answers

1 the countryside
2 we sing
3 perform in a play or film
4 is drawn quickly in pencil
5 the people who watch a play or a concert
6 a person
7 actors or bands perform

ADJECTIVES ENDING IN -ING AND -ED

3 Students complete the sentences with the -ing or -ed form of the words given.

Answers

1 tired **2** embarrassing **3** confused
4 disappointing **5** surprised **6** disgusting

HOMEWORK

Assign students page 73 in their Workbook or the relevant sections of the Online Workbook.

Use of English p108

1 Students look at the photo and say what they think the sport is and what the rules are.

2a Students read the text and answer the questions in exercise 1. Remind them to ignore the gaps at this point.

Answers

The sport is Chess Boxing. The rules are: there is a round of chess, then boxing, then more chess and more boxing. The winner is the person who gets checkmate or knocks out their opponent first.

2b Students complete the text with the correct words.

Answers

a by **b** whose **c** who **d** is **e** the **f** out **g** where **h** and **i** is **j** up **k** them **l** to

3 SPEAKING **What about** *you*? Students ask and answer the questions about the sport in the text.

Listening p108

4 In pairs, students take it in turns to describe what they think the photo shows.

Suggested answers

The photo shows a woman running down a corridor. She is wearing running clothes (trainers and a tracksuit), but the place looks like a public building, perhaps a museum or art gallery.

5 LISTENING 48 Play the track for students to listen to two people at the scene of the photo and find out what is happening in the scene. See p156 for the audioscript for this exercise.

Answers

The two people are in an art gallery watching a work of art by the artist Martin Creed where runners run, as fast as possible, from one end of the gallery to the other.

6 ▶ 48 Play the track again for students to decide if the statements are true or false.

Answers

1 T **2** T **3** F **4** T **5** F **6** T **7** F **8** F

7 SPEAKING **What about** *you*? Students discuss what they think of this work of art.

Suggested answers

I think it gets people talking about what art is.
I think it's a publicity stunt for a sports clothes company.
I think it's a very interesting idea and you are free to think what you want.

Speaking p109

8 Students look at the three sentences and say which tense is used in each one and why.

Answers

1 Past continuous – describes a past action in progress.
2 Past perfect – expresses an action in the past before another action in the past.
3 Past simple – expresses the idea that an action started and finished at a specific time in the past.

9 Students look at the task. Individually, students prepare what they are going to say.

10 SPEAKING In pairs, students take it in turns to do the task. Less confident students may want to use the model answer below before preparing their own.

Model answer

The best match I've ever seen was Brazil vs Germany in the football World Cup. It was in 2014 in Brazil because they were the hosts of the World Cup. It was the semifinal and at first, no one knew who was going to win as they are both amazing teams. But then Germany scored seven goals. The atmosphere had been tense, but then everyone became shocked. In the end, Brazil scored one goal, but it wasn't enough to go to the final!

Writing p109

> **TIP FOR WRITING EXAMS**

Elicit why it is important to read instructions carefully. Ask students to read the tip and look at Exam success on page 146 for more ideas.

11 SPEAKING Students read the announcement and work with a partner to discuss their answers to the questions.

12 Students read the task and write an article for next month's magazine. Remind them to include all the necessary information within the word count. Photocopy the model article below for less confident students.

Model article

Are you a regular cinema-goer or a film geek? Or are you someone who only goes once a year?

I'm somewhere in the middle. I go to the cinema about once or twice a month with my brother and usually watch one film a week at home on DVD or online. I prefer going to the cinema because the screen is so big and the sound is better quality. However, it is more comfortable and cheaper to watch films at home.

I like lots of different types of films, from comedy to action. I like films that make me think after the film has finished. I don't really like modern romantic films – they're so unrealistic!

HOMEWORK

Assign students pages 74–75 in their Workbook or the relevant sections of the Online Workbook.

1 Ask students to read the 'can do' statements and mark from 1–4 how well they can do these things in English.

2 Ask students to look at their marks and decide what they think they need to do to improve. Elicit other suggestions.

9 Future leaders

KEY LEARNING OUTCOMES

CEF

Students will be able to:

- make speculations and deductions in the present and past using modal verbs
- name words connected with state and politics
- understand written and spoken texts about politics and society
- describe photos and speculate or make deductions about them
- write a simple story using different narrative tenses

UNIT OVERVIEW

Vocabulary	Nations State and politics
Reading	Queen Elizabeth I and the boy from Bisley CRITICAL THINKING Discussing conspiracy theories
Grammar in context	Modal verbs of speculation and deduction – present and past PRONUNCIATION Strong and weak forms of *have*
Developing vocabulary	Adjective suffixes
Life skills	Citizenship: Considering social issues
Listening	An important event
Grammar in context	Third conditional
Developing speaking	Describing photos – 2
Developing writing	A story
✓ **Exam success**	Use of English: Word formation cloze activities Listening: Completing notes

DIGITAL OVERVIEW

Presentation Kit

- ▶ Flipped classroom video unit 9: Third conditional
- ▶ Life skills video unit 9: Considering social issues
- ▶ [V] **Vocabulary tool:** Nations
- ▶ Interactive versions of Student's Book activities
- ▶ Integrated audio and answer key for all activities
- ▶ Workbook pages with answer key

Teacher's Resource Centre [TRC]

- ▶ Flipped classroom video Unit 9: Third conditional
- ▶ Life skills video Unit 9: Considering social issues
- ▶ Grammar communication activity Unit 9: Six things
- ▶ Worksheets for this unit, including:
  - Grammar Practice worksheet Unit 9
  - Flipped classroom video worksheet Unit 9: Third conditional
  - Literature worksheet Units 9 and 10
  - Culture worksheet Unit 9
  - Life skills video worksheet Unit 9
  - Everyday English worksheet Unit 9

Student's App
Gateway 2nd Edition wordlist for the award-winning Sounds App (available for download)

TESTING AND ASSESSMENT

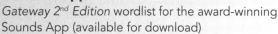

Resources for exam preparation and measuring student progress

- ▶ Test Generator Units 1–9
- ▶ Printable tests Unit 9 and Review (Units 7–9)
- ▶ Gateway to exams Units 9 and 10 (end of Unit 10)

Vocabulary p110

Talking about nations, states and politics

>>> FAST TRACK

You could ask students to do exercise 1 at home so that less confident students can take the necessary time to look up the vocabulary in the Macmillan Online Dictionary.

WARMER

In pairs, students discuss the meaning of the unit title *Future leaders* and what they think the unit is going to be about. Teach students the verb *to lead* if they are struggling, so they can then deduce the meaning of *leader*. Give students three minutes to work in pairs and come up with as many current leaders of countries, of important businesses, or in other fields of endeavour, as they can.

v Nations

1 In pairs, students match the words to the photos of the United Kingdom. Provide dictionaries if necessary.

Answers

a currency b flag c royal family
d capital city e national anthem
f prime minister/president

2 SPEAKING In pairs, students talk about the US using the words from exercise 1. Draw students' attention to the examples.

Suggested answers

The capital city of the US is Washington DC (though each state also has its own capital).
The currency of the United States is the dollar.
The flag of the United States is red, white and blue.
The US national anthem is 'The Star-Spangled Banner'.
The president in 2015 was Barack Obama.

State and politics

3 Students match the types of government with the explanations.

Answers

1 republic 2 democracy 3 monarchy
4 constitutional monarchy

+ EXTRA ACTIVITY

Students mark in the primary stress on the words in exercise 3 and practise saying the words with the correct pronunciation.
1 /rɪˈpʌblɪk/ 2 /dɪˈmɒkrəsi/ 3 /ˈmɒnəki/
4 /ˌkɒnstɪˈtuʃənl ˈmɒnəki/

4 In pairs, students think of a country, in the present or past, for each type of government.

Suggested answers

democracy – Sweden
republic – Republic of Ireland
monarchy – Saudi Arabia
constitutional monarchy – The United Kingdom

5 Students read the text about the United Kingdom and match the underlined words with the definitions.

Answers

1 general elections 2 member 3 political parties
4 run 5 laws 6 policies 7 vote 8 campaigns

6 SPEAKING In pairs, students discuss the questions. With a less confident class, students write down their answers before they do this as a speaking activity. You may like to practise this in open pairs across the class before students continue in closed pairs.

+ EXTRA ACTIVITY

Students write a short description of a country of their choice using the vocabulary from exercises 1, 3 and 5. They could read out their texts in small groups at the beginning of the next class, without saying the name of the country. Other students guess the name of the country.

HOMEWORK

Assign students page 76 in their Workbook or the relevant sections of the Online Workbook.

Reading p111

Reading for general understanding and specific information

>>> FAST TRACK

Students could complete exercises 2 and 3 at home, using their Macmillan Online Dictionary if necessary.

WARMER

Play *Hot Seat* to start the class. Divide the class into two teams, A and B. A volunteer from Team A sits with their back to the board. Write a word from the previous lesson on the board. Team A defines the word for the volunteer student to guess in one minute. After one minute, it is Team B's turn to define words. The team that describes the most words in one minute wins the round.

1 In pairs, students ask and answer the questions. Nominate students to give their answers.

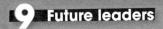

ℹ CULTURAL INFORMATION

Queen Elizabeth I was the daughter of Anne Boleyn and Henry VIII. She ruled from 1558–1603 and her reign was known as the Elizabethan era, where playwrights such as Shakespeare and explorers such as Sir Francis Drake flourished. She was, on the whole, a popular monarch with an almost cult-like following in the 16th century, and her 45-year reign became known as a 'golden period' in English history. Despite pressure, she remained unmarried and preferred to say she was 'married to her country'.

2 READING Students read the text and explain the title.

Answers

There is a conspiracy theory that Elizabeth I was really a boy from the village of Bisley. The real Elizabeth died unexpectedly and they were too afraid to tell the king so they used the boy from Bisley to pretend to be her.

3 Students read the text again and answer the questions. Check that less confident students understand the words *significant, relationship* and *discovery*. Encourage students to write full sentences for their answers.

Suggested answers

1 Elizabeth I was born in 1533 and died in 1603. She reigned for almost fifty years. During the time her government was stable and England became an international power.
2 So that they formed links with other nations.
3 Elizabeth was staying at a house called Over Court in Bisley to avoid the plague.
4 Henry did not visit his daughter often and Elizabeth was quiet and uncomfortable in front of her father.
5 A boy from the village of Bisley took Elizabeth's place because Elizabeth had died after falling ill. There was only one boy with red hair, so they dressed him up as a girl and lied.
6 Because perhaps they were literally true.
7 She always wore a lot of make-up and wigs.
8 A coffin was found in Bisley. Inside it there was a young girl dressed in very fine clothes. Nobody in the village could have had such fine clothes, only a princess.

⁺⁺ EXTRA ACTIVITY

Students write another reading comprehension question to test their partner or the class (e.g. *Do historians believe the theory?*).

4 ⚙ CRITICAL THINKING Students think of their own response to the questions then compare their ideas with the class.

Suggested answers

Conspiracy theories exist to explain strange behaviour. There are lots of conspiracy theories because they are exciting and interesting and in history we never really know the whole truth.

5 Students look at the underlined words in the text, and guess their meaning before checking in a dictionary. Fast finishers can look up the meanings to other words they don't know and teach the rest of the class when they've finished the task.

Answers

reigned = ruled/was the leader of the country in the position of queen or king
stable = stays the same and doesn't change
the plague: a dangerous illness like the flu which is very catching
skin = the covering on your body
speech = important words said at an important moment
wigs = pretend hair, you put it on your head to cover baldness
coffin = wooden box for dead bodies that is used for burying the body

6 SPEAKING **What about *you*?** Students ask and answer the questions in pairs.

⁺⁺ EXTRA ACTIVITY

Students make a mind map of the vocabulary they have come across so far, related to the unit theme of history.

HOMEWORK

Assign students page 77 in their Workbook or the relevant sections of the Online Workbook.

Grammar in context pp112–113

Using modal verbs of speculation and deduction in the present and past tense

⟩⟩⟩ FAST TRACK

Using their Macmillan Online Dictionary, students could do exercise 1 at home and compare the spelling and pronunciation in the next lesson.

Test before you teach

Choose ten small objects at home and put each one in a paper bag numbered from one to ten. The items should not be visible. Pass the bags round the classroom for students to put their hands in and guess what the objects are. Some should be easy – a pen, some keys – but others should be more difficult to identify correctly, e.g. a CD that could be confused with a DVD. Elicit sentences using modal verbs in the present, e.g. *It could/may/might/must be a CD, it can't be a credit card*, etc.

Modal verbs of speculation and deduction – present

1 Students look at the sentences and the verbs in blue and answer the questions. Check answers and ask students to compare the spelling of the words in blue with the way they are pronounced. In particular draw attention to the silent *gh* in *might* and *l* in *could*.

Answers

a must **b** can't **c** might/may/could
d infinitive without *to*

Modal verbs of speculation and deduction – present

Modal verbs of speculation and deduction are used to express our degree of certainty about the present.

- To speculate about a present situation/state, use modal verb + infinitive, e.g. *He must be the king.*
- To speculate about an ongoing action, use modal verb + *be* + *-ing*, e.g. *He might be waiting inside the shop.*
- If the situation is 90% impossible, use *can't.*
- If the situation is 50% possible, use *might, may, could.*
- If the situation is 90% (im)possible/(un)likely, use *must, can't, couldn't.*

Remind students that modal verbs do not take *s* in the third person present tense.

✚ EXTRA ACTIVITY

To focus on form and meaning, set up a drill as follows. Write on the board: *not true, possible* and *true.* Say different phrases and point to the words on the board. Students say the sentence with the appropriate modal verb, e.g.
He is Russian. (point to *not true*) = *He can't be Russian.*

2 Students choose the correct alternative.

Answers

Country 1
1 can't **2** might **3** must
Country 2
1 could **2** may **3** must

3 Students make deductions about these flags using *may, might, must* and *can't.*

Answers

Flag 1
1 may/might **2** can't **3** must
Flag 2
1 can't **2** may/might/could , may/might/could **3** must

✚ EXTRA ACTIVITY

Students write three sentences to give clues about a country or flag of their choice. Tell them to model their sentences on the ones in exercises 2 and 3. They could read out their sentences for other students to guess the flag or country.

4 SPEAKING In pairs, students discuss where the place is in the photo. Remind them to use *can't, may, might, could, must* to make speculations and deductions. Draw students' attention to the example.

✚ EXTRA ACTIVITY

Bring into class more photos of different places around the world. Number them and pass them round the classroom. In pairs, students write down where they think the places are using modal verbs of speculation and deduction. Collect in the photos and elicit sentences about each photo. Each grammatically correct sentence wins a point. Sentences which identify the places score five points. The pair with the most points wins the game.

Modal verbs of speculation and deduction – past

5 Students look at the sentences and answer the questions.

Answers

a must **b** can't/couldn't **c** may/might/could
d past participle

Modal verbs of speculation and deduction – past

Modal verbs of speculation and deduction + *have* + past participle are used to express a degree of certainty about a past action or situation.

If we are guessing about a situation/state in the past: modal verb + *have* + past participle

If we are guessing about an ongoing action in the past: modal verb + *have* + *been* + *-ing*

6a PRONUNCIATION ▶ 49 Play the track for students to listen to the two sentences and decide if we pronounce *have* the same way in both sentences. See p156 for the audioscript for this exercise.

Answers

1 strong form of *have*: /hæv/
2 weak form of *have*: /əv/

6b ▶ 50 Play the track for students to note down if they hear the strong form (/hæv/) or weak form (/əv/). See p156 for the audioscript for this exercise.

Answer

the weak form

6c ▶ 50 Play the track again for students to listen and repeat the sentences.

TEACHER DEVELOPMENT: PRONUNCIATION

Modal verbs of speculation: strong and weak forms

Function words have 'strong' and 'weak' forms depending on whether they are stressed or not. Point out to students that it is not necessary to pronounce the weak forms to be understood, but it will help them understand English much better if they learn the strong and weak forms of the most common words. Students should know that if they want to improve their accent, it's important to use the weak form of function words because it will help them speak faster and make their speech sound more natural.

The difference between the strong and weak forms is that vowel sounds will be much shorter and less distinct in the weak form. Students cannot see this difference in the spelling so this is a good opportunity to point out the value of phonetic transcription as a key to English pronunciation.

In the negative past modal form, *have* is often reduced to *'ve* and connected to *not*, e.g. *He might not've known.* This only occurs in the spoken form; we never write it this way.

7 Students complete the sentences with past modals of speculation and deduction and the verbs given.

Answers

1 may/might have existed   **2** must have been
3 can't have used   **4** must have liked
5 can't have disappeared   **6** could/may/might have lived
7 must have believed
8 may/might/could have taken, may/might/could have received

✚ EXTRA ACTIVITY

Describe a situation which is open to speculation and deduction and elicit some possible conclusions, e.g.
When I walked into my house, the furniture was broken and there were papers all over the floor.
No students came to class this morning. The lights have gone out.

Then ask students to work in pairs and write as many sentences as possible about what may/might/could have happened, using a modal verb + *have* + past participle.

Refer students to the Grammar reference on page 120 if necessary.

HOMEWORK

Assign students page 78 in their Workbook or the relevant sections of the Online Workbook.

Developing vocabulary p113 (Aa) (Bb)

Talking about people, places and things using adjectives and suffixes

⟫⟫ FAST TRACK

Students could do exercise 2 as homework, using a dictionary if necessary. Ask them to compare their answers in class.

Adjective suffixes

1 Students write the words in two columns: noun or adjective.

Answers

Nouns: aristocracy, care, comfort, fame, luck, science, terror
Adjectives: aristocratic, careful, careless, comfortable, famous, lucky, scientific, terrible, uncomfortable

2 For each adjective, students underline the suffix which makes it an adjective, as in the example. Remind students that a suffix is a letter or group of letters added to the end of a word to make another word. A good knowledge of English prefixes and suffixes will help students develop vocabulary. Point out that *uncomfortable* is an example of a word that has both a prefix and a suffix added to the root (*comfort*).

Answers

care<u>ful</u>, care<u>less</u>, comfort<u>able</u>, fam<u>ous</u>, luck<u>y</u>, scient<u>ific</u>, terr<u>ible</u>, uncomfort<u>able</u>

3 Students turn the words into adjectives and write them in the correct column. Remind them to be careful to make any necessary changes in spelling. Students could check the words in their dictionaries.

Answers

-y: hungry
-able: enjoyable
-ible: sensible
-ful: helpful, useful
-less: helpless, senseless, useless
-al: natural, official
-ous: dangerous, mysterious

✓ EXAM SUCCESS
Students discuss how they know if they need to add a suffix, a prefix or both to the word given in a word formation cloze activity. Tell them to turn to page 146 and compare their answers.

4 Students read the text and use the words given in capitals to form a word that fits in the gap. You could do the first one together as an example.

Answers

a official   **b** mysterious   **c** terrible/terrifying
d uncomfortable   **e** careful   **f** dangerous   **g** unlucky
h sensible

✚ EXTRA ACTIVITY

Students think of more adjectives to write under each suffix in exercise 3, using their dictionary to check their words. They underline the primary stress in each word and practise the pronunciation.

Gateway to life skills pp114–115

Considering social issues

To learn about the youth parliament and the social issues that affect young people

>>> FAST TRACK

You could ask students to do exercise 1 at home and compare their answers in pairs during the next lesson.

ℹ BACKGROUND INFORMATION

Citizenship covers being part of a society, or a certain group within a society. Focusing on citizenship allows students to analyse society, and what their part in it is. Being able to see their importance as individuals in a wider system will encourage students to think of the positive impact they can have on society. The focus of this lesson is the UK Youth Parliament, what they do and what they hope to achieve. Students look at a variety of issues that young people can address, before putting together their own manifesto for an issue they consider to be important.

WARMER

Ask students to work in pairs and think of three things they would change in their town or city. Elicit ideas from students. Ask them to think of how they would go about changing these things. Do they think it would be easy to make these changes or difficult? Allow students time to read through the Life skills objectives and the Key concepts before starting the lesson.

1 In pairs, students look at the advert and answer the questions. Nominate students to give their answers.

Answers

1 a political party for young people
2 people between 11 and 18 who are interested in issues that affect society.

2 **READING** Students read the information in the advert and answer the questions.

Answers

1 The UK Youth Parliament provides opportunities for young people to bring about social change.
2 MYPs are members of the Youth Parliament and they are elected every year. They organise different events and projects and they run campaigns.

✚ EXTRA ACTIVITY

Ask students to close their books and write the following numbers from the text on the board: *11–18; 600; one million; 850,000; zero.* Ask students to work in pairs and see if they can remember what each of the numbers refers to.

Answers

11–18: the age of UK Youth Parliament members
600: the number of representatives in the UK Youth Parliament
one million: the number of people who have voted in UK Youth Parliament elections in the last two years
850,000: the number of people who voted to choose the topics for campaign
zero: tolerance to bullying in schools

3 Ask students to read the text again and say if the sentences are true or false. Fast finishers can correct the false sentences.

Answers

1 T 2 T 3 F 4 F 5 F 6 T 7 F

4  **51** Tell students they are going to watch or listen to a video of four teenagers explaining why they are standing for election. Students write which issue from the text in exercise 2 each speaker talks about. See pp156–157 for the audioscript/videoscript for this exercise.

Answers

Olivia: letting 16-year-olds vote in general elections
Jack: bullying in schools
Luke: changing the school curriculum
Chloe: fighting youth unemployment

5 ▶ **51** Students watch or listen again and match sentences a–h with the speakers. Give students time to read through the sentences first.

Answers

Olivia: e, f **Jack:** b, d **Luke:** a, h **Chloe:** c, g

6a **SPEAKING** In pairs, students talk about the issues that appear at the end of the text in exercise 2 and grade them in importance from 1 to 5. You could add up the scores to have an idea of what the class thinks is important.

6b Students say what they think they can do about these issues. Help less confident students by giving an example, e.g. 'Give all young people a week of work experience, by allowing them to take time off school after important exams and having organised programmes in big companies for 16- to 17-year-olds.'

6c Students think of other issues that are important to young people and what positive action can be taken to solve them.

LIFE TASK

Tell students they are going to prepare a manifesto for an important issue to present to the class.

- *Step 1*

  Students decide what they think is the most important issue for people their age. Remind them to look back at their ideas in exercise 6c.

- *Step 2*

  Students prepare a short manifesto explaining the issue and what should be done.

- *Step 3*

  Students present their manifesto to the class. At the end of the presentation, students have a class vote to choose the best three manifestos.

Listening p116

Listening for specific detail

WARMER

Write *South Africa* on the board and give students two minutes to brainstorm in pairs all the things they associate with the country (e.g. *Nelson Mandela, Cape Town, wine, safaris, hot weather, rugby,* etc.).

1 In pairs, students look at the photo, describe it and answer the question. If they don't know the answer, tell them to guess.

Answers

1995 Rugby World Cup final; Nelson Mandela, the South African president, appeared at the match wearing a South African rugby top.

✓ EXAM SUCCESS Tell students they are going to do a gap completion activity and to think about how it can help them to read the notes before they listen. Then ask them to turn to page 146 to check their ideas.

2 **LISTENING** ⏵ 52 Play the track for students to listen to two people talking about the event in exercise 1 and complete the notes with one to three words or numbers. With a less confident class, pre-teach the words *prison* – somewhere a criminal goes when he/she has committed a crime; *slogan* – a short, memorable statement often used in advertising or political campaigning. See p157 for the audioscript for this exercise.

Answers

1 1995 **2** 27 years **3** white South Africans **4** England
5 One Country **6** new national anthem
7 the whole nation **8** ill **9** their hotel

3 **SPEAKING** **What about *you*?** Students talk about the film *Invictus* and give their opinion on it. If they haven't seen it, would they like to?

✚ EXTRA ACTIVITY

Ask students to research another important historical sports event and find out what happened and why it was so important. Students present their findings to the rest of the class.

TEACHER DEVELOPMENT: CLASSROOM TIPS AND PLANNING

Carrying out listening tasks (part 2)

- Always give students a clear purpose for listening to motivate them. For example, if students know they have to do a speaking exercise on the same topic as the listening, they will probably pay more attention.

- Make sure the context is clear (describe the situation and topic) and encourage students to predict content from key words in the questions, visual clues, etc.

- Give students time to read the questions before they listen and ask if there is any vocabulary they don't understand.

- With less able students, it is a good idea to play the listening in short sections. After each section, ask students to discuss what they have understood in pairs or groups. Discussion in pairs is motivating, makes listening activities less threatening and gives you more information about how much students have understood.

- If there is a difficult key phrase, pause the track and see if anyone can repeat it. Write the phrase on the board and then play that section again before continuing.

- After the task is complete, give students a copy of the audioscript and allow students to listen again. This helps to reduce anxiety and confirms that they have understood.

- After the listening, have a class discussion based on students' reaction to the text: *Have you had a similar experience? What would you do in this situation? Do you agree with the speaker? Would you like to do this?*

- For the European Language Portfolio dossier (see Unit 1, Teacher development box, *Portfolio assessment – learning diaries*) students could record the listening activities they have done in class on a self-evaluation sheet. Ask them to write the subject, date and evaluate their progress.

I understood the first time I listened.	1 2 3 4 5
I understood when we had finished listening.	1 2 3 4 5
I understood after listening with the audioscript.	1 2 3 4 5

HOMEWORK

Assign students page 79 in their Workbook or the relevant sections of the Online Workbook.

Grammar in context pp116–117

Using the third conditional

>>> **FAST TRACK**

You could ask students to complete exercise 1 for homework.

 Test before you teach: Flipped classroom
Set the Flipped classroom video and tasks for homework <u>before the lesson</u>. This will allow you to assess the needs of the students before the class. Students can then move on to the relevant grammar practice activities.

Test before you teach

In order to find out how much students know about the third conditional, ask some questions about South Africa. If students seem confident answering them in the correct tense, move through the initial exercise quickly in open class.

What would have happened if South Africa hadn't won the World Cup?

What would have happened if the New Zealand team hadn't been ill?

1 Students look at the sentences in the third conditional and answer the questions.

Answers

1 We use the past perfect in the *if* clause.
2 We use *would have* + the past participle of the verb.
3 No, it can come second.
4 We know '*d* is *had* if it is in the *if* clause.
5 We use the third conditional for imaginary situations in the past.

TEACHER DEVELOPMENT: LANGUAGE

Third conditional

The past is past and cannot be changed. We use the third conditional to speculate about the past and what could have happened if things had gone differently. The third conditional gives the imaginary result, or consequence, of an unreal past.

- The third conditional is formed by an *if* clause and a main clause. The *if* clause can come first or second: if it comes first, the clauses are separated by a comma, but if it comes second, a comma is not necessary, e.g. *I would have got to work on time if my alarm clock had gone off.*

- The main clause in a third conditional sentence can contain any of the modal verbs *would*, *could* or *might* according to the meaning we wish to convey.

- Remind students that we often use just the main clause if the *if* clause can be implied rather than spoken, e.g. *I wouldn't have said so.*

- It is common to use contractions with this language, particularly when it is spoken, e.g. *If I'd studied harder, I'd have passed the exam.*

2 Students read the sentences and choose the correct alternative.

Answers

1 ended, have   **2** had landed, have
3 have survived, hadn't   **4** thought, hadn't fallen
5 have, had   **6** hadn't, would have

3 Students read the text and complete the sentences with the correct form of the verb given.

Answers

1 hadn't thought, wouldn't have been
2 would have taken, had found
3 hadn't defended, would have become
4 hadn't been, wouldn't have taken
5 had been, would have kept
6 would speak, had remained
7 hadn't been, would be

4 Students read the situations and write sentences in the third conditional. Draw their attention to the example sentence.

Answers

2 If I hadn't studied a lot, I wouldn't have got ten in the exam.
3 The road wouldn't have been wet if it hadn't been raining.
4 I would have bought you a present if I had had some money.
5 I wouldn't have known her secret if you hadn't told me.
6 If we had known they were such horrible people, we wouldn't have become their friends.
7 If he had trained, he wouldn't have done badly in the race.
8 She wouldn't have arrived on time if she hadn't got up early that morning.
9 If my dad hadn't given my brother £20, he wouldn't have had enough money to buy the tickets.

5 Students complete the sentences with the third conditional using their own ideas. Nominate students to share their answers in open class.

✚✚ EXTRA ACTIVITY

Ask students to read out their sentences practising the pronunciation of the contracted forms in the third conditional.

6a SPEAKING In pairs, students take it in turns to ask and answer the questions. With a less confident class, students can make notes that they refer to during the speaking activity. They then swap partners and try again without using their notes.

6b SPEAKING Individually, students write five similar questions. They take it in turns to ask and answer the questions with their partner. Draw their attention to the model dialogue.

✚ EXTRA ACTIVITY

If students are finding it difficult to understand the concept and form of the third conditional, give them extra practice. Tell students a story about a terrible day you have had. List the events (your alarm clock didn't go off on time, you overslept, you couldn't find your car keys, you left your house keys inside the house, etc.). Ask students to re-imagine the story as a different past, and ask them to give you correct third conditional sentences, e.g. *If your alarm clock had gone off, you wouldn't have overslept,* etc. Students could then write a similar story.

Refer students to the Grammar reference on page 120 if necessary.

HOMEWORK

Assign students page 80 in their Workbook or the relevant sections of the Online Workbook.

Developing speaking p118 💬 💬

Describing photos

⟫⟫ FAST TRACK

Students could do exercise 1 at home and ask their questions in pairs in class.

WARMER

Write the following sets of vocabulary from the unit on the board.
king queen prince president
monarchy republic democracy election
currency flag anthem aristocrat
Students find the odd one out in each group and give reasons. Students could then invent another odd one out with vocabulary from the unit.

Answers

president is the odd one out because it is not a member of the royal family
election is the odd one out because it is not a type of state
aristocrat is the odd one out because it is not a national symbol

1 SPEAKING In pairs, students think of questions to ask about the photo. Draw students' attention to the example questions. Remind students of the key question words (*who, what, why, where, when* and *how*).

Suggested answers

Who can you see in the picture?
What do you think the man is doing? Why do you think he is there? How do you think he feels?
Who are the other people in the photo?
How long have the people been waiting?
Would you like to be there?

2 LISTENING 53 Play the track for students to listen to a student talking about the photo. Students listen to find out if she answers any of their questions and make a note of her answers. See p157 for the audioscript for this exercise.

3 💬 53 Students listen again and tick the expressions they hear.

Answers

I imagine …, I'm not sure but …, It must be …, The people on the right might be …, It's probably …, It looks as if …, It looks like …, They must have been …

PRACTICE MAKES PERFECT

4a Students look at the task. In pairs, students each choose a photo and, individually, spend three minutes preparing to talk about it.

4b SPEAKING Students take it in turns to do the task. Remind them to use the expressions from the Speaking bank. For students who are less confident, photocopy the model description below for extra support during the speaking task. Ask them to change the information to include their own opinions. Remind them that if their partner stops, they should ask questions to help them. Monitor students, noting important errors and good use of language to go over in a short feedback slot at the end of this activity.

Model description

Let me see, I think this photo might be an important sports event. There are lots of people in the crowd and they are waving their arms in the air. Everybody is looking in the same direction. William and Kate are there. They seem very entertained by what they're watching. I'm not sure which city or country they're in. It could be Britain or another European country. I think it must be an important sports event because everyone looks a bit nervous, too. Personally, I wouldn't like to be there because I don't really like big crowds!

HOMEWORK

Assign students page 81 in their Workbook or the relevant sections of the Online Workbook.

Developing writing p119

Writing a story

>>> FAST TRACK

You could ask students to do exercises 2 and 3 at home and check their answers at the start of the lesson. Alternatively, you could set the writing task in exercise 5 as homework.

WARMER

Hold a *Spelling match* as a fun, competitive way of revising vocabulary and practising spelling. Choose vocabulary you wish to test from the unit so far and divide the class into two teams (A and B). First, read out word one to Team A for them to spell it together, letter by letter. If they spell the whole word correctly, they score one point. However, if at any point they call out an incorrect letter, the 'part-word' is handed over to Team B to complete (and back again if they make an error). This proceeds until one team finishes off the word. The team with the most points wins the game.

1 READING Students read the story about a girl who met the Prime Minister and answer the questions.

Answers

1 She won the chance to meet the Prime Minister after entering a competition where she had had to write ten things she would do if she were the Prime Minister.
2 10 Downing Street in a big black car
3 excited and happy

2 Students read the story again and underline the words and expressions in the text that helped them understand when or in what order the events in the story happened.

Suggested answers

A few months ago, At first, On Wednesday, after school, After about 40 minutes, By the end,

3 Students look at the Writing bank and match the tenses and verbs with their uses in the story. Refer students to the Writing bank on page 151.

Answers

1 d **2** e **3** a **4** b **5** c

4 Students read the story again and find an example of each of the narrative tenses in the Writing bank.

Answers

1 past simple: When Amy finished reading the email, she thought …
2 past continuous: Amy was waiting nervously at home …
3 past perfect: A few months ago, Amy had entered a competition.
4 *used to:* Amy used to dream of a moment like this …
5 *must/may/might/can't have:* She thought the email must have been a mistake or a joke.

✂+ EXTRA ACTIVITY

Play a variation of the popular English parlour game *Consequences* where each person writes one line of a story. Hand out sheets of paper and give instructions to students, for example 'write a female name' (and the student writes 'Lucy'). The student does this, then folds over the paper so the text is hidden, before passing it along to the next student on their right and receiving a new paper from the student on their left. They then wait for your next instruction, for example 'complete the sentence using the past continuous' (and the student writes 'was swimming in the sea'). Continue using a variety of tenses. Then have each student open out the paper and read out the complete story they have ended up with.

PRACTICE MAKES PERFECT

5 Students do the task. Remind them to use narrative tenses carefully and include words and expressions that explain when or in what order the events happen. For students who are less confident, photocopy the model story for extra support during the writing task.

Model story

When Amy finished reading the email, she thought 'It can't be true!' She was sitting in her bedroom with her laptop and she was drinking a can of cola. She almost dropped it as she was so shocked!

Six months before she had entered one of her paintings into a competition. She used to paint when she was younger, but she had given it up until she saw the competition and thought 'I know, I'll start painting again'. She waited patiently for the results, but after a few months she gave up. But then the email arrived in her inbox. At first she thought 'This must be a mistake', when the email said she had won 500 euros. But then she phoned the competition organizer to check it was real. The organizer confirmed she had won. 'Wow!' thought Amy, I must be quite good at painting after all!

✂+ EXTRA ACTIVITY

In pairs, students use their personal checklists to review and give feedback on their partner's work.

HOMEWORK

Assign students page 82 in their Workbook or the relevant sections of the Online Workbook.

Language checkpoint: Unit 9

>>> **FAST TRACK**

Students read the Grammar reference and Vocabulary sections on page 120 before completing the revision exercises on the following page.

Grammar revision p121

Modal verbs of speculation and deduction – present

1 Students complete the sentences with *must, may* or *can't*.

Answers

1 can't **2** must **3** must **4** may **5** can't **6** may

Modal verbs of speculation and deduction – past

2 Students complete the sentences with *must, might* or *can't* and the correct form of the verb given.

Answers

1 can't have seen **2** might have been
3 must have come **4** must have rained
5 can't have snowed **6** might have done
7 can't have eaten

Third conditional

3 Students use the correct form of the verbs in the box to complete the third conditional sentences.

Answers

1 had passed **2** would have bought **3** had died
4 had cooked **5** had shone **6** would have sent
7 had played

Vocabulary revision p121

NATIONS

1 Students complete the sentences with the correct words.

Answers

1 capital city **2** national anthem **3** flag **4** president
5 monarchy, king **6** currency

STATE AND POLITICS

2 Students match the words and write simple definitions.

Answers

1 general elections – occasions when you can vote for a government
2 run a country – manage the way a country works
3 political party – a group of people with similar political ideas
4 prime minister – the person who leads the government that is in power
5 constitutional monarchy – a country ruled by a king or queen whose powers are limited by a set of basic laws

ADJECTIVE SUFFIXES

3 Students complete the sentences with the adjective form of the words in the box.

Answers

1 hungry **2** careless **3** artistic **4** sensible
5 comfortable **6** natural **7** enjoyable **8** mysterious

HOMEWORK

Assign students page 83 in their Workbook or the relevant sections of the Online Workbook.

KEY LEARNING OUTCOMES

CEF

Students will be able to:

- use indeterminate pronouns correctly, and intensify meaning with *so* and *such*
- talk about wishes using *I wish* and *If only*
- talk about shops and shopping

- understand written and spoken texts about shopping and money
- ask for things and explain problems in a clothes shop
- write a formal email of complaint

UNIT OVERVIEW

Vocabulary
Shops
Shopping

Reading
An article about shopping
CRITICAL THINKING Discussing whether knowing supermarket tricks would change the way we shop

Grammar in context
Indeterminate pronouns: *some-, any-, no-, every-*
so and *such*
PRONUNCIATION *so* and *such*

Developing vocabulary
Collocations with *money*

Life skills
Money and finance:
Managing your money

Listening
Shopping dialogues

Grammar in context
I wish and *If only*

Developing speaking
At a clothes shop

Developing writing
A formal email of complaint

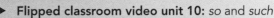
Exam success
Reading: Multiple-choice
Speaking: Getting a good mark

DIGITAL OVERVIEW

Presentation Kit

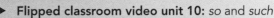

- ▶ Flipped classroom video unit 10: *so* and *such*
- ▶ Life skills video unit 10: Managing your money
- ▶ **V** Vocabulary tool: Shops; Shopping
- ▶ Interactive versions of Student's Book activities
- ▶ Integrated audio and answer key for all activities
- ▶ Workbook pages with answer key

Teacher's Resource Centre

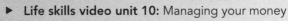

- ▶ Flipped classroom video Unit 10: *so* and *such*
- ▶ Life skills video Unit 10: Managing your money
- ▶ Grammar communication activity Unit 10: Do-it-yourself bingo
- ▶ Worksheets for this unit, including:
  - Grammar Practice worksheet Unit 10
  - Flipped classroom video worksheet Unit 10: *so* and *such*
  - Literature worksheet Units 9 and 10
  - Culture worksheet Unit 10
  - Life skills video worksheet Unit 10
  - Everyday English worksheet Unit 10

Student's App

Gateway 2nd Edition wordlist for the award-winning Sounds App (available for download)

✓ TESTING AND ASSESSMENT

Resources for exam preparation and measuring student progress

- ▶ Test Generator Units 1–10
- ▶ Printable tests Unit 10 and End-of-year
- ▶ Gateway to exams Units 9 and 10 (end of Unit 10)

Vocabulary p122

Talking about shops and shopping

WARMER

Write the following quote on the board: 'It is preoccupation with possessions, more than anything else, that prevents us from living freely and nobly.' *Bertrand Russell*

In pairs, ask students to think what the quote means and if they agree with it. Help with any vocabulary. Elicit the concept of 'materialism' and ask students how they think this could relate to the unit title, *The material world.* Finally, ask what things students think they will learn within the unit.

V Shops

1 **SPEAKING** In pairs, students play 'vocabulary tennis' choosing one of the shops from the box. Go through the rules with the students, and draw their attention to the example.

TEACHER DEVELOPMENT: PRONUNCIATION

Homophones

Point out that things used for writing such as paper and pens are called *stationery*. A similar word is *stationary*, meaning 'standing still, not moving'. To remember the difference between these two words, they could remember the link between the 'e' in *stationery* and the 'e' in *envelope*.

EXTRA ACTIVITY

In pairs, students plan a short role-play going into one of the shops in exercise 1 and asking for an item. Other pairs have to guess the shop they are in.

2 **LISTENING** ▶ 54 Play the track for students to listen to the four dialogues and decide where the people are and what they want to buy. See pp157–158 for the audioscript for this exercise.

Answers

1 Shoe shop: They want to buy some comfortable shoes or trainers.
2 Department store: They want to buy a birthday present/a watch.
3 Clothes shop: The man wants to buy a jacket.
4 Post office: He wants to buy some stamps to post some letters to Australia.

EXTRA ACTIVITY

Ask some comprehension questions to follow up the activity in exercise 2:
1 Where do they want to go walking?
2 What ideas for presents do they have?
3 What colour do the jackets come in?
4 How long do normal letters take to arrive in Australia?

V Shopping

3 Students look at the photo and use the words in the box to talk about it.

Suggested answers

cashier, checkout, cash/debit card, queue

4 Students match the words in exercise 3 with the definitions. Allow students to use a dictionary if necessary.

Answers

1 debit card **2** cashier **3** cash **4** checkout
5 queue **6** afford **7** discount **8** bargain **9** receipt
10 refund **11** trolley **12** changing room

EXTRA ACTIVITY

Students mark the stressed syllables in each word (underlined in the key above) and practise the pronunciation of the words.

5 Students complete the text with words from exercise 3.

Answers

a trolley **b** discount **c** bargain **d** queue
e checkout **f** cashier **g** debit card **h** refund
i cash **j** receipt

6 **SPEAKING** In pairs, students discuss the questions. With a less confident class, students write notes on their answers to each question before they do this as a speaking activity. You could also model this activity in open pairs before students do this as closed pairs.

EXTRA ACTIVITY

Students make up a story similar to the one in exercise 5 using as many words as they can from exercise 3.

HOMEWORK

Assign students page 84 in their Workbook or the relevant sections of the Online Workbook.

Reading p123

Reading quickly for general understanding then for specific information

⟫⟫ FAST TRACK

Students could do exercise 2 at home and focus on checking vocabulary. Ask them to compare their answers in the next lesson.

WARMER

Ask students to look at the photo on page 123 and describe the scene.

1 READING Students read the magazine article and think of a good title. Elicit titles from around the class and ask students to explain their choices. Set a time limit of four minutes to stop students from focusing on difficult vocabulary at this stage and encourage them to read rapidly to get the general idea of the text.

✓ EXAM SUCCESS Students read the information in the Exam success box and discuss what they should do in a multiple-choice activity. Tell students to turn to page 146 to compare their answers.

2 Students read the article again and choose the best answers. Ask students which words or sentences from the text helped them choose the right answers.

Answers
1 a **2** b **3** c **4** c **5** a

3 Students make a list of techniques used by supermarkets to make us buy things. Draw their attention to the example.

Answers
Making shopping trolleys bigger
Offering cheap prices on basic items like eggs and milk
Putting red stickers on products so shoppers think they are at a discount
Putting things like milk at the back so the shopper has to pass all the shelves
Putting the expensive products at eye-level and the cheap ones lower
Putting slow music to make you relaxed and move slower
Creating queues at the checkout to make you buy from checkout shelves while you wait

✚ EXTRA ACTIVITY

In pairs, students think of three more ideas to add to the list in exercise 3.

4 ⚙ CRITICAL THINKING Ask students to read the question and think of their own responses before sharing ideas as a class.

5 Students look at the underlined words in the text and guess their meaning before using a dictionary to check.

Answers
pop into = go inside very quickly
items = the things you intend to buy
tendency = something we usually do or choose to do naturally
deliberately = on purpose, done with a reason
stickers = labels that supermarkets stick to food
eye-level = the height where people's eyes are

6 SPEAKING **What about *you*?** In pairs or small groups, students discuss their supermarket shopping habits.

✚ EXTRA ACTIVITY

Ask students to work in small groups and come up with some more tips for shoppers to avoid the supermarkets' methods for making them spend more.

HOMEWORK

Assign students page 85 in their Workbook or the relevant sections of the Online Workbook.

Grammar in context pp124-125

Using indeterminate pronouns, so and such

⟫⟫ FAST TRACK

Students could complete the table in exercise 1c at home before the next lesson.

Test before you teach: Flipped classroom
Set the Flipped classroom video and tasks for homework <u>before the lesson</u>. This will allow you to assess the needs of the students before the class. Students can then move on to the relevant grammar practice activities.

Indeterminate pronouns: some-, any-, no-, every-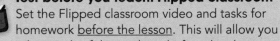

1a Students read the sentences.

1b Students now match the sentence halves to the rules.

Answers
1 c **2** a **3** b **4** d

1c Students complete the table.

Answers

some- somebody/someone
any- anywhere
no- nothing, nowhere
every- everything, everywhere

TEACHER DEVELOPMENT: LANGUAGE

Indeterminate pronouns

Anybody, *nobody* and *somebody* mean the same as *anyone*, *no-one* and *someone* respectively. *No-one* can also be written as *no one*.

Point out to students that there is a difference in emphasis between *nothing*, *nobody*, etc. and *not ... anything*, *not ... anybody*:

I don't know anything about it. (= neutral, no emphasis)
I know nothing about it. (= more emphatic, maybe defensive)

✛ EXTRA ACTIVITY

Draw a 4 x 4 grid on the board with the 16 possible combinations as in exercise 1c. Divide students into two teams. Tell students that they have to race from one side of the grid to the other making correct sentences using indeterminate pronouns, e.g. *There's something in my shoe. Can somebody lend me a pen?* If they say a correct sentence, they win the square and the other team must go round it. If their answer is incorrect, they do not win the square and the square is blocked so that they must now go round it.

2 Students choose the correct alternative.

Answers

1 everything **2** somebody **3** anywhere **4** No-one
5 anything **6** Everybody **7** everyone, anyone
8 anybody

3 Students complete the dialogue with the indeterminate pronouns in the table in exercise 1c.

Answers

a something **b** Anything **c** something
d anything **e** everywhere **f** nothing
g Somebody/Someone **h** anyone/anybody

4a Individually, students complete the questions with *anybody, anywhere, anything.*

Answers

1 anywhere **2** anything **3** anybody
4 anybody **5** anywhere **6** anything

4b SPEAKING In pairs, students take it in turns to ask and answer the questions and see if their answers are similar or different. Elicit answers from different students around the class to close the activity.

so and such

5 Students look at the sentences and choose the correct alternative.

Answers

1 adjectives and adverbs
2 nouns (with or without adjectives)
3 that

6a PRONUNCIATION ▶ 55 Play the track for students to listen to the sentences. Ask students what they notice about the pronunciation of *so* and *such*. See p158 for the audioscript for this exercise.

Answer

The words *so* and *such* are stressed.

6b ▶ 55 Play the track for students to listen again and repeat.

7 Students complete the sentences with *so* or *such*.

Answers

1 such **2** so **3** such **4** such **5** so
6 so **7** so

✛ EXTRA ACTIVITY

Students take it in turns to read the sentences to each other, emphasising the stress on *so* and *such*.

8a Students complete the sentences in a logical way using their imagination.

8b SPEAKING In pairs, students compare their sentences in exercise 8a. Elicit sentences from different students around the class and vote on the most imaginative sentence.

✛ EXTRA ACTIVITY

Students write two or more sentence stems like the sentences in exercise 8a for their partner to complete.

Refer students to the Grammar reference on page 132 if necessary.

HOMEWORK

Assign students page 86 in their Workbook or the relevant sections of the Online Workbook.

Developing vocabulary p125

Talking about money using specific collocations

>>> **FAST TRACK**

You could ask students to do exercise 2 before the class.

WARMER

Write the word *money* on the board and ask students some questions to elicit the verbs we use with this word, e.g. *What can people do with money? (spend, waste, make, earn, win, deposit, withdraw it).* Tell the students that these words collocate, or sound 'good' together, and are better remembered in phrases.

TEACHER DEVELOPMENT: LANGUAGE

Collocations

A collocation is two or more words that often go together.

These combinations just sound 'right' to native English speakers, who use them all the time. Other combinations often just sound 'wrong' (e.g. *a fast train* not *a quick train*). If students learn the words that commonly go together – collocations – they will take an important step in their vocabulary learning. Word combinations are often adjective + noun, verb + noun, and noun + verb pairs. Encourage students to learn collocations in groups, e.g. by topic (time, number, weather, money, family) or by a particular word (*take action, take a chance, take an exam*).

Collocations with *money*

1 Students use the verbs that frequently go with *money* to complete the definitions. Fast finishers make their own sentences using the verbs.

Answers

1 win **2** waste **3** borrow **4** donate **5** earn
6 lend **7** spend **8** save **9** make **10** raise
11 owe

2 Students use the correct form of the verbs in exercise 1 to complete the sentences.

Answers

1 earn/make **2** spends **3** borrow **4** won
5 donates **6** lent **7** made **8** saving **9** wasted
10 owe **11** raised

✚ EXTRA ACTIVITY

In pairs, students use the verbs in exercise 1 to make a questionnaire about money. Students then take it in turns to interview another pair.

HOMEWORK

Assign students page 87 in their Workbook or the relevant sections of the Online Workbook.

Gateway to life skills pp126–127

Managing your money

To learn about the best ways to save money and how and when to spend it

>>> **FAST TRACK**

Students could complete the quiz in exercise 1 at home, later sharing and comparing their results in class.

ⓘ BACKGROUND INFORMATION

Many teenagers are just starting to have some form of financial independence – either through an allowance from parents or a part-time job. Learning how to manage money early on with relatively small amounts will prepare students for events later on, such as going to university and buying a house, where being able to budget is a vital skill. This lesson encourages students to reflect on how they spend or save and ways they can consider spending less. Be aware that money and financial issues may be a sensitive subject for some students, so keep class discussions general rather than specific where necessary.

WARMER

In pairs, ask students to think of one thing in the past they wasted their money on, and one thing that was a good purchase. Elicit ideas from different students, asking them to give their reasons. Then tell them that today's lesson focuses on how to manage money. Allow students time to read through the Life skills objectives and the Key concepts before starting the lesson.

1 **READING** Students read the quiz and tick their own answers. Have a 'show of hands' for each answer, and ask students if they think as a class they are good at managing money.

2a Students look at their answers and see if they have mostly a, b or c.

2b Ask students to look at the results for the quiz to see what it says about them. Ask individual students if they agree or disagree with the results and to explain why.

3a **LISTENING** ▶ 56 Tell students they are going to watch a video or listen to a recording of four British teenagers talking about how they manage money. Ask students to mark the speakers' answers to questions 1 and 2 with a tick or cross. See p158 for the audioscript/videoscript for this exercise.

Answers

a Do you get an allowance? Toby ✗, Callum ✗, Naomi ✓, Rachel ✗

b Do you ever borrow money from others? Toby ✗, Callum ✓, Naomi ✗, Rachel ✓

3b LISTENING ▶ 56 Ask students to make notes of the students' answers to the third question, about how they make their money go further. If necessary play the video or audio again for them to check their notes.

Answers

Toby: spend half of money and save rest
Rachel: avoid designer clothes
Naomi: look for the best price
Callum: think before buying, only buy important things

4 ▶ 56 Play the video or track again for students to decide which speaker says each sentence. Remind students that there may be more than one answer. Help less confident students by pausing the video or track in places so they have time to think.

Answers

1 Rachel and Callum **2** Naomi **3** Naomi **4** Callum
5 Toby **6** Naomi **7** Rachel **8** Callum

5 SPEAKING In pairs, students say which speaker they are most similar to and in what ways.

✛ EXTRA ACTIVITY

Teach students the following English expression: 'Look after the pennies and the pounds will look after themselves.' and ask them what they think it means. (If you save money on a small scale, you won't have to worry about saving money on a larger scale.) In pairs, ask students what money expressions they can think of in their own language and ask them to try to translate them into English.

LIFE TASK

Tell students they are going to make a leaflet or poster to give advice to other teenagers about money.

■ *Step 1*
In groups, students think of more ways they can save money and spend less. Circulate and help with ideas while they are brainstorming.

■ *Step 2*
Students organise their ideas in a logical way and decide how they are going to illustrate their ideas.

■ *Step 3*
Students make their leaflet or poster. Give students the necessary materials to do this or ensure they have access to computers and printers.

■ *Step 4*
Students look at the leaflets and posters and discuss what they think are the five best ideas.

Listening p128

Listening for gist and specific detail

WARMER

Choose vocabulary you wish to test from the unit so far and divide the class into two teams (A and B) for a spelling match. First, read out word one to Team A for them to spell it together, letter by letter. If they spell the whole word correctly, they score one point. However, if at any point they call out an incorrect letter, the 'part-word' is handed over to Team B to complete (and back again if they make an error). This proceeds until one team finishes off the word. The team with the most points wins the game.

1 SPEAKING In pairs, students look at the photo and describe what they can see.

Suggested answer

I can see a boy shopping. He's looking at some trousers on a clothes rack. Behind him I can see lots of shirts. He seems to like the clothes he's looking at. He's probably buying something.

2 LISTENING ▶ 57 Play the track for students to listen to four conversations and match the conversations to the descriptions a–d. See pp158–159 for the audioscript for this exercise.

Answers

a 4 **b** 2 **c** 1 **d** 3

3 ▶ 57 Play the track again for students to tick the correct column. Give students time to read the first column and help with any vocabulary.

Answers

1 4 **2** 1 **3** 2 **4** 3 **5** 4 **6** 3 **7** 1 **8** 2

4 SPEAKING **What about *you*?** In pairs, students ask and answer the questions.

✛ EXTRA ACTIVITY

In pairs, students think of three ways to make the shopping experience more enjoyable. Ask them to make notes and then share their ideas with the rest of the class.

HOMEWORK

Assign students page 87 in their Workbook or the relevant sections of the Online Workbook.

Grammar in context pp128-129

Talking about wishes and regrets using I wish and If only

Ask students to complete exercise 1 at home in preparation for a deeper examination of the grammar in class.

Test before you teach
In order to find out how much students know about *I wish* and *If only*, write these situations on the board and ask students to reword the statements using these two structures.
I'm angry because I've spent all my money on clothes this month.
I regret not going to university.
You hardly do any sport.
I haven't got a job.

Answers
I wish/If only I hadn't spent all my money on clothes.
I wish/If only I had gone to university.
I wish/If only you did more sport.
I wish/If only I had a job.

1 Students look at the sentences and choose the correct alternative.

Answers
1 past simple, present
2 past perfect, past
3 *would*, wants

TEACHER DEVELOPMENT: LANGUAGE

I wish/If only
There are three distinct types of *I wish/If only* sentences:
1 with the past simple: to express a wish, wanting change for the present or future
2 with the past perfect: to express regret
3 with *would* + verb: to express a complaint
Remind students that when we use the verb *to be* after *I wish*, we often use *were* in the first person and third person, e.g. *I wish I were a millionaire! He wishes he were richer.*
If only takes the same verb forms as *I wish*. This form is used as a means of stressing the importance of the wish or hypothetical situations. The form is often also used with an exclamation point.
It is common to use contractions, particularly when we speak, e.g. *If only I'd studied harder. / I wish I'd studied harder.*

2 Students look at the situations and the words given. Tell students to write what the people wish was different about the present situation. Draw students' attention to the example sentence.

Answers
2 He wishes he were/was taller.
3 She wishes she had a cat.
4 She wishes she were/was on a beach.
5 He wishes he had long hair.
6 He wishes he could ski well.

3 SPEAKING In pairs, students look at the ideas. They then take it in turns to tell their partners if they wish each item were true for them or not and write their answers first before doing this as a speaking activity. You could practise this exercise as an open-class activity before students do it in closed pairs. For a less confident class, write the dialogue below and the example in the Student's Book on the board.

A: I don't wish I was a millionaire.
B: Why not?
A: Because I think money could bring problems.

4 Students complete the regrets by putting the verbs in brackets in the correct tense.

Answers
1 hadn't told **2** 'd chosen **3** 'd treated
4 'd studied **5** 'd learnt **6** hadn't listened
7 hadn't said **8** 'd paid

5 Students look at the pictures and decide what they think the people are saying. Students write sentences with *I wish you would/wouldn't …* You could do this as a speaking activity in open class first and brainstorm ideas before students write their sentences.

Suggested answers
1 I wish you'd come to the class on time!
2 I wish you wouldn't watch such frightening films!
3 I wish you'd tidy your room up!

Ask students to read out their sentences, practising the pronunciation of the contracted forms of *would/wouldn't*.

6a SPEAKING In pairs, students decide what the people and animals are wishing. Remind them they can use one of the three types of *wish/if only* (+ past simple + past perfect or with *would*).

Suggested answers
a I wish he would share his food with me.
b I wish the lesson was more exciting.
c If only I had brought my umbrella.
d I wish I was back in the sea.
e I wish I could cook better. / I wish I had taken them out of the oven earlier.

6b Students read out their ideas to the class. Other students listen and try to match the sentences to the correct pictures. Point out the example dialogue.

Tell the class you are going to talk about a few regrets you've had in your life and ask them to take notes about what you say. Ask students to report back your regrets to you, and insist on the correct form of *wish/if only*. Ask students to write five sentences with regrets of their own (tell them they can make them up if they are not comfortable talking about their past).

TEACHER DEVELOPMENT: STUDENT TRAINING

Reflecting on the year

When students take part in setting goals and charting progress, they tend to make faster progress. Self-assessment encourages students to take responsibility for their progress and raises students' and teachers' awareness of areas they feel they need to work on.

You could encourage students to look at the contents list of the Student's Book and use this as a checklist. The students can tick each language skill or activity that they are confident of having mastered. Another idea is to provide ability statements for students at this level.

You could use this opportunity to reflect on the course with your students and ask them some general questions: *What was your overall impression of the course? What were some of the lessons you learnt most from? Can you think of a lesson in particular that you really enjoyed? What key areas do you need to spend more time on improving before the end of the course?*

Refer students to the Grammar reference on page 132 if necessary.

HOMEWORK

Assign students page 88 in their Workbook or the relevant sections of the Online Workbook.

Developing speaking p130

Communicating at a clothes shop

>>> **FAST TRACK**

Students could do exercise 3 at home and compare their conversations in pairs.

WARMER

In pairs or small groups, students think of an item of clothing or an accessory for every letter of the alphabet except X and Y. Set a five-minute time limit. The team with the most correct words wins the game.

Suggested answers

anorak, belt, coat, dress, elastic band, flip-flops, gloves, hat, ice skates, jacket, kimono, linen, moccasins, necklace, overcoat, pyjamas, quilted jacket, raincoat, socks, trainers, underpants, vest, waistcoat, zip

1 **SPEAKING** In pairs, students look at the photo and describe it. Elicit what clothes they can see.

Suggested answer

There's a woman in a clothes shop who is wearing an orange shirt. She might be shopping for more shirts in different colours for herself. Or she could work in the shop and they could be men's shirts.

2 **LISTENING** ▶ 58 Play the track for students to listen to the dialogue in a clothes shop and answer the questions. See p159 for the audioscript for this exercise.

Answers

hoodie, blue, size large

3 Students put the lines in order to make a logical conversation.

Answers

1 e **2** a **3** c **4** g **5** d **6** f **7** b

4 **SPEAKING** Students work with a partner and use the lines in exercise 3 to make and practise a conversation in a shop. Tell them to change the words in bold to make their conversation different.

5 **LISTENING** ▶ 59 Students listen and read the conversation with the same customer from the listening in exercise 2 a week later and answer the questions. See p159 for the audioscript for this exercise.

Answers

1 The hoodie shrank when it was washed.
2 The shop assistant offers to replace it or give her a refund.
3 She gets a refund because she has the receipt.

Have students read out the dialogue in pairs, paying attention to the intonation.

6 Students look at the expressions in the Speaking bank and use their dictionary to check any new words. Ask them to match the expressions to the functions.

Answers

1 I'd like to make a complaint. It shrank the first time I washed it. It's faulty.
2 Sorry about that.
3 Can I help you? How about this/these? We can replace it.
4 Yes, I'm looking for … No, thanks. I'm just looking.
5 What size are you? What seems to be the problem? Have you got anything in blue/green/medium/large? Can I bring it back? Can I have a refund?
6 I like it/them. I'll take this one/these. It's the wrong size.

PRACTICE MAKES PERFECT

7a **SPEAKING** In pairs, students look at the task, choose a role and perform the role-play. Remind students to use the dialogue in exercise 5 and the expressions from the Speaking bank to help them. For students who are less confident, photocopy the model dialogue opposite, and either read it aloud yourself, or alternate the roles with you and a strong student. Then instruct students to read aloud in pairs, alternating between the roles. Then ask them to read it again, changing the underlined information.

7b Students practise their dialogue and act it out for the class.

Model dialogue

Shop assistant: Good morning. Can I help you?

Customer: Yes, I'd like to make a complaint.

Shop assistant: Oh dear. I'm sorry. What seems to be the problem?

Customer: Well, I bought this T-shirt here last week, but when I got home I found it's got a hole. Here, look.

Shop assistant: Oh, I see. Sorry about that. Do you have the receipt?

Customer: Yes, here it is.

Shop assistant: Well, we can replace it for you or we could give you a refund. Which would you prefer?

Customer: I'd like a refund, please.

Shop assistant: Of course. £30. There you are.

✔ EXAM SUCCESS Students discuss what they think they need to do in order to get a good mark in a speaking exam. Tell students to turn to Exam success on page 146 to compare their ideas.

HOMEWORK

Assign students page 89 in their Workbook or the relevant sections of the Online Workbook.

Developing writing p131

Writing a formal email of complaint

⟫⟫ FAST TRACK

You could ask students to prepare for the writing task in exercise 7a by completing exercise 4 at home.

WARMER

Draw these objects on the board and elicit all the different types of problems you could have with each one.

1 a sock
2 a mobile phone
3 a jumper

Suggested answers

1 It's got a hole in it. It's faded.
2 It doesn't work. It's faulty.
3 It's the wrong size. It shrank when I washed it.

1 SPEAKING In pairs, students discuss whether they have ever bought something that didn't work or was faulty and say what happened. Elicit some anecdotes from different students around the class.

2 READING Students read the email and answer the questions.

Answers

1 Oliver bought an e-reader.
2 The screen was broken.
3 He took it back to the store.
4 The shop assistant didn't change it because he didn't have the original box. When he went back with the e-reader in the original packaging, there was a new assistant who said he couldn't have a refund as he had broken the screen himself.
5 He wants a full refund and a written apology for the treatment he received.

3 Students put the pieces of information in the order they appear in Oliver's email.

Answers

1 c 2 e 3 a 4 d 5 b

4 Students read the email again and underline or copy expressions that are useful for a letter of complaint.

Answers

I am writing to complain about …
When, As a result, However,
I demand a full refund.
I would like a …
If I do not … I will …
I look forward to hearing from you soon.

5 Students look at the words and phrases from the email and put them in the correct list in the Writing bank.

Answers

a since **b** In the end **c** However **d** As a result
e Furthermore

6 Students complete the sentences in a logical way.

Suggested answers

1 As a result, I would like to ask for a full refund.
2 Furthermore, she was rude to me in front of other customers and staff.
3 However, the service today was terrible.
4 I would like a full refund since I brought the product back in perfect condition.
5 In the end, I received an apology.

PRACTICE MAKES PERFECT

7a Students look at the task and write their email of complaint. Remind them to use the email in exercise 2 as a model and use linkers from the Writing bank. For students who are less confident, photocopy the model email on the next page for extra support during the writing task. Refer students to the Writing bank on page 150.

Model email

Dear Sir or Madam,

I am writing to complain about your service.

On 10th March, I bought two tickets for a Pharrell Williams concert on 1st April. I've done this many times before, and I am usually very happy with your service (although your tickets are very expensive!). However, this time the tickets arrived two days after the concert, and as a result I couldn't go.

I phoned three times before 1st April. Each time, the staff promised me that the tickets would arrive on time. They finally arrived on 3rd April.

In the end, I missed my favourite band and spent many hours on the phone trying to get help from your support centre.

I would like a full refund and compensation for the wasted telephone calls. Furthermore, I would also like an apology from the Support Centre who treated me so badly.

If I do not hear from you in the next two weeks, I will take my complaint to the Consumer Advice Centre.

I look forward to hearing from you soon.

Yours faithfully,

Charlie Watson

✚ EXTRA ACTIVITY

In pairs, students use their personal checklists to review and give feedback on their partner's work.

7b Students swap emails with a partner and write a reply to their partner's email.

HOMEWORK

Assign students page 90 in their Workbook or the relevant sections of the Online Workbook.

Language checkpoint: Unit 10

>>> FAST TRACK

Students read the Grammar reference and Vocabulary sections on page 132 before completing the revision exercises on the following page.

Grammar revision p133

Indeterminate pronouns: some-, any-, no-, every-

1 Students complete the sentences with the correct indeterminate pronouns.

Answers

1 anything 2 anywhere 3 something 4 Somebody
5 Everybody 6 anyone

so and such

2 Students rewrite the *so* sentences with *such* and vice versa.

Answers

1 This is such a big country.
2 The students are so good.
3 It was such a difficult exam.
4 It was such bad weather that we stayed in.
5 The film was so loud that my ears hurt.
6 My headache is so bad.
7 It's such a dangerous road.
8 It was such a painful experience.

I wish and If only

3 Students choose the correct alternative.

Answers

1 had 2 would 3 understood
4 had met 5 would stop 6 hadn't failed

Vocabulary revision p133

SHOPS

1 Students complete the names of the shops.

Answers

1 butcher's 2 greengrocer's 3 electrical goods store
4 department store 5 stationery shop 6 bakery

SHOPPING

2 Students complete the sentences with words connected to shopping.

Answers

1 cash 2 cashier 3 queue 4 afford
5 bargain 6 receipt 7 changing rooms
8 discount

COLLOCATIONS WITH *MONEY*

3 Students decide if the sentences are correct or not. If not, students change the word in italics.

Answers

1 borrow 2 earn 3 (correct) 4 waste 5 (correct)
6 lend

HOMEWORK

Assign students page 91 in their Workbook or the relevant sections of the Online Workbook.

Reading p134

TIP FOR READING EXAMS

Discuss tips for multiple-choice activities. Tell students to look at Exam success on page 146 for more ideas.

1 In pairs, students look at the FAQs and see if they can answer any of them. Elicit ideas from different students around the class.

2 Students read the text again and check their predictions. They then match the questions to the paragraphs.

Answers

1 B **2** A **3** C **4** D

3 Students read the text and choose the best answers.

Answers

1 b **2** c **3** b **4** c

Speaking p134

TIP FOR SPEAKING EXAMS

Elicit from students how they think they should speak in oral exams to get the best results. Tell students to compare their suggestions to the tip for speaking exams and to look at Exam success on page 146.

4 Students work in pairs and assign themselves roles A or B. Student A looks at the photo on page 147 and Student B looks at the photo on page 148. Ask students to spend three minutes making notes about their photo. Encourage students to speculate about who the people are and what they are doing.

5 SPEAKING Students read the instruction points. In pairs, students take turns talking about their photo and answering the questions.

Listening p135

TIP FOR LISTENING EXAMS

Students read the tip for Listening Exams and discuss strategies for completing notes. Students refer to Exam success on page 146 to compare their ideas.

6 LISTENING ▶ 60 Play the track for students to listen to a history programme on the radio and answer the questions. See p159 for the audioscript for this exercise.

Answers

1 A ship which brought 500 Caribbean people to Britain in 1948.
2 It created modern multicultural Britain.

7 ▶ 60 Students listen again and complete the notes with one or two words or numbers.

Answers

a Jamaica **b** Britain **c** 500 **d** work **e** the weather
f Commonwealth countries **g** India **h** 14% **i** food
j music

Use of English p135

TIP FOR USE OF ENGLISH

Students read the tips for being successful in word formation cloze activities and look at Exam success on page 146 for more ideas.

8 Students read the text and use the words given in capitals to form a word that fits in the gap in the same line.

Answers

a dangerous **b** interested **c** historian **d** inspiring
e employee **f** tiring **g** uncomfortable **h** helpful
i cooperates **j** multinational/international **k** official
l excited **m** surprising **n** director

HOMEWORK

Assign students pages 92–93 in their Workbook or the relevant sections of the Online Workbook.

1 Ask students to read the 'can do' statements and mark from 1–4 how well they can do these things in English.

2 Ask students to look at their marks and decide what they think they need to do to improve. Elicit other suggestions.

Unit 1

Vocabulary p6

2 01

Build

| thin | overweight |
| strong | well-built |

Height

| short | medium-height |
| tall | |

Hair

short	bald
blonde	curly
dark	fair
long	medium-length
spiky	straight
wavy	

General

| attractive | cute |
| good-looking | pretty |

Vocabulary p6

6 02

Rose:

Well, yes, I suppose that it is fair to call me that. I dunno, it's just that I love sleeping. I hate getting up early. And if you give me a choice between doing something active like sport or just lying on a sofa watching TV all day, I'd definitely go for lying on the sofa. And even better if I can stay in my pyjamas all day.

William:

No, the thing is that I don't *think* I'm the best, the most intelligent and the most attractive. I *am* the best, the most intelligent and the most attractive. In fact, I'm the best at *everything*.

Jessica:

I *hate* it when people move my things. In my room, everything is always in exactly the right place. I never leave my clothes out and my desk is always ready for work. The thing is that when you're like me, you always know where to find things.

Brandon:

Oh, I really hate that. When my friends arrive late and make me wait, I get really angry with them. And waiting for buses or trains just makes me lose control. Even waiting for just two or three minutes gets me angry.

Pronunciation p9

3b ▶ 03

beautiful	difficult
elderly	sociable
attractive	good-looking
outgoing	

Gateway to life skills p11

5a and 5b ▶ 04

Callum:

I'm really good at computer games! Definitely! I like games that make you think. Sometimes there are moments in a game when it's really difficult to go up a level. So I'm really proud of myself when I finally manage it. I'm good at thinking of different strategies or solutions.

Naomi:

That's a difficult question. I'm not very good at sports or music. Oh, I'm quite good at listening to people, does that count? I think that's because I'm a patient person and I don't interrupt people all the time. My friends come to me when they have problems. Oh, and I'm also a quiet person. Maybe that's why they trust me. They know I won't tell everyone their secrets!

Rachel:

I'm good at art and I'm good at making things. Art has always been one of my favourite hobbies. I'm really proud of some of my drawings and paintings and my friends like them, too. In fact, some of my friends even ask me to do paintings for them! I've got lots of my own paintings on the walls of my bedroom and it's a really good feeling looking at them all.

Toby:

What am I good at? Um, I'm quite good at tennis. Most of my friends at school play football, but I prefer tennis. I started playing with my dad when I was small. He encouraged me to take it seriously because he could see I was good at it. Now I have classes with a tennis coach twice a week and I'm getting better and better. Just playing a sport outside helps me to relax, but I'm quite competitive too and I enjoy playing matches … especially when I win, of course!

Listening p12

2 and 3 ▶ 05

Speaker 1:

Well, here's my picture. You can see that it's very simple. I knew immediately what I wanted to draw when I saw the circle. I mean, I love warm weather and the summer, so the sun was my first idea. The magazine says that your picture says a lot about your personality, but I don't believe that's true at all! Apparently, drawing a sun means that I'm very confident, and maybe a little bit bossy. Actually, I think I'm exactly the opposite.

Speaker 2:

When I see a circle, I always think of a face. So that explains my picture. I think it looks like me, you know, because of the long, wavy hair. There's a lot of detail in the picture because art is my favourite hobby … It's quite a funny face, I suppose. The analysis here says that if you draw a funny face it means you're a funny and cheerful person. That seems a good description of me. It's true that that's what my friends always say.

Speaker 3:

This magazine here says that your picture says a lot about your personality. It's a clever idea, and I think my picture certainly says a lot about me. That's my foot there, kicking the circle in the middle, which is, of course, a ball. I mean, I play football four times a week, I watch every football match that I can. My mum says it's the only thing I think about. Please don't show her this picture! I don't want her to see it because she thinks I need to spend more time studying instead of playing football.

Speaker 4:

My first idea was to draw a face in the circle. But then I changed my mind and I turned the circle into a big eye. It says here that an eye means that I like to control my life, and that I like to control other people. I see why they say that. The eye is watching others, like a big brother. The thing is, I know that *sometimes* I can be bossy, but I really don't believe that's an important part of my personality.

Speaker 5:

I have a big, beautiful garden and when it's sunny I like sitting out there. So, when I saw the circle I immediately decided to draw a big flower. Perhaps it sounds arrogant, but I agree with the analysis of my picture. It says here that when you draw a flower it's because you like your own appearance and that you're a very friendly person. I think that in my case both things are true. But I think another reason why I drew a flower is just because I love flowers – the way they smell, the way they look. And I was in the garden when I drew it. So, it isn't just about personality.

Developing speaking p14

1 and 2 ▶ 06

Megan: Hi. You're Lucy's cousin, aren't you?

Ellie: Yes, that's right. My name's Ellie.

Megan: I'm Megan. This is your first year at this school, isn't it?

Ellie: That's right.

Megan: Hey, you don't play basketball, do you? We need new players for the team.

Ellie: I play a little, but I'm not mad about basketball.

Megan: Do you play any other sports?

Ellie: Yes, I really enjoy swimming.

Megan: Great! What are your other hobbies?

Ellie: I love music.

Megan: Really? What kind of music?

Ellie: I like all sorts, but my favourite is rock.

Megan: Now I remember! You can play the guitar, can't you? Lucy told me once.

Ellie: Yeah, I'm in a band. We're really good.

Megan: Do you know Josh, Josh Smith? He plays in a band, too. Come on. Let me introduce you to him …

Unit 2

Vocabulary p18

4 07

When you go to the station to catch a train, if you don't already have a ticket, you go and buy one at the ticket office. You can buy a single (if you're only going one way) or a return (if you're coming back). The fare is more expensive when you travel first-class because it's more comfortable and you have more space. There isn't an extra cost for luggage – you can take at least two or three big bags.

When you have your ticket, you need to find the platform where your train is leaving from. If you arrive late, you may miss your train. But sometimes, there can be a delay and your train doesn't arrive on time. And sometimes there's no train at all because they cancel it! It's important to keep looking at the information screens which show the arrivals (the times that trains are coming into the station) and the departures (the times that trains are leaving).

Vocabulary p18

7 08

1

This is to announce the arrival of the 5.15 to Torquay, the 5.15 to Torquay, stopping at Telmouth and Newton Abbot. This train is running approximately 20 minutes late due to a delay at London Paddington. Please stand back when the train makes its arrival, and mind the gap when you board the train.

2

Man: Excuse me, do you have any vacancies?

Woman: How many nights did you want to stay?

Man: Just two.

Woman: And did you want a single room or a double?

Man: A single.

Woman: Hmm, well, we are very small, we only have three rooms and two of those are doubles. Ah! But somebody cancelled a reservation for a single room this morning, so I think we do have a room free for you. Do you want to have a quick look round the place?

Man: Yes, that'd be nice.

Woman: Here's the living room, you can come and watch TV here when you like. And here's the breakfast room. You can make yourself coffee here at any time of the day. I serve breakfast from 7.30 to 9.30. And upstairs are the bedrooms. We have three other people staying here at the moment. If you'd like to come this way, I'll show you your room …

3

Woman: Hello. I would like to go to Yarmouth, please.

Ticket officer: Yarmouth? Are you coming back today?

Woman: Sorry?

Ticket officer: Are you coming back today? It's a cheaper fare if it's a same-day return.

Woman: I am sorry. I do not understand.

Ticket officer: Do you want a single ticket or a return?

Woman: Oh, a single, please.

Ticket officer: OK, madam. A single ticket, standard class for Yarmouth. That's £22.50, please.

4

Girl: Oh no! I don't believe it!

Man: What?

Girl: Look outside. It's raining. It *always* rains when we come here.

Man: Yeah. When we were driving up here it was sunny all the way, and now as soon as we get everything fixed up in the campsite the weather changes.

Girl: Oh, the journey took forever, didn't it?

Man: I know. But it's not easy pulling one of these things behind the car.

Girl: Oh, look at those people over there. I think their tent has got a hole in it. The water's definitely getting in.

Man: You see! It could be worse. At least inside this thing we won't get wet!

Pronunciation p21

2b 09

1 We need to check in at seven o'clock.
2 Here's the check-in desk.
3 What time does the plane take off?
4 What time is take-off?
5 The car didn't break down.
6 There is a car breakdown service.

Gateway to life skills p23

8 🎬 ▶ 10

Jasmine:

Hi there! Welcome back to my vlog. I've just come back from my trip to New Zealand to visit my aunt, uncle and cousins. It was fantastic! And I learned a lot about being a responsible tourist. New Zealand is so beautiful that New Zealanders really look after their environment (especially my aunt who's a really eco-friendly person!). A strange thing happened when we got off the plane at Wellington airport. In our suitcases we had some yummy English food to give our family – English tea, some honey and some cheddar cheese. But when we arrived at the airport, they took them all away. Why? Well, the thing is that New Zealand has a unique island environment. So to protect the plants and animals, they check to see that you don't bring in any food or plants that are new to New Zealand. In fact, they even took away my brother's smelly, old trainers. Why? Because they were dirty! Outdoor shoes with soil on them might contaminate the environment. My brother was very upset about his trainers – they were his favourite pair – although my mum was very pleased! There are some amazing national parks in New Zealand. Look! Here's a photo of Tongariro National Park in the centre of North Island. It's so cool – there are three active volcanoes there and they filmed parts of *The Lord of the Rings* in this park. The problem is that tourists leave rubbish there. So, please, if you ever go to New Zealand and visit any of the national parks, don't leave any rubbish. The parks have all sorts of special wildlife. The original people from New Zealand, the Maoris, consider Tongariro to be a sacred place, so respect that!

Talking about the Maoris, many tourists buy Maori art to take back as souvenirs from New Zealand. But if you want to be sure that a product really is made locally, by Maoris, then look for a sign that says 'Toi Iho', spelt T-O-I , I-H-O.

And when you want to buy something basic in New Zealand, look for a sign or label that says 'Environmental Choice'. That label is important. It means that the product is more environmentally friendly than other similar products. New Zealand is a beautiful place! If you go there on holiday, make sure it stays beautiful! Oh, and it's fine to bring back food from there – we brought back some delicious kiwi fruits! Yum!

Listening p24

2 and 3 ▶ 11

Presenter: Today on the History Programme we have with us Kate Summers. Kate, you've just written a book about the history of travelling around the world, haven't you?

Kate: That's right. I find it fascinating that today anybody can fly round the world in just two or three days. But people forget that it used to take weeks, months or even years to travel round the world.

Presenter: The first person to travel round the world was the Portuguese sailor Ferdinand Magellan, wasn't it?

Kate: People usually say that. But he in fact died before he could complete the journey. So really the first person to travel round the world was the Spanish captain Juan Sebastián Elcano. And, of course, the 17 other members of the expedition who survived with him.

Presenter: When was that, and how long did it take them?

Kate: They arrived back home in 1522. It had taken them just over three years! Of course, that was without maps or anything.

Presenter: People have always been interested in travelling round the world faster and faster, haven't they? You only have to think of the famous novel by Jules Verne, *Around the World in 80 Days.*

Kate: Yes. The truth is that Jules Verne probably got the inspiration for his book from a *real* journey that somebody actually made in 1870, two years before Verne wrote his novel.

Presenter: Oh! So who made this journey?

Kate: It was a man called George Francis Train. He was a rich American businessman who helped to build the Union Pacific Railroad. The building of the railroad was very important. Before the Union Pacific Railroad it used to take about six months to go from New York to California. Once the Union Pacific Railroad was built, it took just two weeks.

Presenter: So how did George Francis Train travel round the world?

Kate: He took the Union Pacific Railroad from New York to California. Then he got on a ship and sailed to Japan. Then he went by sea to Hong Kong and Singapore. After that he took the Suez Canal.

Presenter: Did it use to take much longer before they opened the Suez Canal?

Kate: Yes, the Canal opened in 1869. Before 1869, sailors didn't use to have any alternative. They would sail right round the bottom of Africa, the Cape of Good Hope. It would take a long, long time, and it was dangerous because of the seas there.

Presenter: So really it was only possible to travel round the world in 80 days because of the new railway in the US and the Suez Canal.

Kate: That's right. Of course, the next big change was flying. Aeroplanes really changed everything. In 1995 the Concord supersonic plane flew round the world in less than 32 hours!

Presenter: Not even Jules Verne could imagine that!

Developing speaking p26

2 and 3 12

Ticket agent: Good morning. Can I help you?

Girl: Yes, please. Could you tell me the time of the next train to Canterbury?

Ticket agent: No problem … Let's see. There's a train which leaves in 30 minutes, at five minutes to four and you arrive in Canterbury at quarter past six.

Girl: That's great. Is it a direct train?

Ticket agent: No, I'm sorry, it isn't. There are no direct trains from Gatwick to Canterbury.

Girl: I see. How many changes are there?

Ticket agent: Just one. You go to London St Pancras and change there.

Girl: OK. Could I buy a ticket?

Ticket agent: Of course. Would you like a single or return?

Girl: Sorry, I didn't catch that.

Ticket agent: Would you like a single or a return?

Girl: A return, please.

Ticket agent: When are you coming back?

Girl: Next Wednesday.

Ticket agent: Pardon?

Girl: Next Wednesday.

Ticket agent: OK. Let's see. The cheapest fare for a return ticket to Canterbury is £41.

Girl: Right. Can I pay by debit card?

Ticket agent: Yes, of course.

Girl: Oh, can you tell me which platform it is for the train to London?

Ticket agent: Yes, it's platform 9.

Girl: And when I get to St Pancras?

Ticket agent: Just look at the departure screens or go to the information desk and they'll tell you.

Girl: OK. Thanks a lot.

Ticket agent: Thank you, and have a good journey.

Gateway to exams: Units 1–2

Listening p31

7 13

Speaker 1:

I'd always wanted to go somewhere really different, somewhere really far away, so I decided to go to Japan one year. When you get off the plane at Tokyo and see all the signs in Japanese, it's, well, it's amazing. But it can create a few problems. One day I went down into the underground and I just got totally lost. I caught one train and arrived on the other side of the city. I asked people for help and they were really nice. But in the end it took 50 minutes to make a trip that usually takes five!

Speaker 2:

I love travelling. When I finished university, I travelled around the world. I think it's because I travel so much that I don't really plan things in advance, I just take each day as an adventure. The only thing with travelling like that is you can sometimes have problems. I remember once when I was in France I arrived at this town late at night because I'd missed a train. I thought there'd be lots of hotels there, but there was nothing. Well, no, there was one bed and breakfast and it was full. In the end, I had to sleep outside in a park. It rained all night! Horrible! Sometimes it's better to think first!

Speaker 3:

Last year I'd planned my dream holiday, going to New Zealand. I hated the flight because it took such a long time, and I never like flying. Anyway, I finally arrived. I was tired and really wanted to get to the youth hostel where I was going to stay. It was a really good place that someone had recommended to me. Anyway, I was waiting for my bags to come out; I'd packed lots of things because I was going to be away for a long time. I waited and waited and my bags never appeared. I had to spend the first week with almost nothing, while I waited for them to find my stuff.

Speaker 4:

Last summer I spent ten days in Cuba. But that wasn't my original plan. My plan was to spend just a week there, but on the day before I was going to make the return flight, we were watching the news, and that's when we heard about the weather. There was a hurricane on its way, a really big one. The next day, we got to the airport with all our luggage and they told us that there was a delay with our flight. Well, not just our flight, all of them! We had to wait for a long time before they gave us any more information and then they suddenly told us that they'd cancelled all the flights because of the weather!

Unit 3

Vocabulary p32

2 ⏵ 14

a semi-detached house
b terraced house
c detached house/bungalow
d cottage

Vocabulary p32

8 15

Speaker 1:

The building I live in is quite tall. I think there are about ten families living there, with about 30 to 40 people in total. The building is quite nice and modern. We haven't got a private garden, but there's a garden that we can all use. I like my home, but sometimes it's noisy because you can hear the people on one side and the other side, and the people upstairs and downstairs, too.

Speaker 2:

My grandparents bought a new place recently. My grandmother has problems walking so they decided to buy a house where she doesn't need to use the stairs all the time.

The new place is perfect for them. It's quite big, but it's easy for them to move about in.

Speaker 3:

Where I live is quite quiet, too quiet for me, but my parents like it. We live a little bit outside the city. It's not too far away, but I do need to catch a bus every time I want to go shopping or eat out or go to the cinema. All the streets are clean and tidy where I live, and there are lots of trees and green areas like parks and stuff. It's nice, but I'd like to live somewhere more exciting, closer to the city centre.

Speaker 4:

I don't mind the area where I live. It's a bit crowded and noisy and our house is quite small. But it's very central. I can get to the cinema and the shops really quickly. One day I want to get out of here, though, and live somewhere that's completely different, like in the middle of the country.

Pronunciation p35

4a   16

1 The view from our window wasn't just beautiful. It was absolutely *stunning*.
2 The city of Athens isn't just old. It's *ancient*. It's existed for over 3,000 years!
3 It was very hot in the city yesterday – over 35°C.
4 At the weekend the shops in the city centre are totally *packed* with people.
5 The streets are usually quite dirty because nobody cleans them.
6 There wasn't a sound in the park. It was completely *silent*.

Gateway to life skills p37

7 and 8

 17

Ben:

For our presentation, we've decided to look at who uses the most common social networking site in New York. Here is the information we found out …

Jasmine:

Let's begin by looking at this pie chart. It shows different groups of people in New York using the most common social networking site. You can see that about two thirds of users are between 13 and 34. One in ten users are aged between 13 and 17.

Ben:

The most frequent users of this social networking site in New York are people between the ages of 25 and 34. Over a quarter of users are at that age. The smallest group of users are between the ages of 55 and 64. Maybe that's not a big surprise. But I think that number is going to increase steadily in the future. And I think we'll have statistics for even older users soon, too.

Jasmine:

If you look now at this bar graph, we have more or less the same information. You can see how the number of users rises steadily from the ages of 13 and 17 to the ages of 25 and 34. And then it falls quite dramatically between 34 and 44. After that, it decreases gradually from 44 to 64. So it's a different way of showing us that 18–34-year-olds are again the most active social networkers!

Ben:

What is also interesting about the bar graph is that you can see the different statistics for men and women. You can see that in every age group there are slightly more women than men using this site, according to these statistics. The difference changes very little at different ages, it basically stays the same.

Jasmine:

And it's not just the age of users, or whether they are men or women. There are many other interesting things that social media can tell us about a city like New York. What we choose to follow and like on social media can give us information about the sports team we support, the schools and universities that we go to, the music that we listen to, the places in our city that we like to visit, and films and shows we go to see … What do you think social media can tell you about your city?

Listening p38

2 and 3 18

Interviewer: So, Deniz, can you tell us about your experience of the Erasmus project? First of all, tell us, where are you from?

Deniz: I'm from Istanbul, in Turkey.

Interviewer: And at the moment you're in Salamanca, in Spain.

Deniz: That's right.

Interviewer: How long have you been living in Salamanca?

Deniz: I've been living here since October. And I go back to Istanbul at the end of May.

Interviewer: How have you found the experience so far?

Deniz: I've been having a great time! I always wanted to visit Spain. And then my university told me I had a place at Salamanca. To be honest, at first I wasn't sure where it was in Spain – if it was in the north or the south …

Interviewer: Salamanca isn't as big or busy as Madrid or Barcelona, is it?

Deniz: No, it isn't. But the university in Salamanca is really famous, in fact it's one of the oldest universities in the world! The city is small, but it's very lively. There are lots of historic buildings, a beautiful main square, museums, you know, that sort of thing. But there are also lots of shows, exhibitions, concerts … I've seen two or three brilliant concerts …

Interviewer: So what's been the best part of your stay?

Deniz: I think just meeting people from so many different countries. I've been living in a residence with other Erasmus students – there are British students, students from Poland, Germany, Italy … I've made friends with people from all over Europe. So every night we get together for dinner. We each make a typical dish from our country and we have these great kitchen parties that last for ages.

Interviewer: How much Spanish have you learnt?

Deniz: I've learnt lots. I've been speaking Spanish every day. But it's true that I've also been speaking a lot of English because nearly everybody in the residence can speak it.

Interviewer: And what do you think has been the worst or most difficult thing so far?

Deniz: Well, I study physics, so understanding explanations of physics in Spanish has been really difficult. But it *is* getting easier. And recently we've been doing lots of exams. I just finished yesterday, in fact. But the exams aren't *too* bad. Really the whole thing has just been a *great* experience!

Developing speaking p40

2 and 3 19

In the photo I can see a big city. I think it's Tokyo because on the right I can see some signs and writing in Japanese. And in the background there are some big buildings. I don't know if they're skyscrapers. Maybe this is Hachiko Square. Because it looks very busy. I mean, the streets are really packed. In the foreground and in the middle of the photo there are hundreds of people walking. Perhaps they're shopping because I think that on the right and on the left there are shops, or maybe restaurants. The unusual thing is that people are walking in the road, but there are also cars and taxis. It looks a bit dangerous to me! I don't really like big cities like this. I'd like to visit Tokyo one day, but I don't think I'd like to live there. It's true that big cities like Tokyo are usually interesting and lively. They have lots of things to see and do, and there's always something happening. For example, in the top right corner of the photo there's a large screen showing a video, I think. But in my opinion big cities like this are too noisy and dirty and crowded.

Unit 4

Pronunciation p44

3c 20

carrot	chicken
dessert	lettuce
olive	pancake
starter	sweetcorn
turkey	

Vocabulary p44

6 ▶ 21

1
A: So, first you put the oil in the pan, like that, and then you put the heat up. Right … can you hear that now?
B: Yes.
A: When you hear that, that's the moment to put the chicken in the pan … Mmm, lovely, just smell that. And we leave it in there until it's a lovely golden colour. Then it's ready to eat.

2
A: Are you really going to eat that?
B: Yeah, of course. Why not?
A: But is it cooked?
B: No, they just take the fresh fish, they mix it with lime juice and they leave it. It's delicious.
A: Yuk! I couldn't eat fish that hasn't been cooked.

3
A: Wow! That's good … What is it?
B: Well, it's beef, but they mix in these special peppers. They're a bit hot, aren't they?

A: A bit? I think my mouth is on fire! This is my fifth glass of water.

4
A: Mmm, that's good.
B: Good?!! Do you know what's in that?
A: No, and I don't want to. It's really tasty, just let me enjoy it.
B: Yeah, but you'll be sorry afterwards. Everything in it is artificial. It's full of chemicals. And it's only tasty because it's got extra salt, extra sugar and it's got too much fat.
A: I don't know why I invite you to this burger place. You always ruin my meal in the end!

5
A: Are you really going to eat that?
B: What, this tuna sandwich? Tuna isn't bad for you.
A: Well, it isn't the tuna that's the problem. It's the bread.
B: What's the matter with the bread?
A: It's been in the kitchen for at least a week! It's probably hard.
B: Oh, yeah, you're right: I didn't know it was so old. Yeurgh!

6
A: Mmm. That turkey smells good. Is it ready to eat?
B: Let's have a look … No, it needs to stay in the oven for another ten minutes, with the potatoes.
A: Mmm. The potatoes look good, too. I know that they're probably healthier when they're boiled. But I think they're much tastier done in the oven with just a bit of oil.

Gateway to life skills p49

5 and 6 🎬 ▶ 22

Harry as Judge 1: So, Jasmine, what are you going to make today?
Jasmine: Today I'm going to make my special fried fish. I'm going to cover the fish with the egg and the breadcrumbs and then fry it.
Harry: OK. But, Jasmine, remember that you're going to have to use your hands a lot, you know, putting the fish into the mixture. So?
Jasmine: Oh, right … sorry, chef. I'll take my rings off.
Harry: Jasmine needs to be careful of jewellery on her hands or wrists. When you wear jewellery it's impossible to wash your hands properly and to get them 100% clean. And that's so important when using your hands!
Georgia as Judge 2: Hi, Ben. That looks interesting. What are you making for your starter?
Ben: Well, it's an unusual Italian salad. It's very healthy, and very cheap too because you just need bread, tomatoes, onions … and of course, olive oil.

Georgia: Yes, I can see the olive oil. In fact, there's lots of it on the floor there, just by your foot!
Ben: Oh yes. I spilled some before. Sorry, chef. I'll tidy it up straight away.
Georgia: It's not a question of being sorry … Safety comes first in the kitchen and somebody could stand on that oil and fall because it's very slippery. And what if they're carrying a knife, or something hot? There could be an accident.
Georgia: Jasmine? Are you still cooking for us?
Jasmine: Yes, of course. For my main course, I'm making an Indian dish …
Georgia: I think you've forgotten something, haven't you?
Jasmine: No … I've got the lamb, got the rice, erm.
Harry: Have you seen Jasmine?
Georgia: Yes, I know. She needs to keep her hair tied back or cover it. It's a simple question of hygiene!
Harry: And where's her apron? An apron is to keep you clean and to keep the food clean, too.
Georgia: They're basics. She needs to do better or she's out!
Harry: OK, Ben. Stop for a second. Explain what you've just done.
Ben: Well, I've just been cutting up some chicken. Oh, and chopping up some lettuce, too.
Harry: With the same knife? On the same board?
Ben: Err? Yeeees?
Harry: OK, listen, Ben, this is important. When you cut raw chicken and use the same knife and board to chop the lettuce, the lettuce now has bacteria from the raw chicken. You could get food poisoning if you eat that.
Ben: So, what do I need to do?
Harry: Simple. Make sure you always wash your knife and board after cutting raw meat. But right now you need to put that lettuce straight in the bin!
Harry: And you've only got 15 minutes left to finish your dish!

Listening p50

2 and 3 ▶ 23

Speaker 1:
Personally, I think we'll all be eating something which is already quite common in Asia. I think we'll be eating seaweed, algae. There are so many good things about it. First of all, seaweed grows faster than any other plant in the world. So it's easy to farm. And because it grows in the ocean, you don't need to use the land or fresh water. That's an enormous advantage because by 2050 water will have become

a real problem. There won't be enough for traditional farming. Anyway, another great thing about seaweed is that it's really healthy. You can use it instead of salt and put it in bread or even fast-food meals and it's much better for you than salt. It's actually very tasty, too! I've tried lots of great meals made with seaweed!

Speaker 2:

I think that by 2050 restaurants will have disappeared. We'll all be using 3D printers at home to create our food. The technology already exists, but it's quite expensive at the moment. But by 2050 3D printers will have become a part of everyday life. You'll be able to decide from a list what you want to eat – a burger, a pizza, a chocolate cake. Then you'll just put the basic ingredients in the machine, press a button, and the machine will do the rest. I'm not sure how quick it will be, but it will save us lots of time in front of a cooker, especially when you need to produce food in large quantities. We'll be spending more time doing other, more important things instead of cooking.

Speaker 3:

Some people won't like what I'm going to say. I think in 2050 we won't be eating meat or fish. Maybe we'll be eating things that *look* like burgers, but we'll be making those 'burgers' with insects. In many parts of the world, people already eat insects – in parts of Africa, Japan, Thailand … We all know that insects can give us lots of protein. And insect farms are cheap. They don't need much water *and* there are probably around 1,400 different types of insect that humans can eat. I've never tried them, but people say they're tasty. Really, there are so *many* good reasons for eating them. I think that the problem is that people have a negative attitude towards insects in general. So they really don't like the idea of eating them. I think we'll all need to change our minds about insects in the future.

Speaker 4:

Have you heard about 'frankenburgers'? They're burgers that they made from 'meat' produced in a laboratory. I think that's what we'll be eating in 2050. Big, traditional farms full of animals will have disappeared by then. There won't be enough water for them, and we'll be trying to protect the environment. So the only solution will be to create food and meat in laboratories. It won't be very natural or very tasty, probably. And some of us think that this laboratory food will be dangerous and have negative effects on our bodies. I hate to say this, but I think that in 2050 we probably won't have any alternative.

Developing speaking p52

2 and 3a ▶ 24

Examiner:

Now, I want you to look at these different places where you can eat out. I want you to imagine that it's the end of term. Your class

is going to organise an end-of-term meal for the whole class. Which of these five places do you think is the best place for your end-of-term meal?

Student A:

OK. What do you think about a fast food restaurant?

Student B:

Personally, I don't like fast food. But I think that a lot of people do, and they go to fast food restaurants quite often, at the weekend, for example. So it isn't a very good place to celebrate a special event.

Student A:

Yes, I agree. It's the same with the school canteen. We eat there every day. In my opinion, we need to choose somewhere we don't usually go.

Student B:

An outdoor picnic area might be nice because we could go to a park or somewhere special.

Student A:

Good idea! Picnics are great because they aren't very expensive either.

Student B:

Yes. That's the problem with an exclusive restaurant. The food and service will be really good. But I don't think most people will want to spend a lot of money on the meal.

Student A:

Yes, you're right … Erm … What about in a classmate's house? That's cheap.

Student B:

Yes. And it's probably quite comfortable. You can have music for example, and people can move about.

Student A:

Yes, but a house is probably going to be small for all the class. And it isn't very special.

Student B:

Well, the way I see it, the outdoor picnic area is the best. It's cheap and easy for a larger group. Why don't we choose that?

Student A:

OK. Let's have it somewhere special, at the beach, for example. And we can organise games and competitions, too.

Examiner:

Thank you.

Unit 5

Pronunciation p58

2b ▶ 25

architecture	art
biology	business studies
chemistry	computer science
drama	engineering
English	geography
history	law
literature	maths
media studies	medicine
music	PE (Physical Education)
physics	psychology

Vocabulary p58

3 ▶ 26

Teacher 1:

OK, now Joe, you stand here, and Kate, you stand here. Now, you remember the situation? Joe, you've just discovered that you've lost your job, you've been working for the same company for 20 years so you feel sad, angry, depressed. Kate, you're Joe's wife. You don't know that Joe has lost his job yet, so when you find out, act really surprised. Don't forget that this is a really tragic play, so I want you to really transmit that to the people watching.

Teacher 2:

Now here we have the water. Now add sugar. That's it. And now add sodium hydroxide. Be careful with that because it can hurt if you get it on your skin. OK? Now mix that solution carefully. OK? You can see that it's transparent. Now add the potassium permanganate and watch carefully. Look at the colours. First, purple, yeah? Then blue. And now green … and finally the solution turns orange. Can you see that? OK, a simple little experiment, but you can clearly see how the solution changes colour. Now what happens …

Teacher 3:

OK, you all have your fish in front of you. Now take your scissors. OK. And I want you to cut here, like … that. Well, it doesn't smell or look very nice, I know. But I want you to look closely at what you can see here. There's the skeleton, but we can also see the gills here. You remember, the organs that fish need to breathe underwater. Now I want you to take the scissors again and cut just here and see what you can see. Isn't it just fascinating to see how different animals' bodies work!

Teacher 4:

Listen hard, get your pencils and paper ready and let's see who can be first to answer the question. There's a sports shop, right? Last week this shop sold 17 footballs and 25 tennis balls. The footballs all cost £30 and each tennis ball cost £3. So, how much money did the shop make by selling these balls? Go on. Quick now!

3a ▶ 27

director	employee
farmer	instructor
scientist	technician
electrician	employer
journalist	librarian
photographer	physicist
professor	trainee

Gateway to life skills p63

7a and 7b 🎬 ▶ 28

Harry: Yes, it's that time of year again. Most of us have assignments to do this term and lots of you want tips about the best way to do them.

Georgia: Yes, in particular you have lots of questions about how to use the web for assignments.

Harry: Well, we asked you to send us *your* questions, so we can give you some advice.

Georgia: So, let's see what you said!

Olivia: Once I used an online encyclopaedia to find information for an assignment, but then I read somewhere that you shouldn't use them. Why not?

Harry: Well, Olivia, it depends which online encyclopaedia. Nowadays you can find popular online encyclopaedias which are not actually written by experts. These encyclopaedias often have very recent information and are updated frequently.

Georgia: But! The problem is they aren't always reliable – *anybody* could be writing these articles! And if there are mistakes, nobody is personally responsible.

Harry: So, our advice is to only use encyclopaedias that you know are written by experts, or use a website of a university, a museum, or a serious newspaper.

Jack: Sometimes I find exactly the information that I need on a website. Why can't I just cut and paste the part of the text that I need?

Georgia: Thanks, Jack! Cutting and pasting is fast and easy. But that's the problem. It doesn't show the teacher that you've learnt or understood anything.

Harry: Yes, anybody can cut and paste Einstein's theory of relativity, but does that mean they understand it?

Chloe: I've heard teachers say be careful with plagiarism in assignments. But I'm not totally sure I understand what plagiarism is?

Harry: Good question, Chloe! Plagiarism is when you take

somebody else's words or ideas and say that they're yours. So if you just copy and paste, it's plagiarism. Plagiarism is basically stealing.

Georgia: That doesn't mean you can't use other people's ideas or words. But you must always make sure you include where or who the ideas or words came from.

Luke: Erm … Of course I would never do this but er, is it easy for teachers to spot cutting and pasting?

Georgia: It's *very* easy. Teachers notice straightaway if your text includes complicated ideas that you haven't seen in class yet. Or if the style or words aren't the ones you usually use.

Harry: And, anyway, nowadays there are online services which teachers can use to find exactly where the information came from. Our advice? Don't even think about it!

Georgia: So, there you have it. We hope we gave you some great tips.

Harry: Join us again soon. Oh, and good luck with those assignments!

Listening p64

2 and 3 ▶ 29

1

Boy: So are you going to do any extracurricular activities this year?

Girl: Yes, I've just joined the Capoeira Club.

Boy: The what club??!!

Girl: Capoeira. C-A-P-O-E-I-R-A. Haven't you heard of it? It's Brazilian. It's a sort of martial art.

Boy: Like judo or karate?

Girl: Yes, but it's very different, too. If it was just a martial art, I wouldn't do it. This is a mixture of martial arts, dance, gymnastics …

Boy: So, do you do it with music?

Girl: Yes, music is an important part of it, too. To be honest, I just saw it on TV once and it looked fun. I want to learn something new. Why don't you join, too?

Boy: When is it?

Girl: Seven o'clock on Mondays and Thursdays.

Boy: Hmmm. I don't know my timetable yet. If I'm free then, I'll think about it.

2

Girl: Have you joined any clubs or anything yet?

Boy: Yes! I've joined the Quidditch Club!

Girl: Quidditch??! Isn't that the game in Harry Potter?! Don't you have to be able to fly or something?!

Boy: Ha! It'd be great if it was like in the films and books! But this is a version of Quidditch where you play on a

football pitch, for example.

Girl: But do you have competitions, matches?

Boy: Yes. There's even a Quidditch World Cup now! It's actually quite difficult! You have to run a *lot*. I think it's more tiring than football!

Girl: Hmm. You do realise you're 18 now. If I were you, I'd stop reading those Harry Potter books and start studying!

Boy: I think it's just the opposite. If you don't find time to relax when you're a student, you become stressed. And that's not good for your studies either.

3

Woman:
OK. Could everybody listen? OK, I'm here to tell you a little bit about our society. It's actually one of the biggest societies here at this college. Maybe one reason for that is because you don't have to be good at dancing to join. In fact, beginners are welcome. We offer classes at all levels and for different styles – ballet, modern dance, street dance … For people who are already good dancers we have advanced classes and we take part in competitions. Last year three of our dancers won!

4

Mum: Hello.

Boy: Hi, Mum!

Mum: Hi, darling. How are you? How's your first week at college?

Boy: Really good! There's a lot happening. Yesterday there was a fair where all the clubs and societies explained what they do, and how you can become a member.

Mum: Mmm, that sounds interesting. Did you join any?

Boy: Yes, I joined the Cooking Club.

Mum: Cooking? You? But you can't cook!

Boy: Well, yeah. That's why I joined. They teach you how to make simple dishes. If I don't go to classes, I'll never learn. I don't want to eat out all the time when I'm living away from home.

Mum: No, you're right. It's a very good idea.

Boy: They also organise special evenings where everybody cooks and then you all eat together afterwards.

Mum: That sounds great. You should invite me to one of those evenings … But only *after* you've had a few lessons!

Developing speaking p66

2 and 3 ▶ 30

In this presentation I'm going to talk about homeschooling.

I'd like to begin by saying that I can see *some* advantages to homeschooling. Firstly, you don't have to wear a uniform. So you can wear comfortable clothes all day. Secondly, you don't have to waste time travelling to school or worrying about arriving late, because you're already *at* your school. What's more, in some classes you can't go at the speed you want because some people understand what the teacher is explaining immediately, but there are others who take longer to get the idea. With homeschooling you're probably the only student so you can go at your own speed.

But personally I can see a lot more *dis*advantages. First of all, if you have all your classes at home, you never meet other students or people of your age. I think that's a really big disadvantage. An important part of school is the social life. It's important to make friends and to be able to talk to people of your age. You also learn a lot from your classmates and by working with them. For example, I think working with others prepares you for the world of work when you're older because in any job you need to be able to work with others as part of a team.

It's also true that in my opinion, not many parents would be good teachers. Maybe they're clever and know lots of things, but I don't think parents can usually teach all the different subjects, from maths to literature. Take my father for instance. He's a journalist. He knows lots of history, geography, art. But he doesn't like maths at all.

Oh, and another thing is that exams and tests aren't much fun, but I think they help you to learn. If I didn't have to do exams, I wouldn't sit down and learn everything, and I wouldn't remember so much information.

To sum up, I think there are some advantages to homeschooling. But I don't think that staying at home all the time is a good idea. The point that I'm trying to make is that school isn't just a question of exams and information. It's also about being with others, working together and learning to be part of a group or team.

Unit 6

Vocabulary p70

5 31

a select a programme
b connect X to Y
c press a button
d charge/recharge a battery
e switch/turn on/off
f plug in
g insert
h tap the screen

Vocabulary p70

6 32

1

Boy: Well, I can't do that, can I? I don't know how it works, do I?

Mum: Don't worry. I'll explain. If you can study advanced maths and physics at school, I think you'll be able to

do this. Look. You plug it in, you switch it on, and you move it all over the floor like this, until it's clean. Do you think you can do that?

Boy: Mmm, I'm not sure. Can you explain again?

Mum: Of course. Let me explain another way. If you don't clean the carpet in your bedroom in the next five minutes, you can't go out this weekend. Now do you understand?

Boy: Err. Yeah.

2

Woman 1: Let's see what the instructions say. It says to switch it on by pressing power, then to take pictures you press the red button. You can select the ones you want to keep by pressing this button here and connect to a computer or laptop to save them. You recharge the battery when the red light flashes.

Woman 2: Oh well, that's easy. It was a good idea to buy this! We'll be able to take hundreds of pictures next week when we are on holiday. Ooh, and it says you can record short videos, too!

3

Woman: So, how does this work exactly?

Man: Oh, it's really simple. You switch the machine on here, like this. If they're really dirty, select a long programme. One hour is normally enough. There, can you see it says 45 minutes? That should do. So, select that one and then press the button here and just leave it. When it's finished, the plates and glasses should be good and clean – sparkling, in fact!

Pronunciation p72

2b and 2c 33

1 The gadget was invented last year.
2 The new phones are sold here.
3 Ten prizes were given.
4 The disc was inserted.
5 Emails are sent every day.

Gateway to life skills p75

5a and 6a  34

Olivia: OK. Now, let me explain what we're doing. The head teacher wants to start a prize system in the school. Each year she wants a ceremony where the best students are going to be given awards.

Jack: That sounds cool!

Olivia: She wants *us* to give her some ideas about this ceremony. So, we are going to have a brainstorming session …

Chloe: Great. I love brainstorming. Would you like me to be the secretary?

Olivia: Yes, please. Now, we need to decide what exactly the prizes are going to be for, what the prizes should be and what we could do for the ceremony. Is that clear?

Jack: Yes. How long have we got?

Olivia: We've got a few minutes to do the brainstorming and ten minutes to analyse the ideas.

Luke: Great, let's start. I think there should be a prize for each subject, you know, so Best History Student in Year 8, or the Best Maths Student in Year 11.

Olivia: OK. Chloe, can you write that one down?

Chloe: Sure.

Jack: I don't think that's a very good idea. I think there should be an overall prize for the best boy and the best girl in the class, because otherwise there'd be hundreds of prizes.

Chloe: But what about sport and music and art? I think there should be a prize for other things that people do at school, not just academic work.

Luke: Going back to school subjects, I think there should be a prize for most hard-working student. You know, a prize for effort. Because that could really inspire us all to work harder. That's important.

Jack: Who decides that?

Luke: I think it could be decided between the teachers *and* the students. We could vote in class.

Chloe: Hey, there could be a prize for the best teacher, too?! The whole school could vote.

Jack: Ha, ha, that's a really crazy idea! The head teacher isn't going to do that.

Olivia: OK, Jack, all ideas are welcome in a brainstorming session.

Jack: Oops, sorry Chloe.

Chloe: No worries.

Olivia: Now what about the actual prize?

Chloe: I think it could be like an Oscar!

Jack: Well, OK and maybe we could present the ceremony like the Oscars, too! We could have a famous person present the prizes. An actor or somebody.

Olivia: Wait! I think there's a famous TV presenter who went to our school. Why don't we contact her?

Luke: What about having a red carpet?! And we could have proper photographers and put the photos up on the school website.

Chloe: Or even try and get the ceremony covered by the local newspaper. It'd be great publicity for the school.

Olivia: OK. Any ideas about what the prizes could be?

Chloe: I was thinking books.

Luke: Or e-readers.

Jack: Money! Or MP3 players. Everybody would want to win something like that! People would work harder.

Luke: What about money to take a group of school friends to the cinema or out for pizza?

Olivia: That's great, we've got lots of ideas. Chloe, can you go through some of those ideas and let's see which ones we think could work and which ones we could adapt.

Chloe: Olivia, we've run out of time. I have to go now.

Jack: Oh, no.

Luke: I have to go, too. I'm going to be late for basketball practice.

Olivia: Oops, sorry, I forgot about the time. We'll have to meet again tomorrow to finish this.

Listening p76

2 and 3 35

Presenter: Today on the Science Programme we begin by looking at smart homes. Here to help us is Jane Forrest, who's a specialist in technology in the home. Jane, what exactly is a smart home?

Jane: The simplest way to explain it is a house where technology and electronic systems make life easier for you.

Presenter: Can you give us some examples?

Jane: Yes. Take fridges, for example. Usually you just use a fridge to keep your food cold. But now there are smart fridges. They know exactly what food and drink they have inside. It isn't really magic, the fridge uses the bar code information on your food products – that's the label with the black lines. So, with that information, a smart fridge can suggest what to make for dinner using those ingredients.

Presenter: I *hate* thinking about what to make for dinner. Especially with what's in *my* fridge!

Jane: In that case, another thing that you'll like about smart fridges is that if you want to eat healthier food, your fridge can suggest healthy alternatives for the things you have in it.

Presenter: Amazing!

Jane: Or, for example, when you take something from the fridge, it automatically makes a note of it. You don't have to write a shopping list or go shopping. The fridge can make a list and send it to an online shopping service. You have all your food delivered to your house without doing anything yourself!

Presenter: That sounds great!

Jane: And the good thing is you can control everything either using a remote control or just your smartphone.

Presenter: Really?

Jane: Yes. Imagine you've gone out for the evening. With your mobile phone you can connect with cameras inside and outside your house to see that everything's OK. You can even turn the lights or the heating on or off, just with your phone, from any distance.

Presenter: That's useful. I've got pets and it's sometimes a problem to feed them. I'd be interested in finding a solution to that!

Jane: That's easy to fix! In a smart house you can have your pets fed automatically, whenever you like, using an app on your mobile.

Presenter: This all sounds great, but isn't it science fiction? Can you really buy smart houses today?

Jane: Bill Gates had a smart house built for over 100 million dollars some years ago. Nowadays lots of people are having electronic systems installed in their houses. Smart technology is everywhere. I mean, look at vacuum cleaners. Many homes have those robot vacuum cleaners, you know, you switch them on and you can have the floors cleaned without doing anything. That's a simple example of what a smart house can do now. But soon the vacuum cleaner will decide for itself when the floor is dirty and it'll switch itself on. You won't even need to press the On switch!

Presenter: But I find that a bit scary. It's like the robots are taking control.

Jane: Remember, *you* are still in control of all these systems. Imagine, in the morning, your alarm clock goes off. It automatically switches on the heating and your coffee machine ... You get out of bed and you don't have to do anything. Everything has been done for you!

Presenter: Don't you think that will make people lazier in the future? If we get everything done for us by robots and technology?

Jane: Aren't you tired of doing housework?! Smart houses will give us more free time to be active, do sport, go running, cycling, and also relax. I think cleaning and shopping for food will be things of the past.

Presenter: You're probably right. I don't like doing housework in my free time either. You know, tomorrow I think I'll buy one of those robot vacuum cleaners you mentioned!

Developing speaking p78

2 and 3 36

Erm ... both of the photos show students doing lessons in a secondary school. In the first photo they're in a normal classroom with a whiteboard whereas in the second photo they're in a laboratory.

Of course, one thing that the photos have in common is that they both show lessons at school. It's interesting because in the first photo they're just listening to the teacher. However, in the second photo the students are actually doing experiments. They have liquids in bottles, and I can see a Bunsen burner in the middle of the photo. Erm ... Another important difference between the photos is that the students are all listening to the teacher in the first photo, but in the second photo they're working on their own. One other similarity between the photos is that in both photos the students look interested in the lesson.

Personally, I like both types of lesson because I think it's important to learn the theories in a normal classroom, but then it's good to have practical lessons where you can do real experiments to check the theories. But if I had to choose one of the two lessons, I'd prefer the second. That's because I think it's more exciting to do things instead of just listening and writing. I'd like to have a job connected with science one day, so I think it's important to have practical lessons, because they help you to get ready for working in a real laboratory one day.

Gateway to exams: Units 5–6

Listening p83

4 37

Well, our next story could be really good news for teenagers. Many teenagers find it really difficult to wake up and get out of bed. Is that because they're lazy? Well, 'no', says Russell Foster, a professor at Oxford University. Professor Foster has tested the memory of 200 teenage students and has discovered that the results are 9% better when they do the test in the afternoon. He thinks that this is because teenagers may have different body clocks from adults and younger children. In his opinion, from the ages of ten to twenty we need to spend more time in bed. Professor Foster has calculated that teenagers should stay in bed for two more hours than younger and older people.

Dr Paul Kelley is the headmaster of a large school in the north of England and he thinks Professor Foster is right. He has decided that, at his school, students should start lessons two hours later than usual. Classes will now start at 11 o'clock instead of 9 am, so that students can sleep for longer. He thinks that by doing this his students will be more awake and will learn better and faster. He believes it will stop what he calls 'teenage zombies' falling asleep in the lessons before lunch. When students at the school heard about the idea, one or two said that they preferred getting up early, but the rest agreed that it was a great idea. This is not the first time that Dr Kelley has done something unusual at his school.

Last year he began science classes with a difference. He taught science for three twenty-minute periods with a ten-minute break between each session. He gave the students time for physical activity. By interrupting the class for physical activity he helped all the students to get much better marks in their exams. Another of his ideas was to start teaching university subjects in the last year of school. In this way he prepared them better for the transition from school to university. So, if you're a teenager and you find it hard to get up in the mornings, maybe you should contact Dr Kelley and see if there's a space for you at his school!

Unit 7

Vocabulary p84

2b 38

[1] golf

[2] baseball	climbing	cycling
diving	football	judo
rugby	sailing	skiing
swimming	tennis	
[3] basketball	horse-riding	ice hockey
ice skating	snowboarding	volleyball
weightlifting		
[4] athletics	gymnastics	karate

Vocabulary p84

8 ▶ 39

1

Boy: So, what do you need to play?
Girl: Just a net and a ball.
Boy: And what do you have to do?
Girl: Well, basically there are two teams and you have to hit the ball over the net.
Boy: But do you hit it with a racket?
Girl: No, no, with your hands.
Boy: Oh, right. So, how do you win the game?
Girl: If the other team can't return the ball and it hits the ground, you win a point.

2

Girl: Ouch, this is a really violent sport, isn't it?
Boy: Yeah. It's like a boxing match, isn't it? The players spend more time hitting each other than trying to score goals.
Girl: I'm cold, too. It's freezing here next to the rink.
Boy: I know. It's a difficult sport to play, don't you think?
Girl: Yeah. You need to be able to skate well, but you need to be strong, too. They wear lots of protective clothes, don't they? It must be difficult to move wearing all that stuff.

3

Boy 1: Did you bring your boots?
Boy 2: Boots? No. I thought we were playing inside.
Boy 1: No, I told you we were playing on the big pitch today.
Boy 2: The big pitch? Oh no. I hate playing on the big pitch. The goal's so big that I never save any goals.

4

Girl: You need to have a really flexible body to do that, don't you?
Boy: Yes, and you can't be afraid of heights, can you?
Girl: It's amazing that their goggles don't come off when they hit the water.
Boy: I love watching it, but you have to be mad to do it, don't you? I mean jumping ten metres into a pool. It's *dangerous*, isn't it?

Gateway to life skills p89

6 and 7 ▶ 40

Jasmine: Hi there, welcome back to our fitness vlog! As you may know, we're trying to get fit so we've started this vlog to help us and others.
Ben: So, how fit are you? You can find out by calculating how quickly your heart recovers after doing exercise. To do that, you need to be able to measure your heart rate.
Jasmine: Your heart rate, or pulse, is how many times your heart beats in a minute. We usually call this the BPM, beats per minute.
Ben: Nowadays lots of people use heart-rate monitors when they run or do exercise. Heart-rate monitors are very accurate and very easy to wear. They measure your heart rate electronically. You can wear a strap around your chest that has sensors on it.
Jasmine: Or use a device that looks like a watch.
Ben: But you don't actually need technology to find your heart rate.
Jasmine: The easiest way to measure your heart rate is by using your radial artery, which is on the inside of your wrist.
Ben: Or your carotid artery, at the side of your neck.
Jasmine: To measure your heart rate, take your index finger and middle finger and place them on your wrist or neck like this.
Ben: It can take time to find your pulse, but don't worry, that's normal. But don't use your thumb to find your pulse, because your thumb often has a strong pulse, too. It can interfere with the results.
Jasmine: When you've found your pulse, you need to use a phone or watch. You can either count how many beats you feel in 60 seconds. This is the most accurate method.
Ben: Or you can count the beats in 15 seconds and then multiply it by four. But this is less accurate.
Jasmine: Your heart rate obviously changes. Your heart rate will be totally different when you're resting and when you're doing exercise. Your resting heart rate is when you aren't doing exercise.
Ben: Take your pulse when you've been resting for 15 minutes. A normal resting heart rate for teenagers is between 50 and 90 beats per minute.
Jasmine: The best way to find out how fit you are is to check your recovery heart rate.
Ben: You need to do moderate or high intensity activity like running or cycling fast for a while. Then stop and take your pulse immediately.
Jasmine: Then, after exactly 60 seconds, check your pulse again. Come on Ben, let's go!
Ben: So imagine that when you stop doing exercise your heart rate is 155bpm. Then one minute later it's 125bpm. To calculate your recovery heart rate you take away the second number from the first. So in this case it's 155 minus 125. This means your recovery heart rate is 30bpm.
Jasmine: A recovery heart rate of less than 12bpm means you're not very fit. A recovery heart rate of 50bpm is excellent and means you're very fit.
Ben: The great thing is when you do more sport and exercise, your heart gets stronger and your recovery rate will get better and better.
Jasmine: But the only way you can make sure this is happening is by checking your heart rate. Remember though – if you haven't done much sport in a while, take it slowly and gently!

Listening p90

2 and 3 ⏵ 41

Presenter: Hello and welcome to another programme in our series about the origin of different popular sports. Today our expert, Anna Philips, is going to tell us about the origin of an incredibly popular sport – basketball. Anna, what can you tell us about the beginnings of basketball?

Anna: Well, in comparison with football, rugby or tennis, basketball is quite a modern game because it was only invented in 1891.

Presenter: Invented?

Anna: Yes. The man who invented it was James Naismith. Naismith, who was born in Canada, was working at a YMCA school. He was a PE teacher. His director gave him 14 days to invent a new indoor sport. It needed to be a sport which would keep students fit, but that wouldn't be aggressive or violent. That's why Naismith made basketball a non-contact sport.

Presenter: So, was this in Canada?

Anna: No, Naismith was born in Canada, but he was working in the US, in Springfield, in Massachusetts, which is really cold in the winter. That's why it had to be an indoor sport.

Presenter: What did they use for baskets?

Anna: They had fruit baskets, peach baskets. Of course, the problem was that when the ball went into the basket they needed to stop the match, somebody came with a ladder, climbed up and got the ball out of the basket! The game stopped for a few minutes after each basket. In fact, it was only in 1906 that they finally changed to the modern nets that we have today.

Presenter: Has the game changed a lot since its invention in 1891?

Anna: Many of today's rules are the same as the original rules which Naismith wrote. There were 13 in total. But in the original rules you couldn't bounce the ball, you could only pass it. Naismith had 18 students in his class, so originally he had nine people in each team, not five like there are now. His students, who were all boys, used a football at first. Later they made a special ball for the new sport. Actually, at one moment somebody wanted to call the sport 'Naismith Ball', but Naismith didn't like the idea.

Presenter: Oh! How long were matches?

Anna: In Naismith's original 13 rules, a match had two halves. Each half was 15 minutes long, with a five-minute break between them. Oh, and you only got one point for each basket you scored, not two like today. In fact, the final score in the first match was only one-nil!

Presenter: That doesn't sound very exciting! Nowadays top teams can score *100* points! … So, was basketball immediately popular?

Anna: Naismith actually admitted that the first time he explained the new game to his class they weren't very excited by it! But the game *was* popular, and it soon became popular with other YMCA centres, too. And after that universities started playing it, too. Around that time they changed the rules to have five players in each team.

Presenter: Did Naismith live to see basketball become one of the most popular sports in the world?

Anna: Yes, In 1936, when Naismith was 75 years old, basketball officially became part of the Olympic Games. An organisation collected money so that Naismith could go to Berlin, where the games took place that year. That was a great moment for Naismith, to see people from countries all over the world playing the sport that he'd invented.

Presenter: I can imagine!

Anna: But the interesting thing is that Naismith wasn't really interested in competition, in winning or being the best. He just wanted to invent a sport that people would enjoy, and above all one that would help to keep them fit and healthy.

Presenter: Well, he certainly did that! Thanks for the information, Anna!

Developing speaking p92

3 and 4 ⏵ 42

Girl: What do you think? Are top sports stars good role models for young people?

Boy: Yes, I think they are. Sports stars are good role models because they live healthy lives. They do lots of sport, and I think that's a good example for young people, because I think that nowadays a lot of teenagers don't get enough exercise.

Girl: I take your point, but I think that a lot of today's sports stars are bad role models because they're too competitive. They do anything they can to win, even if that means cheating. That gives the wrong idea to young people. If a football player cheats, then some young people think it's OK to cheat in exams, for example.

Boy: I see what you mean, but top sports people usually play in a team. So they're a good example to young people because they help their teammates and show the importance of teamwork.

Girl: That's true, but I'm not sure sports people today really care that much about their team. They change teams all the time! I think they're more interested in money than in their team. Maybe in the past sports people played for the same team all their life, but not now.

Boy: I totally disagree with you. Some sports people are very loyal to their team and they stay with them. And they're also loyal to their fans. I know a lot of top sports stars who do lots to help their fans. They often give money to help others, children who are ill, for example.

Girl: Hmm, you've got a point. I know a lot of sports people who help with charities. They often visit hospitals and schools. But remember that they have lots of money, and they have lots of free time too, so it's normal that they do those types of things.

Boy: I agree to an extent that they do those things because they have time and money. But that isn't the only reason. I think a lot of top sports people were poor when they grew up and they worked really hard to get to the top of their sport. I think that's another reason why they're great role models – they show young people that anybody can get to the top if they work hard.

Girl: Hmm. Maybe you're right.

Unit 8

Vocabulary p96

6 ⏵ 43

1 (sounds of an orchestra tuning up)
2 (someone playing a guitar)
3 (people clapping)
4 (someone performing Shakespeare: 'To be or not to be …')
5 (someone speaking to an orchestra)
6 (people cheering as a rock band plays)
7 (someone chipping stone and talking about what they're doing)
8 (someone talking about a painting they're working on)
9 (a group of people thanking an audience)
10 (someone trying compositions on the piano)

Pronunciation p99

3b ▶ 44

amazed	bored
confused	depressed
disappointed	disgusted
embarrassed	excited
fascinated	frightened
inspired	interested
relaxed	surprised
tired	uninspired
worried	

Gateway to life skills p101

4 and 5 ▶ 45

Clue 1

Olivia: Well, the first thing to say is that I love this painting. As soon as I see it I feel happy. To be honest, I don't know exactly what the subject is. I mean, it's definitely abstract. But I don't think you always have to 'understand' art. I mean, what I notice most about the painting are the colours …

Jack: The first word that comes into my head about the painting is 'comic'. In some ways, I think it's a very funny painting. But the title isn't funny. Really my interpretation of the painting should be that it is tragic, because it's quite a serious theme. So, actually, there is a difference between the serious title and the comic book picture …

Luke: This painting is easily explained by the title. The title and painting go really well together. It's quite a normal street, nothing special, maybe New York I expect. But it seems very sad to me. Maybe that's because there's nobody in the picture. It certainly makes me think of a typical quiet Sunday morning …

Clue 2

Olivia: … Yes, I love the green in this painting, and I love the contrast with the orange, the red, the yellow. I get a feeling from the colours and shapes. Actually, although it's abstract, it reminds me of writing. It looks to me like somebody practising the letter e or the letter o, writing it again and again …

Jack: … I think good art makes you think and I like this painting because it makes you think about what art is. You know, you expect art galleries to be full of serious old paintings, but this painting is modern and fun. I don't think art always has to be serious and traditional. I often read comics and I think comic artists are really good artists, too.

Luke: … I think the artist wants to express sadness and loneliness in the painting I'm describing. I think that's why art is important – it helps us express and feel certain emotions.

It's interesting because the street where I live looks different from this place, but the feeling of an early Sunday morning is very similar. In fact, it makes me want to take a photo of where I live early on a Sunday morning …

Clue 3

Olivia: … I know that it looks a bit childish, for example you can see some of the paint dripping. It isn't perfect. But I don't think a painting has to be perfect. What it has got is energy and life. I don't think it's easy to paint something like this, and I like it because it makes me want to try to paint something similar myself. I find it very inspiring. Personally, I think that's what art is for, to inspire you to make something yourself.

Jack: Actually, this painting is also quite surprising because it has words in it too, which doesn't usually happen in traditional painting. But then again, in some ancient Egyptian and Greek paintings they also have words, so maybe this isn't so unusual. Anyway, art doesn't have to follow any rules. And that's what makes it exciting.

Luke: … although the picture I'm talking about is sad, it is also beautiful and in some ways optimistic. I mean, I like the way you can see the light of the early morning. Perhaps it's symbolic. Maybe it's going to be a good day in the end. A painting like this is like a scene in a film or a novel. You want to know who lives in this street, and how are they're going to spend Sunday. I think art helps you escape your world and imagine other worlds.

Listening p102

2 and 3 ▶ 46

Presenter: And now on the Six o'clock Show today we have some interesting news from the arts world …

Co-presenter: Yes, that's right. Apparently, it's bath time. Has anyone seen this?!

Presenter: Ha! That's amazing! It's a rubber duck, just like the one I used to play with in the bath when I was a kid.

Co-presenter: What? Was yours over 16 metres tall, too?!

Presenter: Er, no, mine was a bit smaller. So what is this? Who made it?

Co-presenter: A Dutch artist, a sculptor. His name is Florentijn Hofman. He's taken the duck all around the world – it's been in China, Japan, France, Australia, the US … People love it wherever it goes.

Presenter: Yes, I agree, there's something special about it.

Co-presenter: In this article here they asked him why he thought it was so popular. He said that it helped to make people feel relaxed and happy. You know, it reminds them of when they were small, they remember when they were young and didn't have so many worries and problems. Actually, in this interview he says that he thinks the duck has been most popular in Asia … like in China, Hong Kong and Japan. He thinks maybe that's because people work such long hours there.

Presenter: Hmm. It can't be very easy to transport. Have they ever had any accidents with the duck?

Co-presenter: Well, they don't actually transport it, I think each one is a new model, but yes, they have had accidents! The duck actually exploded in Taiwan!

Presenter: Oh no! Why?

Co-presenter: Reporters asked them what had happened, but I don't think they really know. They said maybe birds had attacked it, or maybe it was a change in the weather. First, it had been raining a lot and then it was sunny …

Presenter: It must be complicated for the artist to make something so big.

Co-presenter: It's like *you're* the toy!

Presenter: You know, I could imagine people using the duck for publicity, you know, putting the name of a company on the side. I'm sure that would be an easy way to draw attention to your company name.

Co-presenter: Oh, companies have tried. But Hofman told them not to do it. He wants people to think of it as art, not as publicity. In Japan they asked him to create a special version to put on the roof of a Museum of Art. But he only wants it to exist in the water.

Presenter: Is there one permanent version of it anywhere?

Co-presenter: No, it just moves around the world all the time. But Hofman says that's part of the idea. The duck makes you look at a public space in a new way when it's there. And when it's gone, it makes the place look new again, even though you've maybe been there hundreds of times.

Presenter: Hmm. I think that's true. You never really look closely at the places that you pass every day.

You stop looking at them.

Co-presenter: True. You know, the funny thing is that somebody asked him if he liked rubber ducks.

Presenter: What did he say?

Co-presenter: No! Except for his giant rubber duck, of course! The thing is, when he became famous for the giant rubber duck, people started to give him rubber ducks as presents all the time. In the end, he had to throw them away!

Presenter: Ha! Well, I hope he doesn't throw his Giant Rubber Duck away and that it swims here one day. I'd love to see it!

Developing speaking p104

3, 4 and 5 ▶ 47

Boy: Do you remember any particular school trips?

Girl: Oh yes! The one I remember the most was a long time ago, when I was in primary school. I went to see a play in English with my class, oh, and with our English teacher, of course.

Boy: Where was the play?

Girl: It was at a small theatre near to the centre of my home town.

Boy: And what happened? Why do you remember it?

Girl: Well, at first the play wasn't anything special. There were only two or three actors and the story was a bit boring. But later, after about half an hour, the actors had a break and two musicians went on stage. They sang one or two songs and then asked if anybody wanted to sing a song in English. I was really shy when I was smaller, but everybody always said I had a good voice and was a good singer. So they started to say 'Ewa wants to sing, Ewa wants to sing!'. One of the musicians came and took my hand and told me to go with him onto the stage. At first, I said I didn't want to, but in the end he kept on insisting and so I went.

Boy: How did you feel?

Girl: I was really frightened! It was embarrassing because I'd never been on a stage before, and I'd never sung in public, apart from with friends. Anyway, the musicians started playing a song I knew. I was so nervous that at first nobody could hear me, but after a minute or two I started to feel more relaxed and enjoy myself. In the end, all of the audience was clapping and shouting my name. It was an amazing experience!

Boy: What happened next?

Girl: Next, they asked me to sing another song, and another. Finally, I had to stop because the actors had come back to finish the play. But later on

everybody said that the best thing about the school trip was my singing! I think that's why I enjoy singing and playing music so much now!

Gateway to exams: Units 7–8

Listening p108

5 and 6 ▶ 48

Woman: Come on, it's about to start.

Man: What's about to start?

Woman: The running.

Man: The running? What is this? A sports event?

Woman: Just watch.

Man: Well, what was *that* all about? A man wearing sports clothes running through the gallery as fast as he can. Oh look, now there's another runner, a woman this time. Are they running away from something?

Woman: No, I don't think so. It's a work of art. It was designed by an artist called Martin Creed. And it's called No. 850.

Man: No. 850? What a title! What's it all about?

Woman: Well, he gives runners £10 an hour to run through the gallery. Apart from the £10, they get free sports clothes and trainers. And then they have to run as fast as they can.

Man: All right. But what does it *mean*, though? Is there a message?

Woman: The artist said that when you're dead, you don't move, do you? So moving really fast, like when you run fast, is the opposite of death. It's like a symbol of life. That's why the runners *have to* run as fast as they possibly can.

Man: Hmm, yeah, right. Where did he get the idea from?

Woman: Apparently, he was in Italy and he arrived really late to see a museum in Palermo. He only had five minutes to see it so he and his friend just ran all the way through the museum as fast as they could. They spent the five minutes running and laughing. He said that he looked at the museum in a totally different way when he was running, not walking slowly. He also said that if you run through a museum it gives you time to do other, more important things in life!

Man: He might be right about that. In fact, I think I'm going to run with the next athlete who goes past.

Woman: No! Don't do that! The general public aren't allowed to run.

Man: You're joking! Anyway, what happens if you get in the way of a runner?

Woman: The artist told them to run round visitors. In fact, one of the runners is the artist himself.

Man: Really?

Woman: Yeah. He said he had to train hard to be part of his own work of art!

Man: If *I* see him, he'll have to run fast! I'd like to say a few things to him, I can tell you!

Unit 9

Pronunciation p113

6a ▶ 49

1 You have to go now.
2 You must have known.

6b and 6c ▶ 50

1 She might have gone.
2 They can't have done it.
3 It couldn't have been me.
4 You must have heard it.
5 We may have lost.
6 They must have known.

Gateway to life skills pp114–115

4 and 5 🎬 ▶ 51

Olivia: My name is Olivia Dawkins and I want you to vote for *me* to be Young Mayor. Why? Because I'm serious about making a difference and improving life for all of us. Young people are the future. So we should be able to take part in deciding the future. To do that, we need to be able to vote at the age of 16. At 16 we have to do important exams. To succeed in those exams we have to be responsible, hard-working and intelligent. If we have to do exams and have other responsibilities, we should also be able to vote. Vote for me and maybe you'll be able to vote in the next general elections!

Jack: Hi. My name's Jack Richards. I'm 15. I would like to run for election as Young Mayor. I would like my campaign to be on the issue of bullying at school. Lots of you have told me it's one of the most important issues that affects young people. Personally, I think it's terrible that some students at school suffer because other students treat them badly. And I think we need to do more to stop this problem. If you vote for me, I will have experts come to explain what the real consequences of bullying are and how to stop bullying. Vote for me and bullying will be history.

Luke: Hello. I'm Luke Clarke and I'm 14. I'm standing for election as Young Mayor. I'm campaigning for changes to what we learn at school. What we learn is very useful – maths, languages, literature, science … But there are other things I think we should learn, too. For example, things connected with citizenship and life skills. When we leave school, we need to be able to do lots of things we have never done before. We need to be able to manage our money and cook healthy meals. I think it should be us, the students, to help suggest things that would be useful for us to learn. Please vote for me. I could help to make a real difference in your day-to-day lives.

Chloe: Hi! My name's Chloe Jones and I'm 16. I hear lots of my friends saying they are worried about the future because there aren't enough jobs. I think it is the young who suffer the most from unemployment. That is why I'm campaigning to make jobs for young people a priority for the government. Youth unemployment is a terrible thing. Young people have lots of energy and lots of great ideas. And that is exactly what businesses and companies need. That is why we need to create more jobs for young people. Please vote for me because I promise to do everything I can to solve this problem.

Listening p116

2 ▶ 52

Girl: Craig, you like rugby, don't you?
Boy: Yeah. Why?
Girl: Do you know anything about the Rugby World Cup final in 1995? I'm doing a project about South Africa. The topic is 'Why was the 1995 Rugby World Cup so important for South Africa as a nation?'
Boy: That's easy. Haven't you seen that film *Invictus*? The one with Morgan Freeman and Matt Damon.
Girl: No, I remember the trailer, but I never actually saw it at the cinema.
Boy: That's a pity. If you'd seen it, you would have learnt a lot about South Africa. It tells the story of the final, but it's more about the political situation in the country at that time.
Girl: OK. So what *really* happened?
Boy: Well, Nelson Mandela had just become the first black president of South Africa. He'd spent 27 years in prison but had been free for four years when he became president. But the country was still very divided. At that time nearly all the South African rugby players were white South Africans, Afrikaner. And generally black South Africans didn't really support the rugby team. A year before the World Cup, Mandela had watched a match between South Africa and England and many black

South Africans wanted England to win, not South Africa!
Girl: Really?
Boy: Yeah. So Mandela wanted to change that. He wanted rugby to help to unite the country. He had to persuade both sides to forget their differences and come together. So there was a new slogan for the South African rugby team: 'One Team, One Country'.
Girl: Hmm. That's a nice slogan.
Boy: Another thing he did was to get the rugby team to learn the new national anthem. You see, the new national anthem was really an old song of black resistance. So when the rugby team sang it, it was a very strong message that this was a new start for the nation. It was like both sides were accepting each other for the first time.
Girl: Did South Africa get to the final?
Boy: Yes, and just before the match, Mandela appeared on the pitch. He was wearing a South African rugby shirt. Some people were surprised at first because they didn't really expect him to be so enthusiastic about the team. And 95% of the people in the stadium were white, and Mandela hadn't always been very popular with them. But little by little everybody started standing up and calling his name. He became a hero for the whole nation. In that moment, he made everyone forget their differences. Some people think that the country wouldn't have felt united at that time if it hadn't been for the Rugby World Cup.
Girl: And did they win the final?
Boy: Yes, they did. But there's a conspiracy theory about that.
Girl: Really? Why?
Boy: Well, they played New Zealand. New Zealand was a really good team. But nearly all the New Zealand players had food poisoning just before the match. I think 27 out of 35 players were ill. Some people think they were poisoned by eating or drinking something at their hotel.
Girl: Really?
Boy: Yes. A lot of people think that if they hadn't been ill, they would have won the final. But it was incredibly dramatic. South Africa won in the last minute of the game. And when Mandela came on to give the South African captain the cup, everybody stood up again.
Girl: Wow! What a story. I can see why they made it into a film!

Developing speaking p118

2 and 3 ▶ 53

Erm, in this picture I can see some people sitting in a semicircle in front of an audience. They're wearing very formal clothes. It must be the ceremony for the Nobel Prize because I can see a big letter

N in the middle of the picture. And in the background near the top of the picture I can see the colours of the Swedish flag – blue and yellow. It looks as if the person standing slightly right of the centre is giving a speech. It's probably about the Nobel Prize. I'm not sure but I think the people on the right might be members of the royal family of Sweden because I think they usually give the prizes. I imagine the people on the left could be famous scientists or maybe writers or politicians, but I don't know who they are. There must have been a lot of people there because the Nobel Prize is really important. It looks like the people in the background are musicians, probably an orchestra, because I can see they are holding musical instruments. Of course, I've never been to a Nobel Prize ceremony, but at my school we have a prize ceremony at the end of each year. Last year's was really enjoyable because two of my best friends got prizes.

Unit 10

Vocabulary p122

2 ▶ 54

1
Girl: I'm not sure. What do you think?
Boy: Well, I don't really know. I like the colour, but I'm not sure. Are they comfortable?
Girl: Not really!
Boy: Well, remember, we aren't going to a fashion show. We're going to be walking in the country for hours. If they aren't comfortable, your feet are really going to hurt.
Girl: You're right. Maybe I should try those trainers.

2
Woman: Now, what else do we need to get?
Man: Well, remember, it's Jamie's birthday next week. What can we get him?
Woman: I dunno. A CD or something? A DVD? I know he likes adventure films.
Man: Mmmm. Maybe not. I was thinking of a watch. The one he's got is a bit old now, maybe we could get a sports watch, with a timer.
Woman: That's a good idea! Now where will we find watches? They might be in the men's clothes department, or maybe electrical goods.
Man: I dunno. This place is enormous. Let's ask that lady over there.

3
Woman: Can I help you?
Man: Yes, I've tried this on and I really like it, but I think it's a bit too small.

Woman: OK. What size was that one?

Man: Medium, I think. Yes, medium.

Woman: Fine. Well, look, try this one. This is large. Is the colour OK?

Man: Well, I usually prefer darker colours for jackets, but I can't find any.

Woman: You might like these jackets over here. They come in dark blue, black or grey.

Man: Mmm, yes, those are nice. Can I try the grey one on?

4

Man: And can I have two for Australia?

Woman: Are they just for normal letters?

Man: Yes, look.

Woman: Right. Well, they go by air mail, of course. Is that everything?

Man: Er, yes, thanks.

Woman: That'll be £3.50 in total.

Man: When do you think the letters will arrive?

Woman: Erm. If you're lucky they should arrive in a week.

Man: OK. Thank you!

Pronunciation p125

6a and 6b ▶ 55

1 That dress is so expensive.
2 It's such an amazing shop.
3 I'm so happy that you're here.
4 It's such a pity that you can't come.

Gateway to life skills p127

3 and 4 ▶ 56

1

Toby: I don't get an allowance exactly because I have to work for it! My parents give me money for helping at home, you know, for doing housework like tidying up, making my bed or taking the rubbish out.

Rachel: I don't get an allowance. But I love arts and crafts and I make things and sell them at craft fairs and markets. I make bags, jewellery, purses and mobile phone covers. It's hard work, but I enjoy it. I don't make a lot of money, but it's usually enough.

Naomi: Yes, I do get an allowance. My parents give me a weekly allowance. But I would like to get a job, maybe doing a paper round for a newsagent or something like that. My friend does babysitting and she really enjoys it. I'd like to earn my own money because that way you can be more independent. You don't have to depend on your parents for money.

Callum: I don't get an allowance. I do different jobs to earn money when I need it. I sometimes wash cars for people who live in our street. I go round to their houses and ask them if they want me to wash their car and we agree on a price.

2

Toby: No, I never borrow money. I don't think it's a good habit to get into. If you borrow from the bank, you will have to pay much more money back in the end. It doesn't make sense to me.

Rachel: Well, I try not to. But I have borrowed money from friends sometimes and once or twice I've had to borrow money from my older brother. But that's a real problem because he makes me pay interest on what I owe him! And he even makes me sign a piece of paper to say that I agree!

Naomi: I don't borrow money. If I haven't got enough money to buy something, I don't buy it. I just wait until I've saved enough. I don't like owing money to anybody.

Callum: I borrowed money once. But that's because when I was smaller, about ten or eleven, I broke a brand new games console at home. And my dad made me buy a new one straight away. So I had to borrow the money from him. Then I did jobs at home until I'd paid it all back.

3

Toby: When my parents give me money, I try to separate it. I spend half of it and save the other half. Little by little, I've saved quite a bit by doing that. If I don't do that, I'll spend it all straight away! There are so many things I want to buy!

Rachel: Some of my friends spend a lot of money on designer clothing. I do buy clothes, I just don't buy expensive designer clothes. Some of my friends pay twice as much as me for a white T-shirt, just because it has a fashionable name on it. You can save a lot of money by avoiding shops that sell designer clothes. I'm saving up for a laptop at the moment, so I really need to make my money go further!

Naomi: I look in different shops or online before I buy something. It's easy to think that things cost the same everywhere. But when you look closely you usually find a big difference in price for exactly the same products. It's stupid to pay more than necessary for exactly the same item. So I really pay attention to that now.

Callum: I make a list of the things that I want to buy. But then I put them into order of importance. That means that I think really hard about whether I really need something. It'd be great to have money to buy everything, but that's not realistic. So I think it's necessary to decide what's important and what is a luxury.

Listening p128

2 and 3 ▶ 57

1

Jenny: Hi, Katie. Where have you been? I was worried. I thought you'd only gone out for five minutes.

Katie: Hmm. Yeah, that's what I thought. I just went to the supermarket to buy a couple of things I needed. And in the end, I bought all of this. If only I'd had my lunch before I went shopping.

Jenny: Why??

Katie: Because they say that if you eat before you go shopping in a supermarket you spend less.

Jenny: Really?

Katie: Yes, because you don't feel hungry, so you don't pay attention to all the biscuits and cakes and ice cream. That's what I bought in the end.

Jenny: What I do is make a list of what I need before I go. And then I only buy those things. If it's not on my list, I don't buy it.

Katie: That's a good idea.

Jenny: Anyway, don't worry. I'll help you eat all those extra biscuits and cakes.

Katie: Great. Thanks a lot, Jenny.

2

Jack: Are you doing anything on Saturday, Harry?

Harry: No, I don't think so. Why?

Jack: I'm going to the shopping centre to buy an MP3 player. You know a lot about electronic stuff, don't you? I wanted you to come and help me choose a good one.

Harry: Yeah, OK. I wish I had enough money to buy a new MP3 player. Mine doesn't work anymore.

Jack: Really?

Harry: Yeah. When I bought it I thought I was saving money because it was so cheap. But it was cheap because it was badly made. I wish I'd bought a better one. But now I know the good from the bad. I learnt my lesson!

Jack: Yeah. That's why I wanted your help. Anyway, I want something in the middle, not too cheap but not the most expensive either.

Harry: Don't worry. Let's go to that new department store. They have lots of different models there.

Jack: OK. Great.

3

Mum: Look at these. They're beautiful, aren't they? And there's a 30% discount on them.

Mia: Let's see. Hmm. They are nice, Mum.

Mum: Let's see if they've got my size. Hmm. No, they're all small sizes. If only my feet were smaller!

Mia: Hmm. They've got my size though, Mum. Do you mind if I try them on quickly?

Mum: Oh, go on then.

Mia: Oh yes, they're perfect. Can I have them? Come on, you did say they're nice. And they are much cheaper than usual …

Mum: Hmmph.

Mia: Mum? What's the matter? Why are you looking so upset?

Mum: It's just … every time we come shopping I find all the nice things and you end up getting them.

Mia: Well, it's not my fault my feet are smaller than yours! Now, Mum, where's your debit card?

Mum: And on top of everything I have to pay!

4

Lucy: I wish you wouldn't do that!

Tyler: What?

Lucy: Every time I suggest going shopping at the weekend you say you've got something else to do.

Tyler: Well, it's true. I just remembered that I have to go and watch my cousin play football. He's got an important match on Saturday, you see?

Lucy: Yeah, this weekend it's your cousin. Last weekend it was your uncle, the time before it was your grandfather.

Tyler: It's just that, er, I've got a big family, and, er, we're very close.

Lucy: But when I said we could go to see a film you said yes. As soon as I say the word shopping you suddenly find an excuse for not being able to go.

Tyler: You're right. Look, Lucy, it isn't that I hate going shopping with *you*. It's just that I hate going shopping with *any*body!

Developing speaking p130

2 58

Shop assistant: Can I help you?

Lily: Yes, I'm looking for a hoodie, you know, a top. It's for a friend.

Shop assistant: What size is he?

Lily: Large.

Shop assistant: Large, OK, we've got some here in blue and grey.

Lily: Have you got anything a bit brighter? These are a bit too dark, a bit too serious.

Shop assistant: How about these? These are new in.

Lily: Hum. Yeah. I like the green one. And the blue one. Do you have them both in large?

Shop assistant: Let me have a look … Erm … We've got the blue one in large, but the green one is only in small or medium.

Lily: OK. I'll take the blue one. Can I bring it back if it doesn't fit or if my friend doesn't like it?

Shop assistant: Yeah, no problem. Just remember to bring the receipt. And you've got 28 days to bring it back.

Developing speaking p130

5 59

Shop assistant: Good morning. Can I help you?

Lily: Yes, I'd like to make a complaint.

Shop assistant: Oh dear. What seems to be the problem?

Lily: I bought this hoodie here last week as a present for a friend. It shrank the first time he washed it! It was a large, but now it's more like a small.

Shop assistant: I'm sorry. We haven't had anybody else with that problem. Are you sure he followed the washing instructions?

Lily: Yes!

Shop assistant: I see. Well, we can either replace it for you straight away, or we could give you a refund. Which would you prefer?

Lily: I'll take the refund.

Shop assistant: Fine. Have you got the receipt?

Lily: Yes, here it is.

Shop assistant: Thank you. £40. There you are. I'm sorry about that.

Gateway to exams: Units 9–10

Listening p135

6 and 7 60

Presenter: Today on the History Programme we're talking about a ship called the *SS Empire Windrush*. You might not know the name, but this ship helped to create modern Britain. Adele, can you explain why?

Adele: Yes, of course. The *Windrush* sailed in 1948 from Jamaica to Britain. And on board the ship were 500 Caribbean men and women, from Jamaica and Trinidad.

Presenter: Why did they decide to come?

Adele: Mainly for work. Some were interested in seeing what Britain and London were like, but they were basically coming to work.

Presenter: Who exactly were these men and women?

Adele: Well, in fact most of them were men, and most of them had been in the Second World War. Jamaica and Trinidad were both old British colonies.

Presenter: And they're still part of the Commonwealth now.

Adele: That's right. After the war Britain needed as many people as possible to help to rebuild the country.

Presenter: How was life for the people on the *Windrush* when they arrived in Britain?

Adele: Well, not terribly good, really. The weather was a great shock at first. The passengers were amazed at how grey, cold and wet Britain was. And life was difficult.

Presenter: Did they find work?

Adele: More than 200 people found work as soon as they arrived, others took longer. The reason that this was such an important event is that this was the beginning of modern multicultural Britain. In the 1950s and 1960s many more people came from other Commonwealth countries to live and work in Britain, particularly from India, Pakistan and Bangladesh. Some people calculate that now about 14% of the British population are from different ethnic backgrounds. There are people from hundreds of different countries who have made their home in Britain.

Presenter: And, of course, they've all brought their customs, their food, their clothes, music …

Adele: That's right. And the arrival of the *SS Windrush* was really the beginning of that great transformation.

Workbook answer key

Unit 1

Vocabulary p4

1

1 serious **2** talkative **3** pretty **4** clever
5 hard-working **6** reliable **7** impatient
8 medium height **9** cheerful **10** untidy
11 overweight

2

2 nervous **3** bald **4** handsome **5** quiet
6 unfriendly **7** nice **8** cheerful
9 selfish **10** attractive

3

1 well-built **2** thin **3** bald **4** selfish
5 arrogant **6** funny **7** bossy

VOCABULARY EXTENSION

4

unattractive, unreliable, unsafe, unfriendly,
unsociable, uninteresting, unintelligent,
unfashionable, unselfish, unhappy

5

talkative – quiet/silent, outgoing – shy,
glad – unhappy, funny – boring,
handsome – ugly, boring – interesting

Reading p5

1

Laura Decker sailed round the world alone
when she was just 14. Romero climbed
Mount Everest when he was only 13.

2

1 T (lines 9–11) **2** F **3** T (lines 26–28)
4 F **5** T (lines 33–34) **6** F
7 F **8** T (lines 44–47)

3

1 peak **2** mature **3** fulfilled
4 autobiography **5** determined
6 encountered **7** inspirational
8 dedicated

4

1 F **2** O **3** O **4** O **5** F **6** F

Grammar in context p6

1

present simple
present continuous

2

1 d **2** c **3** g **4** a **5** e **6** b **7** f

3

1 I don't usually enjoy cleaning my
bedroom. **2** Tom rarely finishes all
his homework. **3** Our teachers are
always telling us what to do. **4** We
occasionally go to school by bus. **5** My
brother and I often play computer games
together. **6** We sometimes spend our
holidays in France. **7** My bossy friend is
always telling me what to do.

4

1 am doing **2** sometimes spends
3 is always taking **4** am writing
5 usually enjoy **6** is studying

GRAMMAR CHALLENGE

5

1 goes **2** text **3** meet up **4** usually
spends **5** is getting **6** isn't **7** is
always talking **8** is taking part **9** wants

Developing vocabulary and listening p7

1

1 slim **2** handsome **3** cute
4 sociable **5** clever **6** glad

2

1 bright **2** short **3** sociable **4** elderly
5 cute **6** untidy

3

a interested

4

1 Speaker 1
2 Speaker 2
3 Speaker 3
4 Speaker 2
5 Speaker 4
6 Speaker 2
7 Speaker 1
8 Speaker 4

VOCABULARY EXTENSION

5

old	elderly	someone you have known a long time
funny	it makes you laugh	strange
smart	clever	well-dressed
hard	difficult	not soft
bright	light/colourful	intelligent

6

1 loud **2** brightest **3** hard **4** smart
5 old

Grammar in context p8

1

1 don't believe **2** sounds **3** like
4 belong

state

2

a 4 **b** 1 **c** 2 **d** 3

3

feeling: feel, like, love, need, prefer, want

thinking: know, mean, remember, seem,
think, understand
of the senses: hear, look, see, smell, sound
possession: have, own

4

1 have got (state) **2** don't
like (state), shout (action) **3** 'm
talking (action) **4** Does he know
(state) **5** speak (state) **6** looks
(state) **7** Do you prefer (state) **8** 'm
wearing (action)

5

1 d **2** e **3** b **4** f **5** a **6** c

6

I've got a lovely dog called Mutt. He is
looking looks sweet, but when a stranger
comes to the door, he often barks and is
sounding sounds really unfriendly. After a
long walk in the rain, he doesn't smell very
nice! His long ears feel soft and his nose is
usually wet. When he is hearing hears my
parents' car, he runs to the window. He's
always seeming always seems to know
when they are coming.

GRAMMAR CHALLENGE

7

2 are you thinking A **3** 'm looking A
4 tastes S **5** looks S **6** weighs S
7 think S **8** 'm tasting A
9 's weighing A

Developing speaking p9

1

table tennis and football

2

1 F **2** T **3** F **4** F **5** F **6** T

3

2 aren't you **3** do you **4** can't
you **5** do you

4 and 5

1 down **2** down **3** up **4** up **5** up

6

1 f **2** d **3** g **4** a **5** h **6** b **7** c
8 e

7

Students' own answers

8

1 A young woman. She's probably about
18. **2** She looks like she's in a library and
she's probably studying.
3 The girl is wearing a blue cardigan and
white T-shirt. She has got dark straight hair
which is tied back in a ponytail.
4 She looks relaxed and interested in what
she is doing. She also looks serious and
rather quiet.

9

Students' own answers

Developing writing p10

1

She has got new neighbours.

2

a 5 **b** 3 **c** 1 **d** 4 **e** 2

3

rather, extremely, very, a bit, quite, really, completely

4

1 looks like **2** looks **3** look **4** looks like **5** looks as if/looks like **6** looks like

5

Students' own answers

Revision: Unit 1

Grammar p11

1

1 's raining **2** 'm listening **3** drink **4** 'm learning **5** are moving **6** comes

2

a Do you want **b** 'm working **c** need **d** know **e** is your project going **f** 'm trying **g** always leave

3

1 Josh usually wears … **2** Marley is never late for school. **3** Anna is always forgetting her … **4** Marcus is having a shower right now … **5** We don't often go to …

4

1 ✓ **2** ✗ She looks **3** ✗ This food tastes **4** ✓ **5** ✗ I think

Vocabulary p11

1

Build	Height	Hair
thin	tall	bald
overweight	medium	curly
big	height	straight
strong	short	short
small		wavy

Looks	Personality
beautiful	reliable
pretty	selfish
good-looking	patient
handsome	calm

2

1 quiet **2** talkative **3** serious **4** arrogant **5** funny **6** untidy

3

1 glad **2** hard **3** outgoing **4** bright **5** elderly **6** impatient

Unit 2

Vocabulary p12

1

1 ferry c **2** van f **3** spaceship b **4** yacht e **5** hot-air balloon d **6** coach a

2

1 ticket **2** delay **3** platform **4** single **5** cancel **6** catch **7** departures **8** arrivals **9** return **10** luggage **11** miss

3

1 tent **2** motel, hotel **3** bed and breakfast **4** caravan **5** hostel

4

1 matches **2** mini-market **3** timetable **4** passport control **5** bill **6** mat **7** boarding pass **8** guidebook

Reading p13

1a and b

a

2

1 a **2** b **3** a **4** b **5** a **6** h

3

generous D	lazy N
adventurous D	fit D
likes danger P	ambitious D
selfish N	arrogant N
boring N	cheerful P

4

1 pedals **2** collapse **3** cope with **4** tandem **5** fancy dress **6** constantly **7** motorised

Grammar in context p14

1

a completed **b** in progress **c** before

2

1 b **2** a **3** c

3

1 had spent, arrived **2** had happened, took **3** Had you already learnt, started **4** stopped, had lost **5** didn't want, had forgotten **6** had never travelled, felt **7** were, had rained

4

1 b **2** a **3** d **4** f **5** e **6** c

5

1 was growing, didn't have, lived **2** was, had learnt **3** started, were flying **4** didn't take, had lent **5** used, was

6

a was **b** had **c** was waiting **d** I decided **e** know **f** am always losing **g** had left **h** had put **i** was paying **j** ran **k** had gone **l** was walking **m** saw **n** had missed **o** wasn't

Developing vocabulary and listening p15

1

1 d **2** a **3** h **4** f **5** b **6** c **7** e **8** g

2

1 in **2** out of **3** on **4** down **5** off **6** back

3

Speaker 1: **1** outdoor escalator **2** (walk up) steps
Speaker 2: **1** metrocable or cable car **2** bus

4

1 b **2** b **3** a **4** a **5** b **6** c **7** b

5

1 get across **2** get around **3** get … down **4** get through to **5** get on with **6** get around to

Grammar in context p16

1

1 b **2** c **3** a **4** d

2

2 He used to eat cakes, but now he eats fruit.
3 She used to have short hair, but now she has long hair.
4 He didn't use to wear glasses, but now he does.
5 He didn't use to play rugby, but now he does.
6 She didn't use to listen to the radio, but now she does.

3

1 ✗ (was very excited) **2** ✓ **3** ✗ (used to live) **4** ✓ **5** ✓ **6** ✗ (used to be) **7** ✗ (won) **8** ✓

4

b didn't use to get **c** started **d** would spend/used to spend/spent **e** grew **f** took/would take/used to take **g** would go/used to go **h** had started **i** used to spend/would spend **j** became **k** was growing **l** had/used to have

Developing speaking p17

1

1 I'd like to go to Dundee, please. **2** Is it a direct train? **3** Early in the morning, if possible. **4** I'm travelling next Saturday. **5** I'd like a return, please.

2

It leaves at 9.26 not 10.26

There are three changes, not two.

At Finsbury Park, you have to change first to London Victoria, not to Clapham

Coming back there are two changes, not three

It arrives at 19.00, not 19.30.

3

1 I'd like a return ticket to Guildford.   **2** Can you tell me the cost?   **3** Can you tell me when the train leaves?   **4** And do I have to change, please?   **5** Sorry, I didn't catch that.

4

Students' own answers

5

1 Could you <u>write</u> it <u>down</u> for me, please?
2 Is it possible to <u>pay</u> by <u>card</u>?
3 Could you <u>print</u> <u>out</u> the <u>times</u> for me?
4 Can you tell me <u>how much</u> it <u>costs</u>?
5 Which <u>platform</u> does it <u>leave</u> from, <u>please</u>?

6

Students' own answers

7

1 On holiday.   **2** A beach and a port, with a cruise ship in water (mountains, smaller boats and people).   **3** They are on a cruise ship in the Caribbean   **4** They are sunbathing and reading.   **5** They are wearing clothes for swimming and also shorts and T-shirts.

8

Students' own answers

Developing writing p18

1

a 3   **b** 5   **c** 6   **d** 4   **e** 2   **f** 1

2

a, c, e

3

what an incredible place! / we did enjoy it. / was such an unforgettable experience / I loved it / there is a really special atmosphere. / I can't wait. / I do love zoos!

4

1 It was such a fantastic experience.
2 People were so friendly and helpful.
3 I do love the food.
4 The shopping centre is such a noisy place.
5 I did enjoy the visit to the zoo yesterday.

5

Students' own answers

Revision: Units 1–2

Grammar p19

1

1 was riding, saw   **2** stole, was looking   **3** arrived, were waiting
4 was trying, noticed

2

1 She had never flown before.   **2** He had spent it on sweets.   **3** My old phone had broken.   **4** I had already read it.

3

1 I used to ride a bike, but now I drive a car.
2 Jess used to hate flying, but now she is a pilot.   **3** Mandy used to like camping, but now she prefers hotels.   **4** Gary used to wear school uniform, but now he wears jeans.   **5** The twins used to have long hair, but now they like short hair.

4

1 used to live   **2** are staying, are mending   **3** think   **4** was cycling, started   **5** had left

Vocabulary p19

1

1 single   **2** cancel   **3** miss   **4** fare
5 delay

2

1 tent   **2** caravan   **3** hostel
4 hotel

3

2 down   **3** off   **4** away   **5** out of

4

1 cheerful   **2** sociable   **3** talkative
4 elderly   **5** luggage

Gateway to exams: Units 1–2

Reading p20

1

1 b   **2** c   **3** b   **4** a   **5** a   **6** c

Listening

2

Speaker 1 c   Speaker 2 e   Speaker 3 a
Speaker 4 d

Use of English p21

3

b to   **c** to   **d** travelled   **e** used
f would   **g** were   **h** because   **i** It   **j** be

Writing

4

Students' own answers

5

1 missed my bus   **2** is   **3** luggage
4 looks like   **5** impatient   **6** used
7 fare   **8** took off   **9** I'd like, return ticket   **10** how much the ticket is
11 were shopping   **12** had checked in

Unit 3

Vocabulary p22

1

2 cottage   **3** bungalow   **4** terraced house   **5** flat   **6** semi-detached house
a 6   **b** 5   **c** 4   **d** 1

2

3

1 clean   **2** lively   **3** crowded/busy
4 historic   **5** quiet

4

a shed   **b** garage   **c** chimney   **d** roof
e porch   **f** front door   **g** drive   **h** path
i gate   **j** front garden

Reading p23

1 and 2

Students' own answers

3

a 2   **b** 4   **c** 5   **d** 3   **e** 1   **f** 6

4

1 because locals did not like the idea of a nuclear power station in the 1970s.   **2** central heating or air conditioning   **3** Rieselfeld and Vauban
4 Disch's home, because it produces five times (not four times) more energy than the house needs.   **5** because they produce more energy than they need   **6** they can invest in green energy projects, e.g. the stadium; they also give energy back to the central power grid, and get money for it

5

1, 3, 4, 5, 6

6

1 residents   **2** generated   **3** awards
4 rotates   **5** impact   **6** shares

Grammar in context p24

1

Present perfect simple: 1, 2, 5

Past simple: 3, 4

2

a the past   **b** the present   **c** started
d continue   **e** completed   **f** specific

3

1 moved **2** had **3** 've been
4 Did he ask **5** hasn't lived

4

2 Has she ever seen an Italian film? Yes, she has. She saw *Cinema Paradiso* last year. **3** Have they ever spent any time in Scotland? Yes, they have. They lived on a Scottish island in 1994.

5

1 just, yet **2** never, ever **3** already
4 since **5** for

6

a Have you ever heard **b** has **c** lies
d has been **e** hasn't existed **f** has only been **g** went **h** (had) finished
i have built **j** like **k** are

Developing vocabulary and listening p25

1

1 absolutely **2** totally **3** absolutely
4 completely **5** really **6** absolutely

2

Suggested answers
2 tiny **3** freezing **4** enormous
5 packed **6** stunning

3

a 2 **b** 3 **c** 1 **d** 5 **e** 4

4

1 8 **2** (two) friends **3** day trips
4 big Italian **5** age **6** 15
7 really hard

5

enormous – gigantic, huge
freezing – bitter, icy
boiling – roasting, scorching
packed – crowded, heaving
stunning – breathtaking, spectacular
ancient – prehistoric
tiny – miniscule, minute
dreadful – awful, terrible

Grammar in context p26

1

1 been **2** has **3** living
4 've/have **5** met
a duration **b** short **c** complete
d how many times **e** finished
f incomplete

2

1 been doing **2** had **3** met
4 been doing **5** been making
6 had **7** made

3

1 He's been cooking for two hours.
2 They've been playing golf since nine o'clock. **3** They've been chatting for four hours. **4** She's been travelling for six hours. **5** He's been sleeping for nine hours.

4

1 How long have you been living in London? **2** When did you arrive? **3** Have you made many friends? **4** Have you met any nice Londoners? **5** How long have you been playing the guitar? **6** Have you been to a concert in London yet? **7** When did you start learning English?

Developing speaking p27

1

Suggested answers
calm, clean, empty, green, historic, peaceful, pretty, quiet

2

1 In the UK or somewhere in Europe. **2** a girl, small building for musicians, deckchairs, trees, lovely old buildings, a road, the top of a bus **3** It looks calm and peaceful.
4 It's nice to have a place like this to get away from the lively city.

3

a the foreground **b** the middle
c the left of the photo **d** the background **e** in the middle **f** between

4

1 /ə/ **2** /v/
3 /v/ **4** /n/
5 /ə/ **6** /v/

5

Students' own answers

6

1 A city in China. **2** Lots of skyscrapers, probably offices and luxury flats; blocks of flats and houses and some green areas; a very busy road. **3** I don't like the skyscrapers, they look very industrial; I like the green areas and the smaller houses. **4** I think it would be busy, crowded and tiring to live in.

7

Students' own answers

Developing writing p28

1

1 Newcastle **2** It was great to hear from you, Thanks for your letter **3** Write again soon, All the best **4** By the way

2

1 T **2** NM **3** F **4** NM **5** F **6** T

3

Students' own answers

Revision: Units 1–3

Grammar p29

1

1 haven't seen **2** bought **3** Have you been **4** have known **5** Did you watch

2

1 yet **2** already **3** just **4** never
5 for

3

2 I've been cleaning my bike for two hours. **3** I've eaten 10 biscuits. **4** I've just seen a ghost. **5** I've just won the spelling competition.

4

1 used to have/had **2** was cleaning, found **3** had picked **4** been saving up **5** has been reading

Vocabulary

1

1 boiling **2** packed/crowded
3 stunning **4** freezing

2

1 square **2** block of flats **3** factory
4 port **5** cottage **6** town hall

3

1 d **2** b **3** a **4** c

4

1 d **2** c **3** a **4** c **5** b

Unit 4

Vocabulary p30

1

1 chicken **2** sweetcorn **3** juice **4** oil
5 turkey **6** strawberry **7** carrot
8 tuna **9** cream **10** plum **11** pie
12 pancake **13** milk (enjoy your meal)

2

a lunch **b** starters **c** main **d** desserts
e dish

3

1 raw **2** vegetarian **3** tasty **4** spicy
5 stale **6** fresh **7** healthy

4

1 vegetarian **2** raw **3** fresh **4** tasty
5 healthy

5

1 d **2** a **3** c **4** e **5** g **6** f **7** b

Reading p31

1

c

2

1 T (line 8) **2** F (lines 16–17)
3 T (lines 22–23) **4** F (line 36)
5 T (lines 44–45) **6** F (lines 49–51)
7 F (lines 54–55) **8** F (lines 60–62)

3

1 discarding **2** incentive **3** produce
4 eliminating **5** opt for **6** rejected

4

1 a **2** b **3** both

Grammar in context p32

1a

a are … going to be   **b** go   **c** 'm cooking   **d** will go

1b

1 present simple   **2** present continuous
3 will/won't   **4** going to

2

1 e   **2** b   **3** a   **4** c   **5** d

3

1 will come, ask   **2** 'll get
3 see, 'll tell   **4** boils   **5** 'll burn

4

1 N   **2** F   **3** E   **4** F   **5** E   **6** F   **7** N

5

a 's going to get   **b** I'll ask   **c** won't mind
d I'll make   **e** opens   **f** I'll get
g are we going to light   **h** is going to
serve   **i** we'll enjoy

6

I'm meeting my friends to watch a football
match. That finishes at six o'clock. Then
I'm going home and I'm going to have my
dinner. I'm helping my little sister with her
homework tonight and then I'm probably
going to watch TV after that. When it's
10.30, I'll go to bed.

Developing vocabulary and listening p33

1

1 rebuild   **2** disapproves   **3** refill
4 pre-heat   **5** mishears   **6** overate
7 undercharged

2

2 co-star   **3** rearrange   **4** dislike
5 over-emphasise   **6** pre-washed

3

Speakers 1, 3 and 4

4

a 3   **b** 2   **c** 4   **d** 5   **e** 1   **f** 5   **g** 1
h 4   **i** 2

5

2 misbehave, misbehaviour   **3** disconnect,
disconnection   **4** dishonest, dishonesty
5 misinform, misinformation
6 misprint, misprint

Grammar in context p34

1a

a future continuous
b future perfect

1b

a continuous   **b** unfinished   **c** perfect
d finished   **e** by

2

a will be swimming   **b** will be running
c will be exploring   **d** will be reading
e will be putting   **f** will be flying

3

2 By 9 am they will have swum a kilometre.
3 By 11 am they will have cleaned all the
windows.
4 By midday Tom will have made lunch.
5 By 3 pm Zac will have painted the
garage door.
6 By 5 pm Tom will have cut the grass.
7 By 9 pm they will have both fallen asleep
in front of the TV.

4

1 (We)'ll be living   **2** will work/will be
working   **3** will be doing/will do   **4** will
have left   **5** gets in/is getting in / will
get in   **6** used to be/was   **7** have
lived   **8** would/used to go camping
9 haven't touched

Developing speaking p35

1

Which of these foods do you think is the
best for your meal?
Picture d – gourmet burger

2

1 **a** opinion **b** way **c** prefer
2 **a** right **b** idea **c** agree
3 **a** fast food **b** seafood restaurant **c** think

3

before / you're
birthday / prefer
don't / go
enough / somewhere
good / should
nice / why

4

Students' own answers

5

1 Some people enjoying a barbecue.
2 At the beach, outside.   **3** They are
standing around a portable barbecue
talking and cooking, and smiling for
the photo.   **4** They are all wearing
comfortable, 'weekend' clothes.   **5** I think
they are enjoying being together.

6

Students' own answers

7

Students' own answers

Developing writing p36

1

1 An end-of-exams party   **2** bring a
dessert to the party and help clean up

2

Email A – he answers all the questions and
uses more informal language
Less formal language in A, e.g. *reckon*
More exclamations in A
Shorter sentences in A

Hi Sean,
<u>Thanks</u> for your email. <u>My exams are
stressful, but I think they're going well</u>.
The party sounds great. <u>Of course I'll be
there!</u> Thanks very much for asking me.
I might be a bit late though. I'm going
out that day with my brother to watch a
football match, but <u>I reckon</u> we'll get back
at around 7 pm. I'll come to yours straight
afterwards. If I remember, <u>I'll bring some
cake</u>. Would you like me to bring anything
else?
Thanks again for the invitation. I'm really
<u>looking forward</u> to it!
All the best,
Finn

3

Students' own answers

Revision: Units 1–4

Grammar p37

1

1 I'll call you when I get there   **2** does …
arrive?   **3** I'll have left   **4** I'm starting

2

1 will be   **2** 's going   **3** will win   **4** 'll
have   **5** are you doing

3

1 will have arrived   **2** will have
started   **3** will be writing   **4** will have
finished   **5** will have found out

4

a be enjoying   **b** Have … had   **c** sent
d been living   **e** coming   **f** 'll be
g were planning

Vocabulary

1

Fruit – plum, strawberry
Vegetables – peas, sweetcorn
Meat/Fish – chicken, tuna
Bakery – pancake, pie
Dairy – cream, semi-skimmed milk

2

1 spicy   **2** vegetarian   **3** raw   **4** junk
5 healthy

3

1 re   **2** dis   **3** co   **4** over   **5** inter
6 under   **7** mis

4

1 c   **2** g   **3** e   **4** h   **5** a   **6** b   **7** i
8 f   **9** d

Gateway to exams: Units 3–4

Reading p38

1

It's cheap and has lots to offer for all kinds
of visitors.

2

1 c **2** g **3** a **4** e **5** d **6** b **7** f

Listening

3

1 food plants/crops **2** third **3** serious
4 wind **5** China **6** several reasons
7 stressed and weak

Use of English p39

4

1 A **2** D **3** C **4** C **5** C **6** A **7** D
8 B **9** C **10** B **11** C **12** D

Writing

5

Students' own answers

6

1 I'll go **2** we will have completed
3 terraced **4** grew **5** We have never
seen **6** for three years **7** has he been
studying **8** filthy **9** dairy **10** comes
11 we'll be living

Unit 5

Vocabulary p40

1

1 music **2** medicine **3** history
4 Media studies **5** maths **6** art
7 English **8** biology **9** engineering

2

1 art – chemistry **2** dislike – love
3 medicine – art **4** geography – history

3

1 exam – all the others are verbs
2 term – it's a period of time not a paper
or assignment
3 timetable – the others are places
4 resit – because it's to do with taking an
exam
5 scholarship – the others are about school
work
6 subject – the others are subjects you
study

4

1 maths e **2** art f **3** geography c
4 chemistry a **5** PE d **6** biology b

Reading p41

1

Because of rain and flooding, because
there aren't any roads, because children
can't get to school.

2

1 more than 20
2 Because of the floods during the
monsoon.
3 Because once pupils stop attending
temporarily, they often don't come back.

4 He saved up and he got sponsors to help.
5 They are solar powered, using panels on
the boats' roofs.
6 70% of homes do not have electricity.
They can now work and study after dark.
7 libraries, training centres, clinics, farming
boats
8 To give them a better chance in life, and
because by 2050 one fifth of Bangladesh
could be under water.

3

1 sponsor **2** deck **3** monsoon
4 poverty **5** low-lying **6** permanently

4

Students' own answers

Grammar in context p42

1a

1 can't, ought to **2** mustn't **3** can't,
had better **4** don't have to **5** have to,
can **6** should

1b

1 c **2** d **3** f **4** a **5** e **6** b

2

1 don't have to **2** mustn't **3** mustn't
4 have to **5** must **6** don't have to
7 can **8** shouldn't

3

1 can't **2** should **3** have **4** ought
5 mustn't **6** had better **7** must
8 can **9** don't have

4

1 g **2** f **3** d **4** a **5** c **6** e **7** b

5

have to, can, don't agree, can, can, have to

**Developing vocabulary and
listening** p43

1

a mechanic **b** photographer
c scientist **d** journalist **e** dentist
f instructor

2

1 employer, employee **2** technician
3 professor **4** physicist **5** farmer
6 trainer, trainee

3

1 a **2** c **3** d **4** b
Speaker 1: instructor
Speaker 2: scientist
Speaker 3: journalist
Speaker 4: photographer

4

a energy **b** responsible **c** sociable
d working **e** detail **f** data **g** patient
h quickly **i** annoying **j** the truth/news
k different/creative **l** style **m** relaxed/
comfortable

5

actor	painter
comedian	solicitor
leader	translator
optician	referee
pianist	chemist
sailor	hairdresser
telephonist	musician
violinist	payee
author	receptionist
editor	teacher
librarian	
politician	

Grammar in context p44

1

a Z **b** S **c** F

2

1 second **2** zero **3** first

3

1 will have **2** studies **3** arrive
4 'll help **5** goes **6** 'll learn

4

2 If I had a yacht, I'd sail around the
world. **3** If I hired a surfing instructor,
I'd become an expert surfer. **4** If I
had an expensive camera, I'd take great
photos. **5** If I had a party, I'd invite my
favourite band. **6** If I were a really good
person, I'd give lots of money to charity.

5

2 get terrible headaches if she didn't drink
coffee all day **3** didn't worry about his
pronunciation, he would speak English
comfortably **4** didn't feel ill, she would
come to the college party **5** train wasn't
late, he would arrive on time

6

a won **b** (had) spent **c** decided
d fell **e** used to go/would go **f** didn't
need **g** gave **h** would come
i have been living **j** will visit

Developing speaking p45

1

for it

2

Arguments against: d 1, a 2, b 3, c 4
Arguments for: d 1, b 2, c 3, a 4

3

1 I'm going to talk about
2 What's more **3** First of all
4 Secondly **5** Another thing
6 Finally **7** The point I'm trying to make

4 and 5

<u>a</u>rgument en<u>v</u>ironment qualifi<u>ca</u>tion
se<u>cu</u>rity edu<u>ca</u>tion uni<u>ve</u>rsity ca<u>ree</u>r
ad<u>vice</u>

6

Students' own answers

7

1 teenager   2 foreground   3 camera
4 girl   5 mountains   6 scenery
7 looks

8

Students' own answers

9

Students' own answers

Developing writing p46

1

1 I   2 F   3 F   4 I

2

1 It would be great if you could give me a ring soon.   2 Give me some help.   3 I'd really like some information.   4 I would be very interested in doing your course.

3

Sports leader on a summer camp.

4

I'm really into; I'd be really happy; I can't wait to hear from you

5

I would be very grateful for the chance; I am very interested in all team sports; I look forward to hearing from you

6

a good level of English, special interest in any of the class topics

7

Students' own answers

Revision: Units 1–5

Grammar p47

1

1 don't have to   2 mustn't   3 can't
4 have to   5 must   6 can

2

1 talk   2 to work   3 had   4 shouldn't
5 revise

3

1 wouldn't be   2 don't go   3 would learn   4 told   5 'll help

4

1 If I had (some) money, I'd buy a new bike.   2 I used to wear shorts all year in primary school.   3 If I was older I could stay out after ten o'clock.   4 I've known Johan since 2008.

Vocabulary

1

1 biology   2 literature   3 engineering
4 medicine   5 geography   6 history

2

1 geography   2 architecture   3 drama
4 psychology   5 chemistry   6 PE

3

employer, employee
journalist
professor
trainer, trainee
librarian
farmer
scientist
technician
instructor
photographer

4

1 coursework   2 resit   3 mark
4 turkey   5 co-operate   6 lively
7 dreadful   8 ancient

Unit 6

Vocabulary p48

1

1 b   2 d   3 g   4 j   5 h   6 a   7 i
8 c   9 f   10 e
Picture numbered from left to right: 9, 10, 4, 8, 7, 1, 3, 6, 5, 2

2

laptop, dishwasher; fridge-freezer is hyphenated

3

1 remote control   2 microwave oven
3 dishwasher   4 digital
camera   5 satnav   6 MP3 player

4

1 plug in   2 Select   3 charge
4 connect   5 Tap   6 press

5

1 the sound   2 the time   3 the button
4 the switch

6

1 switch off   2 insert   3 turn up
4 disconnected

Reading p49

1

Students' own answers

2

Velcro – one photo shows how Velcro is used and the other one shows the plant which was the inspiration for Velcro.

3

1 D   2 F   3 A   4 B   5 C   6 E   7 B
8 F

4

1 steel   2 adopted   3 reverted
4 trampoline   5 hook   6 transplant

5

Students' own answers

Grammar in context p50

1

1 past simple   2 present perfect
3 present simple   4 present continuous
5 future with *will*

2

a to be   b past participle   c action
d agent   e by   f do not know
g not obvious

3

1 given   2 seen   3 were taught
4 is dropped   5 are created, is found
6 have been learnt

4

2 is … published   3 has … been done
4 will be won   5 was invented   6 are made

5

2 The criminal was arrested.
3 The news is being read by Anna Williams tonight.
4 The latest research has been published by the Japanese team.
5 The professors will be met at the train station.
6 The man was sentenced to four years in prison.
7 A book called *Bad Science* was written by a British journalist.
8 A reading system for the blind was invented by Louis Braille.
9 Four windows were damaged by the wind.

Developing vocabulary and listening p51

1

1 good at/interested in   2 aware of   3 different to/from   4 good for/at   5 interested in   6 worried about   7 bored of/with   8 afraid of   9 responsible for   10 similar to

2

Nice to hear from you. Your new course sounds similar <u>to</u> mine. I'm really pleased <u>with</u> the choice I've made, but you sound like you're disappointed. Do you know about the student counselling service? Don't be worried <u>about</u> feeling embarrassed, because they are very understanding there. If you've realised that you're tired <u>of</u> your course, just go and see them. They are responsible <u>for</u> helping students switch courses. I think it's good that you're aware <u>of</u> the problem so soon.

3

c

4

1 c **2** c **3** b **4** c **5** a

5

1 f **2** e **3** g **4** c **5** h **6** b **7** a
8 d

Grammar in context p52

1

a subject **b** object **c** past participle
d *have* or *get* **e** don't **f** does
g formal **h** preposition

2

2 How often do you have/get your teeth
checked at the dentist?

3 When did you last have/get your hair
cut?

4 When are you next going to have/get
your car checked at the garage?

5 When will you have/get your eyes tested
at the optician?

6 How often do your grandparents have/
get their blood pressure taken at the
clinic?

7 Are you having/getting a pizza delivered
to your house tonight?

3

1 e **2** f **3** b **4** a **5** d **6** c

4

a cut **b** Going **c** going **d** to change
e to have **f** arguing **g** to think
h wasting **i** have **j** to do **k** Showing
l having

Developing speaking p53

1

Students' own answers

2

Students' own answers

3

1 d **2** c **3** f **4** e **5** b **6** a

4a and 4b

1 Both **of the** photos show young peop**l**e.
2 You **can** tell because **of the** wood**e**n
table **and** the **e**quipment.
3 Howev**e**r, there are several diffe**re**nc**e**s.

5

Students' own answers

6

1 I can see three students, two girls and
one boy and they're probably friends.
2 They're probably somewhere in the
school yard or playground, or they could
be in a park. **3** I think they're either
texting or looking at social media websites
on their mobile phones. **4** I suppose
they're a bit bored because they're more
interested in their mobile phones than each
other.

7

Students' own answers

Developing writing p54

1

For: fascinating programmes, e.g. nature,
culture; company for lonely people;
educational, e.g. language learning;
relaxing, e.g. makes people laugh
Against: stops people reading, listening to
music, talking; advertising – bad influence;
unsuitable programmes for children

2

A 3 **B** 1 **C** 4 **D** 2

3

c

4

However, What's more, In addition, In
conclusion, on the other hand, Firstly,
Furthermore, Finally

5

1 In my opinion **2** Personally, I think

6 a and b

Students' own answers

Revision: Units 1–6

Grammar p55

1

1 Millions of illegal DVDs are sold each
year.
2 The next Olympics will be held in my
country.
3 My computer has finally been fixed.
4 Latin isn't often taught in schools these
days.

2

2 We always have our TV fixed when it
breaks down.
3 I had my bike mended last month.
4 My dad's had a website designed for his
new company.
5 We are having all the bedrooms painted.
6 I usually have my boots repaired.
7 My parents had portraits painted of me
and my sister.

3

1 speaking **2** to eat **3** thinking
4 watching **5** Learning

4

1 were taken **2** is being repaired
3 would check **4** was travelling
5 have been waiting **6** is delayed, 'll
call **7** don't pass

Vocabulary

1

a dishwasher **b** vacuum cleaner
c satnav **d** remote control

2

1 for **2** to **3** of **4** of **5** about

3

1 tap **2** select **3** connect
4 recharge, plugging

4

1 good at **2** ready for **3** tired
of **4** bored with/of **5** good at

Gateway to exams: Units 5–6

Reading p56

1

When scientists, environmentalists and
inventors use ideas from animals and
nature.

2

1 A **2** C **3** A **4** D **5** C **6** B **7** B
8 D

Listening

3

1 c **2** c **3** b **4** a **5** a **6** b

Use of English p57

4

2 was taken **3** had more money **4** are
responsible for **5** having my eyes
tested **6** don't have to

Writing

5

Students' own answers

6

1 I'd **2** about **3** coursework
4 mustn't **5** should wear **6** I'll meet,
Being **7** switch on, reach **8** are
done **9** afraid of **10** are having a pizza
delivered

Unit 7

Vocabulary p58

1

1 snowboarding **2** basketball
3 skiing **4** golf **5** ice hockey
6 athletics **7** volleyball **8** diving
9 football **10** tennis **11** climbing
12 sailing **13** gymnastics
14 weightlifting

2

tennis	court	racket
football	pitch	goal post
skiing	slope	goggles
ice-skating	rink	skates
golf	course	club
athletics	track	trainers

3

1 bounce **2** hit **3** beat **4** scored
5 score **6** game

4a

1 play **2** do **3** go **4** playing **5** go
6 do

4b

1 play **2** do **3** go

Reading p59

1

Students' own answers

2

1 c **2** b **3** a

3

1 T **2** T **3** T **4** F **5** F **6** T **7** F
8 T **9** F

4

1 retain **2** unpredictable **3** entirely
4 absorb **5** vary **6** layer

5

Students' own answers

Grammar in context p60

1

1 who/that **2** which/that **3** where
4 which/that **5** whose

2

a who and that **b** which and that
c whose **d** where **e** when
f who, which or that **g** person, thing,
place or time

3

1 where ✓ **2** that **3** that ✓ **4** that ✓
5 who **6** that ✓ **7** that ✓ **8** who

4

1 where **2** when **3** when **4** which
5 whose **6** whose

5

1 e (who) **2** f (whose) **3** b (when)
4 a (where) **5** g (when) **6** d (whose)
7 c (where)

6

Elephant polo is played

a front rider whose job is to guide the
elephant

Riders use sticks which/that … they always
hit …

The pitch where they play … when the
elephants are changed.

The size or weight of the elephants which/
that compete …

… health and safety of the animals which/
that take part.

Developing vocabulary and listening p61

1

1 out **2** in **3** out **4** up **5** for
6 up

2

2 That shy girl never joins in with the

others. **3** Professional athletes always
warm up before a race. **4** She's
a confident diver who's going for
gold! **5** The less experienced team was
knocked out in the first round.

3

Students' own answers

4

Anti-gravity yoga is good for your heart
and core muscles and it's relaxing.
Reverse running is good for balance,
general fitness and stamina.

5

1 F **2** T **3** F **4** F **5** T **6** F **7** T
8 F

6

1 b **2** c **3** a **4** e **5** f **6** d

7

1 pass out **2** catch up, keep up **3** drop
out **4** send off **5** carry on

Grammar in context p62

1

a people **b** things **c** places **d** times
e can't **f** can't **g** always

2

1 who **2** where **3** which **4** whose
5 when **6** whose

3

2 The university sports centre, where my
son works out, is brand new. **3** This
pool, where Tom Daley used to practise,
is 50 metres. **4** The cricketers, who got
very dirty by the end of the match, were
wearing white. **5** The French runner,
whose family was sitting next to us,
surprised us all by coming first.

4

1 D **2** D **3** ND **4** D **5** ND

5

1 a In baseball, which is popular in Japan,
it's bad luck to touch one of the lines.
2 b In football, which was first played
internationally in 1872, it's lucky to have
a double number on your shirt. **3 a** In
ice hockey, which is the national sport of
Canada, it's bad luck to put down your
sticks crossed. **4 a** In basketball, whose
most successful team is the Boston Celtics,
it's good luck to wipe the soles of your
trainers. **5 a** In tennis, which first became
an Olympic sport in 1896, it's bad luck to
hold more than two balls when serving.

Developing speaking p63

1

Jimmy

2

1 T **2** F **3** F **4** T **5** T **6** F **7** T
8 T

3

(Sometimes), I agree … ✓ (A)
I (totally) agree (with you) (that …) (A)
(I think) You're right (about that) … ✓ (A)
I take your point. ✓ (A)
That's true. ✓ (A)
I agree to an extent, but … (D)
I see what you mean, but … ✓ (D)
I'm not sure that's true. ✓ (D)
You've got a point. However, … (D)

4

1 cricket **2** exercise **3** optimistic
4 argument **5** importance

5

Students' own answers

6

1 In this picture there are five teenagers,
one boy and four girls. **2** I think they are
in someone's garden. **3** They are eating
pizza. **4** Maybe this photo was taken
after doing some sport or perhaps it is
someone's birthday.

7

Students' own answers

8

Students' own answers

Developing writing p64

1

a Why and how video gaming is important
to you.
b the editor of the magazine **c** by email
or letter

2

That video gaming is a type of sport.

3

1 Personally **2** convinced **3** believe
4 see **5** far as I'm concerned **6** opinion

4

1 c **2** a **3** d **4** e **5** b

5

1 His heart beats quickly.
2 He talks about it with friends.
3 Very popular: stadiums can attract
thousands of spectators.
4 No, only the mental scores.
5 There is less physical exercise.
6 He says the professional gamers he
knows keep physically fit so that they are
mentally fit, too.

6

Students' own answers

Revision: Units 1–7

Grammar p65

1

1 where **2** that **3** whose **4** when
5 who

2

2 that **3** which **6** that

3

1 In 1975 Junko Tabei, who is from Japan, became the first woman to climb Everest.
2 The very first Olympics™, which were held in 776 BC, were won by a chef called Coroebus.
3 The first modern Olympic Games™ were held in Greece, where the ancient games also took place.
4 Golf balls, which are now solid, used to contain liquid.
5 Richard Williams, whose daughters Serena and Venus are both multi-millionaires, was extremely poor as a child.

4

1 played **2** gave **3** which **4** got out
5 were leaving **6** reminded
7 'm going to make

Vocabulary

1

1 ice hockey **2** football **3** sailing
4 athletics **5** snowboarding **6** diving

2

1 pitch, boots **2** slope, goggles
3 rink, skates **4** course, club **5** net, court

3

1 up **2** in **3** out **4** up **5** for

4

1 e **2** a **3** f **4** d **5** b **6** c

Unit 8

Vocabulary p66

1a

1 gallery **2** sketch **3** still life
4 abstract **5** exhibition **6** self-portrait
7 sculpture **8** landscape

1b

a still life **b** sketch **c** abstract
d self-portrait **e** landscape **f** sculpture

2

1 landscape **2** self-portrait **3** still life
4 exhibition **5** sculpture **6** gallery
7 abstract **8** sketch

3

1 drawing **2** landscape **3** sketch
4 audience **5** sculpture

4

2 tunes **3** plays/films **4** sculptors
5 pianists

5

1 interval **2** tickets **3** visitors
4 applauded **5** programme

Reading p67

1

Students' own answers

2

Each character is about one centimetre tall.

3

1 b **2** b **3** a **4** c **5** c **6** a

4

Students' own answers

5

1 miniature **2** blob **3** empathise
4 touching **5** projected **6** puddle
7 installation

Grammar in context p68

1

was visiting; had visited; had visited; would visit; could visit; might visit; had to

2

2 didn't know **3** might take **4** could get
5 walked past his installations

3

1 He said his dad had made him a train set when he was younger, but he had never really been interested in the trains.
2 He said that when he had got down to street level, he had realised that everywhere was the same.
3 Slinkachu said, 'I like to think my stories continue after I leave them'.

4

1 she had always hated modern art **2** they were going to the sculpture park the following week **3** he was painting a picture just for me **4** they were hoping to make a new album that year **5** she couldn't sketch anymore that night because it was too dark

5

a asked **b** been/become **c** which
d told **e** had **f** us **g** there **h** were
i going

Developing vocabulary and listening p69

1

1 amazed **2** interesting **3** surprising
4 uninspired **5** frightening **6** relaxed
7 bored **8** disappointing

2

1 terrifying **2** worried **3** satisfied
4 entertaining

3

2 Tom's maths homework is very confusing. / Tom is very confused by his maths homework.
3 Tonight's birthday party is exciting. / We are excited about the birthday party tonight.
4 The number of people at the modern art exhibition was surprising. / I was surprised by the number of people at the modern art exhibition.
5 The cancellation of the school concert is very disappointing. / The children are very disappointed by/about the cancellation of the school concert.

4

2

5

1 c **2** a **3** a **4** c **5** b **6** b

6

1 thrilling **2** moving **3** exhausted
4 pleased **5** annoyed **6** amusing

Grammar in context p70

1

1 same, statements **2** subject, not
3 do **4** whether

2

1 could **2** this had happened **3** made
4 if it had changed

3

1 if/whether he had seen the portrait of the Queen **2** why he was putting his chewing gum under the desk **3** who his/her favourite singer was **4** if/whether he often went to the theatre **5** where the paintings by Lowry were **6** if/whether they would be able to clean the marks off the painting

4a

The interviewer asked Will to speak up a bit.

4b

a infinitive **b** necessary **c** told
d asked

5

2 'Please split into smaller groups.'
3 'Don't use your mobile phones.'
4 'Please move a little faster'.

6

1 The guide asked them to leave all their things at the entrance.
2 The guide told one of the boys not to go too close to the paintings.
3 The guide told two girls not to eat their sandwiches in the gallery.
4 The guide asked the teacher to take the children into the next room.

7

a He told me I could have a major part.
b He told us to be quiet and (to) listen.
c He told us we all had to wear our costumes that day.

d He said we could all finish early, because it was the first day.

e He said he would see us tomorrow.

Developing speaking p71

1 and 2

1 i **2** e **3** a **4** c **5** h **6** f **7** g
8 d **9** j **10** b

3

1 At first **2** First **3** Then **4** Later
5 After that **6** next **7** A few
minutes later **8** after a few minutes
9 Finally **10** In the end **11** Afterwards

4

At the beginning of a description: at first, first

In the middle of a description: a few minutes later, after a while, after that, next, then

At the end of a description: finally, in the end

5a

per<u>for</u>mance

5b

<u>af</u>terwards, at <u>first</u>, in the <u>end</u>

5c

Students' own answers

6

Students' own answers

7

1 There's a female artist, maybe in her 20s or 30s. **2** She's in a field in the countryside. She might be in Spain. **3** She's painting a landscape. **4** The photo was taken in the middle of the day.

8

Students' own answers

9

Students' own answers

Developing writing p72

1

1 e **2** g **3** a **4** b **5** f **6** c **7** d

2

action, drama, science fiction, thriller

3

Type of film: science fiction and thriller
Yes, the writer thinks it's amazing.

4

1 C **2** D **3** B **4** A

5

1 T **2** F **3** F **4** T **5** T **6** F

6

Any of the following:

science fiction, thriller, main characters, well-known actors, plot, happy ending, acting, special effects

released in X, She plays an X, The film was directed by

to sum up, I would definitely recommend
Positive adjectives:

amazing, fantastic, convincing, interesting, incredible, exciting, memorable, tense

7

Students' own answers

Revision: Units 1–8

Grammar p73

1

1 The boy told the guide he was 14.

2 He said he couldn't see his parents anywhere.

3 He also told her (that) he wasn't worried (and that) they would be there very soon.

4 His parents arrived and said they'd been in the gallery shop.

5 They said they were leaving (as/because) they didn't want to miss the train.

2

1 He wanted to know if I had visited the gallery. **2** They asked him where he was born. **3** The teacher asked us if we had touched it. **4** She wanted to know how long we had been there.

3

1 told the boys not to touch the sculptures **2** asked us not to talk in the library **3** told me not to mix all the colours at the same time **4** at the desk told the visitors to get their tickets from her

4

1 b **2** g **3** h **4** a **5** c **6** e **7** f
8 d

Vocabulary

1

1 d **2** e **3** a **4** b **5** c

2

1 musician **2** audience **3** composer
4 songwriter **5** performer

3

1 exhausting **2** surprised **3** depressing
4 embarrassed **5** interested

4

1 characters **2** conductor **3** excited
4 disgusting **5** stage **6** freezing
7 tiring

Gateway to exams: Units 7–8

Reading p74

1

1 F (lines 8–9) **2** F (line 17) **3** T (lines 13–14) **4** NM **5** T (lines 19–22) **6** F (lines 26–27) **7** T (lines 33–34) **8** F (lines 34–35) **9** NM **10** F (line 38)

Listening

2

1 F **2** F **3** F **4** T **5** T **6** F **7** T
8 F

Use of English p75

3

a to **b** which **c** be **d** which
e which **f** can/might/could **g** of **h** to
i where **j** up **k** then **l** before

Writing

4

Students' own answers

5

1 who I admire **2** how long the pictures took to paint **3** beat the Dutch **4** which has been an Olympic sport since 1992 **5** agree with you **6** where the tennis courts were **7** whose coach **8** visitors were … to be quiet **9** excited **10** act **11** he would soon paint a self-portrait **12** in a pretty village, where I grew up

Unit 9

Vocabulary p76

1

1 **p**rime minister

2 nati**o**nal anthem

3 political **p**arties

4 q**u**een

5 **f**lag

6 capital

7 presiden**t**

8 election

9 **p**olicies

10 currency

11 the number of people who live in one particular country

2

1 the US **2** Poland **3** Switzerland
4 Spain **5** Japan **6** Wales

3

1 b **2** a **3** c **4** d

4

1 vote **2** reigned **3** dictates
4 predictions **5** higher **6** kingdom

Reading p77

1 and 2

Students' own answers

3

1 It was sudden and unexpected. Some thought he might have been poisoned. He was only 40.

2 His young son, Edward.

3 to keep him safe

4 The boys disappeared. Their uncle, Richard, was then the King of England.

5 We don't know, but it is thought that either King Richard or the later king, Henry VII killed them.

6 Because the authorities decided they couldn't be tested using modern forensic methods.

7 Richard III, the boys' uncle

8 He was a bad man – a villain, who killed his own nephews.

4

1 villain **2** poisoned **3** skeleton **4** legitimate **5** heir **6** throne **7** orders

5

Students' own answers

Grammar in context p78

1a

1 A **2** B **3** B **4** A

1b

a without **b** have **c** past participle **d** must **e** 50% **f** can't **g** 100%

2

1 can't **2** must **3** might **4** must **5** must **6** may **7** can't **8** could

3

1 d **2** c **3** a **4** b

4

2 He might/may have got stuck in traffic.

3 They must have been very hungry.

4 It must have blown over in the storm.

5 It might have been the wind.

6 She might/may not have marked it yet.

7 I must have ridden over some broken glass.

8 I can't have put it in my bag this morning.

5

a might **b** sure **c** been **d** have **e** could **f** might **g** where **h** already **i** told **j** had found **k** sounds **l** called

Developing vocabulary and listening p79

1

Nouns: aristocracy, danger, sense, help, terror

Adjectives: official, terrible, natural

2

1 helpless **2** careful **3** useless **4** careless **5** useful **6** helpful

3

1 thirsty **2** mysterious **3** famous **4** dangerous **5** comfortable **6** hungry

4

Students' own answers

5

1 Tutankhamun, King of Ancient Egypt

2 3,300 years ago

6

a in 1922 **b** 10 **c** hippopotamus **d** physically fit **e** bone disease **f** 130 **g** his/a leg **h** falling/a fall/breaking his leg **i** DNA

7

beautiful	democratic
dramatic	fearful/fearless
heroic	homeless
hopeful/hopeless	meaningful
peaceful	poetic
romantic	thoughtful/
wonderful	thoughtless
	worthless

Grammar in context p80

1

1 If Carter hadn't made that incredible discovery, his life would have been completely different. **2** If he had been healthy, these activities would have been normal for a king.

2

1 b **2** b **3** a

3

1 f **2** a **3** b **4** e **5** c **6** d

4

1 had **2** have **3** hadn't been **4** 'd **5** would have **6** had

5

2 I hadn't dropped the book in the bath. **3** I hadn't broken my glasses. **4** my little brother hadn't drawn on my book. **5** I hadn't spilt my drink on it.

6

1 If I'd seen Martin's sister, I would have given her his wallet.

2 If Nathan hadn't got food poisoning, he would have taken the exam.

3 If you hadn't told me to use that shampoo, my hair wouldn't have turned green.

4 If Luke's train had been delayed, he would have arrived late for school.

5 If Ella hadn't helped her dad mend the car as a child, she wouldn't have become a mechanic.

6 If I'd had an eye test, I would have realised I needed glasses.

Developing speaking p81

1

Students' own answers

2

1 Some young people on a demonstration, probably students. In the foreground, there are two boys waving flags. On the left there are some police officers and on the right there's a red double-decker bus.

2 They are holding up signs and shouting or protesting.

3 They could have heard an announcement at their colleges or some news online or on the TV which has upset them.

4 They probably feel angry.

3

a waving flags **b** on the right **c** Most of the **d** I mean **e** more young people **f** It seems **g** I imagine **h** could have heard **i** which is bad **j** really angry

4

1 noun (stress is on the first syllable)

2 verb (stress is on the second syllable)

5

They all follow the same pattern (stress first syllable in noun and second in verb): contrast contrast, increase increase, permit permit, refund refund, reject reject, upgrade upgrade

6a

1 N **2** V **3** V **4** N **5** V **6** V

6b and c

1 They re<u>jec</u>ted my application for a scholarship. It's very disappointing.

2 After all that <u>research</u>, Tom got a really high mark.

3 I've just had an <u>upgrade</u> on my phone.

4 We have to con<u>trast</u> the two political systems for our assignment.

7

Students' own answers

8

Students' own answers

Developing writing p82

1

1 past perfect **2** past simple **3** past continuous **4** used to **5** modal verbs

2

1 D **2** B **3** A **4** C

3

1 T **2** F **3** T **4** T **5** F **6** F

4

Students' own answers

5

If <u>I had known</u> what was going to happen, I would never have left the house. My parents <u>were</u> away for the weekend. A new girl in my class <u>had asked</u> me to go for a swim with her. I <u>used to love</u> swimming, but something made me uncertain. I don't know why. I could have said no, but I <u>didn't want to be</u> unfriendly so I <u>agreed</u>.

Marie <u>had made</u> some sandwiches and <u>had packed</u> fruit and drinks for us. The sun <u>was shining</u>, so it <u>was</u> a perfect day to be by the river. As we <u>cycled</u> to the river, I <u>began</u> to feel happier, light-hearted. The water <u>was</u> lovely and we <u>swam</u> for hours. After that, we <u>had</u> our picnic. Marie <u>was</u> nice. She <u>didn't talk</u> much, but I just <u>thought</u> she might be shy.

Later, when <u>we were cycling</u> back, I <u>invited</u> Marie to come to my house to watch a DVD. But she <u>smiled</u> and <u>said</u> that she had to get home. I <u>was feeling</u> tired anyway, so we <u>said</u> goodbye and <u>left</u> each other at the end of my road.

When I <u>was walking</u> up to my front door I <u>started</u> to feel that something was wrong again. The door <u>was</u> wide open. I might have forgotten to lock it, but I can't have left it open. My heart <u>was beating</u> quickly as I <u>walked</u> slowly inside. I <u>said</u> 'hello!' but nobody <u>answered</u>. Somebody <u>was</u> in the house. I <u>called</u> out again, and that's when …

6

Students' own answers

Revision: Units 1–9

Grammar p83

1

1 must **2** can't **3** must **4** may
5 can't **6** may

2

1 It can't have been Paul. **2** The wind might have frightened off your cat. **3** It must have taken months to prepare for the royal visit. **4** It must have been Jamie who rang the doorbell. **5** They may have won because their political campaign was quite successful. **6** They must have changed the national anthem, it sounds different.

3

1 would have sent **2** would have
3 had **4** wouldn't have believed
5 hadn't lost

4

1 got/taken/had, would **2** whose
3 had, 0 **4** me/us **5** taken/brought, known **6** to **7** may/might/could

Vocabulary

1

1 capital **2** national anthem **3** flag
4 population **5** currency

2

1 king **2** president **3** members of parliament **4** laws/policies

3

1 careless **2** sensible **3** comfortable
4 natural **5** helpful

4

1 scientific **2** mysterious **3** helpless
4 possible **5** artistic **6** enjoyable
7 unlucky **8** sociable **9** impatient
10 uncomfortable **11** overcrowded
12 quiet **13** unhealthy

Unit 10

Vocabulary p84

1

1 i **2** j **3** d **4** e **5** g **6** a **7** f
8 c **9** b **10** h

2

1 a bakery **2** a butcher's **3** a bookshop
4 a bakery **5** a sports shop **6** a shoe shop **7** a post office

3

1 trolley **2** refund, receipt **3** queue
4 changing room **5** discount, bargain
6 debit **7** debit card, cash

4

1 fish counter **2** aisles **3** products
4 escalator **5** receipt **6** customer services **7** shopping

Reading p85

1

3, 4

2

1 c **2** a **3** d **4** b

3

1 b **2** c **3** b **4** a **5** b

4

1 approval **2** came up with **3** hassle
4 assume **5** accessible **6** fussy

5

Students' own answers

Grammar in context p86

1

some-: something, somewhere

any-: anybody, anyone, anywhere

no-: nothing, nobody, no one

every-: everything, everybody, everyone, everywhere

2

1 Everyone **2** something **3** anything, anywhere, nobody **4** everywhere, something **5** somewhere

3

1 something **2** anywhere
3 everywhere **4** anything **5** anybody
6 everybody **7** someone **8** anything, nothing

4

a adjectives and adverbs **b** nouns
c that

5

2 such a busy road, so dangerous **3** such a friendly shopkeeper, so helpful **4** are such crowded places, so noisy

6

2 She's such a fast cashier.

3 Mine's not such a cool skateboard.

4 He'd lost so much weight that I didn't recognise him/Frank.

5 There was such a bad smell (in the café) that we decided not to stay.

6 I've been at this school since 2014.

7 That's the restaurant where I had my birthday party.

8 All of my birthday cake was eaten by my friends.

9 People will have started living on Mars by/in 2030.

Developing vocabulary and listening p87

1

1 lend **2** waste **3** win **4** donate
5 earn **6** spend **7** borrow **8** save

2

1 waste **2** won **3** spent **4** save
5 make **6** lends **7** donate **8** borrow

3

Speaker 1: d

Speaker 2: a

Speaker 3: b

Speaker 4: c

4

1 Speaker 3 **2** Speaker 4 **3** Speaker 4
4 Speaker 3 **5** Speaker 2 **6** Speaker 1
7 Speaker 1 **8** Speaker 3

5

1 g **2** f **3** a **4** h **5** d **6** b **7** c
8 e

Grammar in context p88

1

1 c **2** b **3** a

2

1 would listen **2** had **3** spoke **4** had known **5** hadn't bought **6** was
7 wouldn't keep

3

2 He wishes she wouldn't eat biscuits in his room.

3 He wishes she would ask before borrowing his stationery.

4 He wishes she wouldn't say rude things about his hair.

5 He wishes she wouldn't embarrass him in front of his friends.

4

1 If only I had bought that jacket in the sale.

2 I wish I'd bought those Nike trainers on eBay yesterday.

3 I wish you wouldn't leave the lights on in every room.

4 If only my mum hadn't put my new jumper in the wash.

5 If only somebody had saved the department store from closing down.

6 I wish I had curlier hair.

5

1 I'd got up earlier 2 It was such a quiet morning/so quiet 3 practically nobody there 4 I could have a coffee break 5 a sandwich or something 6 when I returned 7 If only he had stayed with me 8 I asked her politely to wait 9 I wish I had stayed calmer 10 he told me

Developing speaking p89

1

b sports shop

2

a I'm just looking b I'm looking for c Have you got anything in d I'll take these e can I bring them back

3

1 b 2 b 3 b 4 a 5 b 6 a

4 and 5

1 c 2 f 3 a 4 g 5 e 6 d 7 b

6

Students' own answers

7

1 expensive clothes shop, perhaps a boutique selling designer clothes and accessories 2 A woman looking at the clothes 3 there aren't many people, there's a plant and it has a big window so it is very light and comfortable, looks like someone's living room 4 people that are rich probably live there

8

Students' own answers

9

Students' own answers

Developing writing p90

1

Carla bought a memory stick from the shop but found when she got home that the box was empty. The shop assistant was rude to her, suggesting that Carla had taken the stick; she also did not tell the truth about the manager being there.

2

1 NM 2 T 3 F 4 F 5 NM 6 T

3

Addition: furthermore, in addition
Contrast: although
Reason: because
Consequence: therefore
Time and sequence: in the end

4

1 a 2 c 3 b 4 c 5 a 6 b

5

Students' own answers

Revision: Units 1–10

Grammar p91

1

1 anywhere 2 something 3 everyone/everybody 4 Nothing 5 anybody/anyone

2

1 such 2 so 3 so 4 such 5 such

3

1 hadn't listened 2 had bought 3 hadn't agreed 4 had arrived 5 hadn't wasted

4

1 not 2 would 3 have 4 such 5 have 6 had

Vocabulary

1

1 stationery shop/newsagent's 2 bakery 3 butcher's 4 jeweller's 5 electrical goods shop 6 chemist's 7 greengrocer's

2

1 d 2 f 3 c 4 a 5 b 6 e

3

1 win 2 lend 3 saving 4 donates 5 raised 6 afford

4

1 bargain 2 discount 3 performance 4 tap 5 assignment 6 mark 7 stale

Gateway to exams: Units 9–10

Reading p92

1

1 b 2 b 3 c 4 .a

Listening

2

1 4,000 2 fighting 3 rectangular 4 long triangle/triangular 5 400 6 US 7 simple/basic design 8 identical/the same

Use of English p93

3

a different b relaxing c international d operates e developer f successful g billionaire h anything i electrical j lucky k exciting l used m sensible n personal o security

Writing

4

Students' own answers

5

1 It can't have been her at the party last night.

2 If you had called me earlier, we would have been able to go together.

3 Seb may have left his coat.

4 We wouldn't have taken that exam, if we'd known how hard it was.

5 It can't be him. He isn't that tall.

6 No one/Nobody knows what the actor's real name is.

7 Laura, come downstairs. Somebody wants to talk to you.

8 The composer was such an interesting person to talk to.

9 In the foreground of the picture, you can see some sheep.

10 I look forward to hearing from you.

11 If only I hadn't lent Bernie my new dictionary. He's lost it.

12 I wish my neighbour wouldn't/didn't play his music so loudly.

Workbook audioscript

Unit 1

Developing vocabulary and listening p7

3 and 4 ▶ 01

Speaker 1:
He said that if the position of the writing is straight up, this shows independence. If it goes to the left, then this shows that you might be shy. My handwriting goes to the left, and I'd say I'm not that confident, so he was right there. But then the size of my writing is large. And he said that meant that you were outgoing and sociable, or that you were *trying* to be. So I suppose he was right again! Anyway, I think I might try and change the direction of my handwriting now, so that I perhaps look more confident.

Speaker 2:
We don't have to agree with his comments. He did seem very intelligent, I mean, imagine being able to read 300 signs in a person's handwriting. But I actually changed my handwriting about two years ago because I decided my old style wasn't very attractive: it was small and spidery. I didn't like it. Now, does this mean that my personality has changed? I don't think so! I don't really believe all this stuff. It *sounds* good, but I'm not convinced.

Speaker 3:
Interestingly, he said that the dots on my letter 'i's were all over the place. That suggests that I'm forgetful and not very organised. And I think my friends would agree! I'm always losing things that belong to me! It drives them mad. But on the positive side, he also said that my *m's*, *n's* and *h's* were large and that shows that I am helpful and sociable. I'd like to hear some more, I think, so I can decide how useful graphology really is.

Speaker 4:
I quite like my handwriting and people generally say it's neat and attractive, but I hadn't noticed anything in particular about it until I spoke to him. He said I had about three different styles in my handwriting but that this was quite normal. He also noticed the wide spaces I have between my words. Apparently, that means that I like my own company, I'm independent. That was interesting. And he also commented on the narrow margins on the right of the page, where I get to the end of the line. He said that these showed I was impatient … impatient to get on with things. I think all this graphology stuff is really interesting.

Developing speaking p9

1 and 2 ▶ 02

Luke: Hello, my name's Luke.
Ben: Hi, I'm Ben. You're Luke Spencer, aren't you?
Luke: Yes, I am. How did you know?
Ben: I'm Maria's friend.
Luke: Oh yes. I remember now, she said that you might be here.
Ben: You're really good at table tennis, aren't you? That's what Maria said.
Luke: Really? Well, I sometimes play, but I don't think I'm very good!
Ben: Oh, well, that's OK. Neither am I! Do you want to play a game now?
Luke: OK.
Ben: You don't have a bat, do you? We need an extra one.
Luke: Look, there's one here.
Ben: Great. You can play football too, can't you?
Luke: Oh yes, I play every week.
Ben: Do you know James? James Kingston? We play on a local team. You don't want to join us one week, do you?
Luke: That would be great.
Ben: Come on, let me introduce you to him.

PRONUNCIATION p9

4 and 5 ▶ 03

1 You're Luke Spencer, aren't you?
2 You're really good at table tennis, aren't you?
3 You don't have a bat, do you?
4 You can play football too, can't you?
5 You don't want to join us one week, do you?

DESCRIBING PICTURES p9

8 ▶ 04

This picture shows a young woman in a library. She's probably about 18. The girl is reading a book. She is probably studying. There are lots of books behind her on the shelves. Maybe it's a college library, or something, or perhaps it's a public library. I'm not sure.

The girl's wearing a blue cardigan and a white T-shirt and she looks really comfortable. She has got dark straight hair which is tied back in a ponytail. She looks relaxed and is interested in what she is doing. However, she also looks a bit serious and rather quiet in this picture. Maybe she enjoys studying or maybe she doesn't – it's difficult to tell.

Unit 2

Developing vocabulary and listening p15

3 and 4 ▶ 05

Interviewer:
So, what's the transport system like where you live?
Woman:
I live in the city of Medellín, in Colombia.

Actually, I live on the outskirts in Comuna 13, but I work in the city of Medellín. These days I can get to my job in the city very easily. I just walk two minutes from my home to the bottom of the huge outdoor escalator. I get on and it takes me all the way up to the city centre, where I get off. There are six stages and it's nearly 400 metres long. When it was first built in 2011 we all thought it was incredible. It cost $7m to build, but it's free for us to use.

Interviewer:
Wow! What was it like in the past?
Woman:
Well, Comuna 13 is on a very steep hillside. Before the escalator, we used to walk up hundreds of big steps. I would leave my house at 6 am, but now I can set off at just before 6.30 as the journey takes six minutes instead of 35. That saves around an hour a day! The old journey was the same as walking the height of a 28-storey building.

Interviewer:
Very tiring!
Woman:
Yes, everyone used to arrive out of breath at the top! I don't think the outdoor escalator has improved our lives financially, but many of us have a bit more free time than we used to. And another thing … we didn't use to feel that we were part of the city, but now we do. We just hope it doesn't break down in bad weather!

Interviewer:
And what about you?
Man:
Well, I'm also from Medellín, but I don't use the escalator, I use the metrocable – that's one of those little bubble boxes that move along a wire in the sky!

Interviewer:
Yes, I've seen them. Do you live far from the city centre, too?
Man:
Yes, I live in one of the favelas of Medellín. They are areas outside of Medellín on steep hillsides and they didn't use to be easy to get to. I used to catch a bus to my job as a mechanic near the city centre. It would often take hours and the buses used to be very overcrowded. Nowadays, I commute by cable car, or metrocable. I use line J. There are three lines, J, K and L – line K is seen as the first city cable system in the world. So, I take the cable, then I get on the metro directly to my workplace. The cable cars give you a great view of the city so they're popular with tourists who get on and take photos and videos. In fact, a group of eight French tourists got into my cabin yesterday. I'm one of thousands of commuters who use the metrocable system. It's brilliant because there are just ten people in each cabin! It's really comfortable. Travelling around used to be a nightmare and we didn't use to enjoy it

at all, but these days, we are very proud of our transport system. Medellín was actually named as the city with one of the top transport systems in the world in 2012!

Developing speaking p17

2 and 4 06

Customer: I'd like a return ticket to Guildford, from Cambridge for today, coming back in two days' time.

Ticket officer: Certainly. So that's departing on the 18th September returning on the 20th …

Customer: Can you tell me the cost?

Ticket officer: It's £33.50

Customer: All right. That's for a return?

Ticket officer: Yes.

Customer: Can you tell me what time the train leaves?

Ticket officer: Well, the next one is at 10.26.

Customer: And do I have to change, please?

Ticket officer: Yes, I'm afraid it's not a direct train. There are two changes.

Customer: Oh dear. Can you tell me where I have to change?

Ticket officer: The first one is at Finsbury Park. You have to change there for Clapham Junction.

Customer: OK, so I get the Clapham Junction train from Finsbury Park. And coming back?

Ticket officer: Well, coming back there are three changes.

Customer: Oh dear. That's a bit complicated. Which platform is it, please?

Ticket officer: You can check on the departure board.

Customer: OK.

Ticket officer: Right. Your return train gets in to Cambridge at 19.30.

Customer: Sorry, I didn't catch that. Could you repeat it?

Ticket officer: Look, it's all written down here for you.

Customer: Oh, thank goodness. Thank you.

Ticket officer: That's OK. Bye.

Customer: Bye.

PRONUNCIATION p17

5 07

1 Could you <u>write</u> it <u>down</u> for me, please?
2 Is it possible to <u>pay</u> by <u>card</u>?
3 Could you <u>print</u> <u>out</u> the <u>times</u> for me?
4 Can you tell me <u>how much</u> it <u>costs</u>?
5 Which <u>platform</u> does it <u>leave</u> from, <u>please</u>?

DESCRIBING PICTURES p17

7 08

I think this photo was taken on holiday. It shows a beach and a port, with a cruise ship in the water. I think the beach is somewhere very hot, perhaps in the Caribbean because there are palm trees and the sea is very green. The cruise ship is very big and modern. It's like a floating hotel! In the background there are mountains and there are also lots of smaller boats in the port.

On the beach at the bottom of the photo, there are lots of people. You can't see exactly what they are doing but I imagine they are on holiday. So they're doing typical holiday activities. Maybe they are the people from the cruise ship. There are sun beds and umbrellas so I think they're sunbathing and reading. And there are some people swimming in the sea. They're wearing clothes for swimming and also shorts and T-shirts.

Gateway to exams: Units 1–2

Listening p20

2 09

Speaker 1:

My last holiday was a camping holiday with my family. We'd done more or less the same holiday for about five years, but last year was too much. My little brother was always trying to get my parents' attention. Because he's seven years younger than me, my parents treat him like a baby. I found his behaviour really selfish. I mean, when the tent was untidy, I had to tidy it up, and so on. I got really impatient with him in the end, and I really wanted to just go home, but I couldn't get away. I was stuck in a tent for two weeks.

Speaker 2:

I usually enjoy going on holiday with my family. My parents are young and sociable and they're generally cheerful and great fun. But last year's holiday was really *not* that enjoyable. We went to Italy and I was hoping to spend time on the beaches, having a lazy time, with lovely Italian food. Well, we did have lovely food, but my parents decided that it was too hot and they got nervous about us getting sunburnt. So we ended up spending more time in the cities, like Florence, Pisa and Lucca. They seemed to find it so interesting, but in my opinion, there are only so many art galleries and churches that you can visit. After we'd seen about ten, I …

Speaker 3:

We went up to Northumberland, near Scotland by train. We were staying in a bed and breakfast. The first two days were wonderful. I was quite happy doing long walks and seeing the beautiful coast. But unfortunately, the weather changed and we ended up being stuck inside, because

of the rain. We didn't have anywhere to go in the day because we were staying in a bed and breakfast, and we didn't have a car. So we spent a lot of time in cafés, playing card games and board games. After it had rained non-stop for three days, I think my parents realised it would simply be easier to come home. So that was it, our big summer holiday! Unfortunately, we'd bought return tickets with a fixed date, so we had to buy new ones, too. It was a total disaster!

Speaker 4:

My last family holiday was about six months ago. We all went to Thailand, for a special holiday, to celebrate my grandparents' 40th wedding anniversary. They came too and paid for us all to stay in a wonderful hotel! We had a few problems on the way, I mean, the flight was delayed for six hours, and our Bangkok taxi actually broke down on the main road from the airport. However, we had a fabulous holiday, and I loved spending time with both my mum and dad and my grandparents, too. I'd forgotten how much fun they can be!

Unit 3

Developing vocabulary and listening p25

3 and 4 10

Chantal: Hi, David, how's it going? I didn't realise you had gone to Scotland. How long have you been living in Edinburgh?

David: I've been here for eight weeks now.

Chantal: And how have you been finding it?

David: Well, at first it was difficult, but now I'm really enjoying myself.

Chantal: Why, what's changed?

David: Well, you know, I've settled in. I've made some friends, well *two*! And, of course, my English has been improving … steadily.

Chantal: Great. And what about Edinburgh, what's that like? Have you been enjoying it?

David: It's absolutely amazing! It's a really ancient and interesting place. I don't mean just in the city itself, but you can do lots of day trips, too. It's really got a lot to offer as a city.

Chantal: Like what? I mean, what kinds of things?

David: Well, for example, on Saturday my host family took me to a town called Musselburgh. It's a really pretty place, with a lovely beach. And the really fascinating thing is that it's packed with ice cream shops! Genuine Italian ice cream shops, with totally delicious ice cream! It's because there's a big Italian community here.

Chantal: Yum, I love ice cream. So what about the host family – would you recommend staying with a host family?

David: Well, I've really enjoyed the experience with my host family. They have a son who's my age, and we have a lot in common, like football and music.

Chantal: Great. So you'd recommend it, then?

David: Yes, I would. And, of course, I've been attending classes too since I got here.

Chantal: Has that helped your English?

David: Definitely. It's also good for making friends. I go to a local language school, 15 minutes' walk away. I've met lots of nice people.

Chantal: Have you had any problems at all?

David: Not really, except that I have an absolutely tiny amount of money left! It's quite expensive. Oh, and it's taken me a while to feel comfortable with the Scottish weather.

Chantal: I can imagine.

David: It was absolutely freezing here on my second week. I had to buy an extra jumper and a jacket!

Chantal: What about the language, have you had any difficulties understanding the Scottish accent?

David: When I first arrived, it was really hard for me. I couldn't understand a word! However, after hearing it for a few weeks, it's become much easier! It does depend on who's speaking, too …

Chantal: Well, it's been really good talking to you, David, thanks for all the information about Edinburgh. It sounds like a great place. I'd better go now. Enjoy your last fortnight!

David: Bye.

Developing speaking p27

2 and 3 ▶ 11

The picture shows a beautiful park. I think it's in the UK or somewhere in Europe. In the foreground there's a little girl running. Just near the middle, there's a small building which is open and it has steps. I think this might be for a group of musicians to play, but I'm not totally sure. On the left of the photo there are chairs, deckchairs, so that people can sit and enjoy the sunshine in the park. In the background, behind the trees, there are some lovely old buildings made of natural stone. One of the buildings, the one in the middle, looks like a hotel. In between the park and the buildings there is a road, I think, as I can see what looks like the top of a bus and a lorry. I'd like to be in that park. It looks calm and peaceful, and a nice way to get away from a lively city.

PRONUNCIATION p27

4 ▶ 12

1 There's a small building
2 The top of a bus
3 A group of musicians
4 It looks calm and peaceful
5 The picture shows a beautiful park
6 On the right of the picture

DESCRIBING PICTURES p27

6 ▶ 13

I think this might be a city in China. It looks really big and very busy. In the background and in the middle of the photo there are lots of skyscrapers. They're probably offices where people work, or maybe luxury flats. In the foreground on the right I can see blocks of flats and houses and some green areas. They are probably parks where people can relax or children can play. I can also see a very busy road or motorway leading into the city. This probably causes a lot of pollution. I don't really like the skyscrapers, they look very industrial, but I like the green areas and the smaller houses. I think this city would be busy and crowded and I think it's a tiring place to live because it's big. It's probably very lively and somewhere there is a historic centre.

Unit 4

Developing vocabulary and listening p33

3 and 4 ▶ 14

Speaker 1:

This is definitely a *global* problem. But if it's true what they say about us getting our protein from eating *insects* in the future, I'm happy to cut down how much meat I eat! I'd much prefer to eat only 2–3 meals a week with meat, than have to eat insects. Eating less meat is healthier too, I mean, you have *half* the chance of getting diabetes. I think it's important for people to get used to cooking and eating vegetarian food now before the situation gets too serious.

Speaker 2:

I am aware that there is a big problem and it's getting worse as the world is becoming more and more overcrowded. And as countries get richer, people eat more meat so the demand grows. But the trouble is I am a meat-lover and I always have been, and so are the rest of my family. Meals without meat or fish are just not satisfying and I don't think it's healthy either. So rethinking how and what I eat is not realistic for me and I'm sure for other people, too. There must be some other solution.

Speaker 3:

I'm vegetarian and I think vegetarian food is delicious! However, for me it's not a question of everyone becoming vegetarian, it's more a case of simply eating *less* meat.

That way there is food for everyone, and we can really reduce global warming. The facts speak for themselves. One third of the world's farmland is used for growing animal feed, not human food, at the moment and the population will have increased to nine billion in 25 years. We have to reconsider how we live our lives.

Speaker 4:

Another reason for us to reduce our consumption of meat is shortage of water, which we know is going to be problematic in the future. I recently watched a documentary and it said that farming uses up 70% of our water supply: animals and their food need a lot of water. Because of all this, in five years' time meat prices will have doubled, which means that many people won't have a choice about eating less meat.

Speaker 5:

Personally, I think all these facts about food shortages are unconvincing. I have faith in technology. I think science can solve the other problems, too. If we don't have enough land, we can create it! We'll soon be growing our food in laboratories. And if we're talking about water – the Earth is 70% water. I know most of it is salt water, but with technology, we can use this water or make more. I think that in 50 years' time, millions of people will be drinking man-made water.

Developing speaking p35

1 and 2 ▶ 15

Carrie: OK, Lisa, let's decide what we're going to eat for Sofie's birthday.

Lisa: OK. Why don't we go to the new fast food place? I know she loves burgers.

Carrie: For a birthday meal? I don't think that's suitable. In my opinion, I think we should have something a bit nicer, as long as it's not too expensive. What about you?

Lisa: Yes, maybe you're right. What do you think about going for pizza? Pizza is nicer than burgers and everyone likes pizza.

Carrie: Yes, but pizza is quite boring. We always have it! What about the seafood restaurant on the High Street? I've heard the food's delicious.

Lisa: But it's also very expensive! You said not too expensive, remember? Most of our friends won't be happy with that!

Carrie: OK. The Chinese, then. It's always good food and it's good to share the dishes, especially when you have a lot of people. I really like their noodle dishes.

Lisa: Yeah. That's a good idea. And I think Sofie likes Chinese food too …, but not everyone else does. It's too unusual for some. Why don't we try the new gourmet burger place instead? I know

Sofie would love that and there are lots of different burgers to choose from, including chicken or vegetarian. The way I see it, that's the most important thing. I think that everyone will find something on the menu that they enjoy eating.

Carrie: Yes, I agree. Personally, I prefer vegetarian burgers, so I think it's a good idea to go there. And the food is good quality, too.

Lisa: OK, great. I'll book it now.

PRONUNCIATION p35

3 16

before / you're
birthday / prefer
don't / go
enough / somewhere
good / should
nice / why

DESCRIBING PICTURES p35

5 17

This looks like some sort of summer celebration. I think it's at the beach. They're having a barbecue – there's a young man doing the food in the middle of the photo and he is turning the sausages. I imagine the other people are his friends or perhaps they are members of the same family. They are all wearing comfortable, 'weekend' clothes. They are waiting for their food and the girl on the left is holding a paper plate. They all look happy and relaxed as if they are having fun. I think they are enjoying being together. They are also looking up and smiling for the photo.

Gateway to exams: Units 3–4

Listening p38

3 18

Interviewer:
Good morning, Mr Eddison.

Mr Eddison:
Good morning.

Interviewer:
Well, I'm sure many of our nature-loving listeners already know something about the bee problems we are facing. However, can you retell us what the main issues are?

Mr Eddison:
Yes, well, basically, the honeybee population is falling very quickly, by billions, in fact. It has halved since 1990. This is an enormous problem, and I'm not just talking about having no honey!

Interviewer:
Because bees pollinate the flowers, and those flowers are necessary for our food. They travel from one flower to another, helping the flowers to produce seeds, which grow into fruit and vegetables.

Mr Eddison:
That's exactly right. They 'pollinate' the flowers, in the way you have said. Pollination is necessary so that we can grow new food plants. Imagine a world without apples, strawberries, plums, peaches, blueberries, pumpkins, courgettes, peas, onions, to name a few. Without honeybees – our food crops cannot grow. Around one-third of our food crops rely on them. Bees contribute around 22 billion Euros to the economy in Europe every year! So it's money, as well as honey.

Interviewer:
Wow! But what about other insects? Can they help with pollination?

Mr Eddison:
Bumble bees are also important, even animals … But honeybees have been pollinating our plants for centuries. We cannot overemphasise their importance.

Interviewer:
So, how serious is the problem?

Mr Eddison:
Very, and if the situation does not change over the next five to ten years, not only will it cost millions, but in a few years, we'll also be eating food which is pollinated by *wind*, not insects. So we will have lost a lot of the colourful food we eat now and consider normal.

Interviewer:
So, what will we be eating then?

Mr Eddison:
In a few years' time, we'll possibly be eating more cereals like wheat and barley, and maize.

Interviewer:
But is there no other way to pollinate these crops?

Mr Eddison:
In a word, 'no'. There *are* places where crops are pollinated by hand even now because of the bee problem … for example, in parts of China. However, there are not enough humans on the planet to hand-pollinate all the crops that we need.

Interviewer:
I see. And exactly why are so many millions of bees dying?

Mr Eddison:
Well, experts actually disagree on the main cause. However, the general opinion is that there are several different problems co-occurring.

Interviewer:
Right.

Mr Eddison:
For example, a virus has been attacking many bee colonies since 2006. There is also a shortage of food for bees in many areas, because of industrial farming. No wild flowers means that bees start to disappear. Then there's climate change. These factors, and others, make the bees stressed and weak. It is thought now that some kinds of chemicals used in farming can be very harmful to bees' memory and behaviour, especially in this weak condition.

Interviewer:
So the future doesn't look …

Unit 5

Developing vocabulary and listening p43

3 and 4 19

Speaker 1:
This job demands a lot of skill and energy. You are responsible for helping people to learn something difficult. It requires a patient and calm person. If somebody had a serious accident, then you would be responsible for helping them. In my opinion, it would also suit a fairly sociable person, someone who loved being outside and working with people. You'd have to be passionate about the sport, too.

Speaker 2:
Well, there are lots of different kinds, but I would say that most people in this field have a very analytical and careful mind. They like to look at detail, and to search for clues and patterns, and to enjoy collecting lots of data. I think you have to be very patient to do this job as it can be very repetitive. If I had this job, I'd go mad as there is no room for creativity. I also wouldn't like to wear that coat or to be stuck in one place all the time!

Speaker 3:
To do this job, you have to be able to think really quickly and to be a questioning person. You should respect people, but you also have to be quite persistent. For example, if these people talk to politicians, they know how to ask the same question in lots of different ways. Some find these people annoying, but they're important because if we didn't have them, we wouldn't get our daily news and we certainly wouldn't find out the truth about what is happening at home and abroad.

Speaker 4:
I think to do this job you have to have a really good eye! You have to be creative and also to know how to do things differently. If you are the same as everyone else, you won't get noticed, so creativity is really important. Lots of people do this for *fun*, but to do it as a job, you must have style. You also need to be able to get on with people to make them feel relaxed, if they are your subject. If people don't feel comfortable with you, your work won't look natural!

Developing speaking p45

1, 2 and 3 20

I'm going to talk about the reasons *for* leaving school at 16. However, I'll start by giving some of the arguments *against* leaving school so young.

Many countries in Europe expect children to stay at school until they are 18. People argue that if you stay longer at school, you get better qualifications, which leads to better job prospects and a better future. Another reason for people staying until they are 18, is that it gives young people more time to grow up, in a safe, school environment. Some children do not have secure home lives, so this may give them much-needed security.

What's more, staying at school until 18 gives young people more time to think about what they would like to do in their working life: when it comes to starting work, they may have a clearer picture of what they want to do as a job.

I'd now like to discuss the points for leaving school earlier. It is true that many of the points I have just mentioned are realistic and, of course, I partly agree with them. However, there are many good arguments for leaving school early, too. First of all, some children simply do not enjoy school. Sitting in a classroom for another two or three years is a waste of their time. Secondly, if this is the case, then these children can also affect other children's learning in a very negative way: if children do not want to be at school, they can be very disruptive. For instance, my sister is 16, and she tells me that at least 40% of her lessons are not effective because there are several children in the classes who are always disrupting lessons.

Another thing is that while many young people do not know what they want to do as a job at 16, some people *do*. Take my cousin, for example. From the age of six, he has always wanted to be a jockey because he has always loved horses and riding. He had to remain in education until he was 18 so this was, for him, a waste of time.

Finally, these days it is very easy to learn and study in different ways, and I think it is easier to study later in life. If people want to leave, then they *should*. This does not mean that they will never go back to education. They may well return to some sort of education, but when they *want* to. The point I'm trying to make is that many people at 16 *do* know their own minds. Being in school might not suit them at that point. For their sake and for other children's sake, children *should* be allowed to leave at 16 if they wish to. However, I do think that they should be given very clear career advice in the school, so that they understand what they are doing.

PRONUNCIATION p45

5 21

presentation	argument
environment	qualification
security	education
university	career
advice	

DESCRIBING PICTURES p45

7 22

In the picture you can see a girl – I think she's a teenager. She has long brown hair in a bun and she's wearing a white T-shirt. In the foreground, you can see her looking through a camera. To the right of the girl there's a town with very old buildings, and in the background you can see the sea and some mountains. I think she might be in Italy. Perhaps she is on holiday with her friends or family. She's taking a photo of the scenery, or maybe she's making a video. It looks like she is happy to be there as she is admiring the view.

Unit 6

Developing vocabulary and listening p51

3 and 4 23

Interviewer:
Today we have Marc Brouwer with us, a keen drone hobbyist and expert ... Hello, Marc.

Marc:
Hello.

Interviewer:
Now tell us, have you always been interested in flying drones, or should I say 'UAVs', Unmanned Aerial Vehicles?

Marc:
I've loved watching planes since I was a boy. We used to go plane-watching in the fields where we lived. I saw my first drone at 14, when my father took me to an exhibition. We were there for hours!

Interviewer:
Right.

Marc:
These days, many of your listeners have probably seen a drone. They can be the size of a pizza box, or a small aircraft.

Interviewer:
So, are they similar to toy planes, run by remote control?

Marc:
Yes, but, of course, they can have a real function. Probably most listeners are aware of drones being used by the military. However, they also have many other much more positive uses.

Interviewer:
Can you tell us a bit more?

Marc:
Well, nowadays, estate agents use them to take photos from the air of new houses they want to sell. And for film-makers and photographers, drones are cheap and exciting ... imagine being able to get close-up shots of the Empire State Building, for example. But drones have more serious uses as well.

Interviewer:
Really?

Marc:
For example, in some countries drones have been used in agriculture for over 20 years. In Japan, spraying rice fields by drone is extremely common. Farmers have their crops regularly sprayed to stop disease.

Interviewer:
Mmmm.

Marc:
An aerial view can be useful in agriculture, too. So the farmers that are responsible for crops can attach a camera to a drone to identify problems – areas of land needing water, diseased crops, bad soil, and so on. And animals, too ...

Interviewer:
Fascinating.

Marc:
Interestingly, in South Africa in the Kruger National Park, park officials are worried about the falling numbers of certain wild animals. 'Falcon' drones now watch their black rhinos, which are in serious danger. Small planes with cameras are used to stop the people who chase and kill the rhinos for their horns ...

Interviewer:
Wow ... And then there's the megastore, Amazon?

Marc:
Yes, Amazon would like future customers to have their goods delivered by drones. They think it will be quicker, safer and cheaper. It sounds like science fiction, and it *will* be difficult to design, but in a few years ...

Interviewer:
So the skies could be full of small planes? I think I would be afraid of that.

Marc:
Mmmm. Safety is an issue. Err, finally, researchers are developing drones which might be able to deliver vaccines and medicines to poor, rural areas in the future, which doctors and nurses cannot reach.

Interviewer:
Really?

Marc:
Yes. And it might not stop at medicines. Perhaps in the future villagers will have food and other goods delivered by drones. This is a possibility ...

Developing speaking p53

2 and 3 24

Both of the photos show young people who look like teenagers. In the first photo, they are in a school classroom or workshop of some sort, and the second photo definitely looks like a workshop. You can tell because of the wooden table and the equipment. In both photos, some sort of woodworking lesson or activity is taking place. One thing they both have in common is that the people in both photos seem very interested in what they are doing, but in different ways. One other similarity between the photos is that the people are making things with wood.

However, there are several differences. One important difference between the photos is that in the first picture the students are working together, whereas the second photo shows a young man working independently. Another important difference is the clothes: in the first picture they are wearing aprons, with the same white shirt, but in the second photo he is wearing overalls, I think, and gloves and goggles. But all the people are wearing something to protect their clothes.

Personally, if I had to choose between the lessons, I'd prefer the first. That's because it looks like you can ask your peers questions more easily, and share ideas.

PRONUNCIATION p53

4a and 4b 25

1 Both of the photos show young people.
2 You can tell because of the wooden table and the equipment.
3 However, there are several differences.

DESCRIBING PICTURES p53

6 26

I can see three students in the photo. There are two girls and one boy, and they're probably friends, because they're standing very close together. I imagine they're pupils at school and they're probably somewhere in the school yard or playground, or they could be in a park. I can see a wall behind them and it looks as if it's got some graffiti on it. I think they're either texting or looking at social media websites on their mobile phones. I suppose they're a bit bored because they're more interested in their mobile phones than each other. Maybe they think the messages are funny, because one of the girls is smiling.

Gateway to exams: Units 5–6

Listening p56

3 27

In the 1860s, around one third of children in England and Wales did not actually go to school. That's one in three children. Children didn't *have to* go to school until 1880, when it became compulsory for 5–10 year olds. This went up to the age of 12 in 1899 and to the age of 14 in 1918. Then from 1918 onwards, if children didn't reach a certain level by their last year, they would have to stay on at school.

If you sat in a school class from 100 years ago now, you would probably recognise most of the lessons. There were the three 'Rs', so reading, writing and arithmetic, that's maths. Children also used to study history, geography and religion. Girls would do needlework, as it was important to learn how to sew clothes and other things in the home, but boys would study drawing. The children also used to do physical education or PE, led by the teacher, which

was called 'drill'. The children would do a series of exercises in the classroom, for example marching or jumping. Even then, educationalists realised that exercising helped children to stay awake and to concentrate.

The children probably quite enjoyed doing physical exercises in winter, when the classrooms were usually freezing cold. Physical exercise was the best way to warm themselves up. There was generally only one small coal fire, near the teacher's desk, so if a pupil was sitting at the back of the class, it would be freezing and that pupil would often shiver with cold.

The teacher used to sit on a high chair at the front of the class, to see everyone. The windows were also high, so that the pupils could not look outside and get distracted by people passing by. The children often sat on wooden benches, with no chair back to lean on, which was quite uncomfortable as the day went on. The desks were heavy and fixed in one place – so pupils couldn't move around, and in the room there was always a picture of the monarch, King George V.

Discipline, as you can imagine, was very strict. Teachers frequently used a stick or a ruler to punish children and keep control. Many classrooms had a corner where naughty children used to stand, sometimes with a pointed hat on their head. On the hat was written 'Dunce', or 'D' for dunce, meaning 'stupid'.

The children used to have a slate and chalk because paper and books were too expensive. They used ink to write, and in those days, even if you were left-handed, the teacher generally made you use your right hand. Learning is certainly much more enjoyable now!

Unit 7

Developing vocabulary and listening p61

4 and 5 28

Speaker 1:

Well, I used to work out, but then I got an ankle injury last spring – while I was warming up – would you believe it! So I decided to take up a new sport. One day a friend whose neighbour is a yoga instructor told me about anti-gravity yoga. We decided to try it together, partly just because we thought it would be fun to do something different!

Anti-gravity yoga *is* yoga, but you are upside down for a lot of the time, hanging from the ceiling like a bat, in a long scarf-like hammock. This helps the blood move around the body. It's good for your heart, as well as your core muscles, which are the deeper muscles inside the middle of your body. It's also very relaxing and helps your body to release 'happy hormones'.

You come out feeling relaxed yet energetic. And, of course, it's weightless, which means it's not a problem for ankles or other joints.

This type of yoga has many of the same positions as in normal yoga, but it is also a little like dance and acrobatics. It started in the US a few years ago, and is now becoming popular in Australia and Europe, too. It's a great way to help your whole body.

Speaker 2:

I took up running backwards, or 'reverse running', about six months ago, and I have never felt so fit! Basically, both my dad and my sister had started doing it and I wanted to join in. At first, I couldn't keep up with them at all!

It's like forward running, but you run backwards. It's not so easy at the start, and it's a good idea to run *with* someone initially so that you don't fall over. You soon get much faster, though. And it's important to warm up really carefully.

It's great for balance and general fitness, as well as stamina, which is necessary for more serious athletes. It also exercises different muscles than forward running, such as your calf muscles on the backs of your lower legs. Running backwards is also better for your knees, where much of your body weight falls in forward running.

Even 100 years ago, there were some athletes who used backwards running to improve their overall fitness. Recently, it's become more popular again. A man called Robert Stevenson, who is an expert in reverse running, recommends practising in an open space, where you don't need to worry about falling over, so for example in a park or on the beach. That's common sense, really. Running backwards in town, where there are pedestrians, roads and so on, can be very stressful.

If anyone is thinking of taking up a new sport which is good for overall fitness, I'd recommend it. And don't give up too soon. You should carry on because it gets easier!

Developing speaking p63

1, 2 and 3 29

Jimmy:
So what do you think?

Sallly:
Personally, I can't imagine school without sports. We do it three times a week. It's as important as a subject like maths. Sometimes, I agree, it is a nuisance: for example, *nobody* likes running or playing hockey in the wind and rain! However, doing sport is necessary, especially for young people, to keep fit and to be part of a team. And I think if some people were given the choice not to do PE in school, then some children would probably say 'no'. That could be bad news for their health.

Jimmy:
I think you're right about that, but even so, I think that teenagers should be allowed to decide for themselves. I mean, most teenagers know which sports they like. They might spend hours doing them *outside* school. Why should someone who spends hours playing football or

table tennis, for example, then do running and cricket during school time – sports they don't enjoy – *inside* school? These students, who do sport outside school, could be doing other things in school, like *studying*!

Sallly:

Well, I take your point. However, PE is really necessary for those children who *don't* do exercise outside school, and who would definitely not do sport if they had the choice. It's the children who don't do it outside school, that are the problem. It's also good to know how to play certain sports.

Jimmy:

That's true, but why make children do something they hate? It might make them really unhappy. It may make them not want to come to school, even.

Sallly:

Yeah. I see what you mean, but how else can we make doing sport a habit, part of your life? For at least *some* children, if they think that doing sports is normal, and that it's fun, they might do it and start to like it. Some kids don't come from sporty families.

Jimmy:

Err … I'm not sure that's true, about changing people's attitude. Aren't you being a bit optimistic? Does doing PE in school make you *like* it, if you are not a lover of sport? I don't think so!

Sallly:

You've got a point, I suppose. But some people don't like sport. They probably never will. However, what about the children in the middle, then, who don't *love* sport, but don't *hate* it either? For them, surely it's important to have PE in school, to make it into a regular, weekly habit?

Jimmy:

Mmmmm. There are strong arguments for doing sport, but I'm still not sure that's true. My mum's a keen runner now. She goes running every other day and loves it, though she wasn't keen on PE at school. I think many people take up sport when they're older, when they've left school and can understand the importance of it. They'll find a sport which suits them, not one which someone else has chosen for them …

Sallly:

Yes, yes. It would be good to ask …

PRONUNCIATION p63

4 30

1 cricket   2 exercise   3 optimistic
4 argument   5 importance

DESCRIBING PICTURES p63

6 31

In this picture there are five teenagers, one boy and four girls. I think they are in someone's garden and they are probably friends. I don't think they're family because they all look different. And they're all eating. They are clearly having lots of fun. They are talking and smiling and obviously enjoying the food. They are eating pizza – you can see the packaging in the middle of the table, and they're all holding slices. I don't know exactly what type of pizza but I imagine it's cheese and tomato. There are drinks too, in glasses on the table. I think it's lemonade. The teenagers look relaxed and comfortable with each other, as if they know one another very well. They are wearing comfortable clothes – jeans and T-shirts and hoodies. Maybe they have been doing some sport and are now relaxing or perhaps it's someone's birthday.

Unit 8

Developing vocabulary and listening p69

4 and 5 32

Interviewer:

And today, in our series *Unusual Music*, we are going to Paraguay, South America to the home of *The Recycled Orchestra*. Our Arts and Culture correspondent, Will Vogel, is on the line. Will, are you there …? Can you speak up a bit?

Will:

Yes, I am. Good afternoon. I'm at the home of The Recycled Orchestra, here in Cateura, in Paraguay, just on the outskirts of the capital, Asunción.

Interviewer:

Great. So, can you tell us something about Cateura, and the orchestra?

Will:

Of course. It's a fascinating story. I'm sitting in a busy café and the air isn't so fresh here. That's because the town, consisting of about 2,500 families, has grown up around rubbish, rubbish from the nearby city of Asunción. The people are surrounded by rubbish, and they earn their living from it, too.

Interviewer:

Can you explain?

Will:

Yes, to earn money, practically everyone who lives here searches through the rubbish and recycles it every day, making it into other things where they can, or washing it, for resale. It's tiring work, and wages are extremely low.

Interviewer:

I can imagine. And yet, this little town has produced a children's orchestra. How did this happen? I'm interested to know.

Will:

It's no *ordinary* orchestra. Two men – Fabio Chavez, the director, and 'Don Cola', who works as a rubbish picker himself, set up this unusual orchestra, … without instruments or money.

Interviewer:

Right …

Will:

These two men made the musical instruments from rubbish and then taught the local children how to play. Don Cola, who makes the instruments, had never even seen a violin himself when he started!

Interviewer:

That's amazing. So what does he make the instruments out of? I'm confused.

Will:

Things that people throw away – oil cans, oven trays, bottle tops, spoons and forks, pieces of wood and metal. You name it …

Interviewer:

Wow! Can you give us an example?

Will:

Well, for example, the cellos are made from oil cans, and an old piece of wood. The clarinets are made from old metal pipes and the keys from bottle tops.

Interviewer:

Unbelievable. And what do they sound like?

Will:

Well, I was listening to them last night, and the sound is surprising. I certainly wasn't disappointed. It's beautiful, actually. It's also a very moving experience to watch these teenagers play. They love music.

Interviewer:

Has it changed the young people's lives?

Will:

Definitely. They have hope now, and so do their families and the community. Until recently, the orchestra was only known locally, but now they have started touring abroad because the story has attracted a lot of media attention. They have actually received some real instruments, too. There is a documentary …

Interviewer:

But will that change the orchestra? I mean, if they aren't playing on recycled instruments?

Will:

That is a good question. Time will tell …

Developing speaking p71

2 and 3 33

Sam: So, how was your evening?

Ben: Terrible!

Sam: What happened!

Ben: Well, I don't know if I told you I was going to the theatre? My mum took me to a modern ballet.

Sam: Really?

Ben: She was supposed to be going with my sister, but Lucy was ill.

Sam: So *you* went.

Ben: Yes. At first, I said I didn't want to go, but she was really disappointed, so I agreed.

Sam: Right. And …?

Ben: Well, first our car wouldn't start, so we had to take a bus. So we ended up getting to the theatre quite late. Then I nearly fell on somebody in the audience while I was walking to my seat. We had to go in when it was all dark and everybody was just waiting for the performance to start. They don't usually let people in that late, but there was a delay so everyone was just waiting with the lights out. But entering in the dark was a good thing, because, later, when the stage lights came on, I realised that everyone was dressed really smartly. And I was just wearing jeans and trainers. My mum did say I should dress up, but I didn't listen. Anyway, after that the curtain went up and the performance started. But it didn't, I mean, it didn't start. Nothing seemed to happen for ages. Eventually, I asked Mum what was happening and the people in the seats behind asked us to be quiet.

Sam: No!

Ben: And next, I'm afraid I started laughing and I couldn't stop. A few minutes later, the dancers came on stage. We were quite near the front, and one of the performers glared at me for laughing. That made me worse! I just couldn't stop.

Sam: So, what did you do next?

Ben: Well, after a few minutes I had to leave. I waited outside until the interval. It seemed like ages. Finally, Mum came out. She wasn't very pleased with me, as you can imagine. In the end, we both decided to just go home, as I didn't want to go back in. My mum didn't talk to me for a while! Afterwards, she told me she wouldn't take me to another performance until I was 18!

Sam: Oh dear!

PRONUNCIATION p71

5c 34

audience	ballet
curtain	dancer
interval	performance
theatre	afterwards
at first	in the end

DESCRIBING PICTURES p71

7 35

In the foreground of the photo, there is a female artist. I think she is in a field in the countryside. The woman could be in her 20s or 30s. She is sitting down in front of an easel and she is painting a landscape. It looks like a lovely bright day and it looks as though she has nearly finished her painting. In the background, you can see an open landscape and some more fields and trees to the left and right. It's quite a beautiful scene and I think it might be in Spain, or somewhere like that, as the grass looks quite dry. I imagine that the artist has been there for a while. I'm not sure when the photo was taken, but as it still looks very light, it might be in the middle of the day.

Gateway to exams: Units 7–8

Gateway to exams p74

2 36

I'm going to talk about the … err … swimmer Michael Phelps, who I think is a very inspiring sportsman. He has won more gold medals in the Olympics than any, err … other person in history.

Firstly, I'll tell you a little bit about how he started. Well, he was born in Maryland, USA in 1985, into a family of swimmers – his two older sisters competed. I was interested to find out that he was, erm, at first nervous about putting his head under water! Anyway, it was his swimming coach who first noticed Phelps's talent, at the age of 11. After years of training and competing, he turned professional at just, err 16 … 16. He trained for six years as a teenager and never missed a single day of training, so he was clearly very determined. Interestingly, Phelps found school hard, finding it difficult to concentrate. I read that one teacher said he would never be able to focus on anything! Phelps has explained that being in the pool actually calmed his mind. This may be one reason why he enjoys swimming so much.

As a young adult, he started to win major competitions. He took part in his first Olympics at just 15. I would say that Phelps became an international sportsman at the age of 19 at the 2004 Olympic Games in Athens, when he won eight medals, including six golds. That began a series of wins at major competitions for him.

Phelps is skilled at using many kinds of swimming strokes, which is surprising as most swimmers at this level specialise in just one or two. This means that he gets little rest in major competitions, for example at the Beijing Olympics in 2008, where Phelps competed in eight races over eight days, winning every single competition. At one point, he had nine minutes between receiving his medal for one race and then competing again in the next!

A lot has been said about his body shape, his physique. Phelps is clearly a talented swimmer, but some say that his natural body shape also helps. He is tall, but with long arms (203 centimetres across, which is about 8 cm longer than his height). His feet are unusually long, while his legs are quite short for someone so tall. However, as far as I'm concerned, it is Phelps' great self-belief and determination that are the most important things. It's well known that he hates losing! The amount he eats has also been, err, well-publicised too: he consumes 4,000 calories just at breakfast!

You probably know that Phelps retired after the London 2012 Olympics at the age of 27. He said at the time he'd finished his career the way he'd wanted to. He explained that he was going to travel and have some fun. However, about a year later, he surprised everyone by announcing his return to swimming professionally. Why did he change his mind? He said that retirement had been boring and that it was good to have some structure back in his life!

Unit 9

Developing vocabulary and listening p79

5 and 6 37

We know that Tutankhamun was the King of Ancient Egypt, about 3,300 years ago. And then in 1922, the archaeologist Howard Carter found his tomb, his mummy, with some amazing gold and fantastic treasure in the Valley of the Kings, in Egypt. Imagine how Carter felt. For an Egyptologist at the time it must have been a life-changing moment. If Carter hadn't made that incredible discovery, his life would have been completely different. But there is one mystery that has puzzled scientists for many years – why King Tut died so young.

We know from DNA testing, that he was just a teenager and that he must have died aged 18 or 19. He reigned from 1333 BC to 1324 BC, so for around ten years. It was suggested that King Tut's death could have been because he was injured when fighting or that he was killed by a hippopotamus when hunting. Or that he fell from a chariot, behind his horse. However, modern DNA tests and scans of his body have shown that Tutankhamun was really not a physically fit man, which would mean that these theories can't be true.

In fact, King Tut wasn't healthy at all. He had a bone disease, which he inherited from one of his parents. And his foot was permanently damaged. So, he walked with a limp and used a walking stick to help him. Inside his tomb, they found 130 walking sticks. Some of them had been used. So, given the evidence, it's very unlikely that he was fighting, hunting or even chariot-racing during his lifetime. If he had been healthy, these activities would have been totally normal for a king.

There was also a theory that he may have been killed because his body was very badly damaged in many places. But modern scientific analysis shows that only one break – a broken leg – happened *before* his death. The other breaks must have occurred *afterwards*, when his body was moved. So, using modern technology, scientists have concluded that with his bone disease and other problems, King Tut probably just fell and broke his leg. Then he must have got some sort of infection which killed him. The good quality of the DNA in the mummy has really helped to solve the mysteries. If the Egyptians hadn't embalmed their pharaohs' bodies with special oils, then the DNA would not have kept so well.

Developing speaking p81

2 and 3 38

I can see some young people on a demonstration, or some sort of protest. In the foreground, there are two boys waving flags. On the left there are some police officers and on the right there's a red double-decker bus. Most of the people are shouting and holding up signs, I mean placards. In the background, there are more young people doing the same thing. They look like students. It seems like they are moving, not standing still, but I imagine they are only walking very slowly. They are protesting about university fees I think. The young people could have heard an announcement at their colleges, or some news online or on the TV which has upset them. I think the government might have announced some sort of new law which is bad for their future. It can't have been good news, and they want to protest. I imagine they feel angry, really angry.

PRONUNCIATION p81

5 39

Nouns

answer	balance
contrast	increase
permit	refund
reject	research
upgrade	

Verbs

answer	balance
contrast	increase
permit	refund
reject	research
upgrade	

PRONUNCIATION p81

6a ▶ 40

1 re<u>ject</u> (N)
2 in<u>crease</u> (V)
3 con<u>trast</u> (V)
4 <u>up</u>grade (N)
5 re<u>search</u> (V)
6 re<u>fund</u> (V)

PRONUNCIATION p81

6c ▶ 41

1 They rejected my application for a scholarship. It's very disappointing.
2 After all that research, Tom got a really high mark.
3 I've just had an upgrade on my phone.

---

4 We have to contrast the two political systems for our assignment.

Unit 10

Developing vocabulary and listening p87

3 and 4 ▶ 42

Speaker 1:

Last year, I ended up in a bit of trouble because I'd borrowed money from my cousin. He'd only lent me £20 originally, but then I'd occasionally borrow more from him for this and that and somehow the amount grew to £250. Then suddenly my cousin wanted his money back for a new bike, and I didn't have a penny. I wish that I'd realised what was happening earlier because the amount I owed him was a real shock! I knew I had to tell my parents. My mum was so angry. I think she was embarrassed because it was my cousin. They had to pay him back and I had to do lots of extra jobs for them, to pay *them* back. It took me nearly a year.

Speaker 2:

Well, my sister and I get an allowance each week, and then we sometimes get some money from relatives as gifts. My dad disapproves. He says he wishes people wouldn't give us money because young people just think it grows on trees! And so Mum and Dad set up a savings account for us. I wish they hadn't because now we have to put most of our money there. They are worried we'll just waste it and won't appreciate how lucky we are. But it's not fair. That money is mine and sometimes I don't have enough to buy what I want. I know they're just trying to teach us to be responsible, but I wish they'd trust us more to make our own decisions.

Speaker 3:

My mum decided to give me an allowance. I was excited at first, about having my own money. The problem was I simply found it wasn't enough. I spoke to my mum, but she said she wouldn't increase it. I have to buy clothes, including shoes, and also go out with my friend, buy presents, extra snacks, you know. It soon disappears! Living is expensive! I'm not sure if it's *me* that is asking for too much, or my *mum*, who needs to be more realistic. I wish she'd listen more, though! I don't feel as if she understands. I might have to get a Saturday job.

Speaker 4:

My parents are really generous with me and I am so grateful. But sometimes, I wish they weren't so generous because I feel guilty. My dad lost his job last year and I know they are struggling to pay the bills at home. But they make sure my brother and I always have everything we need. I'm determined to pay them back one day so I got a Saturday job in a café and I make sure I save something every month. And one day I want to get a really well-paid job so that I can take care of them instead. Some of my friends don't understand why I'm so sensible

---

and I do get frustrated. If only my dad hadn't lost his job, we'd be OK.

Developing speaking p89

1 and 2 43

Shop assistant: Hello, can I help you?
Katya: No, thanks. I'm just looking.
Shop assistant: OK. Call me if you need anything.
Katya: Oh! Actually, yes, I'm looking for some sports socks.
Shop assistant: What size are you?
Katya: They're for my dad, so … size 45, 46 maybe?
Shop assistant: What about these?
Katya: Have you got anything in white?
Shop assistant: Of course. We have them in a pack of four.
Katya: That's great, thanks. I'll take these. But can I bring them back if they're the wrong size?
Shop assistant: Yes, we can replace them if you bring your receipt.

PRONUNCIATION p89

5 44

size / my	another / funny
choose / blue	maybe / grey
middle / damaged	bought / sort
replace / complaint	

DESCRIBING PICTURES p89

7 ▶ 45

This is a photo of some sort of expensive clothes shop. It looks like a boutique, selling designer clothes, like you might see in Paris or Barcelona, somewhere like that. I think it sells clothes and accessories like bags. It probably just sells one expensive brand. In the foreground, there's a customer looking closely at a blue top. She's wearing a striped shirt and sleeveless sweater and is talking on her mobile phone. She is maybe describing the top to a friend. In the background, you can see other clothes on shelves, a plant and a large window looking onto the street.

This makes the shop feel very light and comfortable, as though the customer is in someone's living room. I think most customers who shop here are probably quite rich as the shop is clearly expensive. What's slightly strange is that there's no one else in the shop. I don't think I'd feel comfortable going into a place like that, but I guess some customers like the individual attention you would get.

Gateway to exams: Units 9–10

Listening p92

2 ▶ 46

Interviewer:

So, as part of our series 'What is a nation?', we are looking at flags. And today we have with us an expert in the field, Philomena O'Brien.

Philomena:

Hello.

Interviewer:

Hello … And you are an expert in vexilol, vexi …

Philomena:

Yes, vexillology, the study of flags! That's right.

Interviewer:

Vexillology … that's it. So, tell us something about them.

Philomena:

Well, the first flags were probably used 4,000 years ago, though they may not have been made of material, but of wood. They were used in both Ancient China and Ancient India. They were first used for identification, when fighting, because you had to be able to recognise your fighters. Today every nation has a flag. It is a symbol of pride and represents a country. And flags are *still* used to show ownership or victory; think of Neil Armstrong on the moon, for example …

Interviewer:

Yes.

Philomena:

The flag is a really powerful symbol. In some countries, it is highly valued.

Interviewer:

Hmm. … Can I ask, are all flags the same size?

Philomena:

No, they aren't. In fact, they are not even all rectangular in shape. The Swiss flag is actually square.

Interviewer:

Really?

Philomena:

Yes. And as for the Nepalese flag, that is unique. It is made up of two long thin triangle shapes, one on top of the other.

Interviewer:

Oh! And can countries put whatever they want on their flag?

Philomena:

Yes, and they might decide to change them, too, at some point in history. Denmark has the oldest flag – their flag has been used for at least 400 years. The US flag has changed through history – a star was added for every new state. It only started with 13! If they'd had a different design, it would have been very difficult to change each time.

Interviewer:

Mmm. They must have designed it like that on purpose.

Philomena:

I think so. Most nations just choose very basic designs, so that the flags are simple. One or two have writing on, like the Saudi flag. The Belize flag is the only one to have a human figure on it.

Interviewer:

That's interesting. Most flags I can think of are very simple.

Philomena:

Indeed. It's important, so that they can blow in the wind and be seen from far away. And, in fact, many countries have flags which look quite similar. You might confuse the flags of Chad and of Romania, for example, as they are identical, with their blue, red and yellow vertical stripes. If you turn an Indonesian flag upside down, it could be the Polish flag!

Interviewer:

And I presume the colours are significant.

Philomena:

Absolutely. The most common colours are red, blue and white, but in Africa …

Macmillan Education Limited
4 Crinan Street
London N1 9XW

Companies and representatives throughout the world
ISBN 978-0-230-47095-8

Text, design and illustration © Macmillan Education Ltd 2016
Written by Anna Cole and Ursula Mallows

This edition published 2016
First edition entitled *Gateway B1+ Teacher's Book* published 2011

Designed by emc design ltd
Page make-up by Expo Holdings Sdn Bhd
Cover design by emc design ltd and Macmillan Education Ltd

The publishers would like to thank the staff and pupils at the following
schools in Mexico and Spain for helping us so enthusiastically with
our research for this second edition of Gateway: Concha Campos, IES
Burgo de Las Rozas, Las Rozas, Madrid; Félix Gaspar, IES Las Encinas;
Villanueva de la Cañada, Madrid; Cristina Moisen, IES Joaquín Turina,
Madrid; Colegio Montessori Cuautitlán; Colegio Conrad Gessner; Colegio
Erasmo de Rotterdam; Colegio Kanic, Centro Educativo Erich Fromm;
Universidad Franco Mexicana; Centro Pedagógico María Montessori de
Ecatepec; Instituto Cultural; Escuela Maestro Manuel Acosta; Liceo Sakbé
De México.

The publishers would also like to thank all those who reviewed or piloted
the first edition of Gateway: Benjamin Affolter, Evelyn Andorfer, Anna
Ciereszynska, Regina Culver, Anna Dabrowska, Justyna Deja, Ondrej
Dosedel, Lisa Durham, Dagmar Eder, Eva Ellederovan, H Fouad, Sabrina
Funes, Luiza Gervescu, Isabel González Bueno, Jutta Habringer, Stela
Halmageanu, Marta Hilgier, Andrea Hutterer, Nicole Ioakimidis, Mag.
Annemarie Kammerhofer, Irina Kondrasheva, Sonja Lengauer, Gabriela
Liptakova, Andrea Littlewood, María Cristina Maggi, Silvia Miranda
Barbara Nowak, Agnieska Orlinska, Anna Orlowska, María Paula Palou,
Marta Piotrowska, N Reda, Katharina Schatz, Roswitha Schwarz, Barbara
Scibor, Katarzyna Sochacka, Joanna Spoz, Monica Srtygner, Marisol
Suppan, Stephanie Sutter, Halina Tyliba, Prilipko, Maria Vizgina, Vladyko,
Pia Wimmer, Katarzyna Zadrozna-Attia and Katarzyna Zaremba-Jaworska.

The author and publishers would like to thank the following for permission
to reproduce their photographs:
Shutterstock/Artem Kovalenco pp11, 13, 17, 18, 19, back cover;
Shutterstock/ivelly p11; Shutterstock/M.Stasy p12, back cover

Full acknowledgements for illustrations and photographs in the facsimile
pages can be found in the Student's Book and Workbook.

Printed and bound in Poland by CGS

2024 2023 2022 2021 2020
24 23 22 21 20 19 18 17 16